LAW OF SEIZURE OF GOODS
Debtor's Rights and Remedies
2nd Edition

LAW OF SEIZURE OF GOODS
Debtor's Rights and Remedies
2nd Edition

JOHN KRUSE

Hammicks Legal
Publishing

Disclaimer

This work is not a substitute for legal advice in relation to any particular case. Although the authors have attempted to produce a work which is designed to assist the practitioner, neither they or the publishers undertake any duty of care to any person or entity whatsoever, without limitation, in relation to any of the statements in, or omissions from this work, and accepts no legal liability or responsibility in respect of any statements in or omissions from this work.

© John Kruse 2009

Produced and Distributed by

for

xpl publishing
99 Hatfield Road
St Albans AL1 4JL
UK

Hammicks Legal Publishing
Ash House
Headlands Business Park
Ringwood, Hants
BH24 3PB, UK

www.xplpublishing.com

www.hammickslegal.com

ISBN 978 1 85811 603 7

Printed and typeset in the UK

CONTENTS

Glossary of Case Reports

This glossary lists the case citations used in the text. The older English reports, if not available directly, will be found in the English Reports or in the Digest (Butterworths). The latter also contains most of the commonwealth cases cited. The mediaeval Year Book cases may be found either in the sixteenth century editions of the Year Book, or in parallel translation in editions by the Seldon Society, the Ames Foundation, or the Rolls Series. Year Book citations are generally by term, regnal year of the monarch and page and plea number. More modern reports are listed by reporter(s), court(s) covered and year of publication.

A&E	Adolphus & Ellis, King's Bench & Queen's Bench, 1834-42
ABC	Australian Bankruptcy Cases, 1928-64
AC	Law Reports, Appeal Courts, 1865-present
Ad & El	see A&E
Adviser	The Adviser, 1986-present
All ER	All England Reports, 1936-present
Amb	Ambler, Chancery, 1716-83
And	Anderson, Common Pleas, sixteenth century
Anst	Anstruther, Exchequer, 1792-7
App Cas	Law Reports, Appeal Cases, House of Lords, 1875-90
AR	Ontario Appeal Reports, 1876-1900
Atk	Atkyns, Chancery, 1736-54
B & Ald	Barnewell & Alderson, King's Bench, 1817-22
B & Ad	Barnewall & Adolphus, King's Bench, 1830-34
B&A	either of above
B&C	Best & Smith, Queen's Bench, 1861-70
Barn KB	Barnes' Notes of Cases, Common Pleas, 1732-60
BCC	British Company Cases
BCLC	Butterworth's Company Law Cases
BCR	British Colombia Reports, 1867-1947
Beav	Beavan, Rolls, 1838-66
Bing	Bingham, Common Pleas, 1822-34
Bing NC	Bingham New Cases, Common Pleas, 1834-40
Bl Rep	Blackstone (either Henry or Sir William - see later under initial)
Bligh NS	Bligh's New Series, House of Lords, 1827-37
Bom Cr Cas	Bombay Reports, Crown Cases
Bos & Pul	Basanquet & Puller, Common Pleas, 1796-1804
Bos & P NR	Bosanquet & Puller New Reports, Common Pleas, 1804-7
Bro CC	Brown's Reports of Cases in Chancery, 1778-94
Brod & Bing	Broderip & Bingham, Common Pleas, 1819-22
Bull NP	Buller's Nisi Prius (see Appendix 3)
Burr	Burrow's King's Bench, 1756-72

C M & R	Crompton, Meeson & Roscoe, Exchequer, 1834-41
C & K	Carrington & Payne, Nisi Prius & Criminal, 1834-53 (also Car & Kir)
C&P	Carrington & Payne, Nisi Prius & Criminal, 1823-41
Cab & El	Cababé & Ellis, Queen's Bench, 1882-85
Cab & E	see above
CBNS	Common Bench, New Series, Common Pleas, 1856-65
CCC	Canadian Criminal Cases Annotated, 1892-present
CCR	Law Reports, Crown Cases Reserved, 1865-75
Ch	Law Reports, Chancery Division, 1890-present
Ch D	Law Reports, Chancery Division, 1875-90
Ch App	Law Reports, Chancery Appeals, 1865-75
Chitt	Chitty, King's Bench, 1770-1822
CI & Fin	Clark & Finnelly, House of Lords, 1831-46
CL	Current Law (monthly), 1947-present
CLY	Current Law Yearbook, 1947-present
Co Rep	Coke, Common Law, 1572-1616
Com Dig	Comyn's Digest, Common Law, 1695-1740
Comb	Comberbatch, King's Bench, 1685-98
Coop	George Cooper, Chancery, 1792-1815
Cowp	Cowper, King's Bench, 1774-8
Cox CC	Cox's Criminal Court Reports, 1843-1945
CP	Upper Canada Common Pleas, 1850-81
CPD	Law Reports, Common Pleas Division, 1875-80
Cr App R	Cohen's Criminal Court Reports, 1908- present
Cr & M	Crompton & Meeson, Exchequer, 1832-4
Cr M & R	see C M & R earlier
Cr & J	Crompton & Jervis, Exchequer, 1830-32
Cr & Ph	Craig & Philips, Chancery, 1840-41
Crim LR	Criminal Law Review, 1954-present
Cro Eli/	Croke, Common Law, in reigns of Elizabeth I,
Jac/Car	James I & Charles I
Cun	Cunningham, King's Bench 1734-5
D M & G	De Gex, Macnaghten & Gordon, Chancery Appeals, 1851-7
D&E	Durnford & East (see TR)
D&L	Dowling & Lowndes, Bail Court, 1843-49
De G & J	De Gex & Jones, Chancery Appeals, 1857-9
De G & Sm	De Gex & SMale, Chancery, 1846-52
De G M & G	see above D M & G
Deac	Deacon, Bankruptcy, 1834-40
Diprose's	Diprose & Gammon, 1897
	Friendly Society Reports
DLR	Dominion Law Reports (Canada), 1912-55, 2nd series 1956-present
Doug KB	Douglas' King's Bench Reports, 1778-85
Dow & Ry	Dowling & Ryland, King's Bench, 1822-27
Dow & L	see above D&L
Dowl PC	Dowling's Practice Reports, Bail Court, 1830-41
Dowl	as above

Drew	Drewry, Chancery, 1852-59
Dyer	Dyer, Common Law, 1513-81
E&B	Ellis & Blackburn, Queen's Bench, 1852-4
East	East, King's Bench, 1800-12
EB&E	Ellis, Blackburn & Ellis, Queen's Bench, 1858-60
EG	Estates Gazette, 1858-present
EGCS	Estates Gazette Cases Summaries
EGLR	Estates Gazette Law Reports, 1985-present
EI & BI	as above E&B
Eq	Law Reports, Equity, 1865-75
Eq Cas Abr	Equity Cases Abridged, Chancery, 1664-1744
ER	Englidh Reports, 1220-1865
Esp	Espinasse, Nisi Prius, 1793-1810
Ex D	Law Reports, Exchequer Division, 1875-80
Exch D	Law Reports, Exchequer Division, 1865-75
F&F	Foster & Finlayson, Nisi Prius & Criminal Courts, 1856-67
FLR	Family Law Reports, 1980-present
Gale	Gale, Exchequer, 1835-6
H Bl	Henry Blackstone, Common Pleas, 1788-96
H&C	Hurlstone & Coltman, Exchequer, 1862-66
H&N	Hurlstone & Norman, Exchequer, 1856-62
Hard	Hardres, Exchequer, 1655-69
Hardr	as above
HBR	Hansell's Bankruptcy Reports, 1915-17
Het	Hetley, Common Pleas, 1627-31
HL Cas	Clark's House of Lords Reports, 1847-66
Hob	Hobart, Common Law, 1613-25
Holt KB	Holt, King's Bench, 1688-1710
ICLR	Irish Common Law Reports, 1849-66
ILT	Irish Law Times, 1867-present
Ir CL	Irish Reports Common Law, 1866-77
Ir L Rec	Law Recorder (Ireland), 1827-38
IR CL	as above Ir CL
ILR	Irish Law Reports, 1838-50
Jeb & Sy	Jess & Symes, Queen's Bench Ireland, 1838-41
Jac	Jacob, Chancery, 1821-23
Jo	Johnson, Chancery, 1858-60; or either Sir T or Sir W Jones later
JP	Justice of the Peace, 1837-present
Jur	The Jurist, all courts, 1837-54, new series, 1855-67
K&J	Kay & Johnson, Chancery, 1854-8
KB	Law Reports, King's Bench, 1901-52
Keb	Keble, King's Bench, 1661-77

Keble	as above
Keny	Kenyon's Notes of Cases, King's Bench, 1753-9
Lat	Latch, King's Bench, 1625-8
Ld Raym	Lord Raymond, Common Law, 1694-1732
Leon	Leonard, Common Law, 1552-1615
Lev	Levinz, Common Law, 1660-96
LGR	Local Government Reports, 1902-present
LJ (NS)	Law Journal, New Series, all courts, 1832-1949
LJ (OS)	Law Journal, Old Series, all courts, 1822-31
Lofft	Lofft, King's Bench, 1772-4
LR Ir	Law Reports, Ireland, Chancery & Common Law, 1877-93
LT	Law Times Reports, 1859-1947
Legal Action	Journal of Legal Action Group
LT(os)	Law Times Old Series, 1843-59
LT Jo	Law Times Newspapers, 1843-1965
Lutw	Lutwyche, Common Pleas, 1682-1704
M'Clel	M'Cleland, Exchequer & Equity, 1824
M&G	Manning & Granger, Common Pleas, 1850-45
M&S	Maule & Selwyn, King's Bench, 1813-17
M&W	Meeson & Welsby, Exchequer, 1836-47
Madd	Maddock, Chancery, 1815-21
Man LR	Manitoba Law Reports, 1883-present
Man & G	as above M&G
Mans	Manson, bankruptcy, 1893-1914
Mod Rep	Modern Reports (Leach's), all courts, 1669-1775
Moo	Moore, Common Pleas, 1817-27
Moo & S	Moore & Scott, Common Pleas, 1831-34
Moo PC	see below Moo PCC
Mood Ind App	Moore's Indian Appeal Cases Privy Council, 1836-72
Moo PCC	Moore's Privy Council Cases, 1836-63
Moo & R	Moody & Robinson, Nisi Prius, 1830-44
Mood & R	as above
Mood & M	Moody & Malkin, Nisi Prius, 1826-30
Moore CP	as above Moo
Morr	Morrell's Bankruptcy Cases, 1884-93
MR	see Mod Rep
NB Eq Rep	New Brunswick Equity Reports, 1894-1912
NBR	New Brunswick Reports, 1883-1929, 2nd series 1949-present
Nev & M KB	Neville & Manning, King's Bench, 1832-36
Nfld LR	Newfoundland Law Reports, 1817-1940
Noy	Noy, King's Bench, 1558-1649
NPC	New Practice Cases, 1844-48
NSR	Nova Scotia Reports, 1834-1929
NSWLR	New South Wales Law Reports, 1971-present
NZ Recent Law	New Zealand Recent Law

NZLR	New Zealand Law Reports, 1883-present
OLR	Ontario Law Reports, 1901-30
OR	Ontario Rports, 1882-1900
P	Law Reports, Probate, Divorce & Admiralty, 1890-1971
Park	Parker, Exchequer, 1743-67; Appeal Court 1678-1717
PEI	Prince Edward Island Reports, 1850-82
Ph	Phillip, Chancery, 1841-49
Poll	Pollexfen, King's Bench, 1670-82
PR	Ontario Practice Reports, 1848-1900
Price	Price, Exchequer, 1814-24
QB	Adolphus & Ellis New Series Queen's Bench Reports, 1841-52
QB	Law Reports, Queen's Bench, 1891-1901, 1952-present
QBD	Law Reports, Queen's Bench, 1875-1890
QSCR	Queensland Supreme Court Reports, 1860-1881
R&G	Nova Scotia Reports (Russell & Geldert), 1879-95
RA	Rating Appeals, 1965-present
Roll Rep	Rolle, King's Bench, 1614-25
RTR	Road Traffic Reports, 1970-presents
Russ & Ry	Russell & Ryan's Crown Cases Reserved, 1800-23
RVR	Rating & Valuation Reports, 1960-present
Ry &	Ryan & Moody, Nisi Prius, 1823-26
Salk	Salkeid, King's Bench, 1689-1712
Saund	Saunders, King's Bench, 1666-1672
Say	Sayer, King's Bench, 1751-56
Scott NR	Scott's New Reports, Common Pleas, 1840-45
Sel Soc	Solden Society series
Show	Shower, King's Bench, 1678-95
Sid	Siderfin, King's Bench, Common Pleas & Exchequer, 1657-70
Sir W Jones	Sir William Jones, Common Law, 1620-40
Sir T Jones	Sir Thomas Jones, Common Law, 1667-85
Sm & G	Smale & Giffard, Chancery, 1852-57
Smith LC	Smith's Leading Cases, Common Law Courts
Sol Jo	Solicitor's Journal, all courts, 1857-present
SRQ	Queensland Reports, Supreme Court, 1860-81
Stra	Strange Nisi Prius, 1814-23
Swa	Swabey, Admiralty, 1855-59
Taunt	Taunton, Common Pleas, 1807-19
Tax Cases	Tax Case Reports, all courts, 1875-present
TLR	Times Law Reports, all courts, 1884-1950
TR	Term Reports (Durnford & East), King's Bench, 1785-1800
UCR	Upper Canada Reports; King's Bench, 1831-44' Queen's Bench 1844-81; Common Pleas, 1850-82

Vent	Ventris, all Courts, 1668-91
Vern	Vernon, Chancery, 1680- 1719
Ves Jen/Jnr	Vesey Senior, Chancery, 1747-56; Junior, Chnacery, 1789-1817
Vin Abr	Viner's Abridgement, see Appendix 3
VLR	Victorian Law Reports, 1875-1956
VR(L)	Victorian Reports (Law)
W&T	White & Tudor's Leading Cases in Equity
W&W	Wyatt & Webb, Australian courts, 1861-63
WALR	Western Australian Law Reports, 1898-1959
Will Woll & Dav	Willmore, Wollaston & Davison, Queen's Bench & Bail Ct, 1837
Willes	Willes, Common Pleas, 1737-58
Wils	George Wilson, Common Law, 1742-74
Win	Winch, Common Pleas, 1621-25
WLR	Weekly Law Reports, 1953-present
WM Bl	Sir William Blackstone, Common Law, 1746-79
Wms Saunds	William's Notes to Saunder's Reports, 1871
WN	Weekly Notes, all Courts, 1866-1952
WR	Weekly Reporter, all courts, 1852-1906
WRTLB	Wilkinson's Road Traffic Law Bulletin
WWR	Western Weekly Reports (Canada), 1912-70
Y&J	Younge & Jervis, Exchequer, 1826-30
YB	Year Books, Common Law, 1273-1535
Yelv	Yelverton, King's Bench, 1602-13

Table of Cases

Table of Statutes

Table of Statutory Instruments

Introduction

This book is written for the use of legal practitioners advising those facing enforcement of debts by bailiffs. It describes the rights of the bailiff, the 'distrainor', and of the debtor/ the distrainee. It then proceeds to examine the practical remedies available to the distrainee, whether by negotiation, less formal non-judicial pressure or by litigation. The practical elements of each remedy will be reviewed.

The reasons for producing a revised edition of this book are fivefold:

- the use of distress as a remedy continues to grow. This is due both to its extension in existing regimes, such as the encouragement of magistrates' courts to employ it more frequently, and also due to the development of new forms by Parliament (and the resurrection of an old form, in one case);

- it is an area of which few legal practitioners have much knowledge. A few specialising in the field of commercial property leasing will have employed the remedy of distress for rent and have expert knowledge of that one rather unique form, but on the whole it is a neglected field. With the growth in legal aid franchising, particularly into such areas as welfare and debt advice, more and more practitioners will encounter the day to day realities of enforcement by seizure of goods and will require information upon the subject;

- the previous edition needed to be updated to reflect changes in case law and statute since 2000 and the amendments to the law which are beginning to be made as part of the implementation of the Tribunals, Courts and Enforcement Act 2007 (TCEA);

- much of the interest that does exist considers only the immediate parties to the process – that is, the creditor and debtor. This book specifically aims to take a broader approach, as by its nature seizure of goods can have an impact on many more interests than just those of the debtor; and,

- the area of enforcement of debt by bailiffs is sadly one where there is scope for and, not infrequently, evidence of abuse. This is partly because the law is so unclear, partly because the enforcement agents are relatively poorly regulated and partly because the debtor - bailiff relationship is one which is liable to exploitation, taking place as it does in the privacy of a person's premises, with a large imbalance in power between enforcer and the subject of the levy.

In response to all these matters this text aims to provide a pragmatic step by step handbook to assist those confronted with enforcement by seizure of goods. It will explore each stage of the levy process and recommend remedies at every point. The first part of the book puts the process of distress in its current political and legal context. The second part examines how the bailiff may be avoided, whether by negotiation etc. or by the more extreme solution of insolvency. The third part goes through the procedure blow by blow, from the issue of a warrant to sale. At each stage the parties' rights and responsibilities are described, both in respect of the general principles of the law of distress and in light of the particular form of distress being levied; remedies are discussed and issues of legal controversy are explored.

Finally in the fourth part of the book general remedies such as creditors' or professional associations' complaints procedures are outlined.

The book is designed for practitioners assisting the following groups:

- *debtors*: whether they are individuals, members of partnerships or limited companies;

- *the debtor's relatives*: whether spouses, cohabitees, children or other family members who might find themselves involved in enforcement;

- *tenants & lodgers of debtors (or their families)*; or,

- *third parties with an interest in property on the debtor's premises*, whether they are holders of bills of sale or debentures, trustees or liquidators in an insolvency, finance companies who have let property on lease or hire purchase, manufacturers with claims under retention of title clauses, other creditors of the distrainee or any other third party whose goods might be threatened.

PART 1

LEGAL CONTEXT

Chapter 1

HISTORY & DEVELOPMENT

The laws of distress and execution have a long history of development. They arise from both common law and statute and have arisen in a piecemeal fashion, leading to the very complex pattern of powers which exists today. I have described this process elsewhere in detail.[1]

The recent history of English enforcement law has been marked by two conflicting aspects. On the one hand, there has been the continued development of new forms of the power of seizure of goods as government creates new liabilities. Child support maintenance and congestion charge are good examples of these. On the other hand there has been a growing appreciation that reform is desirable and, indeed, essential. A number of initiatives, partly responding to other current events, have marked this:

- *community charge* - the public concern generated by the very well publicised issue of poll tax enforcement led to the first initiative of Lord Chancellor's Department to reform enforcement law. Little substantive came of this other than some modest changes to the process of bailiff certification by amendments to the Distress for Rent Rules in 1999;

- *Civil Justice Review* - the re-examination of civil court enforcement procedures prompted by the introduction of the Civil Procedure Rules led to discussion of the desirability of harmonising county court and High Court rules on execution;

- *a review of bailiffs' law* was undertaken for LCD by Professor Jack Beatson in 1999. His report and recommendations provided the basis for the lengthy process of consultation that followed, which led through a series of reports to the Green and White papers and, eventually a Bill before Parliament;

---

[1] *Bailiffs Law*, volumes 1 & 2, Wildy, Simmonds & Hill, 2009.

- *the Access to Justice Act 1999* enabled magistrates' courts to transfer the powers of arrest of defendants from the police to civilian enforcement agencies. This was a significant extension of the powers of private bailiffs, although a new system of approval' of enforcement agents was also introduced. At the same time various amendments were also made to the power of distraint for magistrates' court orders (see Kruse, 2001);

- *the National Standard for Enforcement Agencies (NSEA)* was introduced by Lord Chancellor's Department in April 2002. Having decided that it wished to reform the law, government decided to bridge the gap by introducing a national code of practice for enforcement agents and creditors which laid down basic core standards of good practice. All the relevant parties committed themselves to the NSEA- this includes the Local Government Association, the bailiffs' trade bodies and the IRRV. The detail of the NSEA will be described at 3.5 and at appropriate points in the text;

- *Office of Fair Trading debt collection guidelines issued.* These are concerned with promoting good practice within the debt collection industry as a whole, but several large enforcement agencies hold licences and are covered by these provisions as well as the NSEA (see 3.8);

- *Courts Act 2003* - several significant changes were brought about by this Act.

    Firstly a new system of fines enforcement was introduced. 'Fines officers' were appointed in magistrates' courts to oversee the recovery process and, under subsequent regulations, new powers of enforcement were created, such as 'clamping orders' enabling defaulters' motor vehicles to be immobilised.

    Secondly, new Criminal Procedure Rules (Crim PR) replaced the former Magistrates Court Rules 1981.

    Thirdly, the role of the High Sheriff in the execution of High Court writs was terminated by section 99(2) of the Act. Instead full responsibility is vested in High Court Enforcement Officers (HCEOs) - formerly sheriff's officers, and their appointment by the Lord Chancellor and their powers generally were amended by Schedule 7 of the Act. There has again been increased consolidation and commercialisation in this sector (in light of which, perhaps, see *R v*

High Sheriff of Greater London, ex p. Roberts [1998] EWHC Admin 753);

Fourthly, administrative control over individual magistrates' courts passed to Her Majesty's Court Service (HMCS) on April 1ˢᵗ 2005. Significantly, for this book, a decision was taken to offer seven regional contracts for enforcement services to tender by private enforcement agencies. In an increasingly competitive sector, the letting of these contracts has been the subject of dispute. However the circumstances in which this is done is a commercial matter and not an issue of public law (see *R (on the application of Menai Collect) v Department of Constitutional Affairs* [2006] EWHC 727 (Admin).

Tribunals, Courts & Enforcement Act 2007- received royal assent in July 2007 and Ministry of Justice is currently working upon its implementation with a target date of April 2012. The Act has four main elements:

- *a single code of bailiff law*- the powers of all enforcement agents are harmonised, regardless of the debt which they may be enforcing. This code is contained in Schedule 12 to the Act, which contains an outline of the new powers of enforcement agents from the point of issue of the warrant through the process of 'taking control of goods' to payment or sale and the recovery of charges and resolution of disputes;

- *a single regulator for the industry*- this is expected to be the Security Industry Authority, but as an interim measure the government has promised an extended and improved system of certification of bailiffs, which will be applicable to almost all enforcement agents. This is discussed at 6.8. The government is also working on the issue of complaints adjudication, which is not a matter currently dealt with by SIA in respect of its other arrears of responsibility;

- *a single scale of fees*- this key issue is currently subject to detailed consultation;

- *distress for rent is abolished.* The final element of the Act is the long awaited abolition of the remedy of distress for rent by s71. For domestic properties, this abolition is a complete end to the landlord's right to seize goods for rent arrears. However, for business tenancies a new remedy is substituted. This is called 'commercial rent arrears recovery' (CRAR) and it perpetuates for landlords of shops, factories and other commercial properties a right to seize goods where rent arrears have accrued. Sections 72-87 of the Act repeat in the statute most of the basic rules relating to rent due and tenancies which previously applied at common law (see chapters 3 & 6 later).

The current timetable is for the Act to be brought into force in April 2012. There will be further extensive consultation before that date on all aspects of the Act and bailiffs' new powers.

Chapter 2

CURRENT REGIME

2.1 Introduction

Any study of the law of distress is complicated by the range of different forms that the remedy takes. In addition to the ten forms described below, numerous other forms of distress exist or have existed but have fallen into disuse or been abolished. These include the following:

- rent charges created under Improvement of Land Act 1864: interest due under s64 of the Act is enforceable by distress in the same manner as a rent charge under s121 LPA 1925; and,

- various shipping liabilities for which harbour authorities or undertakers may levy distress.

The above list contains forms of distress that are very rarely seen, as a consequence of which no further reference will be made to them in the text.

As is outlined below, there are currently ten forms of distress in active use, enforced by four different types of bailiff, with the law for each subtly different. Despite these differences between the various forms of the remedy, there are common principles running through every form of seizure which will be discussed in detail in Part Three. The ten active forms may be divided into three categories as follows.

2.2 Execution

Execution generally refers to the process of enforcement of civil court judgments, whether by charging order, garnishee order etc. More specifically it refers to the seizure of goods to recover judgment debts.

High Court execution
The High Court enforcement officer (HCEO) may enforce the following judgments by seizure and sale of the defendant's goods:

- High Court judgments of any amount;

- all county court judgments for over £5000 where the debt does not arise from an agreement regulated by the Consumer Credit Act 1974; and,

- county court judgments of between £1000 and £5000 which do not arise from an agreement regulated by the Consumer Credit Act 1974 and where the creditor requests transfer from the county court to the High Court for this purpose - see article 8 High Court & County Courts Jurisdiction Order 1991.

HCEOs are private bailiffs, but also officers of the Supreme Court. They are regulated by the Sheriff's Act 1887 plus the relevant provisions of the Courts Act 2003. HCEOs were formerly termed sheriff's officers and it is by this name that they continue to be described in the following text.

County court execution
The Court Service employs bailiffs in each county court who are responsible for enforcing all warrants and serving process within that court's area. The bailiff may enforce the following judgments by seizure and sale of the defendant's goods:

- all judgments based on debts arising from agreements regulated by Consumer Credit Act 1974 ;

- all county court judgments of less than £1000; and,

- any other judgment of an amount up to £5000 (see above).

Road traffic penalties
Local authorities may use execution to enforce unpaid orders for road traffic penalties (that is, parking contraventions and penalties issued for "moving traffic violations", as well as for congestion charges and unlawful vehicle emissions in greater London). Any sum payable for a road traffic contravention in England & Wales is recoverable by a warrant of execution issued by the Traffic Enforcement Centre at Northampton county court as if payable under a county court order. These warrants are enforced not by county court bailiffs but by private certificated bailiffs contracted to the enforcement authority. Because of the partly privatised nature of this form of execution, the law concerning it is a complex amalgam of county court execution, distress for rent and special provisions all of its own. It is a confusing area to deal with, as there are seven different statutes regulating the process.

2.3 Statutory distraint
Throughout the text, the term 'distraint' is preferred to 'distress' to describe the seizure of goods by bailiffs to enforce liabilities due under statute. This distinction is made because of a tendency to equate statutory distraint with common law distress and to seek to import common law powers into statutory procedure. It is well established that this is a false analogy and that,

in fact, statutory powers of seizure are far more like execution than distress (*Hutchins v Chambers* (1758) 1 Burr 579; *McGregor v Clamp* [1914] 1 KB 288; *Potts v Hickman* [1940] 4 All ER 491 HL).

A number of debts can be recovered by statutory distraint.

Local taxes
Both council tax and national non-domestic rate (NNDR) for businesses are enforceable by seizure of goods. Distraint may be levied by either local authority officers or by private bailiffs. The legislation is expanded upon by guidance such as the codes of practice produced by local authorities (see chapter 12).

Drainage rates
Under Land Drainage Act 1991 s54(1) a drainage board may recover arrears of drainage rates by a levy of distress in the same manner as a local authority may recover NNDR. Rates are raised by assessment on agricultural land and buildings and special levies on non-agricultural properties in order to finance flood defences and the like. The occupier of a chargeable agricultural property may appeal to the valuation tribunal about the determination of the annual value (s45). Any other matter can be appealed to the Crown Court (s51). These matters cannot be raised as a defence in recovery proceedings. A liability order made by the magistrates court may be enforced by distress only upon the goods and chattels of the liable person (s54(5)(a)) though the drainage board need not enforce if it feels that the expenses of collection won't be met (s54(6)).

Income tax
The Collector of Taxes may levy distraint to collect any unpaid taxes in exercise of powers found in ss61-62 Taxes Management Act 1970. Distress is used by the Revenue over 30,000 times per annum, but in seventy five percent of these cases it is against companies who have not paid PAYE. In addition to income taxes HMRC also has identical powers to distrain for arrears of stamp duty land tax under Sch.12 of the Finance Act 2003 and for arrears of windfall tax under Schedule 2 of the Finance Act (No.2) 1997.

Indirect taxes
There is a range of indirect taxes (most of which are unlikely often to be encountered by practitioners) which are enforced by HMRC by means of distraint. These are all recoverable in the same way under s.51 of the Finance Act 1997. These liabilities include the following:

- *VAT:* Customs & Excise may use their own officers or private bailiffs to levy for arrears of VAT. The power to distrain for VAT exists under para.5(4) Sch 11 VAT Act 1994 and reg.65 VAT (General) Regulations 1985, as amended by Part XXV, reg 212 VAT Regulations 1995. Interference with seized goods is an offence under s.68 of the 1994 Act.

- *Insurance premium tax:* Customs & Excise may also levy distress to collect tax due from any insurer which they are refusing to pay (Sch 7 Part III para 7(7) Finance Act 1994). The tax is charged at 2.5% on any taxable insurance contract made after October 1st 1994. These contracts include most policies except those for motor vehicles for the disabled, credit facilities and various ships and aircraft. Like VAT tax may be assessed in the absence of a return, there is a right of appeal to tribunal, and various penalties for non-payment and non compliance. Like VAT these include a penalty for breach of a walking possession agreement (para 19, Sch 7). The tax is enforced by distraint in the same manner as VAT and interference with impounded goods is an offence under s.11 of the 1994 Act.

- *Landfill tax* is also collected by C&E under Part III, Finance Act 1996. It is a tax on the disposal of waste in landfill sites throughout the UK. Site operators are liable for the tax at a rate of £7 per tonne on any disposal made after October 1st 1996. Tax can be assessed where C&E feel that too little is being paid. There is again a right of appeal to tribunal, interest and penalties for non-payment and a penalty of 50% of the tax due for breach of walking possession (Part V, para 24, Sch 5). The tax is enforced by a levy of distress in the same manner as VAT.

- *Climate change levy* - this is recoverable by distress under Schedule 6 of the Finance Act 2000 in the same manner as VAT. Interference with goods impounded under a walking possession agreement is an offence s.90(3) of the Act.

- *Aggregates levy* - this is recoverable under Sch.5 of the Finance Act 2001 by distress. Interference with goods impounded under a walking possession agreement is an offence s.15(3) of the Act.

Magistrates' court orders
Private bailiffs may be used by magistrates' courts to collect unpaid fines, compensation and costs orders, maintenance and civil debts; alternatively the court may employ its own civilian enforcement officers. Where a defendant defaults on payment of any sum adjudged to be paid following summary conviction or an order, the magistrates court can enforce by distraint. These sums recoverable by this means are civil debts (i.e. tax and national insurance contributions), damages, compensation orders and fines, including those from the Crown Court, Court of Appeal and House of Lords. Many

courts restrict distress for fines to fixed penalty offences (e.g. fines for motoring offences) or for sums under a level of £100-150.

National insurance contributions
The Secretary of State for Work & Pensions has the power to distrain for arrears of unpaid class 1 & 2 National Insurance contributions under s.121A of the Social Security Administration Act 1992. A JP may issue a warrant permitting entry to be forced by an 'authorised officer' to business premises for the purposes of levying and constables may be called upon to assist in this. Entry cannot be forced to private dwellings unless there is reason to believe that a trade or business is being carried on there. The goods levied shall be kept for five days before being appraised and sold by public auction.

Child support maintenance
The Secretary of State for Social Security is empowered by section 35 of the Child Support Act 1991 and by the Child Support (Collection & Enforcement) Regulations 1992 to levy distraint to collect arrears of maintenance due to the Child Support Agency (CSA). They may also collect other amounts of maintenance due to a parent with care at the same time and may enforce 'interim maintenance orders' (provisional assessments imposed as a penalty on the absent parent for not supplying the information required) by distress. Private bailiffs are employed. Additional guidance on the manner of levying distraint exists in the contract which exists between the CSA and its enforcement agents.

2.4 Common law distress

Distress for rent
Arrears of unpaid rent may be collected by means of distress, either by the landlord or by using a private certificated bailiff. A range of provisions govern the remedy, some very old. The remedy not only applies to rent but also to rent charges (*Dodds v Thompson* [1866] 1 CP 133).

Distress damage feasant
A statutory remedy in the Animals Act 1971 has replaced the power of distress as a remedy for damage to crops caused by stray cattle. Nonetheless, the remedy of distress damage feasant remains available for trespassing chattels (see for example *Reynell v Champernoon* (1631) Cro Car 228 or Ambergate, *Nottingham & Boston & Eastern Junction Co v Midland Railway Co* (1853) 2 El & Bl 792), and has recently been used to provide a legal basis for the practice of clamping cars wrongfully parked on private land. This application of this form of distress was considered by the Court of Appeal in *Arthur v Anker* [1996] 3 All ER 783.

PART 2

PRE-LEVY TACTICS

Chapter 3

PREVENTING SEIZURE

This chapter examines the strategies open to the client to avoid or prevent a levy by the bailiff actually taking place. Enforcement may have been threatened, a warrant may even have been issued, but it will be assumed in most cases that the bailiff will not have made great progress with the levy itself.

3.1 Staying enforcement of warrants

It may be possible to persuade a creditor to voluntarily withdraw a warrant, but this will normally only be in a situation where terms of payment have been agreed. Only in three situations is it possible to apply to court to have a warrant stayed by order.

3.1.1 *High Court*

If a defendant responds to a claim, it is likely that terms of payment will be set at the time of entering judgment. If no admission is submitted, then a default judgment, usually for payment forthwith, will follow. This will give rise to an immediate right of enforcement. Alternatively, execution may issue following defaults upon the terms of payment set by the Court.

Application to stay execution can be made at any time after the judgment is entered, which will normally be after the HCEO has visited the premises and levied (CPR Sch.1 RSC O.47 r.1). Such an application may be made even though the judgment debtor failed to respond to the original claim.

Application is on form N244 under CPR Part 23 stating the grounds for the application and providing evidence to support these, particularly details of the debtor's income, expenditure, assets and liabilities where inability to pay is the reason for seeking the stay (CPR Sch.1 RSC O.47 r.1(3)). It is obviously also important to notify the HCEO of the request and it can be possible to arrange extra time to make the application by speaking to the HCEO.

The court can stay execution if it is satisfied that the conditions set out in RSC O.47 r.1 are met and either there are "special circumstances which render it inexpedient to enforce the judgment or order" or "the applicant is unable from any cause to pay money". The court may well require the defendant to attend to be examined on the evidence given in the affidavit and to produce supporting documentation such as details of current bills, salary and debts. The court has broad discretion to stay the execution either absolutely or for such period and subject to such conditions as it thinks fit. All these considerations must however be conducted in light of the fact that the claimant should only be deprived of an immediate opportunity to enforce the judgment if there is good reason (*Winchester Cigarette Machinery Ltd v Payne (No. 2)* (1993) *The Times*, 15/12).

Orders staying execution that the court may make include the following:

- a stay on terms of payment, whether by instalments or by a lump sum or sums;

- an indefinite stay with liberty to apply or for a set period with a review at the end thereof;

- a stay subject to a moratorium for a set period; or,

- a stay subject to a charging order (if the debtor consents).

Readers should also note that under CPR Sch.1 RSC O.45 r.11 the Court has a general power to stay execution of a judgment or order, and to give other relief, on the ground of matters that have arisen since the date of judgment being entered. This may be done on whatever terms the Court thinks just. It has been held in *London Permanent Building Society v De Baer* [1969] 1 Ch 321 that the effect of this provision is to enable the court to consider matters which would have prevented the original order being made, or would have led to a stay if they had already occurred at the date of the order. The predecessor of O.45 r.11 (O.42 r.27) spoke of "facts which have arisen too late to be pleaded" - which makes clear the real intention of this rule. Application should again be made by N244.

Execution may also be stayed where a judgment is being appealed. This by application under CPR Part 52.7 and special circumstances will have to be shown to persuade the Court of the need to deprive claimants of their rights. These may include the possibility of enforcement ruining or precipitating the bankruptcy of the defendant (*Linotype-Hell Finance Ltd v Baker* [1993] 1 WLR 321) or the likelihood that if the debt or damages were to be paid to the claimant, they would not be recoverable if the appeal were successful (*The Annot Lyle* [1886] 11 P 114). Such stays may be on terms such as a requirement that the claimant be paid without undue delay if the appeal fails or that the appellant's assets are preserved in the meantime, other than for satisfying essential liabilities.

3.1.2 *County court execution*

Under s88 CCA the county court has a general power to stay any execution issued in proceedings, whether for the whole sum due or an instalment thereon, where the paying party is unable for any reason to satisfy the order. This stay may be on such terms and for such periods as the court thinks fit, and may be renewed periodically until the cause of the inability to pay has ceased.

In respect of execution warrants, the power to suspend the warrant is exercised under CPR Sch.2 CCR O.25 r.8. The debtor applies on prescribed form N245, providing details of his/her income, expenditure and other liabilities, both those subject to court orders and those which as yet are not, and making an offer of payment. This form is copied to the judgment creditor, who is given fourteen days in which to object to the application. If no objection is received the court office will suspend the warrant on the terms proposed. If the judgment creditor objects to the payment terms offered on the N245, a court officer will determine the rate of payment and suspend the warrant accordingly. Either party may challenge such a decision within fourteen days by application for 'reconsideration' on N244. The matter will be transferred to the court local to the debtor if necessary and will be heard before district judge, who may confirm, set aside or vary the order as s/he thinks fit.

Where the judgment creditor's objection is to suspension of the warrant as such, rather than to terms of payment, a hearing will be arranged before district judge, with at least two days' notice being given to each party. Under CCR O.25 r.8(10) where the district judge suspends a warrant the debtor may at the same time be ordered to pay the costs of the warrant and any fees or expenses incurred before its suspension, and sale of sufficient of the goods may be ordered to cover such fees, expenses and costs. Probably because most warrants are suspended very soon after issue without any hearing taking place, other than the fee being added onto the judgment debt - which is automatic upon issue of the warrant- the author has never encountered such orders being made to recover costs.

If any of the terms of the suspension are not complied with, the judgment creditor may apply for the warrant to be reissued. This actually rarely seems to happen, and generally once a warrant is suspended, one may regard it as effectively set aside or cancelled.

The court also has powers under s.71(2) CCA to suspend or stay any judgment or order where the person cannot pay the whole sum or any instalment. This can be done for such time and on such terms as the court thinks fit, and can be renewed periodically. This provision is slightly broader in its application than s.88 and CCR O.25 and can be of particular help where the defendant cannot pay at all. This is because when court staff analyse applications made on N245, a nil offer must be treated as a failure properly to complete the form.

As in the High Court, execution may be stayed on application where a judgment is being appealed either to Circuit Judge (CPR Part 52.7) or to the Court of Appeal (s.77).

3.1.3 *Road traffic penalties*

As described in chapter 2, these penalties are enforced by warrants of execution issued by the Traffic Enforcement Centre at Northampton county court. The relevant local authority in turn passes these to private bailiffs for execution. The bailiffs' powers are set out in the Enforcement of Road Traffic Debts Order 1993, which applies parts of the County Courts Act 1984 to these warrants. Section 88 of the Act does not apply and, as a consequence, it is not possible to apply to a court to suspend these warrants on N245.

3.1.4 *Magistrates' court distraint*

A magistrates' court may, if it thinks it 'expedient', postpone the issue of a warrant until such time and on such conditions as it thinks just (s77(1) MCA). Applications for postponement may be made as often as necessary (*Re: Wilson* [1985] AC 750). This means that, at the hearing at which the decision is taken to issue a warrant to bailiffs, the court can further delay the enforcement provided certain terms- usually for instalment payment- are met.

There is however no specific power to suspend warrants after they have been issued, unlike in the civil courts. However magistrates' courts do have discretionary powers to grant 'stays of execution' in very exceptional cases. Victorian authorities indicate that these exist. For example it has been held that the court may suspend, on terms, the enforcement of 'a sum of money claimed to be due and recoverable on complaint to a Court of Summary Jurisdiction' (*R v Paget* [1881] 8 QBD 151); whilst more recent cases have confirmed the power to grant a stay (*Re S (an infant)* [1958] 1 All ER 783 and *B(BPM) v B(MM)* [1969] 2 WLR 862).

However these cases also show that magistrates have only a discretionary power, not a duty, to grant a stay and that this power is only likely to be exercised where there are exceptional circumstances. This may be, for example, where an appeal is pending or where the welfare of a minor might be effected (*Smith v Smith* (1971) 115 Sol Jo 444). Equally it has been held that an appeal against a maintenance order is not grounds to stay its enforcement (*Kendall v Wilkinson* (1855) 24 LJMC 89) and that once the court has confirmed liability, it cannot suspend a warrant (*Barons v Luscombe* (1835) 3 Ad & El 589). Most recently a Divisional Court decision on this has been reported - *Crossland v Crossland* [1993] 1 FLR 175. In this matrimonial case a distraint warrant was issued to collect unpaid arrears of maintenance and a levy occurred. The husband applied by complaint for the magistrates to suspend the warrant and, on their refusal, appealed by way of case stated. Sir Stephen Brown P held that there was no inherent jurisdiction to suspend and "that once having issued (the warrant) ... the matter was out of the court's hands" and the justices were *'functus officio'* - they had discharged their duty.

Thus, although some courts will allow defendants to apply to vary the terms of payment of an order under s75(2) MCA and at the same time suspend a warrant, many more will refuse to entertain any application whilst the warrant is in the bailiff's hands. There is no way round such a problem and the client's only option then will be to deal with and perhaps try to negotiate with the bailiff, for which see later.

Once the warrant has been passed to the enforcement agent for collection, it is possible under Crim PR Pt.52.8(8) to postpone the sale of any seized goods from the present minimum period of 6 days from the date of seizure for up to sixty days (but no longer). This is applied for by the enforcement agent as a result of successful negotiations over instalments with the debtor and is approved by the clerk of the relevant magistrates' court without a hearing taking place.

3.1.5 *Other cases*

In all other forms of distress the decision to issue the warrant lies solely with the creditor, so any stay on enforcement will be solely a matter of negotiation with that creditor. As in the courts, the agreeing of terms of payment will be essential to any concession given to the debtor.

3.2 Liability for the sums claimed

This section will examine the nature of the liabilities for which distress may be levied, and the various means available to dispute a claim. In many cases these arguments will be commenced after the distress has been taken, and it will be necessary to try to agree a stay of enforcement as described at 3.1 in order to allow negotiations to take place.

3.2.1 *Distress for rent*

When may the landlord distrain? The right of a landlord to distrain exists automatically when land or premises are let (*Manchester Brewery v Coombes* [1901] 2 Ch 608). It need not be expressly reserved and there is no need for a written tenancy agreement (*Walsh v Lonsdale* [1882] 21 Ch D 9) although it may be excluded by the terms of the tenancy agreement or lease. The following specific conditions must also be satisfied:

- the rent payable must relate to occupation of land upon which distress may be levied and formerly only applied to 'rent service' payable as an incident of tenure for possession of premises. Rent cannot be levied in respect of rent for incorporeal hereditaments (*Talentine v Denton* (1605) Cro Jac 111; *Capel v Buszard* (1829) 6 Bing 150), but by statute it may be levied for a rent charge (s121(2) Law of Property Act 1925) and for a 'rent seck' (s.5 Landlord & Tenant Act 1730).

- the rent must be in arrears on a current tenancy and must be certain (*Regnart v Porter* (1831) 7 Bing 451; and see 6.4.1). There are no 'arrears' for which distress can be levied until the day after payment falls due (*Dibble v Bowater* (1853) 2 E&B 564), the tenant being able to pay the rent at any time during the day on which it falls due (*Duppa v Mayo* (1669) 1 Saund 287). Longer may have to be allowed if time to pay is given by the landlord (*Clun's Case* (1613) 10 Co Rep 127a). It does not alter this situation that the rent is payable in advance, if it is not paid on the day it is due (*Lee v Smith* (1854) 9 Exch 662). Payment of course terminates the right to distrain, though it has been held that giving a cheque in payment does not suspend the landlord's remedy until it is cashed (see *Harris v Shipway* (1744) Bull NP 182a and 10.3 later). The rent due must be certain (see 6.4.1 later) - even if the rent varies if it can be calculated or a minimum figure is set, distress may be levied.

- the distrainor must hold the reversion no matter how short, even if s/he is a tenant who has sublet for their term less just one day (*Wade v Marsh* (1625) Lat 211). The reversion must be vested in the landlord at the time the rent fell due, even though it is not necessary to hold the reversion for the whole period over which it accrued (*Thompson v Shaw* (1836) 5 LJCP 234). A joint landlord may distrain for the full sum due, with or without the consent of the other joint landlords (*Pullen v Palmer* (1696) 3 Salk 207; *Robinson v Hoffman* (1828) 4 Bing 562).

- although distress cannot normally be used after the end of a tenancy (see below), if any tenant gives notice to quit and then fails to leave, under DRA 1737 s.18 the landlord can levy (or sue) for double the former rent for the period during which the former tenant remains (*Timmins v Rawlinson* (1764) Bl Rep 533; *Johnstone v Huddlestone* (1825) B&C

922). The landlord thus can levy for mesne profits which otherwise would not be the subject of distress. This right ceases as soon as the tenant leaves (*Booth v Macfarlane* (1831) 1 B & Ad 904). The notice received from the tenant must be valid, in the sense that it complies with the common law requirements as to period and expiry date (*Farrance v Elkington* (1811) 2 Camp 591). Section 18 only applies in cases where the tenant is holding over as a trespasser and the landlord treats him as such. If the notice served by the tenant is valid, but the landlord refuses to accept it, there will be no right to claim double rent (*Oliver Ashworth (Holdings) Ltd v Ballard* [1999] EWCA Civ 1027/ [2000] Ch 12).

• rent must be lawfully due. This is to be determined by the true construction of the agreement (*C H Bailey v Memorial Enterprises* /1974] 1 All ER 1003) and it may be that they sum due can only be ascertained after the due date for payment. Thus where the rent may be subject to a review clause, any higher sum ascertained by this procedure will become payable retrospectively once it has been determined (*United Scientific v Burnley Council* [1978] AC 904). In this connection it is worth noting that a distinction is sometimes made between the 'distrainable rent' (the certain sum due) and other amounts that may be due under the lease (e.g. extra sums due on review)- see for example *ex p Voisey* [1882] 21 Ch D 442. The Court in *United Scientific* questioned whether this distinction was any longer applicable, but did not rule upon it in order to reach their decision. Reference was made to Foa's *General Law of Landlord & Tenant* which suggests that the common law right to distrain only applies to rent in the strict mediaeval sense and not to other contractual sums due under the agreement. *N.B.* if separate agreements exist between landlord and tenant, related to but distinct from the letting of the land, these may not be the subject of distress. See *Pulbrook v Ashby* (1887) 56 LJQB 376 or *Stevens v Marston* (1890) 60 LJQB 192 in which brewers who were landlords of pub premises sought to distrain in respect of sums due under agreements to supply drink to the licenced premises. Such agreements should be registered as bills of sale and as they were not, the levies were illegal.

If rent has been tendered, albeit late, then unless time was made of the essence in the lease, it is no longer unpaid and is not lawfully due (*Bird v Hildage* [1948] 1 KB 91). In this case the tendered rent was refused and was paid into court. The landlord was held liable for the costs of the proceedings. *Bird v Hildage* also held that permitting unpunctual payment of the rent in the past without protest does not justify the tenant assuming it will be permitted in the future, nor waive a right to levy for arrears. Even if the landlord has accepted a reduced sum of rent for a period, on default the whole sum may be levied (*Re: Smith & Hartogs* (1895) 73 LT

221). If the rent is due, the landlord may then distrain on the day immediately after the rent has fallen due for all or part of the arrears. If the rent is due on a Sunday, the landlord can distrain on a Monday (*Child v Edwards* [1909] 2 KB 753).

- the nature of the tenancy is immaterial. It may agreed orally or in writing; it may be a tenancy at will (*Morton v Woods* [1869] 4 QB 293) or a normal weekly tenancy (*Yeoman v Ellison* [1867] 2 CP 681). Clauses in the tenancy extending the right to distrain do not destroy the common law entitlement to the remedy (In *Re: The River Swale Brick & Tile Works Ltd* (1883) LJ Ch 638). Thus clauses permitting distress on privileged goods are legal (*Re: River Swale*), as are clauses permitting distress for sums that are not rent (*Doe d Elney v Benham* (1845) 7 QB 976) or permitting distress off the rented premises- provided that those premises are associated with the demised property (*Daniel v Stepney* [1874] 9 Exch 185). If several tenants occupy the land subject to one rent, the landlord can levy distress on any one for the rent due from all (*Woodcock v Titterton* (1864) 12 WR 865).

- if the tenant is allowed to hold over at the end of the term, the landlord can distrain (*Beavan v Delahey* (1788) 1 Hy Bl 5). Under ss6 & 7 Landlord & Tenant Act 1709 distress can be used within six months of the end of the lease or tenancy provided that the landlord does not change and that the tenant personally remains in occupation. If the tenant remains in occupation at the end of the term of a tenancy in such a manner as to indicate that the tenancy has been renewed, distress may be levied in the normal manner, and the Act will not apply (*Dougal v McCarthy* [1893] 1 QB 736). The Act also does not apply if the tenant remains in occupation of only part of the premises under a new tenancy agreement (*Wilkinson v Peel* [1895] 1 QB 963). Indeed, if a new tenancy is granted, any arrears under the old tenancy cannot be the subject of distress (*Stanfill v Hickes* (1697) 1 Ld Raym 280). The Acts do not apply where the tenancy has been terminated by forfeiture (*Kirkland v Briancourt* (1890) 6 TLR 441) but do seem to apply where the tenant remains under a notice to quit (*Williams v Stiven* (1846) 9 QB 14) or as a statutory tenant. Note that in levies under these provisions the tenant loses the protection of basic household goods and tools granted by statute (see 9.23).

- the landlord need not demand the rent or give notice before distraining unless this is stipulated for in the tenancy agreement (*Cranley v Kingswell* (1617) Hob 207). The distress itself is a demand and the common law rules on demanding rent need not be complied with (that is, a demand made on the premises for the sum due on the day it falls due - *Thorp v Hurt* (1886) WN 96). Thus if the lease allows the rent to be demanded in advance at any time during a rental period, this may be done and distress may be levied immediately without the need for 'reasonable notice' to the tenant (*London & Westminster Loan & Discount Co v London & North Western Railway Co* [1893] 2 QB 49).

When may the landlord not distrain? Distress cannot be employed if any of the following conditions apply:

- if the tenancy has come to an end, whether this is because it has expired; if a tenancy has been terminated by forfeiture (*Grimwood v Moss* [1872] 7 CP 360; *Serjeant v Nash Field & Co* [1903] 2 KB 304); or by a notice to quit (*Murgatroyd v Dodworth & Silkstone Coal & Iron Co.*(1895) 65 LJ Ch 111). Acceptance of rent, or levying distress, after the issue of a notice to quit does not act as a waiver of any breach of the tenancy unless the clear intention is to create a new tenancy (*Clarke v Grant* [1950] 1 KB 104 but see *Zouch v Willingdale* (1790) 1 H Bl 311). If the old tenancy has ended, and a new tenant has entered the premises, distress may not be levied even though a few goods of the old tenant may remain behind (*Taylerson v Peters* (1837) 7 A&E 110). Note the decision in *Rahman v Benwell Properties Ltd* (1997) EWCA 2133 in which the Court of Appeal refused leave to appeal the decision of a recorder in a county court. Mr Rahman argued that a levy of distress for rent the day after a purported forfeiture of the lease waived preceding breaches of the lease. The Court upheld the decision of the Recorder that even though the bailiff had issued a notice of seizure, drawn up an inventory and, apparently, entered into walking possession with Mr Rahman's wife, he was still at this stage entitled to conclude that there were insufficient goods to justify the costs of the seizure and sale and to withdraw from the levy, thus not prejudicing the landlord's position in respect of the forfeiture.

- if there is no demise. A contract for a lease is not sufficient to entitle a person to levy distress (*Dunk v Hunter* (1822) 5 B & Ald 322), nor is entry by a tenant in anticipation of a grant of a lease or an agreement for a lease, unless the conditions for a tenancy at a fixed rent can be implied (*Pinero v Judson* (1829) 6 Bing 206) or unless there is subsequent execution of the lease or a clause in an agreement permitting distress (*Carrington v Saldin* (1925) 133 LT 432; *Manchester Brewery v Coomb* [1901] 2 Ch 608). A landlord also cannot distrain if conditions precedent to a tenancy remain to be satisfied - for example if a house is to be furnished by the landlord prior to the letting, he may not distrain until this is done (*Mechelen v Wallace* (1836) 7 Ad & El 54n).

- if new premises are involved; if a new lease has been granted or if an action has been commenced against the ex-tenant as a trespasser (*Bridges v Smyth* (1829) 5 Bing 410).

- if the tenant has been led to believe that the remedy will not be used by the landlord (*Miles v Furber* [1873] 8 QB 77) or if agreement is made to postpone distress (*Giles v Spencer* (1857) 3 CBNS 244; *Oxenham v Collins* (1860) 2 F&F 172).

- if the tenancy has been terminated by death: in *Scobie v Collins* [1895] 1 QB 375 a tenancy at will ceased on the death of the tenant therefore a distress was trespass. However if a tenant dies and their personal representative enters and holds over, distress may be levied. This cannot be done if the spouse alone remains in occupation (*Turner v Barnes* (1862) 2 B&S 435).

- where the distrainor does not hold the reversion. If there has been an assignment of the lease, the distrainor must have reserved the express power to distrain if assigning his/ her whole interest (*Preece v Corrie* (1828) 5 Bing 24). A demise of the whole term or longer equals an assignment (see s5 L&TA 1730 and *Langford v Selmes* (1857) 3 K&J 220). Thus in *Lewis v Baker* [1905] 1 Ch 46, the defendant sublet the property for a term exceeding the original lease. When he levied distress for the rent, the court held it to be illegal. See too *Tadman v Henman* [1893] 2 QB 168 in which a reversion by estoppel was held to justify distress, but not against third party goods.

- against the assignee of a lease if the landlord consented to the assignment, knowing the assignor owed rent (*Pape v Westacott* [1894] 1 QB 272; *Wharfland v South London Co-operative Building Co* (1995) Times 25/4). However the assignee is bound by the power of distress in the pre-existing lease and cannot object to its use against them (*Daniel v Stepney* [1874] 9 Exch 185).

- if court action has been commenced (*Chancellor v Webster* (1893) TLR 568; *Potter v Bradley & Co* (1894) 10 TLR 445). Conversely the landlord cannot sue so long as distress is held even if it is insufficient because as long as the distress is held in the manner of a pledge, the debt is suspended (*Edwards v Kelly* (1817) 6 M&S 204; *Lehain v Philpott* (1876) 35 LT 855).

- if a person with a license to occupy is involved (*Rendell v Roman* (1893) 9 TLR 192; *Provincial Bill Posting Co v Low Moor Iron Co* [1909] 2 KB 344; *Interoven Stoves Co Ltd v F W Hubbard* [1936] 1 All ER 263).

If a tenant wishes to dispute the right of the landlord to levy distress, for any of the reasons outlined, this may be done by an action for illegal distress or by replevin. See, respectively, chapters 7 and 9. The entire development of the remedy of replevin was driven by the need to define the limits and nature of the landlord and tenant relationship, and almost all the early year book reports dealing with replevies of illegal distresses are concerned not with the manner of the distress itself but the exact terms of the lease upon which it was based.

For what may the landlord distrain? The landlord may distrain for the full sum due, or only a portion, and may include with that all sums treated as rent in the reddendum (see 6.4 below). It used to be held that there is no right of set off even for repairs (*Absolon v Knight & Barker* (1743) 94 ER 998). However the Court of Appeal in *Eller v Grovecrest Investments Ltd* [1995] 2 WLR 278 held that there was no difference between a claim for rent arrears by court action and a claim by distress. In both the respective rights of landlord and tenant should be considered. A cross claim for damages by the tenant could be used by way of set off as a defence against a claim for rent by distress. An injunction was granted in the Eller case to restrain a levy where the damages claim exceeded the rent due. This principle was more recently applied in *Fuller v Happy Shopper Markets Ltd* [2001] EWHC Ch702. The tenant's business property had become partially unusable and after continuing payments for some time, he withheld rent. Distress was levied and the goods seized were sold. The court decided that the tenant was entitled to reduce the rent arrears by the overpayment before the proceeds of sale were applied.

Set off can be excluded by the agreement, but it will have to be an explicit term and a covenant to pay "without deductions" is not sufficient (*Electricity Supply Nominees v IAF Group* [1993] 2 EGLR 95).

3.2.2 *Income taxes*

By the time enforcement proceedings for tax are commenced, whether by distress or by court action, the time for challenging liability has, in theory at least, been lost and cannot be raised to challenge enforcement (*Rutherford v Lord Advocate* (1931) 16 Tax Cases 145; *IRC v Pearlberg* [1953] 1 All ER 388). Even if the tax is improperly assessed, the taxpayer cannot replevy after distraint (*Allen v Sharp* (1848) 2 Exch 352). If however there has been no valid assessment, or if the demands cannot be proved to have been received by the debtor, the distraint may be unlawful (*Berry v Farrow* [1914] 1 KB 632).

3.2.3 *Road traffic penalties*

Enforcement of a penalty follows the making of an order by the Traffic Enforcement Centre at Northampton county court (CPR Part 75). Before this stage is reached, the defendant has opportunities to challenge the penalty, initially with the enforcement authority and subsequently before the adjudicator- although strict time limits apply. Once the court order is made it is difficult to dispute liability, although it may be possible on prescribed grounds, by applying to the court to set aside the order. If such an application succeeds, the court order is revoked and the matter is referred back to the enforcement authority. One issue that is unclear is the status of any charges that the bailiffs have incurred in levying the warrant. The court rules state that "any execution issued on the [cancelled] warrant shall cease to have effect". It is unclear if this is intended to have retrospective effect, so that monies paid to the bailiffs by the owner should be refunded.

3.3 Refusing entry

As will be fully described in chapter 7, entry cannot be made against the debtor's will. If this is ignored or if a forced entry is discovered it is permissible for the debtor to resist entry within limits (*Green v Goddard* (1704) 2 Salk 641; *Leward v Basely* (1695) 1 Lord Raym 62). However, ejecting a bailiff who has entered legally can lead to forced re-entry and to the commission of an offence.

3.3.1 *Lawful resistance*

The courts have sanctioned the use of reasonable force by the debtor to prevent an entry in three different contexts:

- *bailiff's status not disclosed*: In *Broughton v Wilkerson* (1880) 44 JP 781 Broughton, a county court bailiff, attended at Wilkerson's house to levy. The defendant held the door open whilst they discussed the matter. An argument developed and when the bailiff forced entry, a fight ensued. The bailiff neither produced the warrant nor made his purpose clear. As the bailiff had no right to force entry he was not thereafter in execution of his duties. As a result there was not an assault on a court officer.

- *entry is forced*: wherever bailiffs exceeds their powers the debtor may resist. In *Rossiter v Conway* (1894) 58 JP 350 the defendant bailiff was seeking to levy distress for rates. He took Mrs. Rossiter by surprise when she opened the door, jamming his arm in as she tried to close it. When Conway entered the house she punched him. Mrs Rossiter was charged with assault but it was held she had authority to admit or exclude any person from the house and was therefore entitled to resist a forced entry. Similarly in *Vaughan v McKenzie* [1968] 1 All ER 1154 two county court bailiffs used force to enter the debtor's home. One was then struck on the head with a bottle but it was ruled that an assault on a court officer had not occurred because of the prior illegal entry.

- *permission to enter refused or withdrawn*: In *Davis v Lisle* [1936] 2 KB 434 two police officers entered premises to make enquiries relating to an offence. They had no permission and no warrant to enter. Davis told them to leave and then punched and abused PC Lisle. It was held that this was not assault upon an officer in the execution of his duty because, as soon as they were told to leave ("not without emphasis"), they had no right to remain and were trespassers. This case highlights an important point which will receive more consideration later, namely that the bailiff's right to enter is a revocable licence (see 7.4)

The problem in these situations is determining the measure of reasonable force that may be employed by the debtor or occupier. The example of *Vaughan* above is not entirely helpful as there could well have been a criminal assault- the issue decided was that it was not an assault upon a court officer. It is probably safe to assume that something less than the amount of force used in that case will be reasonable and lawful, whether from the debtor or from others. In *Collins v Renison* (1754) Say 138/ 96 ER 830 the defendant was found liable for trespass in upsetting a ladder upon which the claimant was standing. Even though this was done "gently... thereby doing as little damage as possible to the claimant" it was still thought that such a degree of force was not justified in the defence of land. More recently this area has been examined in *Revill v Newberry* [1996] 2 WLR 239, which held that trespassers are still owed a duty of care. There should be a warning or alternative attempt to repel an intruder before any action likely to cause significant injury to the trespasser, if s/he is not posing a threat to the occupier or likely to do irreparable damage to the property. This elaborates on the existing authorities which held that force may be used to remove a peaceable trespasser after a request to leave has been ignored (*Hall v Davis* (1825) 2 C&P 33). If force is used to enter, no request to leave is necessary (*Weaver v Bush* (1798) 8 TR 78)- this is also the case if force is employed after a peaceable entry (*Polkinhorne v Wright* (1845) 8 QB 197). If the occupier meets with resistance, more force may be employed, the limits on this escalation being defined by the value of the property concerned, the amount of harm threatened to it and the above mentioned duty of care.

Regarding the control of dogs on the premises, the law is that it is an offence to set on or urge a dog to attack, worry or put any person in fear and that the keeper will be liable for any damage or injury caused. Even if the dog is kept to guard a property, the owner may be liable if the animal prevents access by or injures innocent visitors on lawful business. The person may sue if their entry is under a legal right.

3.3.2 *Debtor's offences*

The use of violence and threats of violence to eject a bailiff from premises which have been legally entered can lead to forced re-entry (see 7.4) and possibly a claim (or prosecution) for assault (*Gregory v Hill* (1799) 8 TR 299). If a person is unlawfully detained in order to compel the release of goods, it will be possible to bring a claim for false imprisonment (*Harvey v Mayne* [1872] IR 6 CL 417) - and the bailiff could also use force to escape. It is an offence at common law to obstruct the execution of powers granted by statute (*R v Smith* (1780) Doug KB 441). The person can be fine or imprisoned up to two years at the court's discretion. A good example is *Southam v Smout* [1963] 3 All ER 104 in which the county court bailiff entered legally by a closed but unlocked door in order to arrest the debtor. The son-in-law of the debtor objected to this entry of his house without his permission and assaulted the bailiff when he refused to leave. This was held to be an offence. However if the debtor (or her goods) had not been in the house, the bailiffs would have been trespassing on third party premises (see 7.4).

A debtor may be guilty of criminal contempt if s/he obstructs a HCEO or county court bailiff in the execution of their duty- for instance, by assaulting the officer (*Lewis v Owen* [1894] 1 QB 102). The court may commit or fine the offender. This will be so even if there are minor errors in the writ. In *R v Monkman* [1892] 8 Man LR 509 it was held unlawful to resist a sheriff's officer executing three writs of fi fa which were incorrect as to the date of judgment on each. The HCEO is under a duty to enforce a writ that is on the face of it regular, and such errors were mere irregularities that could be amended.

If an HCEO is resisted, he may arrest and imprison the guilty parties (s8(2) Sheriff's Act 1887). The county court may, under s14 CCA, may commit and/ or fine any person who assaults an officer whilst in execution of his duty. The bailiff may arrest the offender without a warrant and take him /her before the judge. A recent example is the two consecutive custodial sentences of three months given to a defendant who attempted to run down two bailiffs with his car (*Read v King* (1997) 1 CL 5). If a person is committed, they can appeal and apply for release pending their appeal, no notice of which need be served on the bailiff (*Brown v Crowley* [1963] 3 All ER 655). The alternative remedy for an officer who is the victim of an assault would be to lay an information before a magistrates' court under the Offences Against the Person Act 1861. Although it has been held that the justices have no jurisdiction over assaults arising during execution (*R v Briggs* (1883) 47 JP 615) the correct procedure for the court would be to treat it as only triable on indictment and accordingly take depositions and commit it for trial at the Crown Court if there is a *prima facie* case to be made out (*R v Holsworthy Justices ex p Edwards* [1952] 1 All ER 411).

3.3.3 *Debtors' defences*

It would be a defence for the debtor to say that s/he honestly, but mistakenly, believed the victim was not a court officer or was not acting in execution of his duty (*Blackburn v Bowering* [1994] 3 All ER 380 CA). The prosecution must show not that the defendant knew that the complainant was an officer acting in execution of his duty but that there was an assault i.e. an intentional or reckless show or application of unlawful force. As the use of reasonable force is lawful in self defence, if such force is applied to an officer as would be reasonable had he not been an officer, in the belief that he was not an officer, then the defendant has a good plea of self defence, even if his belief was unreasonable. Thus if the defendant believed he was being attacked by persons who were not court officers, and only reasonable force necessary to repel the attack was used, the use of force was not assault and the prosecution must prove he did not act reasonably or honestly in self defence.

Equally, if a county court order is void or *ultra vires* resistance by the owner of the goods is not unlawful obstruction (*R v Finlay* [1901] 13 Man LR 383). It is not illegal obstruction to prevent entry where an HCEO is entering third party premises when neither the person nor the goods of the debtor are present (*R v Gazikom Aba Dore* (1870) 7 Bom Cr Ca 83; see also 7.3 later).

3.4 Protecting goods from seizure

The debtor may resist a seizure which is unlawful by taking back the goods which are being seized. However, if used at the wrong time or in the wrong circumstances, such an action risks being an offence- either rescue or poundbreach. The latter is most likely to occur, though both offences are often referred to simply as rescue (e.g. s92 CCA). Both are offences at common law as well as being torts for which the bailiff may sue in trespass. In the cases of an alleged illegal resistance, it is up to the prosecution to show that all the elements of the offence have been committed (*R v Harron* [1903] 6 OLR 666).

3.4.1 *Lawful recaption*

It is legal for a person to simply seize back their own illegally distrained goods before they are impounded, where:

- the distress is illegal in respect of place, goods being seized or because there is no debt due (*Cotsworth v Betison* (1696) 1 Ld Raym 104; R v Pigott (1851) 1 ICLR 471; *R v Walshe* [1876] IR 10 CL 511);

- where seized chattels are being abused or neglected by the distrainor who has taken them out of the place where they were originally impounded for an illegal use (*Gomersall v Medgate* (1610) 80 ER 128);

- where a valid tender is refused (*Bevils Case* (1585) 4 Co Rep 11b);

- the levy is on an order of which there is no record at court (*R v Carroll* (1828) 2 Ir L Rec 53); or,

- where the warrant is invalid because it does not comply with the prescribed form (*R v Williams* (1850) 4 Cox CC 87) and provided that the relevant statute does not contain an exception in such circumstances (see c.10- irregular seizures).

The levy being resisted must be illegal in its execution, and rescue cannot be used to challenge some other aspect of the process- for example, an objection to being held liable to rates is a matter of appeal, and does not justify rescue (*R v Higgins* [1851] 21 ICLR 213). Both forcible recapture and forcible resistance to wrongful seizure are lawful and are defences in claims for assault (*Leward v Basely* (1695) Hawk PC 130), though the level of force permissible may be difficult to determine (*Blades v Higgs* (1861) 10 CBNS 713). The more recent case of *Devoe v Long & Long* [1951] 1 DLR 203 confirms that the right of recaption may be exercised to recover goods wrongfully taken using whatever force is reasonably necessary and entering onto another's property to do so if necessary, provided that that can be peaceable and without any breach of the peace (see too *Rich v Woolley* (1831) 7 Bing 651). Rescue must be by the owner of the goods, or by his agent, but not by a stranger. Thus, if the goods of two persons are wrongfully taken, each must rescue his own (*Jennyngs v Playstowe* (1621) Cro Jac 568).

It is stated in *Bullers Nisi Prius* (7th edition, p.61) that it is not rescue to disturb a bailiff who is in the process of making a distress but who has not yet secured possession. This is cited also in paragraph 9.168 of *Woodfall on Landlord & Tenant*, though there are no modern authorities. By contrast *Coke* (2 Inst p161) and *Viner's Abridgment* state that resisting distress is as much an offence as actual rescue. In modern practice of impounding on the premises, disturbing the initial stages of the levy is probably best regarded as recaption.

3.4.2 *Rescue*

Rescue (or rescous) is interference with seized goods not yet impounded. In earlier times there was a distinct time lag between seizure and impounding during which the debtor could seek to recover items (*Cotsworth v Betison* (1696) 1 Salk 247). To constitute rescue there must be something equal to a breach of the peace, or likely to prove a breach of the peace, plus taking in the presence of the keeper (*Lodge v Rowe* [1875] 1 VLR 65).

Rescous is both a criminal offence under the Distress for Rent Act 1689 and a civil wrong leading to a penalty of treble damages, based on the debt due. The bailiff can also use the right of re-caption, i.e. pursue and re-take the goods and an attempt to rescue justifies an assault (*Anon* (1705) 11 MR 64).

The common law remedy for rescue which would be applicable for instance to statutory distraint is a special action for trespass by the creditor on the goods seized, in which a claim for any assault on the bailiff may also be made. The person sued may defend on the grounds outlined earlier.

3.4.3 *Poundbreach*

Poundbreach is interference with impounded goods and is the offence most likely to be committed in these days of walking possession agreements. It is an offence to breach a pound even if the distress was unlawful, as the impounded goods are now in the custody of the law and the poundbreach is thus a trespass to the Crown and a breach of the peace (*Anon* (1535) 1 And 31; *R v Nicholson* (1901) 65 JP 298). To constitute poundbreach there must be a criminal intention (*Lodge v Rowe* [1875] 1 VLR 65 and see *Abingdon RDC v O'Gorman* below).

Poundbreach is an offence, whether or not there is a breach of the peace and whether or not the seized items have been improperly stored, simply because it is a violation of legal custody (*R v Beauchamp* (1827) 5 LJOSMC 66). The offence of poundbreach can apply to statutory distraint as well as distress for rent (*R v Higgins* [1851] 2 ICLR 213). The bailiff's warrant is prima facie evidence of his authority and there is no need to prove that the sum was properly due in order to prosecute poundbreach (*R v Brenan* (1854) 6 Cox CC 381). It is not a defence to say that the distress was illegal- the breach of the pound is the gist of the proceedings, and it is not necessary to examine the cause of the distress in detail (see for example *Company of Proprietors of Parrett Navigation v Stower, Trott & Munckton* (1840) 6 M&W 564). It can also be an offence for a person to attempt to commit poundbreach (s.1 Criminal Attempts Act 1981).

The offender can be prosecuted for an indictable offence at common law (*R v Butterfield* (1893) 17 Cox CC 598; *R v Bradshaw* (1835) 7 C&P 233). For a person to be convicted, it has been held that there should be clear evidence of them knowingly engaging in or assisting in the commission of the offence (per Lord Hanworth MR at p.218 in *Lavell & Co v O'Leary* [1933] 2 KB 200). The committal can be for an unlimited period (*R v Castro* [1880] 5 QBD 490) or a fine can be for an unlimited amount, though based on the person's means and the gravity of the offence (*Beeches Case* (1608) 77 ER 559).

In addition to the criminal remedy, there are two civil remedies for poundbreach available to the impounder. One is a common law right of action for damages which would be applicable to most forms of statutory distraint. There is also right of recaption, which would bar the civil action (*Vaspor v Edwards* (1702) 12 MR 662)

3.4.4 *Statutory remedies for rescue*

In addition to the common law remedies of rescue and poundbreach, there are a number of statutory remedies applicable to certain forms of seizure of goods.

- *Distress for rent* There is a specific remedy for landlords under s3 Distress for Rent Act 1689. The landlord may sue in the local county court by a special action for the wrong sustained. Such an action is a penal action and the claimant is not therefore entitled to an affidavit of documents or the other preparations normal prior to trial (*Jones v Jones* [1889] 22 QBD 425). Action may be taken against either the owner or actual offender, but if the landlord recovers against the offender, action may not later be taken against the owner (Sir Bartholomew Shower's Observations, fo.162/3).

  The penalty is treble damages for both rescue and poundbreach. Treble costs can also be awarded (*Lawson v Story* (1694) 1 Ld Raym 19). The basis upon which the damages are calculated is the value of the goods seized (*Cyril Morgan (Holdings) v Dyer* (1995) 11 CLY 193). No special damages need to be proved by the landlord (*Kemp v Christmas* (1898) 79 LT 233). The same case also indicated that although the claimant may have already recovered damages in respect of the offence (in this instance, an action for negligence against the bailiff) this does not provide the offender with a defence, although it may be used in mitigation of the damages awarded. Note that in *Firth v Purvis* (1793) 5 D&E 432 the pound was breached after tender was refused by the claimant landlord, who insisted on the goods seized. In the circumstances treble damages were held excessive and were reduced to single damages. For the remedy to arise it is not important where the goods were impounded but if they are fraudulently removed to third party premises and then rescued by a third party the DRA probably does not apply (*Harris v Thirkell* (1852) 20 LTOS 98). Normally it is held that the landlord may not protect seized goods by issuing a claim for trespass or conversion, though a claim for the common law tort of rescue may be possible (*Iredale v Kendall* (1879) 40 LT 362).

• *Indirect taxes* Interference by a debtor with goods impounded under a walking possession agreement will lead to the automatic imposition of a civil penalty in all cases of distraint for indirect taxes, as described in chapter 2. For example, under s68 VATA there is a civil penalty for breach of any walking possession agreement of fifty percent of the VAT due. The debtor will not be liable if s/he can convince the Commissioners or, on appeal, a VAT Tribunal, that there is a reasonable excuse for the breach. Lack of funds is not a reasonable excuse.

• *County court executions* In respect of county court execution section 92 CCA states that any person rescuing seized goods is liable to prison of one month and/or a fine up to level 4 (£2500). S/he may be arrested and brought before a judge by the bailiff. Arrest will either be on the spot if they are caught by the bailiff, or alternatively following a summons from the court (see *Newman t/a Mantella Publishing v Modern Bookbinders* [2000] EWCA Civ 2, in which the Court of Appeal considered the impact of ECHR art.6 upon this procedure). In High Court execution retaking seized goods can be treated as a criminal contempt- see 3.4 earlier.

• *Magistrates clamping orders* It is an offence to remove, or to attempt to remove, a vehicle clamp or a clamping notice. Under Courts Act 2003 Sch.5 para.49 the penalty is a fine up to level 3.

3.4.5 *Abandonment*

Naturally in instances where an offence is alleged, arguments can arise as to whether poundbreach or rescue have indeed occurred and these will involve questions as to whether impounded goods had been abandoned (*Dod v Monger* (1704) 6 Mod 215) or were properly impounded in the first place. There will be no abandonment, and therefore an offence will have been committed, where possession is adequately retained or the bailiff intends to retain it. See for example *Jones v Biernstein* [1900] 1 QB 100, in which a rent bailiff took an inventory and then remained in close possession until he left the house over the weekend. The tenant re-took the goods in his absence but was held guilty of poundbreach as abandonment had not occurred. The bailiff had abandoned actual possession of the goods for no necessary reason, but as he intended to return (as shown by the inventory), the distress was not abandoned completely and the bailiff remained in 'constructive possession'. Abandonment has occurred and/ or no offence is committed where:

- the authorised bailiff is not in possession: even where possession had been abandoned due to threats and violence by the defendant, it was held not to have been rescue because the goods had been left in the care of bailiffs' assistants and not the officer named on the warrant (*R v Noonan* [1876] 10 ICLR 505);

- there is no adequate impounding: in *Alwayes v Broom* (1695) 2 Lutw 1262 it was held that it is not poundbreach to remove goods from a pound left unsecured. Equally it is not an offence for the debtor to change the lock on the pound (for example, the room selected by the landlord on the tenant's premises) provided that no goods are removed. The distrainor may, though, have a special action on the case against the tenant (*Anon* (undated] cited under *Holman v Tuke* (1672) Win 80);

- the bailiff fails adequately to maintain a walking possession: in cases where an 'oral' walking possession is taken but is not followed up every few days, abandonment may take place very quickly. Even in cases where there has been a written agreement, if the debtor does not pay and the bailiff neglects to follow up the default with removal in a reasonable period of time, it may be possible also to claim abandonment (see 8.3.2 and *Lloyds & Scottish Finance v Modern Cars & Caravans (Kingston) Ltd* [1966] 2 All ER 732;

- poundbreach occurs before removal: in *Lavell & Co v O'Leary* [1933] 2 KB 200 a tenant, Mr. Wong Gee, signed a walking possession agreement with bailiffs who distrained for rent arrears on goods in his business premises, the 'Canton Cafe'. Wong then got a removals firm to take the goods away. The firm was found not guilty of poundbreach because they took the goods from the landing outside the property. Wong Gee was guilty as he had moved the goods there after they had been impounded within his premises. The court asserted that a walking possession agreement is valid against all the world (but contrast this with the next case);

- removal is by an innocent third party: in *Abingdon RDC v O'Gorman* [1968] 3 All ER 79 CA a landlord distrained for rent upon a hired television set, amongst other things. Notice was given to the tenant who signed a walking possession agreement. However he later asked Mr O'Gorman from the television hire firm to remove the rented set. The firm was not informed of the levy when doing this. The bailiff began an action for treble damages. The Court of Appeal held that the hire firm was not guilty of poundbreach because the walking possession agreement did not validly impound the goods against strangers. A person cannot be guilty of poundbreach unless s/he has a guilty mind, i.e. knows of the impounding. O'Gorman was not guilty as he was not covered by the agreement. If he had been, he should have been notified of the seizure so that he could serve notice on the landlord of his claim to the goods (see 9.31); or,

- the creditor fails without good reason to take adequate steps to protect and maintain their levy. In *LCP Retail Ltd v Segal* [2006] EWHC 2087 Chancery Division felt that a landlord's failure to protest when impounded goods were sold by the debtor company, and later to notify the liquidator in the company's winding up of the existence of a walking possession agreement, amounted to an abandonment of their claim over the goods.

As will be returned to in Chapter 8, the courts have frequently manifested dissatisfaction with the common lack of notice of walking possession on third parties and the consequent risk of poundbreach. In *Dixon v McKay* (1903)[1912] 21 Man LR 762 seizure by means of walking possession was 'reasonably sufficient' as far as the debtor was concerned, but might not have been for third party buyers, and in *Dodd v Vail* [1913] 9 DLR 534 walking possession was held to be valid seizure against those with notice of the seizure, but third parties would not necessarily be aware of it. Ideally bailiffs should secure effectual and continuous possession (*Little v Magle* [1914] 7 WWR 224, citing Dixon above) if they wish to ensure that the seized goods are protected from interference by all parties with a possible interest in them.

3.5 Concealing or removing goods

Depending upon when it occurs, it may be a legal and effective stratagem, or a criminal offence, for a debtor to hide or carry away distrainable goods and chattels.

3.5.1 *Lawful concealment*

It is not illegal for the debtor to hide items of value on the property prior to the levy. Most bailiffs tend to make only a fairly cursory search, despite a common law duty to use "reasonable diligence" in a search, so this strategy may succeed. Removing items from the property prior to a levy is also legal, except that in distress for rent the debtor risks the offence of fraudulent removal (see below) and in execution by the HCEO entry may be forced to third party premises (see 7.4). Other bailiffs can peaceably enter third party premises to search for goods (see 7.4). The debtor is not obliged to say where any goods are, so it is usually extremely unlikely that a bailiff will be able to discover their new location. The only factor operating in the bailiff's favour is that, after a while, the debtor is likely to tire of not having the use of goods, so that they will be retrieved. At this point if the levy has not been terminated it is possible for the bailiff to return and try again.

3.5.2 *Fraudulent removal*

The offence of fraudulent removal occurs when a tenant removes goods in order to defeat a levy of distress for rent, leaving insufficient goods for distress behind. The landlord can pursue and sell goods fraudulently or clandestinely removed within thirty days of their removal (s.1 DRA 1737), provided that they have not been sold in good faith and for valuable consideration to a person not privy to the fraud (s.2 DRA), and if s/he can also show that the following conditions apply:

- there is a right to distrain- there must of course be rent arrears, although the landlord does not need to show that distress was actually contemplated (*Stanley v Wharton* (1821-22) 9 Price 301). Any distress that is levied must be lawful (*R v Gopalasamy* (1902) ILR 25 Mad 729). There is no presumption by the court that the distress was lawful, and the prosecution must prove this. In the absence of such proof, the defendant cannot be convicted as the court will regard them as exercising their right of private defence of their property against unlawful interference. If the tenancy has been terminated and the tenant is no longer in possession the landlord cannot follow goods and seize them. In *Gray v Stait* [1883] 11 QBD 668 the landlord terminated the tenancy and the same day the tenant moved out, leaving a quarter's rent unpaid. The landlord seized goods at the tenant's new home. This was wrongful. If the tenant holds over under 8 Anne c14 s6 the power to distrain continues (see 3.2).

- the removal was fraudulent- that is, if it was done wilfully, knowingly and deceitfully to deprive the landlord . The burden of proof is on the landlord (*Inkop v Morchurch* (1861) 2 F & F 501). Removal need not be clandestine to be fraudulent (*Opperman v Smith* (1824) 4 Dow & Ry KB 33) but a secretive removal at night is very likely to be fraudulent (*Watson v Main* (1800) 3 Esp 15; *Furneaux v Fotherby* (1815) 4 Camp 136; *Vaughan v Davis* (1793) 1 Esp 257). It has been suggested that if the tenant removes goods, thinking that s/he has a right to do so, this removal is probably not fraudulent (*John v Jenkins* (1832) 1 Cr & M 227);

- the removal was to defeat a levy of distress. The court must decide if it was fraudulent even if the tenant admits it was to avoid distress (*John v Jenkins* (1832) 1 Cr & M 227);

- no sufficient goods remained (*Gegg v Perin* (1845) 9 JP 619; *Gillan v Arkwright* (1850) 16 LTOS 88): readers need to note the complex rules on goods seizable in distress for rent, for which see chapter 9;

- the removal occurred after the arrears accrued (*Watson v Main* (1799) 3 Esp 15; *Rand v Vaughan* (1835) 1 Bing NC 767). The tenant has all day to pay the rent due, and distress cannot be made until the next day therefore it appears that goods removed on the day rent falls due are not fraudulently removed (*Dibble v Bowater* (1853) 2 E&B 564; *Re: Aspinall* [1961] Ch 526); and,

- removal was by the tenant or by a third party acting at his/ her instigation. The tenant need not personally remove goods so long as s/he allows it to be done (*Lister v Brown* (1823) 1 C & P 121/ 3 Dow & Ry KB 501). The tenant will still be liable for the acts of a third party if privy to the fraud. A third party is only liable if s/ he knew of the fraudulent purpose of the removal (*Brooke v Noakes* (1828) 8 B&C 537): see also the next paragraph.

- the goods removed belonged to the tenant and were distrainable (*Thornton v Adamson* (1816) 5 M & S 38). This exemption from the offence applies regardless of whether the creditor is aware of an imminent distress (*Bach v Meaks* (1816) 5 M&S 200). Goods not the property of the tenant (e.g. on a bill of sale in arrears) are outside these provisions (*Tomlinson v Consolidated Credit & Mortgage Corp* [1889] 24 QBD 135) therefore when the goods were seized on default by the mortgagor, there was no fraudulent removal. The fact that this may be in breach of the terms of the Bills of Sale Acts is not an issue for the landlord as these statutes exist to protect the mortgagor, not third parties.

If the landlord has grounds to suspect that fraudulently removed goods are inside any premises entry may be forced during day time to any locked or secured premises, that is any house, barn, stable, outhouse, yard or close (DRA 1737 s.7). If entry is to be forced a constable must be present (*Rich v Woolley* (1831) 7 Bing 651; *Cartwright v Smith & Batty* (1833) 1 Mood & R 284) but the landlord need not request the goods first (*Williams v Roberts* (1852) 7 Exch 618). If entry is to be forced to a house, an oath should be made before a justice of the peace first, to the effect that there is a reasonable ground to suspect that goods are present.

Section 3 of the 1737 Act created a civil penalty for fraudulent removal by the tenant, and any person wilfully and knowingly assisting (which can include the trustee of a bankrupt tenant - *Welsh v Myers* (1816) 4 Camp 368). This is payment of double damages to the landlord and is recoverable by action. The damages are to be measured by the value of the goods removed (*Gwinnet v Philips* (1790) 100 ER 780; *Brooke v Noakes* (1828) 8 B & C 537). In such a penal action, the normal directions and rights as to discovery etc. do not apply, therefore the claimant landlord cannot for instance administer interrogatories to the defendant (*T W Hobbs & Co Ltd v Hudson* [1890] 25 QBD 232).

Alternatively a criminal sanction is available. Under s.4 DRA 1737, when the goods do not exceed £50 in value, the landlord may lay an information in the magistrates' court, either that in the area where goods were removed or where they were taken (*R v Morgan* (1780) Cald 156). The landlord's right to sue still applies even if the debt is under this ceiling (*Horsefall v Davey* (1816) NPC 147; *Stanley v Wharton* (1821) 9 Price 301). The court can order a penalty of double the value of the goods removed which is payable as a fine within a time set by the court. If prosecuted before the magistrates it must be shown that the offence was committed 'wilfully and knowingly' (*R v Radnorshire JJ* (1840) 9 Dowl 90). The justices do not need to specify the goods removed, so long as they find that the value is below the prescribed level (*R v Rabbitts* (1825) 6 D&R 341). The magistrates' decision can be appealed to the Crown Court under s5 DRA 1737 (*R v Cheshire JJ* (1833) 5 B & Ad 439) and if the party appealing enters into a recognizance with sufficient sureties for double the sum ordered to be paid and on condition that s/ he appears at the crown Court, enforcement of the justices' order shall be stayed in the meantime (s6).

3.6 Consequences of a failed levy

If the bailiff fails to gain entry or find any adequate goods, a return of 'no goods' or 'no sufficient distress' is made to the creditor and other enforcement may then be attempted by them. Case law makes it clear that the bailiff must have made reasonable efforts to actually enter or search for goods to be able lawfully to make such a return. Nil returns can be made where:

- the goods are hidden (*Doe d Haverson v Franks* (1847) 2 Car & Kir 678);

- entry is either obstructed (*Doe d Cox v Roe* (1847) 5 Dow & L 272) or refused (*R v Dudley Justices ex p Blatchford* (1992) RVR 63); or,

- the goods found are already subject to seizure, or become so under a claim for priority by the Crown - for which see 6.6.2 (*Grove v Aldridge* (1832) 9 Bing 428).

The link between a failed levy and further enforcement is important because the various regulations specify the conditions that must be satisfied by the bailiff to enable other steps to be taken. In local tax recovery the billing authority may seek to have the debtor committed to prison where the bailiff reports that "he was unable (for whatever reason) to find any or sufficient goods of the debtor on which to levy the amount" (reg 47(1) CT(A&E) Regs; reg 16(1) NDR(C&E) Regs). If the bailiff fails to make any proper levy at all, then a nil return is not correct and an application for committal cannot be based upon it (*R v Burnley JJ ex p. Ashworth* (1992) 32 RVR 27).

Similar rules apply to civil court executions where, following a failed levy by a HCEO or county court bailiff, the judgment creditor wishes to enforce by petitioning for bankruptcy on the basis that execution has been returned unsatisfied in whole or in part (s268(1)(a) Insolvency Act 1986). This was examined *in Re: A Debtor* (No 340 of 1992)[1994] 3 All ER 269 CA and the court held that the failure of the sheriff to gain access on unstated occasions at unstated hours did not justify a return of the writ as 'unsatisfied'. The court made a distinction between an unexecuted and an unsatisfied writ (see also *Re: Worsley ex p Gill* [1957] 19 ABC 105) and stated in this case that the return that the writ was unsatisfied was merely the bailiff's opinion on the effect of what he has done (or failed to do)- the court is not bound by this opinion. The writ orders goods to be seized: where this has not been done at all the return in question was at least irregular as it could not be justified by what the bailiff had actually done. In executions for road traffic penalties, under CPR Part 75.10, an enforcement authority can try other means of recovery through the county court- attachments of earnings, charging orders, 3rd party debt orders or 'oral examination'. To do any of these, though, the authority needs to confirm the following in the application. If no execution was attempted, why not; or, if execution was attempted, the authority must certify that 'no relevant return' was made to warrant- that is that bailiff unable to seize goods because:

- access was refused;

- goods had been removed;

- the goods seized were insufficient to cover the sums due; or,

- the goods seized were insufficient to cover the costs of removal and sale.

3.7 Transfers to third parties

Transferring goods to relatives, children or friends puts them beyond the reach of bailiffs in many cases and in genuine cases, if a third party then removed his/her goods before distress, they could not be sued (*Pool v Crawcour* (1884) 1 TLR 165). The fact that the debtor has disposed of goods to a third party just prior to a levy in order to defeat the seizure does not necessarily void the disposition merely because of the circumstances in which it occurred. If the bargain was for good consideration with a genuine intention to pass property it will be valid (*Wood v Dixie* (1845) 7 QB 892). It is not necessary for both parties to act in good faith, so long as there is good faith on the part of the purchaser (*Mackintosh v Pogose* [1895] 1 Ch 505). The same might apply to bills of sale and purchase and lease back (*Tower Finance & Furnishing Co v Brown* (1890) 6 TLR 192). The deal will not be invalidated by the purchaser's knowledge of the intended execution provided that proof of payment and change of possession can be shown (*Hale v Saloon Omnibus Co* (1859) 4 Drew 492).

If items genuinely transferred to third parties are taken, the person generally has a remedy - interpleader in the courts, a declaration of ownership versus the landlord or an injunction and action for wrongful interference. A third party may prove ownership by making a statutory declaration. If a third party's goods are in the hands of the debtor through fraud or theft they may be recovered by the true owner (*Earl of Bristol v Wilsmore* (1823) 2 Dow & Ry 755).

Various means of transfer have been tried. The most common are outlined below.

3.7.1 *Gifts*

A gift, properly undertaken, will put property beyond the reach of bailiffs. Gifts may be effected by several means - by deed, by declaration of trust or by delivery. It is likely that the last is the method most commonly tried by individuals, though trusts are discussed at 3.4.2.

To make (and prove) an effective gift, the debtor will have to demonstrate the following:

- that the transfer of property was made with no intention of its return; and,
- that there was clear and distinct act of gift.

All property, real and personal, corporeal and incorporeal, may be given. We are interested in personal property and the main means of giving personal chattels is by transfer and retention of possession. Without actual delivery a gift of chattels won't be effective, thus if the donor wishes to retain possession, a gift will have to be by bill of sale instead, for which see 3.7.3. Actual manual delivery is not essential, though an oral gift without some act of delivery will be ineffective (*Smith v Smith* (1733) 2 Stra 953). Examples of successful and failed gifts follow.

- *donee is put in possession by donor* In *Kilpin v Ratley* [1892] 1 QB 582 a father verbally gave furniture to his daughter. They were in a room in her home where some of the furniture was stored. There was no manual delivery and after the gift the furniture remained where it was. The court held that he had done all he could to complete the gift and there was no need to go through "the mere formality of handling furniture in order to complete the gift".
- *donee is put in constructive possession by the donor* For example by handing over the key to a warehouse where goods are stored (*Rowles v Rowles* (1750) 1 Ves Sen 348); by touching and words (*Rawlinson v*

Mort (1905) 93 LT 555); or by delivery of part as representative of the whole (*Lock v Heath* (1892) 8 TLR 295 - the gift of a chair).

- *the nature of the donee's possession is changed* For example in *Winter v Winter* (1861) 4 LT 639 a barge was given to the donor's employee who had previously been in possession of it as employee, but who subsequently used it as his own. In *Cain v Moon* [1896] 2 QB 283 it was held that prior delivery, such as for safe keeping, can be converted into delivery as a gift by changing the capacity in which the item is held.

- *intention alone is not enough* In *Jones v Lock* [1865] 1 Ch App 25 a father put a cheque into his baby son's hand and declared it to be the son's. The father died soon after and the cheque was found still to be in his possession. His declaration in favour of his son was never followed through by investment or the like and thus was not an effective gift.

Gifts between family members can be problematic. There is no reason why a gift cannot be made to a child provided that it is effected properly (*Shephard v Cartwright* [1955] AC 431). Between husband and wife the situation is more complex. They may give each other gifts of chattels and so on, but the need for a clear and distinct gift and evidence of intention is even more important. A gift must be unequivocal. If the facts are consistent with both a gift and an intention to share use with a spouse, no gift has occurred. See for example, *Re: Cole ex p Trustee of Bankrupt's Property* [1964] 1 Ch 175 - the husband told the wife that goods in a house were all hers, but they continued to live together and share the chattels. No delivery or change of possession could be shown, and as a result title remained vested in his trustee. In *Bashall v Bashall* (1894) 11 TLR 152 a husband allegedly gave a pony and trap to his wife. Again both continued to use it and the wife's claim was held unproved. Delivery is needed to affect a gift to a spouse who does not have existing possession (*Hislop v Hislop* (1950) WN 124). An act showing an intention to change ownership may be sufficient, even if chattels are still shared, but mere letters written and signed by one spouse giving furniture to the other are not enough (In *Re: Bretton's Estate* [1881] 17 Ch D 416).

3.7.2 *Trusts*

It is not unheard of for debtors, particularly small firms, to try to protect property by putting it in trust. As noted above this may be done by declaration of trust.

A valid trust of personal property may be created in writing (*Gee v Liddell (No 1)* (1866) 35 Beav 621) or by oral declaration of the trust (*M'Fadden v Jenkyns* (1842) 1 Ph 153). If the trust is created in writing no particular form must be followed so long as all the material terms of the trust are contained-the parties, the property concerned and the objects of the trust. The written instrument will have the advantage of being proof that can be shown to any bailiff calling to seize. However the problem is that written assignments of chattels will tend to fall under the Bills of Sale Acts (see 3.7.3) unless they are covered by one of the statutory exemptions- amongst others, they are for the benefit of creditors of the grantor, they are marriage settlements or they are in the ordinary course of business. As none of these exemptions are likely to apply, the trust may have to comply with the technicalities of the Acts. One way to escape this problem and still have some written proof of the trust is where the bargain is complete without writing, such as by delivery, and the document simply refers to or confirms this transaction. Such evidence of the declaration of trust can be prepared at a later date to the creation of the trust itself. At common law although only an absolute interest in chattels could be created by a trust it is now possible to create limited interests in all chattels except those exhausted by personal use. This does not include a business' stock or farming stock (*Myers v Washbrook* [1901] 1 KB 360; *Breton v Mockett* [1878] 9 Ch D 95).

A trust is effective as most bailiffs cannot seize equitable interests in property (see 9.1). As against strangers, the trustee and beneficiary are one person in equity, so possession of the trust property by the beneficiary is regarded as possession by the trustee (see *White v Morris* (1852) 11 CB 1015). Thus the trustee may sue in conversion even if the trust property is retained and enjoyed by the beneficiary (*Barker v Furlong* [1891] 2 Ch 172). Note however that it has been held that where the whole beneficial interest is vested in the debtor(s), the trust will not be allowed to defeat the creditor (*Stevens v Hince* (1914) WN 148). Clearly, this strategy is only going to succeed where the property can be held on trust for more than one person, perhaps the debtor and spouse/ cohabitee jointly (provided that they are not joint debtors).

Finally we may note that trusts that are created for an illegal purpose or against the public interest are void. We may speculate whether a trustee in the circumstances described, who is forced to sue or interplead to protect the alleged trust property, may meet with some scepticism on the part of the courts as to the validity of the trust they seek to defend.

3.7.3 *Bills of Sale*

Assignment of goods under bill of sale is a means of transferring the property in goods whilst retaining the possession of them. It can afford effective protection for them against bailiffs, whether the purpose is the benefit of another creditor by the provision of security for the credit extended or the debtor's own protection, where the bill of sale is made with a friend or relative. For instance, it has been successfully used between husband and wife in respect of household goods that both continue to use (*French v Getling* [1922] 1 KB 236; *Re: Satterthwaite* (1895) 2 Mans 52). This strategy is not uncommon but can face considerable problems. Bills of sale are regulated by the Bills of Sale Acts 1878 and 1882 and numerous formalities and procedures must be followed for them to be effective against bailiffs. The following outlines the key elements to which attention should be paid.

The bills of sale legislation is concerned with documents rather than transactions. Thus any transfer of property, if put into writing, can be liable to be treated as a bill of sale and will have to comply with the following requirements (*Hopkins v Gudgeon* [1906] 1 KB 690). Gifts by deed or by declaration of trust can be included if the property remains with the donor and no effective transfer to another can be shown. Mortgages and charges of goods by companies are in the main outside the Acts, but instead see 9.21 on debentures. The statutory requirements which must be complied with are described below.

A bill of sale document must exist in the correct form. The 1882 Act contains a standard form in its schedule which must be closely, though not exactly, followed (*Roberts v Roberts* [1884] 13 QBD 794). The statutory form identifies the parties, the loan and the terms of its repayment and allows the goods to remain in the possession of the owner unless s/he is in breach of the bill under s.7 of the 1882 Act, for instance by default, bankruptcy or by allowing the goods to be taken in execution. If two or more individuals grant a bill of sale over their goods, their shares should be identified if they are unequal, otherwise the bill will be void (*Saunders v White* [1902] 1 KB 472). Repayments of the loan do not have to be in equal amounts (*Re: Cleaver ex p Rawlings* [1887] 18 QBD 489) nor do the instalments have to comprise equal amounts of interest (*Edwards v Marston* [1891] 1 QB 225). Bills will be void where the times of payment are unspecified (*Hetherington v Groome* [1884] 13 QBD 789) or the interest rate is not stated (*Blankenstein v Robertson* [1890] 24 QBD 543). A bill failing to comply with the statutory requirements is wholly void (s9 1882 Act and see *Davies v Rees* [1886] 17 QBD 408).

An inventory of mortgaged goods must be attached. The bill of sale document itself does not describe the goods and chattels mortgaged, therefore an inventory will be attached (s.4 1882 Act). This must specifically describe the goods concerned (*Thomas v Kelly* [1888] 13 App Cas 506) and too vague an inventory will render the bill ineffective in respect of any personal chattels not properly described (*Witt v Banner* [1887] 20 QBD 114). If there could be no problem identifying the items concerned, more general words may be permissible (*Davidson v Carlton Bank* [1893] 1 QB 82).

A bill of sale may be made in respect of most goods and chattels, including furniture, growing crops and fixtures. Trade machinery are for the purposes of the Acts treated as personal chattels rather than fixtures (s5 1878 Act), so all machines, plant and equipment in factories and workshops may be assigned, but the bill must be registered - see below (*Hawtry v Butlin* [1873] 8 QB 290). Trade machinery does not, however include machines supplying power or gas, water or steam: any assignment of such items does not require registration (*Topham v Greenside Glazed Firebrick Co* [1887] 37 Ch D 281). Even if a bill is void in respect of personal chattels, it will not prejudice the status of other items included in it, such as fixtures (*Re: North Wales Produce & Supply Co Ltd* [1922] 2 Ch 340) or excluded trade machinery (Re: Burdett [1888] 20 QBD 310). If the bill includes an assignment of real chattels as well as personal chattels, it is void (*Cochrane v Entwistle* [1890] 25 QBD 116). The grantor of the bill must be owner of the personal chattels comprised in the bill otherwise it will be void (s.5 1882 Act)- this includes after acquired property, but not fixtures, plant and trade machinery acquired to replace items mentioned in the schedule to the bill (s.6 1882 Act).

Consideration must have been given and must be stated in the document. A minimum advance of £30 is prescribed; anything less than this renders the bill void (s.12 1882 Act). The loan should have been made at the same time as the bill, unless it is to be made by instalments, in which case this should be disclosed in the bill (*In Re: Young* (1880) 43 LT 576). If the consideration is not truly stated, the bill is not wholly void, but is void only in respect of any personal chattels comprised in it (*Heseltine v Simmons* [1892] 2 QB 547).

Witnesses should attest the making of the bill (s.10 1882 Act). Failure to do this renders the bill void. An affidavit should accompany the bill detailing its proper execution and attestation, the true date of execution and the residence and actual occupation of the grantor (the debtor) and every witness. Again failure to comply with these provisions avoids the bill (*Matthews v Buchanan* (1889) 5 TLR 373).

Registration of the bill must take place to make it valid (s10 1878 Act and see *Pickard v Marriage* [1876] 1 Ex D 364; *Youngs v Youngs* [1940] 1 KB 760). The bill and inventory, a copy of these and the affidavit must be presented within seven days to Queens Bench Division of the High Court (s.8 1882 Act), otherwise it will be void in respect of any personal chattels assigned. Registration must be renewed every five years (s.11 1878 Act) and failure to do this makes the bill wholly void (*Fenton v Blythe* [1890] 25 QBD 417), as a result of which it will be ineffective against a *bona fide* execution creditor (*Jenkinson v Brandley Mining Co* [1887] 19 QBD 568).

Enforcement of the bill of sale is by the mortgagee (the secured lender) taking of possession of the goods given as security. This seizure would put the goods beyond the reach of the bailiff just like seizure by another bailiff (*Taylor v Eckersley* [1877] 5 Ch D 740; *Donaghue v Campbell* [1901] 2 OLR 124). If goods subject to a bill are seized in distress before the debt secured by the bill has been called in by the creditor, that creditor would have no right to possession of the goods and could not sue the bailiff for conversion. A bill dated after the date of a levy will not be effective (*Gladstone v Padwick* [1871] 6 Exch 203). However this statement needs to be qualified as the effectiveness of a bill differs according to the debt being enforced by distress:

- execution cannot be levied on mortgaged goods (*Holroyd v Marshall* (1862) 10 HL Cas 191; *In Re: Cuthbertson ex p Edey* [1875] 19 Eq 264) and the execution creditor may be liable to the grantee of a bill for a levy on assigned goods (*Condy v Blaiberg* (1891) 55 JP 580). Interpleader can protect the goods if this happens (see 9.26). If interpleader is begun by the mortgagee it is normally the practice to order sale and divide the proceeds (CPR Sch.1 RSC O.17 r.6);

- magistrates' court distraint is prevented on mortgaged goods;

- local tax distraint on mortgaged goods is prevented;

- income tax distraint can take place under s.14 of 1882 Act;

- rent distress is not prevented, unless a Consumer Credit Act default notice has been served by the mortgagee (s4A LDAA 1908). However the mortgagee could remove the goods without it being fraudulent (see 3.5). If the landlord distrains, it seems he is not liable to account to the grantee for any surplus (*Evans v Wright* (1857) 2 H&N 527). The grantee may pay off the distress and then sue the grantor (*Edmunds v Wallingford* [1885] 14 QBD 811).

In all cases the validity of a bill may be open to challenge by a bailiff through the courts. In *Miller v Solomon* [1906] 2 KB 91 it was observed that bills of sale could be used to try to defeat seizure but that "It could not be right that a bill of sale holder, whose security is for a small sum on goods of large value, should be allowed to put an execution creditor in this dilemma and permit goods to escape execution..". Thus the court might not allow "the furtherance of a dishonest purpose". See also *Reed v Thoyts* (1840) 6 M&W 410: if a person purports to dispose of goods under a fraudulent bill of sale, although it may be valid as against the other party to the agreement, from the point of view of creditors seeking to levy distress or execution, the bill is void and the property in it remains in the debtor.

3.7.3 *Furniture Leases*

Another quite common approach, especially amongst small firms, is for the debtor to transfer his/her assets to a friend or relative and then lease the items back again. Distress for rent would not be prevented by this technique if the transfer were to a spouse or business partner: in most other cases it might be effective protection against seizure. For example see *Withers v Berry* (1895) 39 Sol Jo 559- a husband gave property to his wife by a deed of gift. After they separated the furniture was leased back to him- but it was held not to be in his possession and thus not seizable in execution. However, the courts may regard these arrangements as simply stratagems to avoid legal enforcement and refuse to uphold them in any action brought by the debtor for wrongful interference following seizure (*Scarfe v Halifax* (1840) 7 M&W 288).

3.8 Personal circumstances & the National Standard

The National Standard for Enforcement Agents requires enforcement agents and creditors to consider extending extra protection to a number of groups and individuals.

There is a general requirement that agents must not discriminate unfairly on any grounds such as age, disability, race, gender, religion or sexual orientation. More particularly, it is stipulated that enforcement agents should respect the religion and culture of others at all times. They should be aware of dates for religious festivals & carefully consider the appropriateness of enforcement on any day of religious or cultural observance or during any major religious or cultural festival. Finally, and in most cases most importantly, it is required that both agents and creditors should protect the vulnerable & socially excluded & should have procedures to deal with such cases. Those who might potentially be vulnerable include:

- elderly people;
- people with disabilities or suffering from serious illness;
- those recently bereaved;
- single parent families and pregnant women;
- unemployed people; and,
- those who have obvious difficulty in understanding, speaking or reading English. Agents should if possible be able to rapidly access translation services & provide on request information in large print or in Braille.

Of course, these categories of potentially vulnerable individuals are not exhaustive and where an advisers identifies an individual who may suffer undue hardship as a result of attempts to levy distress or execution, this should be brought to the bailiffs' attention.

3.9 Office of Fair Trading Guidelines

In July 2003 (revised December 2006) the Office of Fair Trading issued guidelines as to the kinds of practice to be avoided by debt collectors. These guidelines are primarily written with the needs of firms collecting unsecured consumer credit debt in mind, but with appropriate changes are applicable to those bailiffs' companies which have chosen to hold Consumer Credit Act licences.

The guidance is mainly concerned with the personal, rather than material, impact of debt collection practices. Its primary purpose is to prevent improper treatment of debtors by collectors and, accordingly, it specifies the kinds of behaviour which are considered to be unfair, oppressive, inaccurate or misleading. The guidance deals with a number of different aspects of the debt collection process: communications, harassment, visits to properties, charges and false representations of the law or a person's authority. Much of the guidance replicates what is found in the NSEA, but particularly useful provisions include warnings against:

- visiting a debtor when it is known that the person is vulnerable;

- continuing with a visit when it becomes apparent that the debtor is distressed or otherwise vulnerable, for example, when it becomes apparent that the debtor has mental health problems;

- deliberately giving misleading information about the collector's powers to create a fear of arrest or prosecution;

- contacting debtors at unreasonable times and at unreasonable intervals; and,

- making threatening statements or gestures or taking actions which suggest harm to debtors.

In addition, the guidelines prohibit:

- claiming collection costs in the absence of express legal provision;

- applying unreasonable charges which are not based on actual and necessary costs or applying charges which are disproportionate to the main debt; or,

The full text of the guidance can be obtained from the OFT website (www.oft.gov.uk) and the register of consumer credit licences may also be searched on-line.

3.10 TCEA 2007- commentary

Although it will be apparent that the common law offences of rescue and poundbreach are largely redundant, the new Act remedies this for the creditor. Schedule 12 of the Act creates two new offences which debtors may in future be at risk of committing. It will be an offence for a debtor either to obstruct a bailiff or to interfere with controlled goods (para. 68). Moreover, if a debtor interferes with controlled goods, a creditor will be able to issue a claim against him/her for any damages arising from this (para. 67). The incorporation of these offences into the new statute must make it much more likely that, when the Act comes into force, they will be actively prosecuted.

Chapter 4

INSOLVENCY

The insolvency of the debtor individual or company can have a major impact on the ability of bailiffs to proceed. The procedures involved in entering insolvency are not dealt with but there are numerous books available describing these aspects of the system. Insolvency procedure is laid down by four separate bodies of statute.

- For individuals and companies the Insolvency Act 1986 and Insolvency Rules 1986 apply. These provide a code for the insolvency of firms and individuals and lay down procedures to be followed in administering their affairs. The legislation splits into two parts. The first part deals with the insolvency of firms, the second with that of individuals. Parliament created parallel forms of insolvency for both companies and individuals.

- The insolvency of partnerships is dealt with separately by the Insolvent Partnerships Order 1994 (IPO) which modifies the relevant provisions of the Insolvency Act as necessary. A partnership may be wound up as an unregistered company (see below) under articles 7 and 9 IPO. Winding up can occur concurrently with the bankruptcy of the partners (articles 8 & 10) or partners can be bankrupted alone on their own petitions or a creditor's (article 11). A Company Administration Order may be made under article 6. Article 4 applies the CVA procedure to partnerships with the relevant amendments though the partners may need personal IVAs too. Everything said about the separate procedures applies to the partnership forms.

- For deceased bankrupts the Insolvent Estates of Deceased Persons Order 1986 applies. This applies the Insolvency Act 1986 to the administration of deceased insolvents' estates with the adaptions contained in Schedule 1 to the Order. Part I of the Schedule applies certain provisions, including s285 dealing with restrictions on enforcement and ss346 and 347 dealing with limitations on distress and execution. Part III applies the IVA procedure.

- A more informal insolvency can be achieved by a person by seeking an Administration Order in the county court. The legislation relating to this is found in the County Courts Act 1984 and County Court Rules 1981. Although as a result this may seem to be a purely civil court procedure, its origin is in the Bankruptcy Act 1883 and it should be viewed as a form of bankruptcy.

Bailiffs must treat claims to be insolvent seriously and take reasonable time to investigate them (*Ayshford v Murray* (1870) 23 LT 470). If a bailiff proceeds to sell after the insolvency has been confirmed, he may be in contempt of court (*Re: Bryant* [1876] 4 ChD 98), although the trustee may simply issue a claim for conversion (*Hitchin v Campbell* (1772) 2 W Bl 829; *Bailey v Bunning* (1665) 1 Lev 174).

This chapter will examine the effects of the different forms of insolvency, rather than the forms themselves, as it will be assumed that readers will have some familiarity with the general structure of the insolvency legislation. Some bailiffs' actions, such as distress for rent and execution, must be singled out for special treatment as they are treated separately in law. All references will be to the Insolvency Act and Insolvency Rules unless otherwise stated.

4.1 Stays on proceedings and other legal process

The general effect of insolvency is to stay all enforcement proceedings against the debtor and the estate, in order to ensure fair treatment of all creditors. This section examines the relevant provisions in the different forms of insolvency and their detailed implications.

4.1.1 *Interim Orders*

The initial stage of the IVA procedure is for the debtor to formulate repayment proposals with an insolvency practitioner who acts as 'nominee' and draws up a detailed scheme for presentation to the creditors. To buy time for this work to be done, the debtor can apply to the court for an Interim Order (s253). The Interim Order lasts for 14 days initially (s.255(6)) and allows the nominee time to prepare a report for the court on the IVA proposal.

Section 252(2) of the 1986 Act makes it clear that the effect of the 14 day interim order is to establish a moratorium during which no execution or other legal process may be commenced or continued and that no distress may be levied, except with leave of court. Under s.254 whilst an interim order application is pending the court may stay any action, execution or other legal process and may also forbid the levying of any distress on the debtor's property, or its subsequent sale, or both. This provides comprehensive protection against enforcement for the debtor.

4.1.2 *Bankruptcy*

Whilst a petition is pending the bankruptcy court may, on application from the debtor (or presumably, any other interested party), stay any "action, execution or other legal process" against the property or person of the debtor (s285(1)). Property includes goods, chattels and money (s436). Equally a court where a case is taking place against the debtor, for instance a magistrates court dealing with a liability order application, may stay proceedings or allow them to continue on terms (s285(2)). In short, court action may be prevented whether in a civil court or criminal court, but the court cannot inhibit distraint, though it is likely to be effected by the 'three month rule' (see 4.6).

A bankruptcy order will be made upon a petition if the person is insolvent and is unable to pay debts as they fall due. Note that it was held in *Leicester v Plumtree Farms* [2003] EWHC 206 (Ch); [2004] BPIR 296 that it is irrelevant to the question of inability to make payment that the debtor claims to be unable to pay because he has been the victim of an illegal or excessive seizure. Enforcement after a bankruptcy order has been made is dealt with primarily by s285(3). Subject to ss346/ 347 (see later for details of these special rules on execution and distress for rent) no creditor whose debt is provable in the bankruptcy may have any remedy or take any steps against the person or property of the bankrupt. The effect of this is to completely bar enforcement of an existing debt. As for other and future debts, see 4.3.4.

4.1.3 *Administration orders*

When any county court is notified of an administration order application by another court, proceedings against the person in that court are stayed. Once an administration order is by a county court made no creditor included on the order can take any action against the person or property of the debtor except with leave of the court and on such terms as may be imposed (s114 CCA). This also applies to any creditor initially listed on the debtor's application, even though their debt is not subsequently included in the order because the court decided that it should be excluded. These creditors too will need leave of court before being able to enforce even though they are not being paid through the Administration Order. This will particularly affect local taxes and fines which are often excluded after objections by the local authority or magistrates' court. There are a couple of exceptions to this as detailed later.

4.1.4 *Debt relief orders*

Section 103 TCEA has amended the Insolvency Act 1986 by inserting a new Part 7A. The contents of this new part are set out in Schedule 17 TCEA, which it creates a new procedure termed debt relief orders (DRO). An individual who is unable to pay his debts may apply for a DRO to be made in respect of his 'qualifying debts.' These are liquidated debts which are not 'excluded'. A debt is not a qualifying debt to the extent that it is secured and certain debts are prescribed and thereby excluded from debt relief orders. A moratorium commences on the effective date for a DRO in relation to each qualifying debt specified in the order. The effect of this is that, whilst it lasts, the creditor to whom a specified qualifying debt is owed has no remedy in respect of the debt, and may not commence any action or other legal proceedings against the debtor for the debt, except with the permission of the court and on such terms as the court may impose. If on the effective date a creditor to whom a specified qualifying debt is owed has any claim or other proceeding pending in any court, the court may stay the proceedings or allow them to continue on such terms as the court thinks fit. Nothing in this section affects the right of a secured creditor of the debtor to enforce his security. It will be interesting to see whether the courts will be prepared to treat pre-existing walking possession agreements as a form of security (see later).

The moratorium continues for the period of one year beginning with the effective date for the order, unless the moratorium terminates early or the moratorium period is extended by the official receiver or by the court. The Official Receiver may only extend the moratorium period for the purpose of carrying out or completing an investigation, taking any action he considers necessary in relation to the order or, in a case where he has decided to revoke the order, providing the debtor with the opportunity to make arrangements for making payments towards his debts. The official receiver may not extend the moratorium period beyond the end of the period of three months beginning after the end of the initial period of one year. The moratorium period may be extended more than once, but any extension (whether by the official receiver or by the court) must be made before the moratorium would otherwise end.

4.1.5 *Company administration orders*

The rules on company administration orders have been altered by the Enterprise Act 2002 which inserted into the Insolvency Act a new Schedule B1, replacing the previous Part II of the 1986 Act. A company in financial difficulty may be protected from its creditors and create a breathing space in which it may restructure by applying an administration order (para.12). The company usually petitions, but it is possible for a creditor or the clerk of a magistrates' court to petition. Under para.44 when an application is presented, and until the order is made or dismissed, an interim moratorium is in effect. A moratorium also applies for 14 days when a notice of an intention to appoint an administrator is filed in court. The terms of the moratorium are as described below under para.43.

If an order is made, an administrator is appointed and must notify all creditors that, for the period that the order is in force, s/he will be managing the company's business and property. To facilitate this process the firm is comprehensively protected from enforcement (para.43). For instance:

- No security may be enforced by the taking of any steps (para.43(2)). As taking steps to enforce security covers more than court proceedings it would appear to include removal under a possession agreement (see *Bristol Airport v Powdrill* [1990] Ch 744);

- No legal process may be instituted or continued except with either the consent of the administrator or the permission of the court (para.43(6). Legal process is defined as including legal proceedings, execution and distress. All bailiffs' actions are therefore prevented by the making of a company administration order. If the court does give permission to proceed, it may impose conditions (para.43(7)).

4.2 Special exception to stays

4.2.1 *Windings up*

An important general point to note is that the wording relating to enforcement against insolvent companies differs from that dealing with other debtors (contrast what follows with the case for bankruptcy at 4.1.1). Reference is made to any 'proceeding' against the company. It has been held that this word includes distraint. A number of decisions, culminating in *Re: Memco* [1986] Ch 86, have expressed discomfort that distraint should be regarded as an "action or proceeding" under ss126 & 130, but have felt bound by the long line of authority. To explain the difference between this and the effect of IVAs and bankruptcy orders we may note that the word used is 'proceeding' not 'proceedings'. Discussing this phrase in *Re: International Pulp & Paper Co Ltd* [1876] 3 ChD 594, Sir George Jessell MR stated that it should be construed as generally as possible. This approach was followed in *Eastern Holdings Establishment of Valduz v Singer & Friedlander Ltd* [1967] 2 All ER 1192 and it has been held that winding up bars a range of procedures, including interpleader (*Eastern Holdings*) and rates recovery in the magistrates court (*Re: The Flint, Coal & Cannel Co Ltd* (1887) 56 LJ Ch 232) as well as distraint.

Under s126(1), between the presentation of a winding up petition and a winding up order being made, any action or proceeding pending against the company in either the High Court or Court of Appeal can be stayed. Also any other pending action or proceeding may be restrained by the bankruptcy court. Clearly this will affect both execution and distraint.

During winding up by the court the assets of the company are protected from enforcement (ss128 and 130). Under s128 any distress or execution is void if initiated after the winding up commenced i.e. after the petition was presented. Two points must be made. Firstly all enforcement is effected. There is no differentiation between that for pre-insolvency provable debts and post-insolvency non-provable debts unlike bankruptcy (see 4.1). Secondly, void means void to all intents so that the creditor retains no interest under an execution, even against third parties (*In Re: Artistic Colour Printing ex p Fourdrinie* [1882] 21 ChD 510). The restriction includes distress for both rent and rates (*Re: Traders' North Staffordshire Carrying Co ex p North Staffs Railway Co* [1874] 19 Eq 60) and, one may presume, all other forms of statutory distraint. However this apparent bar on enforcement is subject to the powers contained in s130(2) (see 4.4.1).

4.2.2 *Partnership insolvencies*

A partnership may be wound up as an unregistered company. Part V of the Act deals with their liquidation. The effect of such winding up on enforcement against the partnership is that, at any time between the presentation of the petition and the making of the winding up order, the court may stay any action or proceeding against the firm (s221(1) applying s126 etc.). Under s227 the same also applies to proceedings against any of its contributories if the application for a stay is made by a creditor. Also, under s228 the making of the winding up order will restrict a creditor's rights to begin or continue enforcement against any contributory of the firm except with leave given on application to the bankruptcy court and on such terms as it might impose (*Gray v Raper* [1866] 1 CP 694).

4.3 General exceptions to restriction

Some forms of enforcement by bailiffs receive special treatment in all forms of insolvency.

4.3.1 *Distress for rent*

Landlords receive special treatment in both individual and company insolvencies and are not covered by the restrictions which apply to many bailiffs, such as those levying executions (see for example the recently confirmation of this by Chancery Division in *Re: Modern Jet Support* [2005] 1 WLR 3880).

Bankruptcies During bankruptcy the landlord is granted a limited right of distress (s347). Generally rent arrears are irrecoverable by distress and will have to be proved for like every other debt of the tenant. However under s347(1) the landlord may distrain for rent due, but only for the six months immediately prior to the beginning of the bankruptcy, i.e. the date when the order was made. Under s116 CCA a landlord may still distrain for rent arrears due after an administration order has been made. The rent recoverable is however restricted to an amount of six month's rent due immediately before the date that the order was made and any other sums due may not be levied- instead the landlord will have to enter a claim in the administration order.

Where distress follows the order, even by minutes, anything other than the six month's element must be proved for and cannot be the subject of distress (*Re: Bumpus ex p White* [1908] 2 KB 330). If the tenant goes bankrupt during a rental period, the Apportionment Act 1870 will apply to apportion sums due before and after the commencement of the insolvency. Distress may be levied at the end of the period for any sum accrued due before the bankruptcy (*Bishop of Rochester v Le Fanu* [1906] 2 Ch 513; *In Re: Howell ex p Mandleberg* [1895] 1 QB 844). If the landlord neglects to distrain and allows goods to be sold by the trustee, the only remedy will be to prove for the rent debt in the bankruptcy (*ex p Descharmes* (1742)1 Atk 102). For the same reason a landlord who fails to actually distrain cannot claim any priority over any creditor who has obtained some sort of security, such as a solicitor with a charge under the Solicitor's Act (*In Re: Suffield & Watts ex p Brown* [1888] 20 QBD 693).

If the landlord distrains between the petition and order, any surplus over and above the six months' rent plus costs, or any sums in respect of rent due after the distress, shall be held by the landlord on trust as part of the bankrupt's estate (subs 2). The trustee may seek a court order to recover such sums (*Re: Crook ex p Collins* (1891) 66 LT 29). An agreement between landlord and bankrupt tenant not to levy distress on terms of taking the dead stock of the rented farm at a valuation, though this may be beneficial to the estate, cannot enable the landlord to recover more rent than the six months recoverable under the Act (*Re: Griffith ex p Official Receiver* (1897) 4 Mans 217).

Where a landlord is entitled to claim rent due from the HCEO executing upon goods under s1 L&TA 1709 etc (see 6.6.1), the claim is restricted to six month's rent (subs 6). The HCEO is under no liability to account to the trustee for any money paid to the landlord before any notice of the bankruptcy order was received (subs 7; *Re: M'Carthy* [1881] 7 LR Ir 437). If the claim is received before the bankruptcy, but not actually paid before the commencement, the trustee will be liable to satisfy the landlord's claim as the goods are already impounded on his behalf (*Re: Driver* (1899) 43 Sol Jo 705). Alternatively, the trustee will have to recompense the execution creditor who has paid the rent but not been repaid by the HCEO (*In Re: Craig & Sons ex p Hinchcliffe* [1916] 2 KB 497). See also *Re: Jermyn ex p Elliott* (1838) 3 Deac 343 in which an injunction was granted to restrain an action by the trustee against the execution creditor for the proceeds of goods sold to recover sums paid to release items claimed by a landlord. These sums do not form part of the bankrupt's estate and the trustee is not entitled to retain them. However if a landlord neglects either to levy or to make any claim until after sale by the HCEO and the supervention of bankruptcy, the preferential rights granted by the statute are lost (*Re: Davis ex p Pollen's Trustees* (1885) 55 LJQB 217). For similar reasons, if a rent claim is met by the supervisor of a voluntary arrangement for a debtor who later becomes bankrupt, the estate can reimburse the supervisor for the sums paid (*Re: Ayshford ex p Lovering* (1887) 4 Morr 164); see too *Re: Humphreys ex p Kennard* (1870) 21 LT 684 where the Official Receiver made a similar payment prior to the appointment of the trustee. The trustee later sought to impugn this arrangement but it was upheld by the court. If the bankrupt wishes to assign the lease but has rent arrears, the arrears may be cleared from the purchase monies and cannot then be reclaimed from the landlord by the trustee. This is because the estate has benefited by the payment and the landlord has waived the right to distrain (*Mavor v Croome* (1823) 7 Bing 261). Equally money paid by a trader after the commencement of bankruptcy to avert imminent distress by a landlord cannot be recovered by the trustee as again the estate has benefited by retaining the goods that may have been seized and the landlord cannot be deprived of his/ her legal rights (*Stevenson v Wood* (1805) 5 Esp 200).

After discharge, the landlord cannot distrain upon any of the goods that were comprised in the bankrupt's estate (s347(5)). Note that these provisions are intended generally to restrict the landlord's rights against property comprised in the estate. The right to seize property not in the estate, but still liable to distress for rent, such as the goods of third parties (see 9.24) is unaffected. Thus in *Railton v Wood* [1890] 15 App Cas 363 the landlord was held able to seize goods subject to a bill of sale and maintain poundbreach when these were wrongfully seized by the mortgagee. As the landlord can seize any goods on the premises, it does not matter whether they have vested in the trustee or not (*In Re: Lundy Granite Co ex p Heavan* [1871] 6 Ch 462). If distress is issued before an insolvency commences it may be completed against the goods found on the bankrupt's premises if s/he is not the tenant (*In Re: Exhall Mining Co Ltd* (1864) 33 LJ Ch NS 595). If a joint tenant has gone bankrupt the landlord may distrain against the non-bankrupt joint tenant for the same arrears, provided no dividends have been paid in the insolvency (*Holmes v Watt* [1935] 2 KB 300). The landlord may distrain on goods, even though they have been sold or assigned by the trustee, if they are not removed promptly from the premises (*ex p Plummer* (1739) 1 Atk 103) but it seems that if they are sold to a person residing on the premises they are held to have been removed (*ex p Grove* (1747) 1 Atk

104). This latter case presumably will not apply if the purchaser is the bankrupt tenant's spouse (see 9.24 later).

It is lawful for a landlord to levy distress even though the property is vested in the trustee (subs 9; *Re: Mead ex p Cochrane* [1875] 20 Eq 282): such property is not in legal custody so as to be exempt from distress (*Re: Collins* [1888] 21 LR Ir 508). It is not possible for the trustee to obtain an order for repayment of sums raised (*Re: Cliffe ex p Eatough & Co Ltd* (1880) 42 LT 95). Injunctions to prevent such distresses may be made, but only on terms that the landlord is paid the rent allowable, or that the sum is secured for him/ her (per Bacon CJ in *ex p Till In Re: Mayhew* [1873] 16 Eq 97). The trustee may agree to make payment to the landlord to avert an imminent distress: these generally give the landlord preference over the trustee's costs, as s/ he would have had if a levy had actually been made (*Re: Chapman ex p Goodyear* (1894) 10 TLR 449). If there are no seizable goods, the only remedy for the landlord will be to prove for the rent as other remedies against the tenant are barred by the bankruptcy (*Thomas v Patent Lionite Co* [1881] 17 Ch D 250). Leave will generally be given to permit distress begun before the petition to be concluded. If the landlord is in possession under a distress when the insolvency begins, and that possession later becomes tortious, the trustee may recover damages in conversion but in deciding the measure of damages the landlord must be allowed what the trustee would have had to pay to obtain possession at the start of the bankruptcy- i.e. the arrears claimed (*Cox v Liddell* (1895) 2 Mans 212).

If the landlord levied before bankruptcy, but the tenant had initiated replevin (see 9.29) and had recovered his/ her goods, but then gone bankrupt before trial of the replevin claim, the landlord may not make any claim against the goods now in the possession of the trustee. The landlord's only remedy will be against the replevin bond (*Bradyll v Ball* (1785) 1 Bro CC 427).

Winding up Rent distress also attracts special provisions in windings up. If rent distress has been initiated before the winding up it may continue unless the liquidator pays any rent due (*Re: Roundwood Colliery Co* [1897] 1 Ch 373). If goods of a company in liquidation are on the premises of a tenant in arrears, for instance as undertenants, they may be seized by a landlord (*Re: Regent United Service Stores* [1878] 8 ChD 616; *Re: Carriage Co-operative Supply Association ex p Clemence* [1883] 23 ChD 154). If distress for rent is put in at premises rented by a company now in liquidation it is illegal if the premises are not retained for the purposes of the winding up (*Re: Progress Assurance Co ex p Liverpool Exchange* [1870] 9 Eq 370). The lessor's only remedy would be to prove for the debt (*Re: Coal Consumers Association* [1876] 4 ChD 625). The landlord can however levy if the property is retained for the purposes of better winding up the firm (*Re: North Yorkshire Iron Co* [1878] 7 ChD 661).

Continued possession If the bankrupt tenant continues to occupy the rented premises, s/ he will still be liable to pay rent. As a result there seem to be no restrictions upon the landlord using distress to collect rent arrears accruing after the order (*Re: Binns* [1875] 1 ChD 285; *Re: Thomas* (1876) Diprose's Friendly Soc Cases 64; *In Re: Wells* [1929] 2 Ch 269). The landlord's rights against third party goods on the premises will not have been altered by the bankruptcy or vesting (*Brocklehurst v Lawe* (1857) 7 E&B 176). The court will not be able to intervene under s285(1) or (2) because, as described earlier, distress for rent cannot be described as a legal proceeding. Even if the lease has been disclaimed, if the bankrupt is still in occupation the landlord can distrain up until the date of termination (*Briggs v Sowry* (1841) 8 M&W 729). If the tenancy is terminated by notice to quit by the landlord, the landlord may only distrain for rent due up until the notice becomes effective (*Re: Wilson ex p Lord Hastings* (1893) 10 Morr 219).

If the tenancy vests in the trustee in bankruptcy and s/ he does not disclaim, s/he may become personally liable for the rent (*Burrell v Jones* (1819) 3 B&A 47). Vesting occurs where the tenancy is not exempt from the effects of the Insolvency Act. Exempt tenancies include those which are assured, secure and protected. Thus it will be business, unprotected and agricultural tenancies and restricted contracts that are most likely to vest. Landlords may therefore prove (or distrain within the limits described) for the rent due before the insolvency, but their rights in respect of rent accruing after the date of commencement are unaffected and the trustee may be liable to distress under privity of estate (*In Re: Solomon ex p Dressler* [1878] 9 Ch 252).

In company insolvencies a landlord may levy if the demised premises are retained for the purposes of better winding up the firm (*Re: North Yorkshire Iron Co* [1878] 7 ChD 661). Rent payments in such circumstances are regarded as a debt contracted for the purpose of the winding up and should be paid in full like any expense properly incurred by the liquidator (*Re: Oak Pits Colliery* [1882] 21 ChD 322). See also *In Re: South Kensington Co-operative Stores* [1881] 17 ChD 161, a voluntary winding up case, in which it was held that rent due must be apportioned under the Apportionment Act 1870- the landlord being entitled to prove for rent due up until the commencement of the winding up, and being entitled to levy distress for the full rent after that date, for which the firm remained liable as it remained in possession of the premises for the purpose of carrying on the business under the liquidator during the winding up. Enforcement may proceed as normal in the event of non-payment. See also *In Re: Brown Bayley & Dixon ex p Roberts & Wright* [1881] 18 Ch D 649, in which it was held that distress could be levied for sums due after winding up began where the liquidator remained in possession, as the terms of the lease will continue to apply.

The area of liquidation expenses was recently in *Kahn v Commissioners of Inland Revenue* [2002] UKHL 6. This was a case of a creditors' voluntary liquidation in which application was made to the court for directions as to whether corporation tax was a liquidation expense. It was held that whilst the court may have a discretion as to how a creditor may recover a liability, it has no discretion as to whether an item is to be treated as a liquidation expense: the Act and Rules lay down what liquidation expenses are and that these should be paid from the assets before paying the creditors. The House of Lords provided a useful summary of the development of the relevant case law on distraint, confirming that *Re: Exhall, Re: Progress Assurance, Re: Lundy,* and *Re: Oak Pits* all remain good law. It was also affirmed that rent may be treated as a liquidation expense if possession is retained by the liquidator for the purposes of the winding up and that, on equitable grounds, liabilities incurred before the liquidation in respect of property retained by the liquidator may also be paid.

County court administration orders Under s.116 CCA a landlord may still distrain for rent arrears due after an administration order has been made. The rent recoverable is however restricted to an amount of six month's rent due immediately before the date that the order was made and any other sums due may not be levied- instead the landlord will have to enter a claim in the administration order.

4.3.2 *Bankruptcy orders and statutory distraint*

It is stated explicitly in section 347(8) that none of the restrictions affecting landlords during bankruptcy apply to other forms of distraint. It has been suggested that the leading decision on committal for non-payment of rates (*Re: Smith* [1989] 3 All ER 897) bars all forms of enforcement, including distraint, after the bankruptcy order. However the remarks on this in the case are ambiguous and obiter and are at variance with both the statute and other decisions. The actual situation is that most forms of distraint are uninhibited by bankruptcy, being exempt from s285(3). Bailiffs may therefore legally levy against a bankrupt for local taxes, road traffic penalties and the like as normal, regardless of the debtor's bankrupt status. Subsection 347(9) emphasises this by stating that property that is included in the estate may be distrained, even though it is vested in the trustee. It is understood that Customs & Excise and the Inland Revenue will not exercise their rights to levy unless, respectively, the debtor continues to trade and incurs further debts or if other creditors also continue to exercise their rights to levy, to the Revenue's possible detriment.

4.3.3 *Execution*

Special provisions are made in both bankruptcy and all forms of winding up for the HCEO and county court bailiff levying execution for any debt, whether provable or not. The provisions for winding up (ss183/4) and bankruptcy (s346) closely mirror each other and will be dealt with together. Although it should already be apparent, the term 'execution' does not include distress for rent, a point recently confirmed by Chancery Division in *Re: Modern Jet Support* [2005] 1 WLR 3880, nor does it include distraint for taxes under the Taxes Management Act 1970 (*Brenner v HMRC* [2005] EWHC 1611 (Ch)).

Statute intervenes in certain executions to deprive the creditor of the proceeds. There must be an execution in progress for the relevant sections to apply- it must not have been withdrawn, completed or otherwise abandoned, for instance due to there being no available goods (*Re: Godwin* [1935] Ch 213). Conversely, there being an execution in progress cannot prevent a bankruptcy order being made (*Rorke v Dayrell* (1791) 4 TR 402). There is also a question as to whether the following provisions apply to partnership goods seized from an insolvent partner. It was held in *Dibb v Brooke & Son* [1894] 2 QB 338 that the execution creditors were entitled to the proceeds of sale of such assets as there is nothing in the sections to show that such joint assets vest in the trustee after seizure by the HCEO. If a bankruptcy is annulled the trustee loses his/ her right to the proceeds, which revert to the execution creditors (*Diggles v Austin* (1868) 18 LT 890). Equally if one petition is dismissed, and the bailiff pays the creditor, if another petition is presented the proceeds cannot be reclaimed by the trustee (*Re: Condon ex p James* [1874] 9 Ch App 609). It should also be noted that the fact that an execution may be inhibited by the insolvency does not mean that later levies by other bailiffs will be inhibited in the same way; a bailiff in possession under a subsequent levy, for instance for statutory distraint, may now be able to remove and sell (*Re: Toomer ex p Blaiberg* [1883] 23 Ch D 254).

Notice The following rights and duties are triggered by the HCEO receiving notice of the insolvency. It will often be important for the debtor, in order to protect him/ herself, to ensure that proper notice is given. The notice must be served on the HCEO or his recognised agent, not on the bailiff in possession (*In Re: Holland ex p Warren* [1885] 15 QBD 48; *Bellyse v M'Ginn* [1891] 2 QB 227). Notice can be verbal (*Curtis v Wainbrook Iron Co* (1884) Cab & E 351) and its service is not covered by the rules for service in the Insolvency Rules (*Lole v Betteridge* [1898] 1 QB 256). The notice should be specific enough for the bailiff to be able to identify the bankrupt as the person against whom a levy has been made: in *Re: Smith ex p Spooner* [1874] 10 Ch

App 168 the sheriff had levied against a debtor who was not apparently a sole trader, but went into insolvency as such.

In the county court notice may be implied if the district judge is responsible both for issuing execution and for making a subsequent bankruptcy order, even though direct notice from the Official Receiver is not received until after the statutory period (*In Re: Harris* [1931] 1 Ch 138). In voluntary windings up notice to the HCEO of the meeting at which a resolution to go into voluntary winding up may be made is adequate notice under the Act (*Engineering Industry Training Board v Samuel Talbot (Engineers) Ltd* [1969] 2 QB 270). Contrast to this *Re: T. D. Walton* [1966] 1 WLR 869 in which notice to the sheriff of a meeting of creditors to consider the possibility of voluntary winding up was held insufficient notice, as the meeting would not consider an actual resolution to wind up. The onus of proof lies on the execution creditor, not the trustee, to show that no notice was received (*In Re: Joy ex p Cartwright* (1881) 44 LT 883; *Pearson v Graham* (1837) 6 A&E 899). If there is insufficient evidence to prove notice was not received any sale is invalid and the proceeds must be returned to the trustee (*ex p Schulte In Re: Matanlé* [1874] 9 Ch App 409; see also *ex p Dawes In Re: Husband* [1875] 19 Eq 438).

If a bailiff seizes the goods of a bankrupt in execution, even though no notice has been given, s/he will be liable in conversion to the trustee (*Price v Helyar* (1828) 4 Bing 597; *Balme v Hutton* (1833) 9 Bing 471). Any damages that the trustee may recover may be reduced by the bailiff's legitimate expenses.

Incomplete executions Where the execution was issued before the bankruptcy order was made but the process has not yet been completed by sale of goods (or by receipt of the proceeds - *Figg v Moore* [1894] 2 QB 690), the creditor must abandon the seizure and is not entitled to retain the 'benefit of that execution'. The benefit of the execution is defined as any title to goods seized, to the proceeds of their sale (including those proceeds paid into court pending the resolution on an interpleader claim (*Heathcote v Livesey* [1887] 19 QBD 285 - though see *Galt v Saskatchewan Coal Co* (1887) 14 Man LR 304 *contra*) or to any sums paid to avoid the execution (s 183(1)/s346(1); see for example *Re: Norton ex p Todhunter* [1870] 10 Eq 425). If the judgment creditor seeks to continue with execution it is wrongful and malicious (see 5.2). After the presentation of a petition, the court can intervene by way of injunction to restrain sale under an execution (*Re: Tidey* (1870) 21 LT 685). The same applies if an execution creditor seeks to enforce a provable debt after discharge (*Davis v Shapley* (1830) 1 B & Ad 54).

If the execution is complete, the claimant may retain the money regardless of the bankruptcy. The onus is on the creditor to prove that the execution had been completed. An execution is not complete where:

- the bailiff has withdrawn upon agreeing instalment payments (*Re: Ford* [1900] 1 QB 264) or has re-entered when such an arrangement has broken down (*Re: Brelsford* [1932] 1 Ch 24);

- the HCEO has withdrawn permanently with the creditor's consent on payment of a lump sum (*Re: Evans* (1916) 2 HBR 111) or at the order of the court on the appointment of a receiver (*Mackay v Merritt* (1886) 34 WR 433);

- the debtor pays all or part of the debt to the HCEO (*Re: Pearson ex p West Cannock Colliery Co* (1886) 3 Morr 157) or direct to the creditor (*Re: Godding* [1914] 2 KB 70; *Re: Pollock* (1902) 87 LT 238). Cheques in payment of the debt given to the HCEO are received as a result of the coercive nature of the writ and are proceeds of the execution still in the HCEOs hands (*Koppers Co v. Dominion Foundries & Steel Ltd* (1965) 8 CBR(NS) 49);

- successive sales occur under the same execution, and although the first is complete and the proceeds have passed to the creditor, other goods remain to be sold to satisfy the full debt. The HCEO's duty is to go on settling the debt until it is cleared. The proceeds of sale in this context mean the whole proceeds of all sales, not just proceeds of a partial sale (*Jones v Parcell & Thomas* [1883] 11 QBD 430;

- there has only been delivery of the writ/ warrant to the bailiff (*Philips v Thompson* (1684) 3 Lev 191; *Arminer v Spotwood* (1773) Loft 114; *Re: Davies ex p Williams* [1872] 7 Ch App 314). There must be an actual levy. Thus where a second writ or warrant is satisfied from the proceeds of a sale made under a prior execution, the proceeds cannot be retained against the trustee unless there has been an actual seizure (*Johnson v Evans* (1844) 7 Man & G 240). Where, however, a prior writ is set aside, for example on interpleader by the trustee, a subsequent executed writ may still be valid and entitle to the creditor to the proceeds (*Goldschmidt v Hamlet* (1843) 1 Dow & L 501; *Graham v Witherby* (1845) 7 QB 491);

- the bailiff has simply seized and is in possession (*Cole v Davies* (1699) 1 Ld Raym; *ex p Rayner In Re: Johnson* [1872] 7 Ch App 732; *In Re: Dickenson ex p Charrington & Co* [1888] 22 QBD 187);

- a sale occurs that is not a sale under the execution (see *Heathcote v Livesley* [1887] 19 QBD 285), and may be fraudulent (*Re: Townsend ex p Hall* [1880] 14 Ch D 132 - 'sale' to a third party with HCEO's consent) or is not a full sale of the goods. In *Ward v Dalton* (1849) 7 CB 643 the sheriff sold some of the goods seized by auction of lotted parts. Deposits were taken on each lot but lots were only separated from the mass of goods and delivered to the buyers after the bankruptcy order had been made. It was held that this was an 'inchoate sale' that enabled the trustee to recover the whole of the proceeds;

- the creditor has only begun to prepare for the sale (*In Re: Chinn* [1881] 17 Ch D 839);or,

- proceeds are still held by the bailiff/ HCEO (*Bluston & Bramley Ltd v Leigh* [1950] 2 KB 554).

It does not matter that the execution has not been completed because sale has been delayed by an injunction under the Insolvency Rules (*Re: Gwynn ex p Veness* [1870] 10 Eq 419) or by an interpleader claim (*O'Brien v Brodie* [1866] 1 Exch 302; *Re: Haydon ex p Halling* [1877] 7 Ch D 157). The trustee will be able to claim any proceeds of sale or possession of the goods from the HCEO (*Re: Johnson ex p Rayner* [1872] 7 Ch App 325). If the trustee recovers the proceeds an action against the execution creditor for conversion by seizing goods after the commencement of the bankruptcy will probably fail as the proceeds are a fairer measure of damages than the value of the goods at the time of seizure (*Whitmore v Black* (1844) 2 Pow & L 445).

An execution is complete if there has been:

- a sale before the presentation of any petition (*In Re: Love ex p Official Receiver v Kingston on Thames County Court Registrar* [1952] 1 Ch 138; *Higgins v M'Adam* (1829) 3 Y&J 1; *Young v Roebuck* (1863) 2 H&C 296);

- the execution has been settled by a payment of cash and sale of goods to the creditor well before the bankruptcy (*In Re: Jenkins* (1904) 90 LT 65);

- a return of no goods (*Re: Fairley* [1922] 2 Ch 791); or,

- an interpleader sale (*Re: Chiandetti* (1921) 91 LJKB 70), as well as normal sale or full payment;

- the HCEO has sold goods by bill of sale (*Christie v Winnington* (1853) 8 Exch 287) and has received full payment (*Loader v Hiscock* (1858) 1 F&F 132 NP).

If before the execution is completed, notice of the debtor's bankruptcy is received any goods or money seized or recovered in part satisfaction of the judgment debt after that time must be surrendered, on request, to the trustee as the right to enforce the security given by seizure is lost and the money is a by product of that security. The provisions refer to the HCEO receiving notice after goods have been "taken in execution" (s346(2)) - this has been held to mean that the HCEO is in possession of them, not that they have had to have been removed as under s1, Landlord & Tenant Act 1709 (*Marylebone Vestry v Sheriff of London* [1900] 2 QB 591). As s346(1) refers to sums paid to avoid execution, we must conclude that 'money recovered' by the bailiff includes these sums.

The costs of the bailiff, up until notice of the bankruptcy was received, constitute a first charge upon the goods, to satisfy which they may be sold by the trustee (s346(2)). These costs do not include poundage (*Re: Ludmore* [1884] 13 QBD 415), or the costs of preparing for a sale that could not proceed because of the insolvency (*Searle v Blaise* (1863) 14 CBNS 856; *Rush v Baker* (1734) Cun 130) nor do the allowable costs include the costs of an interpleader as this procedure is initiated by the HCEO without the trustee being a party (*In Re: Rogers* [1911] 1 KB 641). The execution creditor or interpleader claimant may instead be liable. Costs also do not include the execution creditor's costs of issuing and serving the writ of fi fa; the HCEO cannot deduct and retain a third party's expenses (*In Re: Woods* [1931] 2 Ch 320).

The wording of the provisions is slightly different for companies and their treatment is consequently also different to bankruptcy. Under s184(1) after an order, resolution for voluntary winding up or appointment of a provisional liquidator the HCEO has duties imposed upon him. If an execution has not been completed by sale or by receipt or recovery of the full amount due including costs the bailiff will have to deliver to the liquidator the goods or money seized (or received) in part satisfaction though the costs of the execution are a first charge upon this and the liquidator can sell items to pay the HCEO (s184(2)). Readers should note that this requirement to pass on goods or money must be read in light of the general voiding of incomplete executions under s183(1). That subsection states that the benefit of an execution may not be retained. It has been established by the courts the benefit is not monies paid to the bailiff to avoid sale. Cases such as *In Re: Caribbean Products (Yam Importers)* [1966] Ch 331, and *In Re: Andrew* [1937] 1 Ch 122 have explored the meaning of the phrase "benefit of execution" and explained that it refers not to the money received (which is the 'fruits of the execution') but to the security of the charge on the debtor's goods obtained by the issue of execution. The charge enables the creditor to proceed to complete the execution and clear the balance of the judgment debt then due by removal and/or sale and it is this benefit that is lost. This charge subsists as long as the goods are unsold or the debt is not fully satisfied. The creditor issuing a warrant is protected by a priority right preventing other dealing with the goods as long as the execution is in force.

To have this priority it does not matter that the security has not been enforced by sale. As a consequence we must take the reference to monies in s184(2) to refer to money seized by, not paid to, the bailiff. The situation is different in bankruptcy. Payments already made cannot, subject to the next section, be claimed back from the creditor (*Re: Samuels* [1935] Ch 341).

Note that the goods only need to be delivered when asked for by the bailiff. In the absence of such a request, the bailiff's duty is to proceed to sale as usual (*Woolford's Estate v Levy* [1892] 1 QB 772).

Executions over £500 There are further restrictions on an officer levying execution in respect of any completed execution for a judgment of over £500, including bailiff's charges (*ex p Lithgow In Re: Fenton* [1878] 10 Ch D 169) leads to the realisation of money by sale or payment to avoid sale. The execution is affected even though the judgment debt is below £500, if the costs take it over the limit (*ex p Liverpool Loan Co In Re: Bullen* [1872] 7 Ch App 732). The bailiff's costs include levy fees and poundage, but possession fees may be a different matter (*Howes v Young* [1876] 1 Ex D 146). A judgment is not affected if it has been reduced below the limit by the time bankruptcy occurs (*Mostyn v Stock* [1882] 9 QBD 432). Also creditors may avoid this provision and retain the proceeds of sale against the trustee in a number of ways: by abandoning part of their claim (*Re: Salinger* [1877] 6 ChD 332; *Turner v Bridgett* [1882] 8 QBD 392); by issuing execution for less than the specified sum of £500 (*Re: Hinks* [1878] 7 ChD 882); or by ordering sale for less than £500, even though execution was issued for more (*Turner v Hinks* [1882] 8 QBD 392).

If the HCEO or bailiff is notified of a pending bankruptcy petition and an order is later made upon that petition, or if notice is served that a winding up petition has been presented against a firm or that a meeting has been called at which a resolution to enter voluntary winding up will be presented, and a compulsory or voluntary winding up results from this, the sums collected will vest in the bankrupt's estate. The proceeds of any execution therefore must be held by the bailiff for fourteen days after the notice, or whilst the petition is pending, in case they should be paid over to the trustee (s346(3)&(4)/ s184 (3) & (4)). The execution creditor's right to receive the proceeds has been described as a vested right, but one which is liable to be divested if insolvency supervenes within fourteen days (*In Re: Greer, Napper v Fanshawe* [1895] 2 Ch 217). The HCEO can deduct the costs of the execution, but this will not include possession fees after the date of the bankruptcy (*In Re: English & Ayling ex p Murray & Co* [1903] 1 KB 680).

Sums paid to prevent sale include any payments made under a possession agreement to the HCEO or payment made to the HCEO when he called in order to levy (*Re: Walkden Metal Sheet Co. Ltd* [1960] 1 Ch 170). However, payments made by a third party to the bailiff to avoid seizure are not effected (*Bower & Co v Hett* [1895] 2 QB 51). Also excepted are sums paid into court by an interpleader claimant subject to trial of the claim in order to prevent sale of their goods - they were unsuccessfully claimed by the trustee as representative of the proceeds of sale (*Shuckborough v Duthoit* (1892) 8 TLR 710). The trustee also has no claim to payments made by the debtor to the HCEO without there being any seizure: such payments made under pressure to buy the forbearance of the HCEO are not paid 'under an execution' (*In Re: Hassall ex p Brooke* [1874] 9 Ch 301- see also *Stock v Holland* [1874] 9 Exch 147- this seems to include payments made to avoid a sale that the execution creditor has agreed to accept). The 14 day 'waiting period' begins with the day of payment or the day that sale takes place and not the day on which the HCEO receives the proceeds (*Re: Cripps, Ross & Co* [1888] 21 QBD 472) and if notice is received after this period has expired, as payment to the HCEO in such circumstances is vested in the creditor and held by the HCEO on the creditor's behalf, the creditor is entitled to receive it (*Marley Tile Co Ltd v Burrows* [1978] QB 241). In county court execution, if the warrant is transferred to a 'foreign court' for enforcement, the 14 day period is reckoned from the date that proceeds are received by the foreign court rather than the court of issue (*D P Toomey v King* (1952) CLY 260). If bankruptcy does occur following notice of a petition, money will have to be repaid whether paid to the HCEO, the solicitor or the execution creditor (*Re: Ford* [1900] 1 QB 264; *Re: Godding* [1914] 2 KB 70). If money is paid over to the creditor despite notice of the bankruptcy, the HCEO may be sued by the trustee (*Notley v Buck* (1828) 8 B&C 160) but the HCEO may in turn sue the execution creditor (*Re: Husband* [1875] 19 Eq 438). NB the fact that the HCEO is holding a debt for fourteen days does not render it a debt, even a contingent debt, upon which a petition could also be issued by the execution creditor (*In Re: William Hockley Ltd* [1962] 1 WLR 555).

Under s346(6) and ss183(2)(c) & 184(5) the court has the power to set aside the trustee's or liquidator's rights to such extent and on such terms as it thinks fit. These rights may again be set aside by the court as it thinks fit but a very strong case will have to be made, the guiding principle being fair treatment of all creditors. However where the creditor failed to complete execution because the debtor firm was stalling it (and all other creditors) there was no reason for the court to exercise its discretion in favour of that creditor and allow the execution to continue (*Re: Redman Builders* [1964] 1 All ER 851). Those who have purchased property in good faith from the HCEO are protected (s346(7); s183(2)(b)). Under s346(8) it seems to be permissible to issue execution for a non-provable debt, provided that only property acquired since the bankruptcy order, and not claimed by the trustee, is seized. If after acquired property is seized for a debt provable in the bankruptcy, the execution will be set aside by the court on application by the debtor or trustee (*Barrow v Poile* (1830) 1 B & Ad 629).

4.4 Leave to proceed

In windings up, bankruptcy and administration orders, despite the general bar on enforcement after the order, special exceptions can be made in some cases.

4.4.1 *Windings up*

Despite what was said at 4.2.2 regarding the effect of liquidation on enforcement it has been held (*Re: Bellaglade* [1977] 1 All ER 319; *Venners Electrical & Cooking Appliances v Thorpe* [1915] 2 Ch 404) that distraint issued before a winding up petition was filed may continue unless there are special circumstances such as fraud or unfair dealing which mean that it should be stayed. The apparent bar on enforcement during a winding up under ss 128 & 130 is however subject to the powers contained in s130(2).

Under s130(2) no action or proceeding can be begun or continued after an order has been made, except with leave of court and on such terms as the court may impose. This supplements the impact of s128 on distraint. Levies may not be begun, nor may they be continued with as the term 'proceeding' has been held to refer to any stage in the levy process - from seizure to sale. However, as stated, leave of court may be given on terms under s130(2) to allow enforcement such as distraint to continue.

Where the enforcement began before the commencement of the winding up and unless special reasons exist which render it inequitable, such as fraud or unfair dealing (*Re: David Lloyd* [1877] 6 Ch D 339; *Re: Herbert Berry* [1977] 1 WLR 617) distress may continue (*Re: Bellaglade* [1977] 1 All ER 319; *In Re: Exhall Mining Co Ltd* (1864) 33 LJ Ch NS 595). The simple fact of the petition being presented is no ground in itself to restrain an execution (*ex p Millwood Colliery Co* (1876) 24 WR 898). Appointment of a provisional liquidator prior to a winding up order is not a necessary bar to distress (*In Re: Dry Docks Corporation of London* [1888] 39 Ch 306). The crucial point is when seizure occurs, rather than the issue of the warrant, so if this follows the presentation of the petition, even by minutes, the levy must be stayed (*Re: London & Devon Biscuit Co* [1871] 12 Eq 190). Even where execution is issued before or at the same time as the petition, if the liquidator takes possession before the bailiff, the bailiff should be restrained (*Re: Waterloo Life (No 2)* (1862) 32 LJ Ch 371).

Leave to continue prior distress may be given:

- if the court feels that the creditor has acted properly and simply been prevented from levying before the petition by the resistance of the debtor (*Re: London Cotton Co Ltd* [1866] 2 Eq 53);

- if there are sufficient assets to satisfy all creditors so that the issue is simply whether a creditor should be paid now or later, having otherwise acted correctly at all times (*Re: Bastow* [1867] 4 Eq 689);

- if subsequent writs have been lodged with the HCEO, even though they have not been levied, provided that he is already in possession under a prior writ (*Re: Hille India Rubber* (1897) WN 20). The court may in such cases restrain sale until the winding up order is made and then order delivery of the property to the liquidator for sale, reserving to the creditors the same priority against the proceeds as if it was a sale by the HCEO (*Re: Plas-yn-Mhowys Coal Co* [1867] 4 Eq 689; *Re: Hill Pottery* [1866] 1 Eq 649); or,

- if the levy is for an ongoing liability such as rates, which should still be payable and enforceable where the liquidator retains beneficial occupation on the behalf of the company, particularly where the business is carried on, otherwise leave to distrain may be given (*Re: International Marine Hydropathic* [1884] 8 ChD 470). Distraint for rates begun before the winding up commenced may proceed unless the liquidator pays the rates (*In Re: Dry Docks Corporation of London* [1888] 39 Ch 306).

Leave to continue with a levy may not be given, where for instance:

- the court doubts that the warrant was properly issued before the order was made (*Re: Perkins Beach Lead Mining Co* [1878] 7 Ch D 371);

- forced sale under an execution or distress would be injurious to the company and its other creditors (*Re: Twentieth Century Equitable Friendly Society* (1910) WN 236); or,

- to ensure fair treatment of all creditors (*D Wilson (Birmingham) Ltd v Metropolitan Property Developments Ltd* [1975] 2 All ER 814) and the *pari passu* payment of all debts (*Mitchell v Buckingham International plc* [1998] EWCA Civ 247/ 2 BCLC 369). It is the court's duty to ensure that there is an 'equality of equities' (*In Re: Dimsons Estate Fire Clay Co* [1874] 19 Eq 202).

Terms may be imposed when granting leave, such as in *Re: Bastow* [1867] 4 Eq 689 in which the court made an order restricting the levy to moveable property i.e. stock rather than plant. Where the value of goods seized before the petition greatly exceeds the debt due the court may order the liquidator to pay the enforcing creditor off (*Re: Withernsea Brickworks* [1880] 16 ChD 337). It is also possible that a sale may be allowed to go ahead as sale is not putting an execution or distress in force as contemplated by s128 (*Re: Great Ship Co* (1863) 9 LT 432).

Where the enforcement is to begin after the winding up, it will only be allowed where special circumstances apply (*In Re: Lancashire Cotton Spinning Co* [1887] 35 Ch D 656; see also *The Constellation* [1966] 1 WLR 272). In the absence of special circumstances the court has to stay or restrain the execution to ensure an equal distribution to all creditors of the same class (*Bowkett v Fullers United Electrical Works* [1923] 1 KB 160). Special circumstances that might justify giving leave to continue with enforcement might be where:

- the creditor delayed the enforcement due to representations for indulgence on the part of the company (*Re: Taylor ex p Steel & Plant Co* [1878] 8 ChD 183 or *Re: Richards* [1879] 11 ChD 676);

- where the actions of the company inhibited the bailiff (*Re: London Cotton* [1866] 2 Eq 53);

- where the execution creditor has delayed enforcement proceedings due to other proceedings disputing the validity of the insolvency itself (*Re: Prior ex p Osenton* [1869] 4 Ch App 690); or,

- where the creditor is secured and is proceeding to recover their own property (*Re: Aro Co Ltd* [1980] 1 All ER 1067).

Exceptional circumstances do not include the fact that the creditor may have no other way of recovering their money (*Anglo-Baltic & Mediterranean Bank v Barber* [1924] 2 KB 410). Where part of the claim relates to before the winding up and part to after its commencement, then the latter debt may be enforced with leave whilst the former will have to be proved for (*Re: North Yorkshire Iron Co* [1878] 7 Ch D 661).

4.4.2 *Voluntary windings up*

As the court need not be involved at all in voluntary windings up, there is as a result no automatic stay on enforcement under ss128 & 130 as in compulsory liquidations as described at 4.2.2. However the liquidator may apply to the court under s112 for such protection and the court may use the powers it would have in respect of a court winding up. The earliest stage at which the court can intervene is after a petition has been presented. If the company plans a meeting of members and creditors to consider plans to deal with creditors, this does not justify the court intervening (*Booth v Walkden*

Spinning & Manufacturing Co Ltd [1909] 2 KB 368). The impact of court orders can be as follows:

- all enforcement action against the company will usually be stayed, unless the circumstances are exceptional, in order to ensure fair treatment for all creditors (*Needham v Rivers Protection & Manure Co* [1875] 1 Ch D 253; *In Re: Thurso New Gas Co* [1889] 42 Ch 486). Where the company has been stalling all its creditors it is not just and reasonable to give one stalled creditor, who has not been able to complete a levy before the winding up began, preference over other stalled creditors, whether they had completed levies or not (*Re: Redman Builders* [1964] 1 All ER 851). The court will stay threatened as well as actual enforcement (*Re: Zoedone* (1884) 32 WR 312).

- this general bar includes distress for rent (*In Re: South Rhondda Colliery Co* (1898) 60 LT 1260), statutory distraint (*In Re: Margot Bywaters Ltd* [1942] 1 Ch 121) and execution (*Westbury v Twigg & Co* [1891] 1 QB 77). However note that in the Bywaters case the distraint was only begun after the resolution. In such cases the costs of the execution will have to be met by the creditor and not the liquidator (*Montague v Davies Benachi & Co* [1911] 2 KB 595).

- distraint begun before the commencement of the insolvency may be treated differently - see *In Re: Roundwood Colliery* [1897] 1 Ch 373. In such cases only if special reasons such as fraud or unfair dealing make it inequitable for enforcement to continue will it be restrained (*Venners Electrical Cooking & Heating Appliances v Thorpe* [1915] 2 Ch 404).

- although leave to enforce may be given under s130(2), terms may be imposed by the court, such as that part of the debt only may be enforced (e.g. *In Re: G Winterbottom Ltd* [1937] 2 All ER 232 where only part of several years' rent arrears were recoverable by distress).

- the manner of exceptional circumstance that may lead the court to allow enforcement to continue include deception of the bailiff (*Armoduct Manufacturing Co Ltd v General Incandescent Co Ltd* [1911] 2 KB 143); use of winding up as a deliberate way of avoiding payment (*In Re: Imperial Steamship & Household Coal Co Ltd* (1868) 32 LJCh 517) or distress where all assets are subject to floating charges that exceed their value (*In Re: Harpur's Cycle Fittings* [1900] 2 Ch 731).

- the court may, when staying enforcement commenced after the commencement of the winding up, impose terms, such as that the creditor be permitted to prove for the debt plus court costs (*In Re: Poole Firebrick & Blue Clay Co* [1873] 17 Eq 268; *In Re: Sabloniere Hotel Co* [1866] 3 Eq 74).

4.4.3 *Administration orders*

The power also exists under s115 CCA for the court, at the request of a creditor, to issue execution against the debtor where it is believed his/her property is worth more than £50. This process will be a normal county court execution.

4.4.4 *Future debts & bankruptcy*

If new debts arise after a bankruptcy order the situation is more complex. If there are no existing debts proved for in the bankruptcy then the creditor can proceed as normal to commence any action or other legal proceedings save that enforcement could be stayed on application under s285(1) or (2) - see 4.4.1. In most cases there may be little reason to bar enforcement as bankruptcy does not absolve the debtor of responsibility for ongoing or subsequent liabilities. However if the creditor has already proved for a debt in the bankruptcy, leave of court is required to pursue any debt arising later- see s285(3(b)). If debts accrue after the bankruptcy order has been made, they are largely unaffected by it and can be collected in the normal fashion. The only possible restrictions are in ss285(1) or (2).

4.5 Security

Certain creditors are given preferential treatment in insolvency. Those with security (e.g. a mortgage on property) are in the most favourable position, getting paid first from the assets before any other claim is dealt with and, as will be seen, being largely unaffected in enforcing their security (s285(4)). This is of relevance in distress and execution because of the decision of the High Court in *Re: A Debtor (No 10 of 1992)* (1995) Times Feb. 1st which held a bailiff's walking possession agreement to be security within the meaning of s383 of the Act. Section 383 reads "a debt is secured...to the extent that the person to whom the debt is owed holds any security for the debt (whether mortgage, charge, lien or other security) over any property of the person by whom the debt is owed". This decision did not create any new legal principle but simply revived an established principle. It could have a profound effect on debtors if the creditor suspects that the person may be contemplating or facing insolvency, as a prompt levy before any order is made would put the creditor in a preferential, secured position. A right of distress in itself is not a form of security (*In Re: Russell* [1885] 29 Ch D 254). It also seems undisputed that a creditor who has both levied distress and removed the seized goods will be regarded as secured (*ex p Birmingham Gaslight & Coke Co, In Re: Adams* [1870] 11 Eq 204).

It would appear that this right of security will be effected where a petition is presented by the execution creditor in question and it will have to be surrendered in whole or in part (see s269 IA 1986 and *In Re: Chidley & In*

Re: Leonard [1875] 1 Ch D 177). Surrender of the security which derives from a levy of distress and a walking possession agreement will also be deemed to have occurred where a creditor fails, without good reason, to mention the levy in any proof of debt submitted to a trustee, liquidator or the like (*LCP Retail v Segal* [2006] EWHC 2087).

Creditors levying distraint against bankrupts enjoy broad powers, which are supplemented by these provisions. Restrictions on enforcement do not apply to secured creditors (s285(4) and see for example *In Re: Longendale Cotton Spinning Co* [1878] 8 Ch D 150). Under s285(5) where any goods of a bankrupt are held by any person by way of any pledge, pawn or other security, the Official Receiver when acting as interim receiver or during the course of investigations into the bankrupt's affairs may, after written notice, inspect them with a view to redeeming the security. The security cannot then be realised without leave of court and unless the trustee has had a reasonable opportunity to inspect the goods and redeem. Equally under s311(5) after the trustee has been appointed, where any goods are similarly subject to some form of security, the trustee may serve notice again with a view to exercising the bankrupt's right of redemption. The notice has the same effect as under s285(5). By rules 6.117 to 6.119 the trustee may give notice to redeem at the creditor's proved value. The creditor then has 21 days in which to revalue the security and call on the trustee to settle for that sum. If either valuation is disputed, the trustee can require sale. It seems that the effect of these latter provisions is that a creditor with walking possession may be paid even sooner than their already preferential position might suggest. They may be compared with similar powers to dispose of goods subject to security and to clear the secured debt that apply to companies (e.g. s15 for administrators and s43 for administrative receivers).

Personal insolvency None of these rights would appear to be exercisable if goods have not been seized before a Bankruptcy Order, after which date the estate vests in the trustee and probably seizure should be before the date of the petition's presentation, otherwise the impounding being challenged as a void disposition. In respect of IVAs, interim orders do not prevent most forms of distraint, so it will be worthwhile creditors seeking to exercise their right of distraint as they will then be in a preferential position for payments and a creditors' meeting could not affect their rights without their consent, as was ruled in the case in question.

Company insolvencies In CAOs no security may be enforced by the taking of any steps (s11(3)(c)). As taking steps to enforce security covers more than court proceedings (*Bristol Airport v Powdrill* [1990] Ch 744) it would appear to include removal under a walking possession agreement. If seizure precedes a winding up, the distraining creditor will be treated as secured as in bankruptcy (*Re: Printing & Numerical Registering Co* [1878] 8 ChD 535; *Re: Blue Bird Mines* [1942] 44 WALR 85) and thus will have priority to any preferential creditors (*Re: D S Paterson & Co Ltd* [1931] OR 777). This is subject to any specific limitations such as the 'three month rule'.

4.6 Three month rule

In both bankruptcy and all forms of winding up special provisions apply to bailiffs levying any form of distress immediately prior to the court making an order against the insolvent firm or individual. The section relating to firms is s176; that relating to bankrupt persons is s347. What may be termed the 'three month rule' applies where the any person, whether landlord or other bailiff, distrains on a debtor and that person or firm is declared bankrupt or is wound up within three months of the levy (ss176(1) & 347(3)).

In the case of companies if the assets of the company are insufficient to cover preferential debts, the seized goods, or the proceeds of their sale, are charged with those preferential debts to the extent that they cannot be satisfied from the assets (s176(2)). Any person who must surrender goods or money as a result of this will also rank as a preferential creditor for payment after the other creditors with priority. Their position relative to other creditors is determined by the proceeds of sale of the goods by the liquidator but they will not be entitled to payment from those proceeds (s176(3)). The provisions do not effect s128 which voids any post petition levy (s176(1)).

In the case of levies against bankrupts, any goods seized or proceeds of sale realised, other than any amount held by the landlord on trust for the bankrupt's estate under s347(2) (i.e. rent arrears accrued more than six months before the bankruptcy or any later rent due), shall be charged with the amount of any preferential debts that cannot otherwise be met from the bankrupt's estate. If the bailiff hands over goods or cash to the trustee as a result of this provision, s/he ranks as a preferential creditor to the extent of the sum paid over or the proceeds of sale of the goods but not so as to receive any money from the sums realised from the distraint.

PART 3

LEVY PROCEDURE

Chapter 5

WRONGFUL DISTRESS: FORMS AND REMEDIES

It is possible for a bailiff to make a variety of errors in his procedure or conduct. These are classed generally as wrongful distress (or execution). It is important to be clear about how and when these may arise and their consequences, in order to ensure that actions to which clients are subject are legal. It should be noted that special rules and remedies apply to the HCEO and are dealt with separately.

5.1 Forms of wrongful seizure

Wrongful distress can take three forms - illegal, irregular or excessive:

5.1.1 *Illegal seizure*

In law an illegality is any act that is forbidden by law: that is a departure from or neglect of the proper formalities. For bailiffs illegality will occur where there is no right to levy (e.g. the debt has been paid, or its amount tendered) or where an unlawful or unauthorised act is committed during the levy, such as a seizure at the wrong time, of exempt or third party goods, with forcible entry or when goods not previously seized are removed and sold. The levy will be void from the beginning (*Attack v Bramwell* (1863) 3 B & S 520 and see 7.5.3 on trespass *ab initio*). Even if a valid warrant is levied at the same time as an invalid one, this will not be a defence against an action for illegal distress on the invalid warrant (*Lamont v Southall* (1839) 5 M&W 416).

Illegal seizure is a trespass, so an action for illegal seizure is simply an action for damages for trespass to land or goods or for conversion. The measure of damages will be the same as in the ordinary tort action, and the claimant may simply sue for damages for trespass or wrongful interference instead of for illegal distress as such. As in all torts nominal damages at least are recoverable for infringement of the claimant's rights, but particularly if special damages are sought some causal connection between tort and loss will have to be shown. It is also probable that only such damages as are reasonably foreseeable and not too remote are recoverable. The claimant has the burden of proof, but this is discharged if s/he shows that, on the balance of probabilities, the tortious distress caused or contributed to the damage.

5.1.2 *Irregular seizure*

Irregular seizure is a creation of statute, and does not apply to all forms of distress (see 10.8 later). An irregularity is anything done in the wrong manner or without the proper formalities. It may be waived or consented to by the other party or rectified by the court by the award of damages for the costs caused by it. The validity of the act done is not affected. Thus in bailiffs' law this offence occurs when the levy is correct but subsequent events are not, e.g. selling goods at an undervalue, sale after the debt and costs have been paid or failing to give proper notices. It is more of a technical offence than illegal distress and as the remedy is only the actual damage suffered by the claimant, which may be negligible or difficult to prove depending on the nature of the irregularity, it is likely that this will be encountered very infrequently.

5.1.3 *Excessive seizures*

There is a common law duty to avoid an excessive levy. This has also been codified in the Statute of Marlborough and has been reiterated in the National Standard, which requires the value of goods seized to be 'proportional' to the sums outstanding. The offence occurs when more goods are taken than are reasonably required to satisfy the debt and costs (for example an excessive levy occurred when £100 of goods were taken for a debt of less than £1- *Baker v Wicks* [1904] 1 KB 743). Judging the value of the goods etc must take into account the nature of the forced sale which will have to take place: the bailiff must therefore exercise a reasonable and honest discretion (*Roden v Eyton* (1848) 6 CB 427). Sale at an undervalue does not necessarily mean the levy was excessive (*Thompson v Wood* (1842) 4 QB 493). The debtor may sue for excessive distress even though the sale, less expenses, does not clear the debt due (*Smith v Ashforth* (1860) 29 LJ Exch 259). It is no defence for the bailiff to say that allowance was being made for possible claims by the landlord, for which see 6.6.1 and *Gawler v Chaplin* (1848) 2 Exch 503, nor is it acceptable to say that excess was seized in case unforeseen circumstances might have rendered a levy for less insufficient (*Aldred v Constable* (1844) 6 QB 370). There will be no basis for a claim if there was only one thing to take, even if its value greatly exceeded the sum due (*Welsh v Bell* (1668) 1 Vent 37; *Field v Mitchell* (1806) 6 Esp 71; *Avenell v Coker* (1828) Mood & M 172). There is no basis for a claim based on an intention to seize alone, such as goods being entered on an inventory, as no actual wrong will have been done (*Beck v Denbigh* (1860) 29 LJCP 273).

Because they often fail to appreciate the nature of sale at auction and the prices likely to be raised by the process, plus the natural tendency to overvalue one's own goods, debtors often feel that there has been an excessive levy when there has not. L J Simon Brown in *Steel Linings v Bibby & Co* [1993] RA 27 observed that "where the allegation advanced was one of excessive distress, debtors should expect a generally sceptical reaction to their own estimation of the goods' worth. In short, the civil courts would not allow themselves to become a ready means of escaping the proper processes and consequences of...distress". Consequently it is fair to assume that successful actions for excessive distress will be rare.

Legality of attempted seizures - an attempt to levy distress may be as wrongful as an actual levy, and the same remedies will be applicable. See for example:

- *Hutchins v Scott* (1837) 2 M & W 809 in which a tenant in rent arrears was visited by the landlord's bailiff and pressed for payment of the due rent plus the expenses of the levy. Nothing was touched and no inventory made but the tenant paid under protest. Hutchins later sued for excessive distress. It was held that the tenant could not say that no actual distress has occurred just because nothing was taken, no one remained on the premises and no inventory was made. The bailiff, Scott, had said "unless you pay...I shall take your goods". The payment made was thus 'an agreement not to go through a mere ceremony'.

- *Bissicks v Bath Colliery* [1877] 2 Ex D 459: in which it was held that going to the debtor's house, showing him the warrant and demanding payment, otherwise a man would remain in possession, was sufficient seizure to entitle the HCEO to fees. "It is enough if the sheriff's officer goes down to the premises with the warrant and gets payment. He can only receive payment by virtue of the warrant, which is his authority, and the debtor can...in order to avoid the inconvenience of a levy and sale...pay." Cockburn CJ went on to say that the warrant was 'virtually executed' if both sides agree to avoid the trouble of seizure and sale by agreeing payment.

- *R v Hampstead Magistrates Court ex p St Marylebone Property Co plc* (1995) Legal Action Sept 1996, p21: recently this case confirmed that *Hutchins v Scott* is still good law and applicable to distraint for local taxes. On judicial review a liability order was quashed, thus rendering the distraint issued under it wrongful. The damages arising from this were the amount paid by the company in excess of the rates that were due. This sum was the court costs and bailiffs' fees plus interest.

5.2 Wrongful execution

The general principles of offences described above apply to both the county court bailiff and the HCEO, but because of their special office and status, the detailed position of the latter is notably different.

5.2.1 *Liability of HCEOs*

As with other bailiffs, the HCEO is liable for any action done in excess of the authority given by the writ, and thus for any fraud, omission or wrongful act. The legal position of HCEOs and county court bailiffs is the same except that an order of a superior court is in all cases a protection to the officer executing it unless he exceeds his mandate. He is not bound to take notice of any defect or irregularity in the writ, even though obvious and apparent (*Countess of Rutland's Case* (1605) 6 Rep 53; *Brown v Watson* (1871) 23 LT 745; *Williams v Williams & Nathan* [1937] 2 All ER 559; *Barclays Bank v Roberts* [1954] 1 WLR 1212). As a public officer with duties to judgment debtors, if he knows, or might by reasonable care have discovered that a writ was void, the HCEO will be guilty of culpable negligence if he seizes under it (*Hooper v Lane* (1857) 6 HL Cas 443). The HCEO must prove the validity of a judgment debt where the debtor has assigned chattels in fraud of creditors (*Hooper v Lane* (1857)). If the HCEO wishes to seize such goods under a writ of fi fa he must prove the judgment, not just rely on the writ (*Grey v Smith* (1808) 1 Camp 387), as the assignment is good except as against the judgment creditor, and the HCEO will trespass by seizing third party goods unless there is a valid judgment (*White v Morris* (1852) 11 CB 1015). Liability arises here from taking the goods of an innocent party, not because the judgment is bad.

5.2.2 *Improper executions*

Improper execution is categorised differently to wrongful distress due to the nature of the writ upon which the levy is based. Execution is at royal command, with the consequence that wrongdoing in its performance is viewed more seriously. Improper execution may be either wrongful or irregular, though the distinction is not absolute and it has been suggested that all improper levies are wrongful, the only differentiating factor being the actual damages that the claimant could prove.

5.2.3 *Wrongful executions*

A wrongful execution occurs in three ways:

- where it is authorised by neither the judgment nor the writ: there are many examples of such execution. The levy may be excessive (provided that the claimant can show it to be 'obviously' so - *Moore v Lambeth*

County Court Registrar [1970] 1 QB 560). The execution may be at the wrong address (*Morris v Salberg* [1889] 22 QBD 614; *Jarmain v Hooper* (1843) 7 Scott NR 663) or against the wrong person's goods (*Hilliard v Hanson* [1882] 21 ChD 69; *Smith v Critchfield* [1885] 14 QBD 873). It may even be because the judgment has been satisfied or valid tender has been made (*Cubitt v Gamble* (1919) 3 TLR 223; *Rook v Wilmot* (1590) 78 ER 465 ; *Clissold v Cratchley* [1910] 2 KB 244) or because there is no writ to justify it (*Cameron v Lightfoot* (1778) 2 Wm Bl 1190; *Parsons v Lloyd* (1772) 3 Wils 341), for example where a writ is executed after it has been set aside by the court (*Belshaw v Chapman Marshall* (1832) 4 B&A 336).

- The remedy against wrongful executions in such circumstances is for the aggrieved party to take an action for trespass (*Hooper v Lane* (1857) 6 HL Cas 443), the measure of damages being the same as if the wrongdoer had no official character. There is no need to prove that malice was involved in such an action (*Clissold v Cratchley* [1910] 2 KB 244). Although wrongful execution is trespass, it is not trespass *ab initio* and the levy remains good (*De Gondouin v Lewis* (1839) 10 Ad & E 117). Such actions will be against the HCEO and may be against the execution creditor if they instructed the HCEO to act in the wrongful manner (*Morris v Salberg* [1889] 22 QBD 614; *Jarmain v Hooper* (1843) 7 Scott NR 663). The HCEO may seek protection from the action by way of interpleader (see 9.26 later).

- However an execution is void and is trespass *ab initio* if the debt was paid (*Clissold v Cratchley* above) and the court may set the execution aside. If execution is set aside restitution of goods, or their value if they have been sold, may also be ordered (see 'irregular execution' below). A claimant can of course issue another writ even if the first is void (*Mackie v Warren* (1828) 5 Bing 176).

- where it is issued without reasonable cause or maliciously: a levy is illegal if malice is involved in its issue or conduct (*Cash v Wells* (1830) 1 B & Ad 375; *Pinches v Harvey* (1841) 1 QB 368; *Gillott v Aston* (1842) 12 LJQB 5). Malice means an act done intentionally without just cause, or any act motivated by a dishonest, irrelevant or improper motive. For example an action lies where a person maliciously and without probable cause procures execution to be levied for a sum higher than the judgment debt (*Churchill v Siggers* (1854) 3 E&B 929), where a judgment creditor issues a second writ whilst the first remains unreturned (*Waterer v Freeman* (1617) Hob 205; *Wren v Weild* [1869] 4 QB 730) or where the judgment creditor maliciously issues execution for the whole debt when part has been paid or refuses tender and proceeds to execution (*Gilding v*

Eyre (1861) 10 CBNS 592). Execution may also be malicious where it is levied excessively (*Wooddye v Coles* (1595) Noy 59; *Jenings v Florence* (1857) 2 CBNS 467) or where the judgment creditor continued to enforce after the judgment debtor became insolvent (*Phillips v General Omnibus Co* (1880) 50 LJQB112).

- The defendant's remedy is to claim damages in an action on the case (*Scheibel v Fairbairn* (1799) 1 Bos & Pul 388), the damages awarded being assessed on the degree of malice proved (*Gibson v Chaters* (1800) 2 Bos & P 129), with an exemplary award possible. In the absence of proof of malice on their part, action cannot be taken against a judgment creditor (*Phillips v General Omnibus Co* (1880) 50 LJQB 112 - an action for detention of goods failed as the 'ingredient of malice' was absent). See too *Crozer v Pilling* (1825) 4 B&C 26 and *De Medina v Grove* (1847) 10 QB 172.

- where the levy is otherwise in breach of court rules or common law powers: an illegal execution also occurs wherever the procedure of the HCEO does not follow that laid down by the Rules of the Supreme Court or fails to comply with the duties imposed by case law. Thus execution is wrongful if goods are seized after a stay of execution has been ordered (*Childrens v Saxby* (1683) 1 Vern 207; *Winter v Lightbound* (1720) 1 Stra 301) or has been agreed between judgment creditor and debtor (*Veal v Warner* (1669) 1 Mod Rep 20; *Bikker v Beeston* (1860) 29 LJ Exch 121). A levy is illegal if there was forced entry (*Curlewis v Lawrie* (1848) 12 QB 640) or if execution occurred on a Sunday without leave of court having been obtained by the HCEO. Execution is also wrongful if the HCEO ignores the orders instructions of the judgment creditor (*Walker v Hunter* (1845) 2 CB 324) or if the HCEO alters the writ or warrant (*Hale v Castleman* (1746) 1 Wm Bl 2). In such cases the debtor can sue for damages for trespass with no need to prove malice (*Percival v Stamp* (1853) 9 Exch 167; *Duke of Brunswick v Sloman* (1849) 3 CB 317). Restitution will be ordered if necessary.

- Although illegal execution is trespass it is not void, even if there has been forced entry (Littleton J in YB 18 Ed IV fo.4 pl.19). The court may void the execution but if the HCEO simply exceeded his authority the execution is not automatically void. If the cause of action is breach of duty by the officer, the measure of damages is the actual loss incurred, though the claimant should at least get a nominal sum (*Wylie v Birch* (1843) 4 QB 566).

5.2.4 *Irregular executions*

An irregular execution will occur if the rules of court are not followed. Essentially it is distinguished from wrongful execution by the fact that it is concerned with the form of the writ or warrant, not the manner of its execution. Typically some mistake will have been made in issue which the court is able to rectify. As irregularity involves genuine error or a technical flaw, no wrong will normally be committed and damages will rarely be awarded unless malice or actual damages are shown (*Rhodes v Hull* (1857) 26 LJ Ex 265). Damages may be allowed if for instance goods have been sold under the irregular execution (*Perkins v Plympton* (1831) 7 Bing 676). If a writ is set aside for irregularity, rather than amended, an action for damages for trespass may be taken against the execution creditor (*Loton v Devereux* (1832) 3 B & Ad 343).

Examples of irregularity include a levy by an unauthorised officer (*Rhodes v Hull* (1857) 26 LJ Ex 265); an execution which does not exactly follow the terms of the judgment (*Fisher v Magnay* (1843) 6 Scott NR 588; *Phillips v Birch* (1842) 2 Dowl NS 97; *Re: Cobbett* (1861) 10 WR 40); a levy for the wrong sums (*Wentworth v Bullen* (1829) 9 B & C 840; *Davis v Shapley* (1830) 1 B & Ad 54; *King v Birch* (1842) 3 QB 425; *Cobbold v Chilver* (1842) 4 Man & G 62).

The remedy in cases of irregular execution is for the debtor to apply for the execution to be set aside and for restitution to be ordered if necessary (*Rhodes v Hull* (1857) 26 LJ Ex 265). The judgment debtor has the option of waiving any irregularity (*Lewis v Gompertz* (1837) Will & Woll & Dav 592). The judgment creditor may seek to have the proceedings amended.

Proceedings are not automatically nullified by an irregularity but can be if it is serious enough. An order is a nullity if it fails to comply with an essential provision and can be set aside by the court '*ex debito justitiae*' under its inherent jurisdiction (*Craig v Kannsen* [1943] KB 256 CA). Normally the court will correct an irregularity by giving leave for the creditor to amend the process (e.g. *Laroche v Wasbrough* (1788) 2 TR 737; *Evans v Manero* (1841) 7 M&W 463; *Re: London Wharfing & Warehousing Co* (1885) 54 LJ Ch 1137). Execution will only usually be set aside where the debtor has suffered prejudice as a result or has become insolvent (*Hunt v Pasman* (1815) 4 M&S 329; *Webber v Hutchins* (1841) 8 M&W 319). When setting aside, terms cannot be imposed on the HCEO, who will be protected from action by the writ provided that it was not obviously void or beyond the court's jurisdiction (*Gillot v Aston* (1842) 12 LJQB 5 and see above). The application for setting aside must be made by summons or motion by the debtor without delay in a reasonable time (*Austin v Davey* (1844) 4 LTOS 160). It has been held one year is unreasonable delay (*Reynolds v Coleman* [1887] 36 ChD 453), as was four months (*Pontin v Wood* [1962] 1 QB 594). The setting aside does not prevent the creditor issuing another writ (*McCornish v Melton* (1834) 3 Dowl 215; *Mackie v Warren* (1828) 5 Bing 176).

Restitution may be ordered if execution is set aside and should be included as a term on the same order. If restitution is not ordered a separate application may be made. If the goods have been sold, the sum to be ordered to be paid as restitution to the owner should be the sale value, not the real value of the goods (*Robertson v Miller* [1904] 3 NB Eq Rep 78). As to the effect of irregularity on sale see 10.5.2.

5.2.5 *County court executions*

An order of an inferior court is not of itself, at common law, conclusive protection to the officer operating under it. The officer must scan the terms of the order and if, on the face of it, it appears to be an order the court could not legally make, he is justified in not enforcing it since he is supposed to know the law and know that the document is a nullity (*Andrews v Morris* (1841) 1 QB 3; *Carratt v Morley* (1841) 1 QB 18; *Watson v Birdell* (1845) 14 M&W 57). If the order is good on the face of it the bailiff is fully protected in its execution - even though aware that in the circumstances it was illegally issued. Wrongful execution by the county court bailiffs is broadly the same as described above for HCEOs. In addition to the general rights to sue, if execution is irregular the court can set it aside in whole or in part under CPR 13.3.

5.3 Remedies

As already suggested, a range of remedies exist, some under statute, some at common law. The debtor may choose to:

- Issue a complaint to the creditor or the bailiff company, with the further option of complaint to a trade body or an ombudsman (see c.12);

- Issue a claim for a tort actionable *per se* (trespass to land, goods or person, and breach of duty by public officers). Proof of the wrong done will suffice (*Williams v Mostyn* (1838) 4 M&W 145);

- Take an 'action on the case' where the damages (general and consequential) claimed must be proved. This would include conversion and negligence and actions for illegal distress (*Messing v Kemble* (1800) 2 Camp 116);

- Issue a claim based on a statutory provision, which provide remedies for various offences that may be committed typically under distress for rent. Examples include actions for distress off the demised property or upon the highway- for which see later. It is also possible to sue on the 'equity' of a statutory provision- in other words, where an Act imposes a duty but creates no specific penalty for breach, it may still be possible to base an action for wrongful distress upon failure to comply (*Johnson v Upham* (1859) 2 E&E 250);

- Seek replevin of the seized goods from the county court;

- Pay under protest and then issue a claim to recover the sums paid;

- Issue a claim for misfeasance in public office - this tort permits an aggrieved person to recover damages for any loss, injury or damage resulting from an administrative action known by the relevant authority or officer to be unlawful or done maliciously. The key elements of the tort of misfeasance are an abuse of power leading to damage, whether financial or loss of reputation and the like. The tort may arise in two ways: from malice, which renders an action both *ultra vires* and tortuous, or from recklessness on the part of officers as to whether their conduct was unlawful. The damages will include compensation for the claimant's losses, but may also include an exemplary element. Any public authority may be sued, as may any individual officer, although an authority is not liable for the officer's action if the person behaved in a way that s/he knew to be deliberately unlawful and beyond his/ her powers. The application of misfeasance to distraint was examined in *R v Hampstead Magistrates Court & another ex p St Marylebone Property Company* (1995) Legal Action Sept. 1996 p.21. Carnwath J felt that the local authority had been aware that the notices it served were unlawful. However, the levy of distress rested upon a liability order, the validity of which had not been challenged, therefore the distraint had to be regarded as lawful. It seems, then, that levies based on some form of court order or judgment are unlikely to be susceptible to challenge by this route. Those warrants issued by public officers without recourse to court (e.g. income tax and VAT) may be; or,

- Issue a claim for negligence - Crown departments and local authorities are vicariously liable for the torts of their servants. There is no need to prove malice or deliberate illegality. It is also possible to claim against a bailiff's employer for negligent acts associated with the person's conduct of their job or against the principal instructing the enforcement agent. In such cases, there would be joint liability on the part of bailiff and employer. The tort arises where an operational task is carried out negligently or in excess of statutory power, without care being not taken to avoid foreseeable and proximate damage. It also arises when a body fails to act fairly or reasonably. A duty of care must be established, but a public body should comply with regulations and should seek to avoid any probable harm that could arise from its activities. There is no duty of care if a body is acting within a statutory discretion. Thus, no claim arises if authority chooses to use distress rather than another remedy, but a claim may lie for the manner in which distress was levied. The claimant can only recover such actual damages as can be proved. As negligence is concerned with the defendant's conduct, it may be possible to claim for both negligence and for another tort committed at the same time, for instance, trespass.

The debtor may only employ one remedy at a time. In *Hilliard v Hanson* [1882] 21 ChD 69 a man applied for interpleader and an injunction successively: the latter was refused until the first proceedings were decided. Reaching an agreement with the bailiff regarding payment or sale does not debar the debtor from later taking action against the bailiff (*Sells v Hoare* (1824) 1 Bing 401; *Willoughby v Backhouse* (1824) 2 B&C 821). If the bailiff tenders amends before an action is begun, the claimant should not get judgment (s.20 Distress for Rent Act 1737).

5.4 Who can be sued?

Normally any action taken will be against the bailiff who levied and any creditor authorising the illegal act (*Hurry v Rickman & Sutcliffe* (1831) 1 Mood & R 126). In illegal distress the action will always be against the bailiff, the creditor may only be sued if they authorised or ratified any unlawful act by their agent (*Gauntlett v King* (1857) 3 CBNS 59 - see 12.1 later). If such authorisation or ratification has been given then, to cite Tindal CJ in *Wilson v Tumman* (1843) 6 M&G 236: "all who procure a trespass to be done are trespassers themselves". The situation is different in execution because of the special liability of the HCEO. Special rules also exist for magistrates' distress. The liability of creditors and bailiffs companies is examined in c.12.

5.4.1 *HCEOs' liability*

The HCEO is an agent of the claimant and must execute a writ if it is regular, dealing with writs in the order in which they were received (*Dennis v Whetham* [1874] 9 QB 345). The HCEO is liable for damages to the creditor if he does not follow this procedure (*Smalcomb v Buckingham* (1697) 12 Mod Rep 146) or if he executes with unreasonable delay or negligence (*Re: Essex Sheriff, Terrell v Fisher* (1862) 10 WR 796) or fails to levy at all (*Pitcher v King* (1844) 5 QB 758). However, the HCEO also has duties to the debtor, the debtor's trustee in bankruptcy and to the debtor's landlord, and is generally liable for any act not covered by the authority of the writ or warrant which would by itself be trespass or conversion (*Re: A Debtor (No. 2 of 1977)* [1979] 1 WLR 956). Thus the HCEO is not merely liable for putting the execution process in train, he is absolutely liable for every aspect of his subordinates' conduct (*Ackworth v Kempe* (1778) 99 ER 30; *Underhill v Wilson* (1830) 6 Bing 697). If the HCEO seizes the wrong goods under a valid warrant he acts on behalf of the court not the execution creditor

(*Wilson v Tumman* (1843) 6 M&G 236; *Woollen v Wright* (1862) 1 H&C 354). The HCEO may be liable to a claim even where the execution creditor's solicitor has issued directions to seize certain goods. It is not within the solicitor's authority to issue instructions as to the conduct of levies, and an innocent execution creditor is not liable for wrongful acts arising from verbal instructions (as opposed to directions on the writ itself) (*Smith v Keal* [1882] 9 QBD 352; *Jarmain v Hooper* (1843) 7 Scott NR 663).

Anything done illegally is imputable to the HCEO as if it was done as part of the execution or was purported to be part of the execution. For example, in *Smart v Hutton* (1833) 8 A&E 568n the sheriff was held liable for false imprisonment where the bailiff arrested a debtor in the absence of sufficient goods for seizure under a fi fa. The HCEO will be liable for any act done in purported exercise of the officer's duty, even if it is contrary to instructions (*Scarfe v Halifax* (1840) 7 M&W 288). Any deputy appointed is also the HCEO's responsibility - see *Gregory v Cotterell* (1855) 5 E&B 571 in which the sheriff was liable when goods were seized after payment. The HCEO is liable despite the fact that there is no proof that the act or omission has been ratified (*Saunderson v Baker & Martin* (1772) 3 Wils 309 - third party goods were seized under the writ). The HCEO can be sued for wrongfully retaining possession of goods after the true facts of ownership become apparent (*Dunstan v Patterson* (1857) 2 CBNS 495) though if the original seizure arises from misrepresentation by the owner, s/he may be estopped from suing (see also Price v Harwood (1811) 3 Camp 108). If a person is silent upon a mistake in process, they may be assumed to have acquiesced to it (*Fisher v Magnay* (1843) 12 LJCP 276) and may be estopped from any remedy. However if the third party protests against the mistaken execution, the HCEO will be liable for any consequent damages (*Walley v M'Connell* (1849) 13 QBD 903) even where the protest is accompanied by a payment to prevent execution (*Baron De Mesnil v Dakin* [1867] 3 QB 18). That money is paid under duress and can be recovered by an action for money had and received- see later.

The HCEO is not liable if the bailiff's action is not under the colour of the writ or done in pretended execution of it and is quite outside his duty and is not done for the purpose of executing the warrant (*Woods v Finnis* (1852) 7 Ex 363; Smith v Pritchard (1849) 8 CB 565). The HCEO is not liable if the bailiff acts after the warrant has been withdrawn (*Brown v Copley* (1844) 8 Scott NR 350). If a person persuades a bailiff to act contrary to his duty, he cannot later complain about that particular breach of duty but the HCEO has a general responsibility in the matter (*Taylor v Richardson* (1800) 8 TR 505) and face a claim for any other misconduct by which the claimant suffered damage (*Cook v Palmer* (1827) 6 B&C 739; *Botten v Tomlinson* (1847) 16 LJCP 138; *Crowther v Long* (1828) 8 B&C 598). Thus, where the debtor persuaded the bailiff not to advertise and to delay the sale this interference did not bar an action for damages arising from the negligent conduct of the sale leading to disposal at an undervalue (*Wright v Child* [1866] 1 Ex 358). The HCEO is not liable for criminal acts committed without his authority (*Woodgate v Knatchbull* (1787) 2 TR 148).

HCEOs are also liable for damages for their wrongful acts. It will be necessary to prove that the HCEO authorised the conduct complained of, so merely showing that the bailiff is bound to the HCEO is not enough (*Drake v Sikes* (1797) 7 TR 113); the original warrant will have to be produced or proved (*Snowballe v Goodricke* (1833) 4 B&Ad 541). Notice of certain facts to the HCEO, such as setting aside of a writ, is notice to the HCEOs too, so that they will also be liable for any wrongful act that occurs (*Belshaw v Chapman Marshall* (1832) 4 B&A 336).

Under s29(2) Sheriffs Act 1887 it is an offence for either a HCEO or bailiff to breach any of the provisions of the Act, or be guilty of any wrongful act or neglect or default in the execution of their office. This will clearly include any wrongful levy of execution as well as making improper charges in violation of s20 of the Act (for which see 11.5). Any such offence may be punished as a misdemeanour (s29(1)) or as contempt of the Supreme Court (s29(5)).

The debtor or other aggrieved person also has a personal remedy in that they may sue under s29(2) in the High Court. The Court may order the officer to forfeit a penalty of £200 and pay all damages suffered by the person aggrieved (presumably to be assessed as in trespass) plus the costs occasioned by the complaint. Proceedings should be commenced no later than two years after the alleged offence (s29(7)). The court may stay any proceedings and order the offence be dealt with by other means (s29(8)). See for example *Bagge v Whitehead* [1892] 2 QB 355 CA in which the debtor sued the sheriff for failing to exempt from seizure the basic wearing apparel, bedding and tools of the trade protected by statute. It was held in this case that the sheriff was not liable for the £200 penalty as only the officer guilty of an illegal act can be subject to the forfeit. However general damages were awarded at common law. Lopes J held "Acts done criminaliter are alone dealt with by s29, not acts done civiliter, in respect of which the remedy against the sheriff remains the same as before the Act."

5.4.2 *County court liability*

The nature of the liability of county court district judges and bailiffs is set out in Part VIII CCA and is modelled largely on HCEOs' liability and partly on constables' liability.

Under s123 every district judge is responsible for the acts of bailiffs appointed to assist him just as a HCEO is responsible for acts of officers, e.g. the district judge is responsible if execution is against the wrong person. These provisions have been explored in several cases. In *Burton v Le Gros* (1864) 34 LJQB 91 it was held that the high bailiff (now district judge) in a county court is liable to the same extent as the HCEO for the wrongful acts of any bailiff or persons employed by them, so that the high bailiff could be sued if the bailiff executing the warrant failed to follow the procedure laid down in the County Court Rules. See 5.4.1 on HCEO's liability. Whilst the position of the high bailiff/ district judge has been said to be that of standing in the place of the HCEO in terms of all relevant legislation (*Bennett v Powell* (1855) 3 Drew 326), caution must be exercised as the county court office is a creation of statute and "it is fallacious to liken a high bailiff in all respects to a sheriff "(per Smith J in *Thomas v Peek* [1888] 20 QBD 727). Although this responsibility is created by statute, the District Judge will also be liable under common law, like the HCEO, and can be sued by anyone injured by the bailiff's failure to carry out his statutory duties. Thus in *Watson v White* [1896] 2 QB 9 it was held that an action will lie against the district judge at the party aggrieved by neglect in the performance of his duties, notwithstanding the powers of the judge, under s124 CCA, to order the bailiff to pay damages. As s124 is only concerned with providing a summary remedy to judgment creditors aggrieved by the bailiff's actions (see for instance *Domine v Grimsdall* [1937] 2 All ER 119), the continued existence of the common law remedy is beneficial to other parties.

There are limits on a district judge's liability. The district judge of a court where a warrant is issued cannot be liable for the wrongful acts of a bailiff in a 'foreign' court in executing the warrant (*Smith v Pritchard* (1849) 8 CB 565)- even though a bailiff from the issuing court may assist in the wrongful execution. Smith v Pritchard shows also that the district judge is responsible only for acts done under the supposed authority of the warrant, such as forced entry, but not unassociated acts such as assault.

Further under s.126 a person cannot take action against the bailiff for anything done in obedience to the warrant unless demand in writing for inspection of warrant is made at the bailiff's office and the bailiff refuses or neglects to comply within six days. The bailiff shall not have judgment made against him if the warrant is produced at the trial, despite any defect or irregularity in it. Compare the Constables Protection Act 1750 s.6 at 5.4.4. This protection was examined in *Aspey v Jones* (1884) 54 LJQB 98 which confirmed that both the district judge and the bailiff are protected, even though there may have been no jurisdiction for the judge to have made the order upon which the warrant is based. If the action is for the mere fact of seizure (not its mode) and if this was done in conformity to the warrant and if this is produced and is regular, then the officers are protected. See *Dews v Riley* (1851) 11 CB 434 which held that the bailiff or clerk of the court are mere ministerial officers and if they act in performance of a duty placed upon them by statute, such as enforcing a warrant, they are not liable for trespass even if the order being enforced is bad (see also *Andrews v Morris* (1841) 1 QB 3).

5.4.3 *Justices' liability*

In the case of magistrates' court distress the scope for action against justices is limited because of the effect of ss44 & 45 Justice of the Peace Act 1979. Under s44 justices may not be sued for any act or omission in the execution of their duty in respect of any matter within their jurisdiction. This is despite negligence on their part (*Everett v Griffiths* [1921] AC 631), informality (*Ratt v Parkinson* (1851) 15 JP 356) or irregularity (*Bott v Ackroyd* (1859) 23 JP 661). Even when the justices act beyond their jurisdiction, any act or omission in purported execution of their duty may only be the subject of an action if done in bad faith (s45). Acting in excess of jurisdiction thus may not be actionable if it is the result of an error or misdirection- for instance, for lack of sufficient evidence (*Palmer v Crone* [1927] 1 KB 804; *R v Cardiff Justices ex p Salter* (1985) 149 JP 721). Under s50 of the Act the High Court or county court may set aside with costs any action wrongly brought against a justice of the peace.

5.4.4 *Constables' and other officers' liability*

Constables or other officers enforcing a warrant issued by justices have a duty to act strictly according to the terms of the warrant. If they do not they can be sued. However if the officer acts in obedience to the warrant, s/he has a good defence to any action in tort as s/he is protected by s6 Constables Protection Act 1750. Provided that s/he complies within six days with any written demand for sight of or an opportunity to copy the warrant, the officer will not face judgment as a result of any defect in the justices' jurisdiction. If the officer complies with the demand for the warrant the justices must be sued as co-defendants and judgment cannot be given against the officer for any defect in the justice's jurisdiction. The officer merely needs to produce the warrant at the trial to be entitled to judgment in his/ her favour. As already described, it may be very difficult to enter any judgment for trespass or conversion against justices nowadays, though if a judgment is entered against them, even though the case is dismissed against the constable or officer, costs can be awarded against the justices. If no demand for a copy of the warrant is made, the constable may be protected from damages for seizing goods under an illegal distress warrant (*Palmer v Crone* [1927] 1 KB 804). A constable is under a duty to enforce a justices warrant, even though it is known to be defective, so resisting the execution can be an offence (*R v*

Royds ex p Sidney [1860] 1 QSCR 8; *R v Rapay* (1902) 7 CCC 170) and the proper procedure will be to challenge the magistrates jurisdiction following the procedure under the 1750 Act.

Section 6 has been held to apply to any person acting by order of a constable (*Jones v Chapman* (1845) 14 M&W 124) and to any 'officer', not just a constable, enforcing a magistrates' warrant. Thus "all inferior officers" enforcing a warrant issued for rates are entitled to protection in any action- for instance for conversion (*Lyons v Golding* (1829) 3 C&P 586) - but not in replevin (*Milward v Caffin* (1779) 2 Wm Bl 1330; *Fletcher v Williams* (1805) 6 East 283), where the validity of the warrant is disputed (*Harper v Carr* (1797) 7 TR 270; *Nutting v Jackson* (1773) Bull NP 24). Today it will probably not be possible to count distraint issued under liability orders for local taxes and child support maintenance as equivalent to distress warrants issued for rates by justices under previous legislation. As a result the 1750 Act will no longer relevant to such bailiffs and will only apply to those enforcing magistrates' orders for fines, maintenance and civil debts by distress.

For details of the nature of the demand, see *Clark v Woods* (1848) 2 Ex 395 or *Jory v Orchard* (1799) 2 B&P 39. A demand is not invalid because it requires compliance in less than six days (*Collins v Rose* (1839) 5 M&W 194). The person charged with execution of the warrant must receive it, not a subordinate (*Clarke v Davey* (1820) 4 Moo 465). If the officer refuses or neglects to comply with the demand, action may be begun immediately, but if it is delayed, the constable may still comply before the writ or summons is issued (*Jones v Vaughan* (1804) 5 East 445). A substantial rather than literal compliance with the section may be sufficient to protect the officer (*Atkins v Kilby* (1840) 11 Ad & El 777).

A distinction needs to be made between cases where an action may lie against the justices for exceeding their jurisdiction and actions against the officer for exceeding the authority of the warrant (*Milton v Green* (1804) 2 B&P 158). Thus in an action against the bailiffs for a wrongful and malicious excessive distress, there is no need to demand the warrant under s6 prior to commencing action as the bailiffs had clearly not been acting in obedience to their authority (*Hoye v Buck* (1840) 1 Man & G 775). Thus an action for unauthorised distraint will not require prior compliance with s.6 (*Kay v Grover* (1831) 7 Bing 312; *Cotton v Kaldwell* (1833) 2 Nev & M KB 399), nor will an action for excessive distraint (*Stirch v Clarke* (1832) 4 B&A 113). If it is doubtful whether the officer was acting in obedience to the warrant, it should be demanded (*Price v Messenger* (1800) 2 Bos & P 158). A constable is protected if s/he obeys an unlawful warrant, but not if s/he executes a lawful warrant in an unlawful way (*Horsfield v Brown* [1932] 1

KB 355), in which case the officer may be sued, but not the justices (*Money v Leach* (1765) 3 Burr 1742). A constable may be sued even though s/he believes that s/he is acting under the warrant for example by taking the wrong persons goods (*Price v Messenger* as above), by levying excessively or by levying without having the warrant available (see 6.1.2).

The Act protects against defects in jurisdiction, not against defects in the form of the warrant. If there are faults with the form, the bailiff's protection may be derived from elsewhere (see 6.1.1).

TCEA 2007- commentary

It is important to note that when the 2007 Act is brought into force, the rights of debtors will be diminished by the fact that most wrongful levies will be treated as 'irregularities' rather than 'illegalities'. Schedule 12, para 66 provides that debtors can claim for damages arising out of breaches of TCEA. It will only be in rare cases that a wrongful levy is treated as a trespass and therefore void *ab initio*. This might arise where the wrong person or property has been visited, or where no debt was due, but in all other cases where the bailiff's error was in neglecting to follow the procedural code laid down by TCEA, it will only be possible to claim for special damages.

Chapter 6

COMMENCING LEVIES: ISSUE

6.1 Warrants

6.1.1 *Form*

The beginning of the process of recovery of debt by distress is the instruction of the bailiff. This is typically done by the issue of a 'warrant', a written authority from the creditor or court to the distrainor. From the warrant the bailiff derives his powers and rights (*Smith v Birmingham Gas Co* (1834) 1 Ad & El 526). Without a warrant the distress would be illegal. In *Symonds v Kurtz* (1889) 61 LT 559 a person other than that named on the warrant carried out the distress. This was held to be trespass. If the bailiff holds more than one warrant against the same person, there is nothing irregular in seizing under more than one at once (*Robertson v Hooper* [1909] 12 WLR 5).

The form of the warrant will vary from one type of distress to another but typically specifies the debt due and commands the bailiff to seize and sell goods and immediately pay over the proceeds to the creditor. In the case of distraint for fines the warrant must be in writing (Crim PR Part 52.8(1)) whilst for VAT prescribed form 823 is used. In other forms of distraint there is no requirement that they should be in writing.

In several regimes it is provided that any defect in the warrant or original order will not invalidate the levy. For instance under reg 45(7) CT(A&E) Regs and reg 14(7) NDR (A&E)(LL) Regs or under reg 30(3) CS (C&E) Regs distraint is not unlawful because of any defect in the liability order and a bailiff will not be a trespasser as a result. Thus a trivial error that does not detract from the general sense of a warrant does not invalidate it (though see *IRC v Rossmeister* [1980] AC 952), but it will be invalid if some important detail, such as the address, is wrong (*R v Atkinson* [1976] Crim LR 307 CA). Damages cannot be claimed for a wrongly calculated sum (*Bavin v Hutchinson* (1862) 6 LT 504).

It is worth noting that many magistrates' courts neglect to correctly issue warrants because they only enter the name of a firm of bailiffs rather than named employees. However, s78(1) MCA provides that a warrant is not void because of any defect so long as it states that the sum has been adjudged to be paid. It would therefore not be possible for the bailiff to be sued for trespass (*Price v Messenger* (1800) 2 Bos & Pull 158) however the defendant can claim any special damages caused by the defect in the warrant (s.78(3)). A similar provision relates to defects in other court process (s.123) and the guidance in *Stones Justices Manual* is that a minor error that does no injustice should be disregarded.

6.1.2 *Production of warrant*

There is no right general for the debtor to see a distress warrant, unlike a police search warrant, and no duty for the bailiff to show it (*Buller's Case* (1587) 1 Leon 50). However, in *Symonds v Kurtz* (1889) 61 LT 559 the court held that it is a general principle of law that every person whose home is entered is entitled to know the authority under which this is done and be able to see whether that authority is followed.

It has been held that at common law a constable enforcing a magistrates arrest warrant can be sued for an illegal act not in execution of his duty by failing to have the warrant with him when levying, as he should be able to produce his authority if required (*Galliard v Laxton* (1862) 2 B&S 363; *Codd v Cabe* [1876] 1 Ex D 352). The warrant doesn't have to be in the officer's physical possession provided that it is under his control and can be easily and quickly produced- for instance in a vehicle parked close by (*R v Purdy* [1974] 3 WLR 367). It is not acceptable that a warrant is available at an office nearby (*Horsfield v Brown* [1932] 1 KB 355; *De Costa Small v Kirkpatrick* [1979] 68 Cr App R 186). This common law rule is explained by Roskill LJ in Purdy - "Where a person is being arrested on a warrant otherwise than for a criminal offence, it is essential that he should be able to know for what he is being arrested...; he can ... 'buy' his freedom from arrest by instant payment of the sum stated on the warrant".

In respect of magistrates' court levies the Criminal Procedure Rules Part 52.8(5) now require that the person executing a warrant either has it with him/her or states where it is and what arrangements may be made to inspect it. The distrainor should also produce identification and/ or a copy of his/her authorisation from the court and should explain in plain English the reason for the levy of distress. Nevertheless, the principles derived from the above cases are capable of being extended to other distress warrants where again the debtor may prevent immediate taking of their goods, rather than their person, by immediate payment.

6.1.3 *Validity & Limitations*

The debtor may be able to challenge the validity of a warrant of the basis that enforcement of the debt is time barred, or that the warrant itself has expired. The Limitation Act 1980 is, in fact, of limited assistance in this matter. The Act is applicable to all classes of action, which includes any proceeding in a court of law (s38(1)). This is defined as including any form of initiating process, such as the summons for a liability order for local taxes (China v Harrow UDC [1954] 1 QB 178). It does not refer to the issue of execution on a judgment, to which special rules apply, nor does it apply to the recovery of taxes and duties by the crown (s.37(2)).

We may accordingly summarise the limitations that apply as follow.

- Execution - in the civil courts it is necessary for the judgment creditor to obtain leave of court before issuing execution where six years or more have elapsed since the date of the judgment (CPR Sch.1 RSC O.46 r.2(1)(a); Sch.2 CCR O.26 r.5(1)(a)). Application is made *ex parte* supported by affidavit, though the High Court may direct that the application is made by summons and the county court may direct that notice be served on the debtor, so that the judgment debtor would have an opportunity to make representations.

- Failure to apply for leave is an abuse of process (*LB Hackney v White* [1995] 28 HLR 219) and the execution may be set aside by the court on application by the debtor. The Limitation Act 1980 does not apply to applications for leave to issue execution (*National Westminster Bank v Powney* [1990] 2 WLR 1084) as there is a distinction between the right to take an action and the procedural right or remedy to issue execution (*Berliner Industriebank Aktiengesellschaft v Jost* [1971] 1 QB 278; W T *Lamb & Sons v Rider* [1948] 2 KB 331).

- High Court and county court warrants are then valid for twelve months from the date of issue (CPR Sch.1 RSC O.46 r.2(3) & Sch.2 CCR O.26 r.6) but they can be extended, or the leave renewed.

- Crown distraint- there seems to be no limit on the validity of warrants (*Elliot v Yates* [1900] 2 QB 370).

- In the case of magistrates' court orders, there is no limitation placed upon criminal proceedings by the Limitation Act (see *AG v Bradlaugh* [1885] 14 QBD 667). There are limitations on the commencement of civil and criminal proceedings within the Magistrates Court Act 1980 (s.127(1)) but there seems to be no time limit on the validity of a warrant issued to enforce an order.

- Road traffic execution is modelled on county court execution. Thus a warrant is valid for twelve months and can only be reissued (for the remainder of the 12 month period) where it is found that the debtor's address has changed (CPR Pt.75.7). Under CPR Sch.2 CCR O.26 r.5 (as applied by Part 75.6(c)) a warrant cannot be issued without leave of court if more than six years have elapsed since the original order.

- There are no limits on the duration of rent distress warrants but there are limits on when distress for rent can be used. Distress should be levied within six months of the end of the lease as long as the landlord still has an interest in the property and the former tenant is still in possession i.e. the person is holding over under s.6 L&TA 1709. The maximum time allowed for enforcement of rent arrears is six years after they have accrued (s19 Limitation Act 1980). Up to six years' arrears are enforceable, even if more than that are due (*Doe d. Davy v Oxenham* (1840) 7 M&W 131).

A distress made upon an invalid warrant or unenforceable debt would be illegal. See 5.1 for details of how to challenge this. In other forms of distraint there is no limit on the validity of the warrant.

6.1.4 *Binding effect of execution warrants & writs*

When a writ of *fieri facias* or warrant of execution is issued a warning notice is usually sent to the debtor. The purpose of this is to notify the debtor that ownership rights over all goods are 'bound in the debtor's hands' from the date the HCEO/ bailiff received the writ/ warrant (para.8, Sch.7, Courts Act 2003; CCA s99; for road traffic penalties article 15(1) ERTDO applying CCA s99). The receipt of the writ is the important date, so a writ received by the HCEO before a writ issued on an earlier judgment will have priority (*Guest v Cowbridge Railway Co* [1868] 6 Eq 619). If a warrant is issued in one county court but transferred to another for enforcement, the time of binding is when the warrant is issued by the second court (*Birstall Candle Co v Daniels* [1908] 2 KB 254). If the creditor loses the right to seize goods because there is delay by the court between the application for the warrant and its issue by the court office, the binding will be held to be effective from the time of issue, thus giving the execution creditor priority (*Murgatroyd v Wright* [1907] 2 KB 333).

'Bound' means that the HCEO has acquired the legal right to seize the goods though, notwithstanding this binding effect, ownership continues with the judgment debtor until sale and does not vest in the HCEO (*Payne v Drew* (1804) 4 East 523). As the property in the goods is not altered the debtor can legally deal with the goods until seizure (*Lucas v Nockells* (1833) 10 Bing 157). However a charge upon the goods has been created for the creditors

(*Woodland v Fuller* (1840) 11 Ad & El 859). Note that this charge is not such as will give priority in bankruptcy if there has only been binding, but not actual seizure (*In Re: Davies* [1872] 7 Ch 314). The HCEO has acquired a special property in the goods which enables him to sell as officer of the court. Any transfer or assignment of the goods from the date of binding will be subject to the HCEO's right to follow and seize the goods (*Ehlers, Seel & Co v Kauffman & Gates* (1883) 49 LT 806). The binding effect of the writ effects any transaction occurring on the same day- such as a deed of gift, which will be rendered ineffective (*Boucher v Wiseman* (1595) Cro Eliz 440).

The binding effect of the writ is only defeated if the goods have been purchased in good faith without notice of the fact that a writ has been issued and remains unexecuted by seizure (*Samuel v Duke* (1838) 3 M & W 622; *McPherson v Temiskaming Lumber Co Ltd* [1913] AC 145). Alternatively the HCEO can recover the value of the goods from the purported purchaser, rather than pursuing and seizing the items themselves (*Cockburn v Jeanette* [1942] 3 DLR 216). Disposal of the goods other than by sale in market overt will be void (*Giles v Grover* (1832) 6 Bligh NS 277). Binding only effects the debtor's general property, not any special property (para.8(5), Sch.7, Courts Act 2003), thus hired or mortgaged goods and the like are not bound until actual seizure and may be removed without any fear of pursuit by the owner (*Allan v Place* [1908] 15 DLR 476). Note also that binding only applies to goods and not to other property e.g. money, which are not affected until actual seizure (*Johnson v Pickering* [1908] 1 KB 1).

At common law the binding power operated differently, being effective from the date of the 'teste' of the writ, that is, the date it was issued by the execution creditor. It has been held that the common law rule still applies to the Crown (*Jeanes v Wilkins* (1749) 1 Ves Sen 194). This will give later Crown writs priority over those delivered earlier (*R v Wells* (1807) 16 East 278; and see 6.6.2), though again a bona fide sale in market overt will defeat the binding power (*Lowthal v Tomkins* (1740) 2 Eq Cas Abr 380). It has also been held that the statutory binding provisions are only for the protection of genuine purchasers of the judgment debtor's goods, and do not apply to executors of the debtor's goods, in whose hands the property is bound from the date of issue, not delivery (*Horton v Ruesby* (1686) Comb 33; *Rawlinson v Oriel* (1688) Comb 144; Anon (1690) 2 Vent 218; *Dr Needham's Case* (1691) 12 MR 5; *Waghorne v Langmead* (1796) 1 Bos & P 571). The same naturally also applies to administrators (*Farrer v Brooks* (1673) 1 MR 188).

It should be noted that TCEA 2007 Sch.12 paragraphs 4-6 extend the principle of the binding effect of the issue of a writ or warrant to all forms of seizure of goods. This will increase the protection of creditors from fraudulent disposals of goods immediately before a bailiff levies.

6.2 Distrainor

The qualifications needed by the distrainor will vary from regime to regime, as will the remedies for failing to comply with these requirements. In most cases complaint can be made to the employer, in some cases to a trade body (see c.12). The county court also has a role in this as it grants certificates to private bailiffs (see 6.10). In many cases there is no statutory stipulation as to who may levy, though creditors may restrict themselves, for instance by insisting that only certificated bailiffs levy.

6.2.1 *Distress for rent*

In distress for rent either the landlord or a certificated bailiff may distrain (*Re: Caidan* [1942] Ch 90). The landlord may include executors and administrators acting on behalf of a deceased landlord, receivers under Law of Property Act 1925 s.109(3) and receivers appointed by the court (*Pitt v Snowden* (1752) 3 Atk 750). If the land is held on trust, only the trustee, not the beneficiary, may distrain (*Schalit v Joseph Nadler Ltd* [1933] 2 KB 79). However if the landlord has simply authorised payment to be made to another person, they cannot distrain (*Ward v Shew* (1833) 9 Bing 608).

Unless the landlord is a corporate body, s/he may distrain in person. In the latter case, and most often otherwise, a private bailiff, who must be certificated, will be used, being instructed by the issue of a warrant. If the landlord distrains in person, the sale may be passed to an agent, who need not hold a certificate. If the landlord is a company, the director most hold a certificate to be able to distrain (*Hogarth v Jennings* [1892] 1 QB 907). Distress without a certificate is trespass (s7 LDAA 1888). The bailiff must produce a certificate and any letter of appointment from the landlord for the tenant or any other person present who appears to be in control of the premises (r.12(1)).

6.2.2 *Road traffic execution*

The Enforcement of Road Traffic Debts (Certificated Bailiffs) Regulations 1993 apply the Distress for Rent Rules 1988 to execution for road traffic penalties. Under reg. 2 any bailiffs holding a certificate for rent can act under the Traffic Management Act and any bailiff wishing to enforce these penalties needs a certificate. On levying the certificate should be produced to the debtor or any other person who appears to be in control of their premises (r.12(1) of the Rules).

6.2.3 *Local tax distraint*

Generally, private bailiffs will be used by the billing authority, though some authorities employ their own staff to levy. Under reg.45(6A) of the 1992 Enforcement Regulations bailiffs making distresses for local taxes must be certificated. Some bailiffs' companies interpret this to mean that only those bailiffs actually levying distraint have to hold a current certificate. This enables them to use uncertificated and trainee staff for other aspects of this work. There seems little justification for this in the wording of the regulations, which does not indicate that any exceptions are intended; rather, this reading relies upon an overly narrow interpretation of the phrase 'making distress' for which it would be difficult to find much case authority. Bailiffs must also carry a written authority from the billing authority, which should be shown to the debtor if requested (reg 45(5) CT; reg 14(5) NNDR).

6.2.4 *HCEOs*

High Court enforcement officers (HCEOs) are appointed under the High Court Enforcement Officers Regulations 2004, made under paragraph 12, Schedule 7 of the Courts Act 2003. They are appointed by the Lord Chancellor on a district basis throughout England and Wales; the country is divided into 105 districts for these purposes.

To be authorised as an HCEO a person must not have a criminal conviction for dishonesty or violence, or which led to a prison term; s/he must have neither unpaid fines nor judgments outstanding and should neither be an undischarged bankrupt or disqualified company director. Once appointed, HCEOs are under a duty not only to execute all writs directed to them but also to maintain adequate insurances and banking arrangements and to undergo appropriate training. The Lord Chancellor may cancel an authorisation whenever it appears to be in the public interest to do so, and particularly whenever it emerges that the person lied upon his/ her application or has behaved in an "unprofessional or unacceptable" manner.

6.2.5 *County court bailiffs*

County court bailiffs are the only bailiffs who are employed as such by a government department or agency. They are civil servants employed by Court Service and are responsible to the senior district judge within each county court.

6.2.6 *Magistrates' courts*

Magistrates' court warrants will be enforced either by the courts' own bailiffs, termed civil enforcement officers, or by private bailiffs contracted with HMCS under large regional contracts for which they have tendered.

These bailiffs will have to comply with the 'approval' process introduced under the Access to Justice Act 1999. Section 125B(1) of the Magistrates Court Act 1980 (MCA) provides that warrants may be executed anywhere in England & Wales by any one of the following:

- an individual who is an approved enforcement agency;
- a director of an approved company;
- a partner of a partnership which is approved; or,
- an employee of an approved agency.

Section 31A Justices of the Peace Act 1997 deals with the approval of such agencies and requires MCCs to maintain a public register showing all persons or bodies approved by them. Approval is by the process set out in the Approval of Enforcement Agencies Regulations 2000. Enforcement agencies may only be approved if they satisfy the conditions laid down in the regulations and if the procedure prescribed there is followed; of course, approvals may also be revoked if there is misconduct on the part of an agent or agency or if the conditions for authorization cease to be satisfied. Before authorising an agency and its individual employees HMCS must be satisfied that the company is financially sound and is properly managed by suitable individuals and that enforcement agents do not have criminal records nor are the subject of bankruptcy orders or civil court judgments. Perhaps more importantly, HMCS also expects all bailiffs acting on its behalf to hold county court certificates (see 6.8 later).

6.2.7 *Customs & Excise*

The distrainor may be any HMRC (formerly C&E) collector or officer empowered by a warrant signed by a Customs and Excise Officer of rank not below Higher Executive Officer (reg. 65(1)). Alternatively a warrant may be issued by the HEO direct to an 'authorised person' to levy distraint. In about seventy five percent of cases C&E now employ private, usually certificated, bailiffs. The levy must be executed by or under the direction of the authorised person.

6.2.8 *HMRC (formerly Inland Revenue)*

The collector of taxes has sole responsibility for carrying out a distraint (s.61(3) TMA) but is normally accompanied by a bailiff. The collector carries a 'Collectors' Warrant' which provides proof of identity if required and confirms that the holder has been appointed by the Commissioners of Inland Revenue to carry out all duties in relation to the taxes for which they are responsible. The accompanying bailiff is required by the Revenue to hold a general certificate or a HCEO's identity card. He may advise on the value of goods, arrange for disposal of goods and act as an independent witness in the event of an alleged irregularity or complaint.

6.2.9 *Child Support Agency*

Any levy of distraint will be by private bailiffs who should carry written authorisation of the SoS, which should be shown to the debtor on request (reg.30(2)).

6.3 Death of parties

In the civil courts leave is necessary in order to issue execution where either the judgment creditor or debtor has died, or any assets of the deceased have come into the hands of his/ her executors or administrators since the date of the judgment (CPR Sch.1 RSC O.46 r.2(1)(b)&(c) & Sch.2 CCR O.26 r.5(1)(b)&(c)). Application for leave is *ex parte* with an affidavit. Leave given to issue execution against an executor is not equivalent to entering judgment against that executor (*Stewart v Rhodes* [1900] 1 Ch 386).

Execution for road traffic penalties follows the county court procedure. Under CPR Sch.1 CCR O.26 r.5 (as applied by CPR Part 75.6) a warrant cannot be issued without leave of court if the defendant has deceased and the estate is in the hands of executors or administrators. In distraint there are no such restrictions.

In distress for rent, it has been held that if the tenant dies, but his/ her executor or administrator continues in possession of the property, the landlord may distrain on the deceased goods in the hands of the executor/ administrator (*Braithwaite v Cooksey & Another* (1790) 1 H Bl 465; *Bolton v Canham* (1670) Pollexfen 20).

6.4 Sums leviable

Typically the sums for which the warrant may issue will be the debt plus any court costs incurred (see for instance s35 CSA or for local taxes reg 45(2) CT; reg 14(2)(b) NNDR). Two cases require special mention.

6.4.1 *Rent arrears*

The landlord may distrain for part of the rent only (*Tutthill v Roberts* (1673) 89 ER 256) so rent for individual periods may be distrained for separately, and in any order (*Palmer v Stanage* (1661) 1 Lev 43). However one sum due on one date must be levied in one levy (*Bagge v Mawby* (1853) 8 Exch 641). If there are several tenancies in one tenant's name, each should be distrained for separately (*Rogers v Birkmire* (1736) 2 Stra 1040).

Service charges, water, fuel and insurance may be recovered by distress if they are treated as rent by the lease- that is, they are reserved or recoverable as rent (*Concorde Graphics v Andromeda Investments* [1983] 265 EG 386; *Escalus Properties v Robinson* [1995] 31 EG 71). If the agreement includes such items as part of the use of the land, the landlord can distrain for the whole balance due (*Selby v Greaves* [1868] 3 CP 594). Though distress may not be levied for the use of chattels, if furniture is included in a lease, rental for its use may be levied by distress (*Newman v Anderton* (1806) 2 Bos & P NR 224).

The rent payable must be certain in the sense that its quantity, extent and time of payment should be known or be capable of being ascertained (*Parker v Harris* (1692)1 Salk 262; *GLC v Connolly* [1970] 2 QB 100). Thus if a service charge treated as rent is variable, the sum due must have been agreed by the tenant or otherwise confirmed (e.g. by tribunal). A rent that fluctuates is not uncertain and distress upon it is valid provided that it may be calculated, though based on factors that may vary (*In Re: Knight ex p Voisey* [1882] 21 Ch D 442). The essential factor is that the sum payable can be worked out (*Daniel v Gracie* (1844) 6 QB 145). If there is no agreed rent, distraint cannot be levied and the landlord must begin a court action (*Dunk v Hunter* (1822) 5 B & Ald 322).

In the case of farms and agricultural holdings, only up to one year's rent may be recovered (s16 Agricultural Holdings Act 1986) unless the terms of the tenancy defer payment of rent to the next quarter or half year after the date when it is due. (s16(2)). The tenant may offset any compensation due from the landlord (s.17).

6.4.2 *County court*

Where a judgment is payable by instalments a warrant cannot be issued until the debtor has defaulted on at least one instalment and so long as no previous execution is outstanding (CPR Sch.2 CCR O.26 r.1(2)). The warrant can be for a part of the debt or the whole outstanding balance. Part warrants are for £50 or one monthly or four weekly instalments, whichever is the greater. Execution ceases if the debt and issue costs are paid. If the bailiff is executing a part warrant and is offered more than the sum being claimed, he may accept any amount up to the full judgment debt and costs.

6.5 Preconditions

For many debts, in addition to simple default in payment, other conditions will have to be satisfied before the debt can be enforced by seizure of goods.

6.5.1 *Local taxes*

Having obtained a liability order in the magistrates court, the 'billing authority' must give 14 days' notice to the debtor of the making of the order and must warn that distraint may follow and the costs which this may entail. However the authority is free to use whichever recovery method it considers most appropriate, although normally a warrant is issued immediately to the bailiff. Certainly distraint must be tried before the authority proceeds to committal. It is not permissible for the first stage to be omitted just because it appears that there would be no goods worth levying upon (*Re: Brown* [1878] 3 QBD 545 and see 'Failed levies' at 3.6).

6.5.2 *Magistrates' court orders*

If instalments are in default, enforcement will be for all instalments still unpaid. A distraint warrant will be issued in the following circumstances.

- Fines - on convicting a person a court can make a collection order regarding payment of the fine. This will specify the sum to be paid and the mode and rate of payment (Courts Act 2003 Sch.5 Part 4). A fines officer will be allocated to oversee the fine's repayment. If the defendant defaults the fines officer can increase the fine by up to 50% (Sch.5 part 7). If there is still no contact from the defendant, the fines officer can either refer the matter to the court or issue a 'further steps notice' (para.37(6)). A further steps notice can include the issue of a distress warrant. If the matter is referred to the court the magistrates can reduce the sum payable, vary the payment terms or order enforcement of the fine themselves, which could include the issue of a distress warrant (Sch.5 Part 9 para.39).

- Maintenance - a warrant will be issued by the magistrates after a hearing to consider whether there is good cause for the failure to pay. The hearing will follow a complaint made by the spouse or collecting officer. A request for a complaint can only be made at least fifteen days after the date of the original maintenance order itself.

In respect of fines, the Queens Bench Divisional Court clarified the procedure that may be followed by a magistrates' court in enforcing a fine by distress in *R. v Hereford Magistrates Court ex p MacRae* (1998) The Times, December 1st. If no payment or response is made following a final demand, it is appropriate to issue a warrant without further proceedings. The court has no duty, and indeed no power, to hold a means enquiry hearing when considering whether to issue distress. Such a hearing is only necessary under ss82-84 MCA when the issue of a warrant of committal is being considered. Thus *R. v Birmingham Justices ex p Bennet* (1983) 147 JP 82, which held that if the evidence reveals a 'reasonable likelihood' that there are distrainable assets, a warrant should be issued, must be understood to apply when the court is "considering committal as an alternative" (see too *R. v Clacton JJ ex p Commissioners of the Customs & Excise* (1987) 152 JP 120. In *R. v Norwich JJ* ex p Trigger (1987) 151 JP 465 it was held that the use of distraint as an option, and the availability of seizable goods, should be considered before committal is threatened: though not cited in *MacRae* the decisions must now be read in light of that case. Nonetheless none of these decisions were an authority for the proposition that there had to be a means enquiry in every case, even if only a distress warrant was being considered. The decision in *R. v German* (1891) 66 LT 264, which states that generally, before issue, the court may require positive evidence of the existence of distrainable goods and of the circumstances of the debtor, held no more than that the justices have a discretion in such circumstances. The justices' discretion will include a consideration of the debtor's payment record. Thus, in *R (on the application of Wallwyn) v Hereford & Worcestershire Magistrates Court Service* [1999] EWHC Admin 299, the fact that the defendant had several times defaulted upon the payment of a relatively small fine persuaded the court that it had not been 'unfair' to have issued a warrant without further notice or hearing.

The decisions in *R. v Guildford Justices ex parte Rich* (1996) Times May 17th 1996, that in every case the defendant should have an opportunity to make representations at a hearing before the warrant is issued and thus there is a chance for distraint to be further postponed (see 3.1.3) on varied terms of payment, must be distinguished. See too *Harper v Carr* (1797) 7 TR 270 - in that case the defaulter had no notice of the possible issue of distress. In the MacRae case the final demand sent specific notice of distress. The decision in *Forrest v Brighton JJ* [1981] 2 All ER 711 that the only exception to the debtor's right to attend is where the person is in prison, though there should still be a hearing, must also now be understood in light of *MacRae*.

MacRae also held that, as no hearing is necessary, it is acceptable for the justices to delegate the task of issuing warrants to a court officer. Whoever makes this decision must still consider the circumstances of the debtor. If the court is satisfied that there are no seizable goods, for instance the debtor's only asset is income, there is no need to attempt to levy, and alternative enforcement such as committal may be used instead. The finding of the magistrates of insufficient goods is a judicial finding that must be set out on the order by them (see no goods - *R. v Mortimer* (1906) 70 JP 542; form of order - *R. v Tyrone JJ ex. p. Patterson* (1915) 49 ILTR 25).

6.5.3 *Rent*

A private landlord must obtain leave of county court to use distress against a protected or statutory tenant under s147 Rent Act 1977 or an assured or assured shorthold tenant under s19 Housing Act 1988. Leave is not required for commercial tenancies, secure tenancies or tenants with restricted contract. Application for leave of court is by originating application. At the hearing the court has the same powers as it has in possession proceedings to adjourn, stay or postpone proceedings. The court's discretion to grant or refuse the application is not limited, but should only be exercised after due enquiry into any question that might arise and the tenant should be permitted to show a reasonable and *bona fide* defence if one exists, for example, whether the rent is due and payable.

Leave may be refused if there is a dispute over the amount payable, though there is no need for a decision to be reached by the court on this question at the hearing of the application for leave (*Townsend v Charlton* [1922] 1 KB 700). If leave is granted, it may be on whatever terms the court thinks fit, and as the court's discretion is absolute an order will only be set aside where it is wrong in principle. Thus in *Metropolitan Properties Co Ltd v Purdy* [1940] 1 All ER 188 the Court of Appeal would not overturn an order suspending leave on condition that a lump sum be paid at once followed by monthly payments thereafter to clear the arrears in under eighteen months. The power certainly exists to suspend leave on conditions that weekly payments are made, provided that the whole weekly rent/ mesne profits are covered, plus a sum towards the arrears (*Blanket v Palmer* [1940] 1 All ER 524).

6.5.4 *Income taxes*

Under s61(1) Taxes Management Act 1970 distraint may be used where tax has been demanded and there has been a neglect or refusal to pay. A taxpayer will be sent demand notes requiring payment and subsequent non-payment is evidence of refusal to pay (*Lumsden v Burnett* [1898] 2 QB 177). However, distraint would be unlawful where the collector distrained immediately after demand and in the absence of the debtor (*Gibbs v Stead* (1828) 8 B & C 528).

6.6 Competing claims

6.6.1 *Landlords' claims*

Landlords are given priority rights to claim payment of any rent arrears in both execution of judgments and for road traffic penalties under s1 Landlord & Tenant Act 1709 in the High Court and s102 CCA for the county court and road traffic cases. Where the goods have been seized in distraint the landlord cannot demand payment of the rent arrears as distraint is not an execution of a

judgment within the meaning of s1 L&TA - see *Potts v Hickman* [1940] 4 All
ER 491 where a bailiff levied for rates arrears on a tenant already in rent
arrears. The landlord failed in his claim against the bailiff.

Restrictions on claim
The extent of the rent that may be claimed is limited:

• the landlord may be entitled to receive no more than four times any
  term's rent where the term is less than one year (s.1 Execution Act 1844)
  with a maximum of one year's rent. The landlord can claim the
  maximum rent to which they are entitled, even if they were in the habit
  of remitting some of the sum due to the tenant (*Williams v Lewsey*
  (1831) 8 Bing 28). If the tenancy is for a fixed term and has just been
  renewed, no claim may be made for rent due under the previous lease-
  even though it falls within the one year limit for claims (*Cook v Cook*
  (1738) Andrews 217);

• there must be an existing landlord and tenant relationship (*Re:
  Eastcheap Alimentary Products Ltd* [1936] 3 All ER 276). *Re: Eastcheap*
  was decided on the basis that there was no tenancy between the
  company and the landlord. Older authority was cited (*Bennet's Case*
  (1727) 2 Stra 787 and *Carr v Goslington* (1727) 11 MR 414) which also
  suggest that if the relationship is of head landlord and subtenant, the Act
  will not apply. There does appear to be an exception to this in that the
  landlord and tenant relationship does not have to be between the
  judgment debtor and landlord as the legislation applies to any landlord
  of a property 'in which goods are seized', so the tenancy may be with the
  spouse of the debtor for example (*Hughes v Smallwood* [1890] 25 QB
  232) If the lease or tenancy has expired but the tenant is still in
  possession, under ss6 & 7 of the 1709 Act the landlord may distrain for
  up to six month's rent (see 3.2.1): however this does not apply to the
  landlord's claim against the bailiff under s1 as this only applies to
  subsisting tenancies (*Lewis v Davies* [1914] 2 KB 469);

• the landlord can only claim rent due at the time of seizure (*Hoskins v
  Knight* (1813) 1 M&S 245). A claim for any sums accruing after the date
  of the seizure is barred, although if the rent is payable in advance and
  has fallen due, it is recoverable (*Harrison v Barry* (1818) 7 Price 690);

• the landlord is entitled to payment of up to a full year's rent even if a
  petition for the debtor's bankruptcy is presented subsequent to the
  seizure and sale (*Gill v Wilson* [1853] 3 ICLR 544) and despite the fact
  that the landlord's right to rent would be less under the bankruptcy (*Re:
  British Salicylates Ltd* [1919] 2 Ch 155). This is so because the 1709 Act
  has impounded the goods for the benefit of the landlord so they are no

longer the debtor's goods. This is contrary to the normal effect of bankruptcy on an execution - (see 4.3 and *Re: Neil Mackenzie ex p Sheriff of Herts* [1899] 2 QB 566). However, if bankruptcy occurs before the sale, the HCEO will only be able to justify payment to the landlord if it was made in ignorance of the bankruptcy order (*Lee v Lopes* (1812) 15 East 230).

There are also limits as to the seizures against which the landlord may claim:

- the execution cannot be one on a judgment for the landlord (*Taylor v Lanyon* (1830) 6 Bing 536);

- the claim can only be made against one execution even if two are levied (*Dod v Saxby* (1735) 2 Stra 1024);

- the section is not confined to seizure of goods that would be subject to distress for rent (*Riseley v Ryle* (1843) 12 LJ Ex 322); and,

- the landlord cannot claim rent accrued due after the execution (*Harrison v Barry* (1818) 7 Price 690).

Generally, however, it has been held that these provisions should be construed liberally in the landlord's favour (*Henchett v Kimpson* (1762) 2 Wils 140).

Bailiff's duties

The bailiff is under no liability to enquire as to the existence of rent arrears or keep the goods in case such a claim emerges and the bailiff cannot be sued for failing to do this (*Arnitt v Garnett* (1820) 3 B&A 440; *Andrews v Dixon* (1820) 3 B&A 645). If notice of a claim is received it may be investigated, and a bailiff would be wise to require production of a current tenancy agreement or lease to confirm the landlord's entitlement to claim (*Augustien v Challis* (1847) 1 Exch 279). This said, it would however appear that even slight evidence of the existence of a lease will then be sufficient (per Lord Ellenborough CJ in *Keightley v Birch* (1814) 3 Camp 521). The form of the notice is not important, so verbal notice from a tenant would be sufficient. Certainly, knowledge of the existence of rent arrears is sufficient notice to the bailiff (*Andrews v Dixon* (1820) 3 B & Ald 645); though again matters may be delayed to enable the bailiff to investigate where the tenant disputes the level or existence of arrears (*Nowlin v Anderson* [1849] 6 NBR 497).

Though the bailiff is liable to make payment to the landlord, and may be sued if this is not done (*Henchett v Kimpson* (1762) 2 Wils 140), it is unlikely that the execution creditor is (*Forster v Cookson* (1841) 1 QB 419). Action against the bailiff should be by way of a special action on the case, rather than an action for money had and received (*Green v Austin* (1812) 3 Camp 260; *Levy v Goodson* 4 TR 687). A restitution order can be obtained against the bailiff by the landlord to ensure payment from the proceeds (*Arnitt v Garnett* above; *Henchett v Kimpson* above). If the landlord sues later, the measure of damages is the amount of rent the sheriff would have paid, though if the goods actually seized were worth less the damages may be reduced to this figure, as it represents their value to the landlord at the time (*Thomas v Mirehouse* [1887] 19 QBD 563). It is interesting to note that in the latter case the sheriff's attempt to mitigate the claim by the landlord against him failed as he was unable to prove the goods' value at the time of removal- simply relying on the proceeds of forced sale as proof of their worth. The bailiff may deduct his costs from any sum adjudged to be paid to the landlord (*Henchett v Kimpson* above), but only such costs as were incurred before notice was received, and not poundage (*Gore v Gofton Stra* 643).

The HCEO can seize enough to cover the rent plus the debt on receiving notice from the landlord within five days of the levy (even after sale). If a separate levy must be made for enough to cover the rent, this is a separate proceeding for which separate possession fees may be charged (*Re: Broster* [1897] 2 QB 429). If the HCEO wrongly removes the goods he can then be sued by the landlord for damages equal to the rent due (*Gawler v Chaplin* (1848) 2 Exch 503).

If the county court bailiff seizes the goods of a third party in error they may not be retained to satisfy a claim by the landlord but must be returned to the owners, even though the landlord could have seized them in distress (*Beard v Knight* (1858) 8 E&B 865; *Foulger v Taylor* (1860) WN 220). However if the HCEO seizes goods belonging to a person who is not the tenant, a claim may be made by the landlord as the L&TA 1709 applies to any "goods and chattels whatsoever" on the premises (*Forster v Cookson* (1841) 1 QB 419; *Duck v Braddyll* (1824) M'Clel 217).

Landlord's duties
The landlord cannot distrain as the seized goods are in the custody of the law (*Peacock v Purvis* (1820) 2 Brod & Bing 362) - whether they are in the HCEO's hands or the hands of a buyer from the HCEO (*Wharton v Naylor* (1848) 6 Dow & L 136), but the goods are "in effect impounded ... for the landlord's benefit" (*Re: McKenzie* [1899] 2 QB 566). The landlord cannot insist on sale of the goods (*Green v Austin* (1812) 8 Camp 260; *Yates v Ratledge* (1860) 5 H&N 249) but s/he can sue the HCEO if payment is not made out of the proceeds of sale (*Henchett v Kimpson* (1762) 2 Wils 140). The landlord cannot sue the execution creditor (*Palgrave v Windham* (1719) 1 Str 212) and cannot interplead against the seizure (*Bateman v Farnesworth* (1860) 29 LJEx 365). It does not affect the landlord's claim that goods were

left after the execution upon which distress could have been levied (*Colyer v Speed*). The landlord may sue in respect of what was distrainable as well as what is not (*Riseley v Ryle* (1843) 11 M&W 16).

If the landlord attempts to recover rent due by distraint it is trespass (*Wharton v Naylor* (1848) 12 QB 673). If the execution is later abandoned, the landlord can proceed with distress as normal (*Seven v Mihill* (1756) 1 Keny 371). Equally if the sheriff fails to seize or impound distress may be levied (*Blades v Arundale* (1813) 1 M&S 711). If the sale is fraudulent, the landlord may distrain (*Smith v Russell* (1811) 3 Taunt 400).

Procedure

Under s102(2) CCA the landlord may within five days of seizure, or before removal of the goods, deliver a written claim stating the rent due and the period to which it applies. The bailiff should then levy for the rent and costs as well and should not sell any of the goods within a further five days unless they are perishable or the tenant has requested their sale (subs 3; *Thomas v Mirehouse* [1887] 19 QBD 563). Under subsection 4 upon sale the bailiff will satisfy firstly the costs of the sale, then the landlord's claim not exceeding:

- four weeks rent where the rent is due weekly; or,

- two terms of payment where the letting is on any term of less than a year; or,

- otherwise, one year's rent; and,

- the sum for which the warrant was issued.

Any surplus or left over goods are returned to the debtor (subs 6). If replevin is commenced, the bailiff can nevertheless sell such portion of the goods as will satisfy the costs of the sale and debt for which execution was commenced (subs 5). The cost of distress will be calculated on the same basis as any execution and no extra fees may be added (subs 7).

A similar procedure is followed by the HCEO except that there must be removal of goods off the premises for s1 to apply- simply seizing the goods will not suffice (*White v Binstead* (1853) 22 LJCP 115). Thus if only a portion of good seized have been removed, this does not enable the section to apply (*Colyer v Speer* (1820) 2 Brod & Bing 67) and this cannot be rectified later. If there is no removal within a reasonable time, the landlord will be able to distrain as normal (*Re: Davis* (1885) 55 LJQB 217). If the HCEO seizes and sells the goods without physical removal the claim under the act will not be effective (*Smallman v Pollard* (1844) 6 Man & G 1001). In the High Court the claim is for up to one year's rent in total (unlike the county court) and once the maximum is paid the levy may proceed as normal. When the claim is received by the HCEO the execution creditor is notified and required to pay the rent due to the HCEO. If this is not done, the HCEO should withdraw from possession and levy only on goods elsewhere in the bailiwick (*Cocker v Musgrove* (1846) 9 QB 223). The subsequent levy by the HCEO will be for both the debt due to the claimant and the rent arrears that they have been obliged to discharge.

6.6.2 *Crown Priority*

It is a long established principle of common law that the Crown is entitled to priority in all recovery proceedings (*New South Wales Taxation Commissioners v Palmer* [1907] AC 171), whether it is enforcing by execution (*R v Cotton* (1751) Park 112) or by distress (*Attorney-General v Leonard* [1888] 38 ChD 622). Thus if the Crown seeks to levy and finds a landlord or other creditor already in possession, it may proceed as its debt takes precedence providing the goods have not been sold (*R v Sloper & Allen* (1818) 6 Price 114). This cannot occur if the earlier levy has proceeded to sale, for then the goods are no longer the debtor's.

This right originates in common law. Now for income tax it is contained in s62 TMA. Where the debtor has not paid PAYE due for the last year or has not passed on sums deducted from sub-contractors, that tax should be paid by the creditor seeking to levy any execution or distraint on demand to the Collector before sale or removal can proceed. If the enforcing creditor will not pay up the bailiff will be obliged to withdraw. If these sums are not paid within ten days of the demand the Collector can then distrain and sell the goods to recover the tax. A landlord is exempt from this. These provisions do not apply to money seized by the bailiff, nor to money paid to him by the debtor.

The other likely Crown creditor to be encountered in this context is Customs & Excise collecting VAT. If the Department have exercised their right to issue summary proceedings in the High Court and enforce that judgment by execution, the writ will have priority. The more normal course of action for VAT arrears is distraint (see later) and, as described above, even a later levy will attain priority

6.6.3 *Previous Distress*

The basic principle is that goods already seized and in the custody of the law cannot be seized again by a bailiff. Properly each bailiff must wait for the one with a prior levy to complete that levy before proceeding (note that an agreement with the creditor whereby the bailiff will not enforce on terms of payment is equivalent to withdrawing a warrant, so that later levies will gain priority - *Hunt v Hooper* (1844) 12 M&W 664). A more pragmatic approach tends to be followed: if the debtor does not pay, the earlier bailiff will remove and sell and will pass on any surplus proceeds of sale to the second bailiff. If the debtor pays by instalments, the second bailiff requests the first to either complete the levy by sale or to withdraw. This will often lead either to sale or an instalment arrangement between the debtor and second bailiff.

Regard must be had to the special rules applicable to civil court bailiffs. In execution upon judgments and for road traffic penalties the date of issue of the writ or warrant determines priority between them (see 6.1.4).

6.7 Final warnings

Most bailiffs will send notice to the debtor of the fact of that a warrant has been issued, as this may provoke payment without the need to take any further steps. Some regulations include a specific charge in the fee scales for such a letter (for example CSA and road traffic penalties). Whatever the situation, it is important to check the contents of such communications to be satisfied that no untoward or illegal threats are made. Although it is an offence under s40 Administration of Justice Act 1970 to harass a person whilst endeavouring to collect debts, this only applies to debts due under contract and, other than rent and certain judgment debts, will not be applicable to most bailiff actions.

The Malicious Communications Act 1988 may be more useful. Section 1 makes it an offence to send any letter or article which conveys a threat or "information which is false and known or believed to be false by the sender" and which it was known would be likely to cause distress or anxiety to the recipient. Malicious communications are a criminal offence leading to a fine on summary conviction of up to £2500. The defendant may show that s/he used the threat to reinforce a demand s/he believed there were reasonable grounds for making and that it was believed that the use of the threat was a proper means of reinforcing the demand.

Finally, the Office of Fair Trading debt collection guidelines may also be helpful- in those cases where they are applicable (see 3.9). When corresponding with debtors, it is stressed that it is considered unfair to communicate, in whatever form, with consumers in an unclear, inaccurate or misleading manner. Examples of such improper conduct include:

- use of official looking documents intended, or likely, to mislead debtors as to their status- for example, documents made to resemble court claims;

- leaving out or presenting information in such a way that it creates a false or misleading impression or exploits debtors' lack of knowledge;

- when contacting debtors, not making clear who they are, who they work for, what their role is, what the purpose of the contact is. This can include implying that an individual is a court officer when s/he is not; and

- acting in a way likely to be publicly embarrassing to the debtor, either deliberately or through lack of care, for instance by not posting correspondence in a sealed envelope, thereby running the risk that it could be read by third parties;

6.8 Certification

Most private bailiffs, or at least senior partners, directors or officers in a firm will hold a county court certificate. A bailiff must be certificated in order to levy distress for rent (s.7 LDAA 1888), road traffic penalties (reg.2 Enforcement of Road Traffic Debts (Certificated Bailiffs) Regulations 1993) and local taxes (see 6.2.3). However, the fact that the court has authorised an individual is used by most bailiffs as a way of demonstrating their suitability and probity when tendering for many other kinds of work.

A bailiff may be fined up to level 1 for levying distress for rent without a certificate (s.2 LDAA 1895)- this will presumably apply as well to levies for local taxes and road traffic penalties. Such distress is also trespass under s.7 LDAA 1888 (*Hogarth v Jennings* [1892] 1 QB 907). It is probably wrongful to use a certificate as a means of identification when levying any other form of distress.

6.8.1 *Application*

The procedure for the granting and challenging of certificates is found in the Distress for Rent Rules 1988, as amended in 1999 and 2009.

A request for a new certificate, or to renew an expired or expiring certificate, is by sworn application on prescribed form 3 to the nearest county court with jurisdiction to issue certificates to where the bailiff lives or works. Information should be provided on the applicant's current employment, his/her criminal record - by means of supplying a copy of their Criminal Records Bureau check (although the Rehabilitation of Offenders Act 1974 applies to applications) - and on whether the applicant has a history of personal indebtedness - a copy of the register of judgments, orders, fines and tribunal awards should be provided. Applications must also reveal whether applicants, or any firm with which they have been involved, has ever been insolvent. Applicants must demonstrate knowledge of the law, for instance by evidence of relevant educational or employment achievements or by having passed a professional examination. The Ministry of Justice announced in March 2009 that it intended to specify minimum training requirements and competencies as part of the application process.

Under r.6 the applicant must also provide a bond or deposit (or satisfy the court that there is sufficient subsisting security) of £10,000. This security covers the 'due performance of the bailiff's duties' and any reasonable costs and fees incurred in investigating any complaint lodged against the bailiff, or in the cancellation of the certificate. This security must be maintained throughout the duration of the certificate (r.6(2A & B).

The application is then heard on oath by circuit judge, who must be satisfied that the applicant is a fit and proper person with sufficient knowledge of the law and does not buy bad debts for a business. Despite the efforts made in 1999 to focus this work on a limited number of county courts, most county court circuit judges are not very familiar with the laws of distress and the hearing is seldom a thorough examination of the applicant's suitability or knowledge. In reality, getting a certificate has, in the past, largely been a formality at most courts. Certificates last two years and then have to be renewed, but the renewal process is seldom problematic for applicants either.

6.8.2 *Register*

Rule 13(1)(a) of the Distress for Rent Rules 1988 states that a list of certificated bailiffs carrying on business within a county court's issuing area shall be exhibited in the public area of the court. This list should also be made available to members of the public upon request.

The HMCS Enforcement Team at the head office in Victoria Street, London, maintains a central register of certificated bailiffs which is updated daily on the basis of information supplied by the county courts. County courts are required to conduct a data cleansing exercise with HMCS twice a year in order to keep the register updated. Local county courts are also required by the HMCS guidelines on distress for rent to notify headquarters every time a new application is made and upon the outcome of any complaint hearings.

It is possible for members of the public to search the central register by means of a telephone, email or letter enquiry to HMCS. This permits an individual to check whether a bailiff is certificated, and if so, which court issued the certificate. This allows the public to confirm that a certificated bailiff is genuine; the information obtained from the central register may also be used when submitting a complaint on Form 4 (see next section).

From June 2009 HMCS have published the central register online under powers provided in an amendment to the Distress for Rent Rules (r.13(1)(b)). This online facility provides a list of all current holders of bailiff certificates and is updated daily. It gives the bailiff's full name, the name of the bailiff's employer or company to which the bailiff is contracted, the issuing court, and date of issue and expiry of the certificate. HMCS has committed itself to maintaining the online register and keeping it as up to date as possible. However, HMCS also states that there is no guarantee that the on-line register will be completely accurate or comprehensive at any given time. This is for two reasons. Individuals working on probation whilst they await their hearing date will not be on the register. Additionally, HMCS are dependent upon the courts for this information and therefore the ultimate check will always remain with the issuing county court.

6.8.3 *Complaints*

A certificating court has a general power to cancel certificates or declare them void at any time (s.1 LDAA 1895). However the matter will normally come before a court by means of a debtor's complaint under the Rules, though a district judge a detailed assessment of a bailiff's bill may also refer the individual for consideration of the certificate if a significant overcharge is felt to have occurred. Creditors may also refer a bailiff to a court if a complaint is upheld under an internal complaints procedure. In fact, case law has shown that the right to initiate a complaint lies not only with the debtor, but with the creditor, and, indeed, affected third parties, such as hire purchase lenders whose goods are wrongfully levied (*Perring & Co v. Emerson* [1903] 1 KB 1).

Any complaint as to the conduct or fitness of a bailiff should be made to the issuing court (r.8(1)). There is a prescribed form (form 4) which simply requires the parties' details and the action(s) which are the subject of the complaint. The court sends written details to the bailiff who must respond in writing within 14 days, or within a longer period if the court allows (r.8(2)).

If the bailiff either does not reply, or if the reply does not satisfy the circuit judge that the person remains fit to hold their certificate, a hearing will be arranged to show cause why the certificate should not be cancelled (r.8(3)). If the judge is satisfied with the bailiffs' written response, no further action is taken on the complaint and a notice to that effect is issued to the bailiff under rule 8(3A)). If a hearing is scheduled, the bailiff is summonsed on notice and the complainant and any other interested party receive a copy (r.8(4)). It is possible for the complainant to have apply to have the hearing transferred to their nearest county court (r.8(4A & B). At the hearing the bailiff may attend and make representations, as may the complainant (r.8(5)). The procedure at the hearing is determined by the judge, including what evidence shall be allowed, and the hearing may proceed even in the bailiff's absence (r.8(6)).

After hearing the parties, if the complaint is upheld the judge may cancel the certificate and/or order that the security be forfeited either wholly or partly to compensate the complainant, to cover any costs and expenses s/he may have incurred and also to cover the court's own costs, expenses and fees. If the certificate is retained but the security is forfeit, the bailiff must provide a new indemnity (r.9(2)). The court publicises the cancellation both locally and nationally if the bailiff operates outside the district of that county court and the costs of this are taken from the security (r.9(6)).

It should be noted that even if a certificate is cancelled, it continues to have effect for any possession agreement entered into before the date of cancellation unless the judge directs otherwise (r.9(4)). It will be necessary for the complainant to make a specific request for such a direction to prevent any levy continuing, presumably most conveniently at the hearing of the complaint.

The attractions of the complaints procedure to the complainant are its simplicity and its cheapness, as no filing fees are incurred. However, there are a number of possible difficulties. LSC funding may rarely be available, unless the potential damages are likely to be considerable; accordingly proper representation before circuit judge may be problematic for the debtor. Secondly there are very few reported cases on certification complaints to give guidance to either party on the circumstances in which bailiffs should have their certificates challenged or cancelled. This compounds the obscurity and neglect of the remedy. The few reported cases are considered in the next section. Thirdly the problem of the obscurity of the remedy is compounded by uncertainty as to its extent. The LCD gave their opinion on this, though it may well not be shared by local judges. LCD suggested that certification complaints may be made in the following situations:

- a levy for rent, council tax or road traffic (obviously);
- a levy of any other form of distraint by a certificated bailiff, on the basis that the basic rules of procedure are common to all forms; and,
- against a certificated employer in respect of a levy by an employee, the argument being that a failure to adequately train or monitor staff suggests a lack of fitness to hold a certificate.

The final issue is that the Rules as a whole are written in the context of distresses for rent. Their application to other forms of work for which certificates are now required is a little uncertain. For example, the security deposit may only be forfeit to compensate the person in cases of wrongful distress for rent, and not other forms.

6.8.4 *Unfit & improper conduct*

From the reported cases, a number of principles emerge on general standards and conduct likely to lead to loss of a certificate.

General standards of behaviour

The certification process was introduced by the Law of Distress Amendment Act 1888 in response to widespread public concern about the behaviour and qualifications of private bailiffs. County court judges from the outset used the new powers enthusiastically and proactively. They saw the new process as a means both of getting rid of undesirable bailiffs as well as raising standards within the industry. For example, HHJ Parry at Manchester County Court in 1910 warned that certificate holders had to act with discretion and discrimination. They had duties to all the parties involved- to the creditor, to the debtor, to the wider community and the court that awarded the certificate by ensuring that the poor were protected and that exempt goods were not seized in distress (*Taylor v Ashworth* (1910) 129 LT 578). Certificated bailiffs must maintain the highest standards of behaviour when levying, avoiding rudeness, violence and drunkenness. Other unfit or improper behaviour which could lead to revocation of a certificate includes criminal acts such as assault, civil wrongs such as negligence and the detention of goods despite payment by the debtor and the misappropriation or mishandling of monies received (see for example *Villeneuve v Clark* (1890) 35 Estates Gazette 458; *Re: Gurden* (1894) 2 Property Market Review 410 & 872; Estates Gazette vol.47 p.171 & vol.48 p.183).

Unlawful fees

Many certification complaints have concerned abuses of the scales of fees which bailiffs are entitled to charge. Helpful cases include:

- *In Re: Longstaffe ex p. Robinson* (1896) 49 Estates Gazette 60 a certificate was revoked because the bailiff had charged extortionate fees and had also left no inventory of the goods seized (in breach of his statutory duty) and had sold the goods at an undervalue to an associate;

- In *Duncombe v Hicks* (1898) 42 Sol. Jo. 393 the bailiff lost his certificate for charging fees for work not actually undertaken by him; whilst,

- In *Mutter v Speering* (1903) 119 LT 134 revocation was ordered because fees not authorised by the fee scale had been charged.

Scope of certification

As already stated, uncertificated bailiffs cannot undertake certificated work; moreover, a certificated bailiff is liable for any trespass by his uncertificated assistant. It is further arguable to no uncertificated bailiff should be involved in any way with work for which a certificate is required (*Hogarth v Jennings*

[1892] 1 QB 907; *Hawes v Watson* (1892) 94 LT 181; *Thomas v Millington* (1892) 2 Property Market Review 472). However, contrast the decision in *Re: Sanders ex p Sergeant* (1885) 54 LJQB 331. Distress was levied by a certificated bailiff- but not within district in which the certificating county court was situated. It was held that no offence had been committed.

Unlawful levying

In *Manchester City Council v Robinson* (1991) the council applied for revocation of the defendant's certificate on several grounds. He had distrained after a suspended possession order had been made in the county court, he had used invalid forms (thus showing an insufficient knowledge of the law), he had used his own pass key to enter the premises and he was director of the landlord company, despite undertaking in his certificate application not to distrain where he was regularly employed in rent collection. The court held that whilst the bailiff may have acted illegally in some respects, his misconduct was not serious enough to warrant cancellation of his certificate. This was justified particularly by the fact that the defendant gave the court an assurance that he would not use out-dated forms again. Whilst it was suggested that the use of the key was illegal entry, only £100 costs were awarded against the defendant (see report in Legal Action, October 1991).

6.8.5 *Summary and TCEA 2007*

Experience has shown that the attitude of courts is that the wrong complained of will have to be very serious, and certainly more than a 'technicality', to warrant revocation or a heavy financial penalty. The certification complaints with the best prospects of success will be those which involve very serious and blatant abuses of powers of entry, seizure or charging, or those which are founded upon a dossier of incidents recorded over a period of time, indicating a pattern of rule breaking, abuse or exploitation.

TCEA 2007 proposes further to extend the scope of certification. Under section 63 enforcement agents will only be able to lawfully take control of goods if they hold a certificate, act under the direction and in the presence of a certificated individual or are exempt from needing a certificate. Exempt individuals will include constables, HMRC officers and court staff, including magistrates' courts' civilian enforcement officers. It will be an offence to knowingly or recklessly act without a certificate, which will be punishable on summary conviction by a fine up to level 5 on the standard scale. Under s.64 of the Act the Lord Chancellor is empowered to make new regulations for the certification process to replace the Distress for Rent Rules 1988. The regulations will cover the fees payable for an application, the security that may be required, the powers of county court judges and district judges to grant limited certificates for special purposes, the conduct of complaints and the suspension or cancellation of certificates. Bailiffs holding certificates issued under the Law of Distress Amendment Act 1888 and the 1988 Rules will be covered by the new Act when it comes into force.

Chapter 7

COMMENCING LEVIES: INITIAL VISITS

PART ONE - BAILIFFS' RIGHTS

7.1 Liable persons

A bailiff is entitled to levy execution or distress against the goods of the liable person, the debtor, whether that person is an individual or a company. Special rules apply to partnership property (see 9.11), but a debt due from a partnership maybe pursued against any partner, even if s/he is the only surviving member of a firm (*Eddowes v Argentine Loan & Mercantile Agency Co Ltd* (1890) 62 LT 602). If the debt in question is a joint debt it may be enforced against the debtors' sole or joint property. The property of any one of the liable individuals may be seized and the others need not be chased (*Herries v Jamieson* (1794) 5 TR 553). The warrant must follow the judgment or order, so a joint judgment must be enforced by a warrant issued against all defendants (*Abbot v Smith* (1774) 2 Wm Bl 947; *Clarke v Clement & English* (1796) 6 TR 525). This point was confirmed also in *Penoyer v Bruce* (1697) 1 Ld Raym 244, which further held that if one of joint debtors has died, enforcement may continue unabated against the other (see also 5.3). Special rules also apply to property jointly owned by the debtor.

Some individuals are specially privileged from enforcement:

- *diplomatic staff* may not have execution levied on them, their family members or their employees (respectively Articles 31(3), 37 (1) & 37(2) Sch 1, Diplomatic Privileges Act 1971). Under Article 22(3) of the 1971 Act the privilege extends to the furnishings of diplomatic missions, other property thereon and to vehicles owned by the mission for the transport of the diplomatic staff.

- *armed forces*: neither execution nor distress may be levied upon those volunteering or called up for service in the armed forces without leave of court (s1(2) & (3) Reserve & Auxiliary Forces (Protection of Civil Interests) Act 1951 respectively). Leave is sought by application on originating summons to the High Court or originating application to the county court. This does not apply to judgments for damages in tort, to orders for costs, to judgments for debts incurred after the military service began or to orders in criminal proceedings. It also refers to other forms of distress than rent, for instance for local taxes (s6(2) & *Stepney BC v Woolf* [1943] KB 202). Furthermore any military equipment, instruments or clothing supplied to a person in the armed forces may not be seized in execution (s185 Army Act 1955; s185 Air Force Act 1955 and s102 Naval Discipline Act 1957).

If execution is levied against a privileged person, or in a privileged place (see 7.3.1), the process can be set aside, but no action lies against those acting in disobedience of a lawful writ or order, even if malice is alleged (*Magnay v Burt* (1843) 5 QB 381).

7.2 Time

Longstanding rules have been developed as to when during the day and when during the week levies may take place.

7.2.1 *Time of Day*

Execution may be levied at any time (*Brown v Glenn* (1851) 16 QB 254). By analogy with execution, it seems to be the case in statutory distraint that bailiffs may distrain at any time (see *Throssell v Leeds City Council* (1993) 41 Adviser 22).

The common law rule applicable to distress for rent is that a levy should not occur between sunset and sunrise (*Aldenburgh v Peaple* (1834) 6 C&P 212, *Brice v Hare* (1824) 2 LJOSKB 194, *Tutton v Darke* (1860) 5 H&N 647, *Nixon v Freeman* (1860) 5 H&N 647). A landlord may enter premises at night to prevent removal by third parties so that goods may be levied the next day, though this may still be trespass (*England v Cowley* (1873) 28 LT 67). If the bailiff levies distress for rent at the wrong hour the distress is irregular (*Perring & Co v Emerson* [1906] 1 KB 1) unless the error is waived by the debtor (*Werth v London & Westminster Loan & Discount Co.* (1889) 5 TLR 521). In the only reported case on the matter (*Lamb v Wall* (1859) 1 F&F 503) only the "real actual damage" suffered was allowed to the claimant - which in this case of distress after sunset and occupation of the claimant's premises by the landlord for several hours, preventing her leaving, was held to be only one farthing. However as distress at the wrong time is illegal and is a trespass, the proper measure should be general damages because the tort has been committed (for which see 7.5 later) without any set off for any debt due.

Over and above all of this case authority, the National Standard lays down what may be called 'reasonable hours' for conducting levies. It is advised that enforcement should only occur between the hours of 6.00am and 9.00pm. An exception to this is allowed where the debtor is conducting a business and it is otherwise impossible to make contact with him/her at the business premises. Otherwise enforcement agents will have to justify why a visit was conducted outside the NSEA 'reasonable' times.

7.2.2 *Day of the Week*

Distress for rent should not be levied on Sundays (*Werth v London & Westminster Loan and Discount Co.* (1889) 5 TLR 520) or on public holidays like Christmas and Easter. Execution may be levied on a Sunday but only with leave of court in an emergency (Practice Direction to CPR Sch.1 RSC O.46 & Sch.2 CCR O.26) and otherwise on any day. These restrictions only apply to the original levy, not later visits to the premises (*Atkinson v Jamieson* (1792) 5 TR 25; *Wells v Gurney* (1828) 8 B&C 769). By implication one may assume that similar limitations will apply in statutory distraint. Certainly the National Standard lays down a rule for all forms of seizure of goods: enforcement should not occur on Sundays, Bank Holidays, Good Friday or on Christmas Day, unless a court orders otherwise or legislation permits it. Failing to comply with the legal restrictions will, as above, render the distress irregular.

7.3 Place

The basic rule is that the debtor's goods may be seized wherever they are, normally from premises belonging to the debtor. Although bailiffs executing statutory distress may go anywhere in England and Wales (for example CSA distraint can be levied anywhere in England and Wales - reg 30(1); as may local taxes - reg 45(6) CT; reg 14(6) NNDR), certain limits are placed on other bailiffs' movements.

7.3.1 *Executions*

The officer levying execution is limited in several respects as to where he may levy:

- the HCEO is restricted to his 'bailiwick' and the county court bailiff may only operate within that particular court's area. The county court provisions regarding execution out of the court's area do not apply to warrants for road traffic penalties, though these are modelled on county court procedure (s103);

- execution may not be levied at royal residences (*Winter v Miles* (1809) 10 East 578; *AG v Dakin* (1820) 4 HL 338) though this does not include the Palace of Westminster (*Combe v De La Bere* [1882] 22 Ch D 316);or,

- at diplomatic premises or the private residences of ambassadors (Articles 22 & 30 Sch 1 Diplomatic Privileges Act 1971).

7.3.2 *Distress for rent*

The bailiff or landlord can only attend at the 'demised', i.e. rented premises (*Capel v Buszard* (1829) 6 Bing 150) unless goods are on common land, have been fraudulently removed elsewhere (see 3.5) or the tenant consents to a levy elsewhere. The landlord may not levy off the premises in the street (see 7.3.4). An exception exists where goods are located in the street immediately outside the premises. Two cases, *Hodges v Lawrence* (1854) 18 JP 347 and *Gillingham v Gwyer* (1867) 16 LT 640, suggest that a property includes half the road outside, so in theory a car parked not only in a drive but immediately outside a house can be seized, whereas one directly opposite in the street or outside a neighbour's house cannot.

7.3.3 *Third party premises*

Rather like the landlord's right of pursuit of fraudulently removed goods mentioned above, the bailiff levying execution may attend third party premises if it is believed that the debtor's goods have been removed there in order to avoid execution (*Ratcliffe v Burton* (1802) 3 Bos & P 223). Force may be used as a house is "only a privilege for himself" and the protection from forced entry only applies to the goods of an occupier and his/ her family and does not protect goods brought in there to prevent lawful execution (*Semaynes Case* (1604) 5 Co Rep 91a, proposition 5). This conclusion was reached by analogy with c.17 Statute of Westminster I: the HCEO may force entry in order to replevy goods wrongfully removed to premises in order to evade replevin. Demand for entry should be made first before force is employed (*Semaynes Case*, proposition 6).

The bailiff of course may enter a third party's premises peaceably in order to search for a debtor's goods (*Biscop v White* (1600) 78 ER 991 - the doors of the stranger's house were found open). However the bailiff will be a trespasser if either no goods are found (*Cooke v Birt* (1814) 5 Taunt 765; *Green v Leney & Another* (1933) un-reported case 11/12/1933), even though the debtor may have resided on the premises immediately before the levy and the bailiff therefore had reasonable cause to suspect and believe that the defendant's property was still there (*Morrish v Murrey* (1844) 13 M&W 52). If inner doors are forced in the process, the bailiff also trespasses (*Johnson v Leigh* (1815) 6 Taunt 246).

What may be defined as a stranger's house? It does not include a property where the debtor's goods are ordinarily deposited, or where the debtor is ordinarily resident, though s/he may not be classed as the occupier (see for example *Cooke v Birt* (1814) 5 Taunt 765 or *Sheers v Brooks* (1792) 2 H Bl 120).

7.3.4 *Goods on the highway*

The common law rule, confirmed by c.15 of the Statute of Marlborough 1267, is that distress for rent may not be levied in the street. It reads as follows:

"It shall be lawful for no man henceforth, for any manner of cause, to take distresses out of his fee, nor in the King's highway, nor in the common street, but only the King or his officers, having special authority to do so." (*extra feodum suum, neque in regia aut communi strata, nisi Domino Regi et ministris suis, specialem authoritatem ad hoc habentis.*)

It is clear from the text of the provision that this only relates to distresses for rent- reference is concurrently made to distresses taken 'out of fee' (see 7.3.2). Expert opinion supports this reading: for example, in his analysis in the second volume of the Institutes, Coke emphasised that the mischief addressed by the statute was wrongful levies of distress for rent and that, for example, distresses upon leet orders are not involved.

That the Statute of Marlborough does not apply to statutory distraints or to executions was confirmed by the Court of Appeal in *Quinlan v Hammersmith & Fulham London Borough Council* (1988)153 JP 180, in which bailiffs levied for rates by seizing the car Quinlan was driving in the street. The Court did not find this to have been a wrongful levy. There is a more recent case at variance with this: *Ba Tu Dinh v Drakes Group Ltd* (2000). In this unreported decision a county court circuit judge held that seizure of a car on the highway for a road traffic penalty was unlawful (Case ref: AC0100422). It is very hard to find support for this judgment in the form of c.15; it may be that the judge was misled by the fact that the seizure was termed a distress, when the recovery of road traffic penalties is very clearly a form of county court execution.

7.4 Entry rights

7.4.1 *Basic rights*

In *Long v Clarke* [1893] 1 QB 119 Lord Esher MR observed that a bailiff may "do that which, if any other person did it, would be a trespass". It is correct that a bailiff, acting lawfully upon a lawful warrant, has a right to enter premises- however this right is qualified by two important conditions.

Firstly, the bailiff's right of entry must be exercised in a peaceable manner. If entry is obtained through force, it is an illegal act which is unauthorised by the warrant and the distress is trespass (*Curlewis v Laurie* (1848) 12 QB 640). A criminal offence may also be committed (see 7.7).

Secondly, as was restated in *Khazanchi v Faircharm Investments* [1998] 2 All ER 901, the bailiff's entry must also be with permission. Morritt LJ commenced his judgment in the Court of Appeal by stating that entry may only be made "with the consent of the occupant or person in possession of the premises".

It will be seen therefore that bailiffs' rights to enter property are in fact subject to very significant provisos and are much weaker than many enforcement agents would like to think. Moreover, some within the enforcement sector entertain serious misconceptions concerning these rights. There is confusion about what is meant by 'force' whilst many are entirely unaware of the need for permission.

7.4.2 *Premises*

Consideration must be given to which premises these basic rights of peaceable entry apply:

- *debtor's home*: since at least the early seventeenth century the debtor's home has been considered his/ her 'castle'. It is protected from any forced or unwanted entry. This protection against forced entry extends to all buildings within the boundary of the premises (*American Concentrated Must Corporation v Hendry* (1893) 68 LT 742). See also *Munroe & Munroe v Woodspring District Council* (1979) CLY 2226 where bailiffs forced entry into a garage in the claimant's garden. The court awarded general damages for trespass, for the value and loss of use of the car and special damages for damage to the garage door.

- *separate, non-domestic premises*: private bailiffs levying distress may enter such premises but must never break in (*Brown v Glenn* (1851) 16 QB 254; *Poole v Longueville* (1680) 2 Wms Saund 284). There is an exception for execution- see 7.4.5 later.

- *flats, maisonettes and bedsits*: A common problem confronted during entry into a block of flats or house in multiple occupation is determining which is the outer door - the common entrance or the door to the premises solely and exclusively occupied by the debtor. The often quoted English case is *Lee v Gansel* (1774) 1 Cowp 1. General Gansel was arrested by a bailiff who entered the property where he lodged by means of an open outer door but then broke into the General's bedroom.

Gansel rented a number of separate rooms in the home of a Mr. Mayo. It was held not to be logical for Gansel to have four outer doors to his premises, therefore the bedroom was legally broken open, for as was held in *Astley v Pinder* (1760) 'an inner door has no protection at all'. This case seems to favour the case for occupiers of flats and HMOs. A more definitive answer is given in *Welch v Kracovsky* [1919] 3 WWR 361. In this it was held that a door connecting a suite of rooms occupied exclusively by a tenant in an apartment block with a hallway used by all tenants and leading to the main entrance is an outer door and therefore cannot be forced.

• *hotels & lodgings*: if the debtor is resident in a hotel or lodgings house, it may be that the debtor would have no protection from forcible entry to the premises in order to seize their goods, and the levy would be valid. However, the actual owner of the premises may have a cause of action against the bailiff (see the discussion in *Kirkpatrick v Kelly* (1781) 3 Doug KB 30; *Piggot v Wilkes* (1820) 3 B & Ald 502).

7.4.3 *Mode of entry*

The strict legal rights of entry apply as by the authorities are reviewed here- but see the later commentary section.

Doors

The bailiff may enter an open door (*Budd v Pyle* (1846) 10 JP 203). It would also appear that a bailiff may open and enter an unlocked door having the legal authority under the warrant to open the door in the ordinary way in which other persons may (*Ryan v Shilcock* (1851) 7 Exch 72). Breaking open a door or gate in a wall is trespass (*Long v Clarke* [1893] 1 QB 119). The use of a locksmith to open a door is illegal and otherwise removing or damaging locks and chains is likewise wrongful in the opinion of Viner's Abridgment. If an obstruction has been placed against the door by a person and s/he permits the bailiff to remove this to enter the door, the entry is legal provided that no force is used (*McKay v Douglas* [1919] 44 DLR 570). If a door is nailed shut, it is illegal to force it open (*Russell v Buckley* [1885] 25 NBR 264). Reasonable force may be used to see if a door is fastened (*McKinnon v McKinley* [1856] 1 PEI 113).

The front doors of all buildings within the boundary of the property are protected from forced entry (*American Concentrated Must Co v Hendry* (1893) 57 JP 521). Even if a door is within the boundaries of a property and can only be reached by passing through other gates or doors, if it constitutes the entrance to a dwelling, it is protected (*Hopkins v Nightingale* (1794) 1 Esp 99). A door leading into a garden or yard within a property is not an outer door.

Windows
A bailiff may climb through an open window (*Nixon v Freeman* (1860) 5 N&N 647; *Tutton v Darke* (1860) 5 H&N 647) or skylight (*Miller v Tebb* (1893) 9 TLR 515) and open one more if necessary (*Crabtree v Robinson* [1885] 15 QBD 812). *Clerk & Lindsell on Torts* at 16-33 questions whether these principles can now apply in the light of the decision in *Southam v Smout* [1964] 1 QB 308. Though a bailiff may open a closed but unfastened door he cannot open a closed but un-fastened window as the former gives an 'implicit licence to anyone with lawful business to enter' whilst the latter gives no such licence as it is not a normal means of entry (*Nash v Lucas* [1867] 2 QB 590). In his text on the *Law Relating to Entry, Search and Seizure* (Butterworths 1986), David Feldman also questions whether, in light of the discussion of the concept of licence to enter in *Nash v Lucas*, it is now safe to assume that an open window is a licence to enter if a door is locked.

The bailiff cannot open a closed, latched window (*Hancock v Austin* (1863) 14 CBNS 634) and the fastening securing a window may not be removed (*Bell v Oakley* (1814) 2 M&S 259). A window pane cannot be broken (*Attack v Bramwell* (1863) 3 B&S 520).

Walls
A bailiff may climb over a wall or fence or walk across a garden or yard provided these are not damaged (*Long v Clarke* [1894] 1 QB 119). A wall cannot be broken down to gain entry, but a hole in an unfinished wall may be passed through (*Whalley v Williamson* (1836) 7 C&P 294).

Keys
Use of a landlord's pass key is illegal as entering by such means is not "the ordinary way in which visitors gain access" (*Miller v Curry* [1893] 25 NSR 537). It does not matter whether the bailiff found the key or it was provided by a landlord - see *Welch v Kracovsky* [1919] WWR 361. If the key is left in the lock it seems it may be permissible to turn it like a door handle to open the door if it has been left in the lock so as to make the premises accessible to all with a legitimate reason to enter (*Ryan v Shilcock* (1851) 7 Exch 72), though whether such a general authority from the householder to enter in such situations can now be assumed seems to be questioned in the judgment in *Southam v Smout* [1963] 3 All ER 104.

Other means
In one case it was even held acceptable for a landlord to take up the floor of his room so as to effect entry into the tenant's room below (*Gould v Bradstock* (1812) 4 Taunt 562). This odd result arises from the fact that the floor was only comprised of boards, and there was no plaster ceiling in the

tenant's premises through which the landlord had to break. Thus the boards were not the claimant's sole property, nor was any force used. The tenant might have had a remedy for disturbance of his use of the ceiling, but the court felt there was no trespass, Lord Mansfield CJ added "What is decided in this case will not do much harm or good as a precedent, for probably the circumstances never happened before, or will ever happen again." This is probably true, though readers may note that it has been held that entry via a loft from an adjoining house is illegal (*Anglehart v Rathier* [1876] 27 CP 97). If the door, window or wall are already broken open, it would seem that the bailiff may enter (*Long v Clarke* above). In *Whalley v Williamson* (1836) 7 C&P 294 a levy was conducted at premises that were only part built. The bailiff entered through a hole in the wall and then forced a boarded over window. It was held that this was trespass because the hole was not intended to have a door or window fitted later, therefore it had to be considered that the 'outer fence' of the house was the boarded window, which was illegally entered by force.

7.4.4 *Permission to enter*

It is clear from the authorities that if the debtor simply verbally refuses entry before the bailiff is over the threshold, the bailiff may not proceed (*Semayne's Case* (1604) Yelv 29; *Vaughan v McKenzie* [1968] 1 All ER 154). The debtor has the legal right to refuse entry and the bailiff has the legal duty to respect this (*Entick v Carrington* (1765) All ER 41; *Morris v Beardmore* [1980] 2 All ER 753).

This rule requiring a 'licence' to enter is of longstanding and is very well established. Nevertheless, a number of issues arise around it:

- *implied licence* - it is accepted that, in some circumstances, an individual on lawful business may imply a licence to enter premises- for example, a bailiff may enter if s/he finds a door unlocked or standing open (*Lambert v Roberts* [1981] 2 All ER 15). A licence may also be implied by a person's conduct- for example, walking away from an opened door (*Faulkner v Willets* [1982] Crim LR 453). It is upon this principle of an implied licence that the right to climb through windows has been developed.

- *revocation of licence* - the occupier of premises may terminate an express or implied licence if s/he chooses. Accordingly, if a bailiff is found to have entered premises through an open door, it is lawful to ask him/her to leave and the bailiff's duty is to comply and to leave (*Halliday v Nevill* (1984) 155 CLR 1; *Bailey v Wilson* [1968] Crim LR 618).

- *strangers* - did the person opening the door have the authority to do so? It is arguable that if they did not, this is not a legal means of entry;

- *minors* - if a child opens the door either in the absence of the parent or whilst the parent is elsewhere in the house, is the entry legal? Very probably this is not a legal mode of entry.

- *under false pretences* - it appears from the older case authorities that entry gained under false pretences will not render a levy illegal. The authorities are not explicit, but the conclusion may be inferred, particularly from *R v Backhouse* (1771) Lofft 61. In the course of executing an arrest warrant an officer gained access by pretending he had a note for the attention of the defendant, Backhouse. When the officer was let in and revealed his true purpose, he was assaulted by Backhouse. At the trial the actual circumstances of the assault were disputed, but Backhouse was held culpable and was fined. The means by which the officer entered initially were neither examined nor criticised, from which it may be implied that they were neither thought wrongful nor a mitigating factor in Backhouse's defence.

Deliberate deception thus seemed not to make an entry and seizure wrongful, so we may regard any mistaken deception as similarly not wrongful. In *Cresswell v Jeffreys* (1912) 28 TLR 413 a bailiff instructed to distrain for rent arrears told the tenant that he could not legally seize his livestock. The tenant had intended to remove them from the property but then did not. The bailiff later seized some of the cattle and was then sued for wrongful distress. It was held that the bailiff's remarks were either a misstatement of law or a declaration of an intention to abandon a legal right, but in neither case could they create an estoppel preventing seizure. A misstatement of law cannot create an estoppel and a representation can only do so if it is regarding existing facts, not an intention. The right to distrain was not waived either, as there was no consideration for the waiver. It seems that entry under false pretences was only wrongful if a court was misled by the bailiff as part of the procedure. See *Anon* (1758) 2 Keny 372 in which a sheriff procured a search warrant by pretending stolen goods were on premises so that he could enter and arrest the occupant. No search was made for any goods. The court regarded the means used to gain entry as 'undue' or improper.

All of the cases reviewed above are old, two being very old, and they predate the elaboration of the principle of the licence to enter which has occurred in the last century. Given this development in the law, it is probably safer now to presume that, if an individual is granted a licence to enter under false pretences, it will be possible later to revoke it or to treat the entry as trespass *ab initio* when the individual's true identity is revealed (*Cundy & Bevington v Lindsay* [1878] 3 App Cas 459).

- *assistance*: in *Nash v Lucas* [1867] 2 QB 590 the court dealt with a question yet to be satisfactorily answered - may a bailiff be let in by a third party already on the premises? In Nash the bailiff encouraged a workman employed by the landlord to let himself into the house by opening a shut window so that he could then open the locked front door to admit the bailiff. As he acted at the behest of the bailiff the whole entry was held to be illegal. However reference was made to *Sandon v Jarvis* (1859) EB & E 935 where a bailiff arrested a man by touching him through an already broken window. This action was held to be legal and the principle could be extended to 'assisted entry'.

The surest course of action for enforcement agents will only be to enter where it is clear that consent has been properly obtained. The words of Atkin LJ in *Great Central Railway Co Ltd v Bates* [1921] 3 KB 578 might be borne in mind "it should be established that nobody has a right to enter premises except strictly in accordance with authority".

If a bailiff enters in violation of the licence to enter, or remains after a licence has been clearly revoked, the occupier has two remedies. One is the use of 'reasonable' force to remove the trespassing bailiff from the premises (*Lambert v Roberts* [1981] 2 All ER 15; *Robson v Hallett* [1967] 2 QB 939). The other remedy will be to bring a county court claim for trespass subsequently.

7.4.5 *Initial entry by force*

There are a several exceptions to the basic rules outlined above which permit entry to be forced. Nevertheless it is probably safe to say that the courts would expect prior demand for entry to be made first before force is used so as to allow the occupant the opportunity of permitting entry and in order to avoid, if possible, violent resistance (see *Launock v Brown* (1819) 2 B&A 592; Burdett v Abbot (1811) 14 East 1).

In three cases initial forced entry is sanctioned by statute. These are:

- *income taxes* - the Inland Revenue collector of taxes may force entry to premises, though some demand for entry should be made first (*Semaynes Case* (1604) All ER 62). A collector may seek a break-open warrant for the purpose of gaining access to premises. This is done by laying an information on oath before a JP. The warrant will be granted if the JP is satisfied there is a reasonable ground for believing the person is "neglecting or refusing" to pay. The collector may only force entry during the 'daytime' (s61(2)). The collector may call for police assistance when forcing entry and every constable shall "aid and assist in the execution of the warrant and in levying the distress". This presumably only extends to preventing a breach of the peace (see 7.4.7). It has been held that the collector cannot break in without a constable being present (*Foss v Racine* (1838) 8 C& P 699). Use of the power of forced entry is very rare.

Despite the judgment in *Semayne* it does not seem that this right of forced entry any longer extends to HCEOs and county court bailiffs enforcing judgments for tax (s.26(1) Crown Proceedings Act 1947) and certainly in other suits by the Crown, except to those in which the monarch is personally claimant, there is no right of forced entry. It does not seem possible to extend the principle in *Semayne* to private bailiffs or local authority officers enforcing local taxes (*Munroe v Woodspring DC* (1979) CLY 2226). Similarly bailiffs enforcing a fine by distraint are held to be enforcing a civil process, so that entry may not be forced in such a levy either (*R v Myers* (1786) 1 TR 265).

- *Magistrates' court distraint* - an amendment to the Magistrates Court Act 1980 has created new powers for bailiffs and civilian enforcement officers collecting fines to force entry in order either to distrain on goods or to arrest a fine defaulter.

These powers of forced entry were created as a deliberate attempt to improve rates of fine recovery. They are concerned only with fines imposed upon criminal conviction in magistrates' courts. Section 27 of the 2004 Act creates a new s.125BA in the MCA 1980; this refers to a new Sch.4A to that Act. Sch.4 of the 2004 Act creates the new Sch.4A. Bailiffs have suggested that these powers apply to road traffic penalties or to any orders made by a magistrates' court (such as council tax liability orders or civil orders for non-payment of income tax): this is incorrect.

A new subsection 125BA 3(1) of the 1980 Act reads "An authorised officer may enter and search any premises for the purpose of executing a warrant of distress issued under section 76 of this Act for default in paying a sum adjudged to be paid by a conviction." Subsection 2 qualifies this by adding "The power may be exercised only to the extent that it is reasonably required for that purpose." Subsection 5 specifically deals with the use of force and states "An authorised officer may use reasonable force, if necessary, in the exercise of a power conferred on him by this Schedule."

The key question for all parties must be- when will it be reasonable and necessary for a bailiff to use force in order to gain entry? The official answer is that the powers are expected to be used only rarely to deal with "the hard core of offenders who wilfully refuse to pay." Here the MoJ clearly (if possibly erroneously) equated wilful refusal to pay with refusal of a right of entry, which is a long established legal right of debtors. However, they go on to state that "reasonable force means force that the average person would consider reasonable in the individual circumstances in order to achieve the execution of a warrant. The circumstances can vary, so it is not possible to give an exhaustive definition of what might be reasonable. The power may be used when all other means of gaining peaceful entry have been exhausted." [emphasis added]

- *National insurance contributions* Under s.121A(2) of the Social Security Administration Act 1992, a JP may issue a warrant permitting an 'authorised officer' of the Department of Work and Pensions to force entry to business premises for the purposes of levying arrears of national insurance contributions. Constables may be called upon to assist in this. Entry cannot be forced to private dwellings unless there is reason to believe that a trade or business is being carried on there.

In a number of other cases, case authority supports a bailiff's right to use force to enter in limited circumstances:

Re-entry
Entry may immediately follow a legal first entry in two circumstances:

- *after forcible ejection*: if the bailiff is obliged to leave premises because of threats or the use of force immediately after a lawful first entry or later during the process of seizure and impounding, he may use force to regain entry. Examples include, after peaceable entry - *Eagleton v Gutteridge* (1843) 11 M&W 465 and during seizure *Francome v Pinche* (1766) Esp NP (3rd Edn) 382. Force may be employed in such cases even after a considerable delay - in the case of *Eldridge v Stacy* (1863) 15 CBNS 458 the bailiff returned three weeks after forcible expulsion. However the bailiff must have made a full entry initially, not just a foot in the door (*Boyd v Profaze* (1867) 16 LT 431).

- *after forcible exclusion*: if the bailiff leaves temporarily, and returns to find his way barred, he may again use force to get back in (*Bannister v Hyde* (1860) 2 E&E 627). It was argued in this case that force is justified as being kept out by force is equivalent to being turned out by force. This right to re-enter will only apply if the bailiff voluntarily leaves for a short time (and on return only goods previously seized may be taken).

The bailiff cannot re-enter after a long delay (*Russell v Rider* (1834) 6 C&P 416) because the goods will have been abandoned (see 8.4). In Russell the landlord's bailiff left in a state of 'high excitement, bordering on insanity'. The landlord broke in six days later to remove the goods and was found to have trespassed.

No demand need be made before forcing re-entry (*Aga Kurboolie Mahomed v R* (1843) 4 Moo PCC 239). This is because, in the circumstances under discussion, the debtor is taken to know the purpose for which the bailiffs entered and have returned and to be unlawfully obstructing them by preventing entry.

Note that David Feldman (1986) also proposes that, in light of the judgment in *Southam v Smout* (above), it may also be held lawful for a bailiff to use force to open a door in order to summon help (see too *R v Clarke* (1835) 4 Nev & M 671).

Separate or non-domestic premises
Such premises may be entered forcibly only in execution, e.g. a workshop (*Hodder v Williams* [1895] 2 QB 663) or a barn (*Penton v Browne* (1664) 1 Keb 698). It is however interesting to note that Bowen J in *American Concentrated Must v Hendry* (1893) WN 67 felt that the decision in *Penton* was a departure from the older law and that it was "a misconception to suppose that an outhouse within the curtilage enjoys less immunity than a disconnected outhouse" i.e. the sheriff had no more right to break in than a landlord or other bailiff. This right does not apply if the non-domestic premises are connected to a dwelling, even though they may have separate entrances and no communicating doors- for instance a flat over a shop (*Hudson v Fletcher* [1909] 12 WLR 15).

The bailiff should make enquiry as to the presence of goods first (*Hobson v Thelluson* [1867] 2 QB 642). These rules refer to premises which are not "connected with or within the curtilage of the dwelling house". Garden sheds and garages are thus protected as they are "parcel of the dwelling house". County court bailiffs will always get the permission of a district judge before such a forced entry. It is understood that HCEOs regularly exercise the right to force entry to business premises.

Stranger's premises
These may be entered forcibly by a landlord with a police officer if an oath has been sworn before magistrates to the effect that there are grounds for believing goods have been fraudulently removed there (see 3.5). The HCEO may also break into a third party's house if goods have been taken there to avoid execution (see 7.3.3).

In all other cases, any use of force against the premises or an occupant for the purposes of gaining entry would be unlawful. Force includes not only active force against a door to push it open, but the obstruction of a door to prevent it being closed. It is very apparent that, within the enforcement industry, there is a widespread belief that 'passive force' preventing an individual from shutting a door is not unlawful force within the meaning of the law. As should be apparent from what has been said, this is a misconception and any levy which has involved the use of such means of obstruction will be as unlawful as one where a door has been forced open.

There is no statutory requirement for a property to be left secure after forced entry. Parallels could be drawn with the duties imposed upon the police under the Police & Criminal Evidence Acts, or the fuel companies in respect of disconnections, and failure to leave a property secure could form the basis of claims for compensation for damage caused by the forced entry, for property lost if the premises were not secure and for losses arising from the occupier's inability to get back into the property.

7.4.6 *Identification & information*

In most cases of distress bailiffs do not have to identify themselves when entering premises. In distress for rent, road traffic penalties, local taxes and child support maintenance only is some document is required by statute. Any such authorisation and the certificate for rent, local taxes and road traffic penalties should be produced upon request. The certificate should only be shown when levying for those debts for which it is required. HCEOs will show their 'warrant card' (their official identification bearing their photograph and name) on entry.

However, the National Standard demands that enforcement agents should always produce identification on request, together with a warrant from the creditor. See also 6.1.2 on the production of warrants.

The National Standard goes on to recommend that agents should not discuss a case with anyone except the debtor if possible. More importantly still, agents must withdraw if the only person present at the premises is, or appears to be, under the age of 18- although they can ask when the debtor will be home - if appropriate. If the only persons present are children who appear to be under the age of 12, then enforcement agents must withdraw without making enquiries at all.

7.4.7 *Police attendance*

A police officer may be called by a bailiff to attend a levy or forced entry if a threat of violence can be shown (*Skidmore v Booth* (1854) 6 C&P 777). The officer's presence would be to prevent a breach of the peace and not to assist in the seizure. A breach of the peace may be defined as a situation when and where:

- harm is actually done or is likely to be done to a person whether by the conduct of the person against whom the breach is alleged or by someone provoking that breach;

- harm is actually done or is likely to be done to a person's property in his presence, provided that the natural consequences of such harm is likely to be a violent retaliation; or,

- a person is genuinely in fear of harm to him/herself or property in their presence as a result of an assault.

The police can arrest the person who commits, or who they reasonably believe will commit, a breach of the peace.

A request for police attendance can only be justified by a bailiff if it can be shown that it was necessary because of threats of resistance or violence or similar circumstances met on a previous visit (*R v Clarke* (1835) 4 Nev & M 671; *Skidmore v Booth* as above). A challenge brought under article 8 of the ECHR (*McLeod v UK* [1999] 1 EHRLR 125) confirmed that the police must strike a fair balance between the right to respect for the home and the prevention of crime and disorder and must ensure that their actions are proportionate to the degree of risk existing at the time. In the absence of a significant and indisputable threat to persons or property their interference cannot be justified. It is clear that the common threat in correspondence to attend with police is at least misleading and should not be made as a matter of course.

Attention should also be paid to the more recent Court of Appeal case of *Bibby v Chief Constable of Essex* [2000] EWCA Civ 113. Bibby was endeavouring to remove goods under a lawful possession agreement; an argument developed and both parties called the police. The officer in charge at the scene concluded that there was a risk of a breach of the peace and as Bibby was refusing to leave, he was likely to precipitate the breach. As a result he was arrested and was taken away in handcuffs, though he was released about an hour later without charge.

Bibby sued for assault and wrongful imprisonment but his claim was dismissed at trial in the county court. The Court of Appeal reversed the decision and in the process set out a clear list of conditions which must be satisfied in order to justify the arrest of a bailiff for breach of the peace. These are as follows:

- there must be the clearest of circumstances and a sufficiently real and present threat to the peace to justify arresting a person who is not acting unlawfully;

- the threat to the peace must be coming from the person who is arrested, who must be acting unreasonably;

- that conduct must interfere with the rights of others, and the natural and not wholly unreasonable response to that conduct must be violence.

The Court held that neither a lawful levy by a bailiff nor a refusal to leave a building lawfully entered could justify a breach of the peace by an occupier. Exercising the rights and duties of a bailiff is not a breach of the peace. Bibby was entitled to remain on the premises and to remove goods and to call for police assistance if there was a genuine fear that violence would be employed. The bailiff's behaviour had been lawful and reasonable whilst the debtor's use of violence had been wholly unreasonable. As a result the arrest of Mr Bibby was unjustified, and the use of handcuffs was particularly unnecessary. However the Court did not go so far as to say that a bailiff could never be arrested. Pill LJ stated "I do not of course exclude the possibility that a bailiff, or someone in a similar position, might behave so outrageously, short of violence, that he is likely to provoke a not wholly unreasonable violent reaction from others, thereby justifying his arrest."

To conclude therefore, both parties are entitled to have the police present if there is a genuine threat of violence. Other attendance or threats of police attendance are inappropriate and should be taken up with the local constabulary as well as with the bailiffs' firm, even if no action is taken for illegal distress.

7.4.8 *Failed entry*

If the bailiff fails to gain entry or find any adequate goods on a first visit the bailiff will try once or twice again, very likely at different times, and may make discrete local enquiries in the neighbourhood as to whether the debtor still trades or lives at the address. If they still do not meet with success a return of 'no goods' or 'no sufficient distress' is made to the creditor. Case law makes it clear that the bailiff must have made reasonable efforts to actually enter or search for goods to be able to make such a return legitimately. Nil returns can be made if the goods are hidden (*Doe d Haverson v Franks* (1847) 2 Car & Kir 678) or entry is obstructed (*Doe d Cox v Roe* (1847) 5 Dow & L 272) or refused (*R v Dudley Justices ex p*

Blatchford [1992] RVR 63). For the consequences of failed entry upon the levy and upon other remedies, see 3.6.

Rights of entry - commentary & conclusions

It will be apparent from the above review of case law on modes of entry that there is no coherent pattern to what is considered lawful or acceptable. One may particularly feel that judicial opinion is moving against means of entry that are not 'ordinary means'. Thus in *ex p. Williams* [1893] 14 NSWLR 395 Windeyer J observed "persons entering premises must take care not to do so in a way that is calculated to provoke a breach of the peace. Climbing over fences is very likely to annoy people and ... very serious consequences might ensue if someone thought a burglary was about to be committed". The judge's recommendation was that only entering premises by normal means was the safest course to pursue in the interests of the public, and for the preservation of the public peace."

More recently a more restrictive view still was enunciated in *Swales v Fox* [1981] 2 WLR 814 by Lord Donaldson. Though he took trouble to stress that he was only concerned in the case with the statutory powers of the police under s3 Criminal Law Act 1967 to use 'such force as is reasonable' in aid of a power of arrest, and not the common law position, his views are probably indicative of the general attitude of the courts to modern property rights. In defining forced entry he stated: "In the context of outside premises of course there is no problem unless there is a gate or something of that sort. The constable simply enters and is authorised to do so. ... But if he meets an obstacle, then he uses force if he applies any energy to the obstacle with a view to removing it. It would follow that, if my view is correct, where there is a door that is ajar but is insufficiently ajar for someone to go through the opening without moving the door and energy is applied to that door to make it open further, force is being used. A fortiori force is used when the door is latched and you turn the handle from the outside and then ease the door open. Similarly if anyone opens a window or increases the opening in any window, or indeed dislodges the window by the application of any energy, he is using force to enter..."

PART TWO -
REMEDIES FOR WRONGFUL ENTRY

A variety of remedies are available for wrongful entries. These include common law claims for damages and specific remedies designed for unlawful levies of distress. Readers should also remember that a complaint against the bailiff's certificate may be considered where there has been a serious breach of the rules on entry- for example an entry with force or an assault upon an individual (see 6.8.3).

7.5 Trespass to land

Readers will often encounter claims for illegal distress in the case reports. These are nothing more than claims for trespass - whether to land, or to goods or the person. Trespass to goods is discussed at 9.27.

7.5.1 *Scope*

Whilst a licence to enter property against an owner's consent may be given by law, for instance, in order to distrain, any unlawful or unjustifiable entry into or upon property is a trespass for which court action may be taken, even though there is no actual damage. Every unjustifiable intrusion is covered, however minor. Every continuance of a trespass, for example from day to day, is a fresh trespass and a fresh cause of action. It is no defence to say that the trespass arose from a mistake as to law or fact, provided that the physical act of entry was voluntary (but see *Papillon v Backne* (1658) 2 Hardr 480, which suggests that the bailiff trespasses only after notice of his error). If the entry is voluntary, the intention renders the person a trespasser, whether or not their purpose was to act lawfully or wrongfully.

Consequently it will be trespass for a bailiff to levy illegal distress (*Etherton v Popplewell* (1801) 1 East 139) or to remain on the property after a legal distress has become illegal (*Ladd v Thomas* (1840) 4 Jur 797). The fact that the bailiff either had no right to enter, or abused a legal right of entry, gives the claimant an automatic right to damages without proof of actual loss. It follows that it is no defence to contend that the trespass was of a trifling nature- though this will go in mitigation of the damages (see 7.5.2 & *The Six Carpenters Case* (1610) 8 Co Rep 146; *Moir v Munday* (1755) Say 181; *Lamb v Wall* (1859) 1 F & F 503). The sheriff remaining too long in premises is trespass, but it is unclear whether it may be possible to extend this to other bailiffs (*Lee v Dangar* [1892] 1 QB 231).

7.5.2 *Measure of damages*

General damages

As explained, if trespass is proved the client is entitled to damages, even though no loss can be shown. The measure of the damages depends on the nature of the trespass. If the trespass caused no identifiable loss damages will only be nominal: see for example *Hogarth v Jennings* [1892] 1 QB 907 where an error in using an uncertificated bailiff was held to be technical and occasioning no real loss. If substantial damage can be proved, the damages award will be increased accordingly to compensate for this. If there has been physical damage to the land the measure of damages will either be the diminution in value of the property (though limited by the claimant's interest in the property) or the costs of replacement or repair. If the trespass has involved severance and removal of fixtures, the common law rule is that the claimant may elect for the action giving the highest amount of damages-either for trespass to land or for wrongful interference (see *Twigg v Potts* (1834) 3 LJ Ex 336 and 9.27).

Consequential damages

These will also be recoverable under such heads as:

- losses such as loss of profits or expenses may be claimed due to disruption of business;

- alternative accommodation, if necessary, such as a stay in a hotel.

Consequential losses may also be recoverable as aggravated damages.

An example of the extent of the general and consequential damages that may be recoverable is *Munroe & Munroe v Woodspring DC* (1979) CLY 2226. During a levy of distraint for rates the bailiffs forced entry into a garage in the claimant's garden and unlawfully seized and sold a car. The claimant was entitled to damages representing the value of the car, general damages for trespass and loss of use of the vehicle and special damages for damage to the garage door.

Aggravated damages may be awarded where the trespass included deliberate or negligent injury to the claimant's pride and dignity or was accompanied by noise or disturbance. Examples may be damages for injury to the reputation of business premises, fear at entry or insult suffered by the claimant.

Exemplary damages may also be awarded on a punitive basis where it is necessary to make an example of the wrongdoer. They may be granted where there was a desire for profit on the part of the creditor or bailiff or where a public officer has acted in an oppressive or arbitrary way. Such awards will be rare, made only in cases of serious misbehaviour which was malicious as well as unlawful. Thus a mistaken excessive levy by a county court bailiff did not justify exemplary damages (*Moore v Lambeth County Court Registrar* [1970] 1 All ER 980).

7.5.3 *Trespass ab initio*

More significant, perhaps, than the right to claim damages is the ability to render a levy null and void from the start. The doctrine of trespass *ab initio* applies equally to trespass to land, trespass to person (see 7.5.4) and trespass to goods (see 9.27). The principle is that if a bailiff enters a property lawfully but, whilst there, abuses his authority by an unreasonable or illegitimate act amounting to trespass, s/he becomes what is termed a 'trespasser *ab initio*' (from the beginning) (*Hickman v Massey* [1900] 1 QB 752). The trespass relates back to render the original entry tortious (Bl. Comm. vol. 3 para 213). Thus the levy will be trespass from the start and consequently void ('void *ab initio*'), as will all associated charges. It will give rise to the normal remedies for trespass, including both actions for damages and replevin (see 9.29). The rule is based on the legal presumption that if the person acted illegally, s/he entered with that aim in mind and as a result all their actions were illegal (*Dye v Leatherdale* (1769) 3 Wils 20; Taylor v. Cole (1791) 3 TR 292).

The bailiff may thus be sued as if the original entry were unlawful. Trespass *ab initio* arises where there is positive misfeasance by a person - mere non-feasance, such as failing to release goods seized on proper tender is not enough (*West v Nibbs* (1847) 4 CB 172). If the tortious act that occurs is not trespass, the tort does not 'relate back' to make the entry illegal. See for instance *Shorland v Govett* (1826) 5 B&C 485 - an overcharge by a bailiff was not trespass ab initio as the court did not feel it could be reasonably supposed the bailiff had entered solely to extort money from the debtor; see also *Moyse v Cocksedge* (1745) Barnes 459).

Examples of acts that do constitute trespass *ab initio* would be:

- legal entry followed by an illegal seizure of third party goods - in *Harvey v Pocock* (1843) 11 M & W 740 damages were awarded for seizure of undistrainable goods when others were available. A legal entry followed by illegal seizure of exempt goods would also be trespass *ab initio*: see *Swire v Leach* (1865) 18 CBNS 479. Readers should not overlook the fact that these levies will be both trespass to land and to goods, so the damages awarded will be the full value of exempt goods seized;

- forced entry: in *Bell v Oakley* (1814) 2 M & S 259 a rates bailiff forced entry into a house, breaking windows in the process, found nothing inside and then removed some timber from the garden. The whole distress was invalid as he was a trespasser *ab initio*; or,

- remaining in possession too long (*Gargrave v Smith* (1691) 1 Salk 221).

The courts may be prepared to award higher damages in a case of trespass *ab initio*, such as a sum equal to the whole amount levied (*Shorland v Govett* (1826) 5 B&C 485). Then again the damages may be limited- to the value of a barrel of beer (*Dod v Monger* (1704) 6 MR 215) or for the loss of use of looms (*Harvey v Pocock* (1843) 11 M&W 740).

The wrongful act will not be trespass *ab initio* if the bailiff does that which he is authorised to do as well as the tort complained of. Thus if only some of the goods seized were third parties', and some were the debtor's and available for distress, the bailiff would not be a trespasser *ab initio* to the land, but only a trespasser to the goods wrongfully taken (*Canadian Pacific Wine Co v Tuley* [1921] 2 AC 417; *Elias v Pasmore* [1934] 2 KB 164; *Owen & Smith v Reo* (1934) 151 LT 274). In such cases it will still be possible to sue for wrongful interference to the goods in question, but the whole levy will not be called into question. There are certain statutory exemptions to trespass *ab initio* (e.g. rent and local taxes - see 10.8), but not in several other forms of distress.

7.5.4 *Trespass to person*

The bailiff could also be sued for damages for trespass to person. This covers both assault and battery. Assault is any intentional or reckless act that causes a person to fear the immediate use of unlawful force or personal violence. Threats, gestures and abuse on their own are not assault, without capacity to carry them out. Battery is the infliction of any unwanted physical contact, force or violence in excess of everyday contact and without the person's consent. It may be a blow, spitting or pushing. There is no need to show that any harm was inflicted or intended. There does not need to be any physical contact or injury in assault, the emphasis being the reaction of the victim. As it is a trespass there is an entitlement to damages as of right and claims for consequential and special damages may be made. Damages for assault are calculated like any personal injury action. They may cover not just illness or injury but injury to feelings (indignity, mental suffering, disgrace and humiliation). For physical injury the claimant may recover both pecuniary and non-pecuniary losses e.g. medical expenses, loss of earnings and compensation for pain and suffering and loss of amenities of life. These may be increased by aggravated damages and exemplary damages may also be awarded. Provocation by the claimant may reduce the award. An assault probably does not render the levy trespass *ab initio* (*Smith v Egginton* (1837) 7 A&E 167; *Wiltshire v Barrett* [1966] 1 QB 312).

7.5.5 *Injunctions*

Injunctions are available in the county court ancillary to a damages claim. Application can be made before the issue of a claim by the claimant in urgent cases and the court may grant an injunction on terms that the action is begun in that court. The courts will take account of several factors when considering applications:

- *if other proceedings have been commenced* to restrain the levy, it is generally improper for the claimant to also seek an injunction. See *Hilliard v Hanson* [1882] 21 ChD 69 in which the claimant was penalised for costs after applying for an injunction despite interpleader being initiated by the sheriff.

- *legal rights*: in *Carter v Salmon* (1880) 43 LT 490 it was stated that the courts do not favour interference by injunction with the legal right to distrain, even if it is excessive. There are remedies to deal with such a situation and in Carter no *prima facie* case could be made out by the tenant for restraining the landlord until trial: he appeared to be in breach of his lease, with no convincing evidence of any defence.

- *protecting the parties*: in *Sanxter v Foster* (1841) Cr & Ph 302 it was held that the court should never interfere in a party's enforcement of a legal right by means of an injunction unless it secures to itself the means of putting any person prevented from enforcing a legal claim in the same position, in the event that the claim turns out to be right, as if the court had not interfered. In *Sanxter* an injunction was discharged on appeal as the court felt unable, in the circumstances, to set a proper level of security to protect the landlord. The sort of terms that may be set in order to do justice between the parties are illustrated by *Shaw v Earl of Jersey* [1879] 4 CPD 359 in which the court granted an injunction that restrained the landlord for 14 days, but its continuance was conditional on the tenant paying all the arrears into court. The landlord was seeking to exercise his legal rights and the court declined to make an unconditional injunction to inhibit these despite the tenants' claims of wrongful and excessive distress. Payment into court ensured that the landlord could have the rent if he was entitled to it and the tenants could recover it if he were not. In *Walsh v Lonsdale* [1882] 21 Ch D 9 an action was started to recover damages for illegal distress with an interlocutory injunction to restrain sale and the landlord's continued possession. The court held that it was not trying the case, but as the landlord's claim seemed justified he was entitled to retain the security given by his distress so he was ordered to withdraw on payment of the disputed rent into court by the tenant. Thus the utility of the injunction is tempered by its possible expense to the claimant.

• *prima facie* case: *Steel Linings v Bibby & Co* [1993] RA 27 is a recent example in which the claimants sought an injunction against a firm of certificated bailiffs to prevent sale following alleged excessive distress. The Court of Appeal underlined that injunctions would be given only in very exceptional cases where a powerful *prima facie* case for wrongful distress could be made.

To summarise, injunctions are probably most likely to be granted where there is a bona fide dispute as to whether there are arrears at all, whether goods seized are exempt or not or whether there is a set off or counter claim. As payment into court may be required, from the claimant's perspective they be a less favourable remedy than replevin, in which only security is necessary (see 9.29). If application is made to restrain the bailiff, the creditor should at least receive notice of this so that they have an opportunity of being heard (*Hilliard v Hanson* [1882] 21 ChD 69).

7.6 Complaint to magistrates' court

The regulations for local taxes and child support maintenance give to any person aggrieved by a levy, or an attempt to levy, a right of appeal to the magistrates' court. This is done by making a 'complaint' and requesting the issue of a summons directed to the creditor. It would appear that no complaint can be made simply because a warrant has been issued to the bailiffs, where no further action has been taken to enforce it (*R v Justices of London* [1899] 1 QB 532).

If, on hearing the aggrieved person's complaint, the court is satisfied that an irregular levy has occurred, it can order the return of the goods distrained. Although the regulations speak of irregularity alone, it has been held by the courts that this term includes any wrongful act by the bailiff i.e. illegality, irregularity or an excessive levy (*Steel Linings v Bibby* [1993] RA 27).

The court may also, as an alternative to ordering return of goods, order an award of compensation for the goods sold equal to an amount which, in opinion of the court, would be awarded by way of special damages if proceedings had been taken for trespass or otherwise in connection with the irregularity. In assessing the level of compensation the court is required to act reasonably and to give proper attention to any evidence placed before it: *R v Epping Magistrates ex p Howard & Leach* (1996) 7 CLY 521. It has been held by the High Court in *Steel Linings v Bibby*, and endorsed in *R v Hampstead Magistrates Court ex p St Marylebone Property Co plc* (1995)

Legal Action Sept 1996, p21 that the reference to special damages has a wider meaning in the regulations than just special damages as opposed to general damages and covers all damages caused by the wrongful levy, including damages for annoyance, injury to credit and reputation. The court can also order the creditor and bailiffs to desist from any levying in an irregular manner.

Several community charge complaints have been reported relating to illegal entry and seizure-

- *Bates v Northampton City Council* (1990) Legal Action 3/91 - the bailiffs wrote to Bates, never having entered his property, claiming to have levied on his goods. He appealed and the council denied that what had occurred was a levy (as indeed it was not). The magistrates dismissed the case as they held no distress had been attempted. Bates was ordered to pay £1300 costs. A similar case is *Brown v LB Haringey* (1986) noted at [1992] 2 All ER 704. The Divisional Court in an appeal from the Crown Court held that as a draft walking possession agreement was ineffective there was no levy upon which the statutory right of appeal could be founded. By contrast in *R v Liverpool JJ ex p Greaves* [1979] RA 119 in which the ratepayer's attempt to appeal to the Crown Court was ignored by the magistrates on the grounds that there can be no appeal before a levy and that no levy had occurred. The bailiffs had made a return of no goods and the High Court held that this was indeed a levy, albeit unsuccessful. The matter was therefore passed to the Crown Court to consider a case stated.

- *H v Sandwell MBC* (1993) Legal Action August p.15: see 8.3.1 for details. On hearing the case the magistrates made an order declaring the attempted levy to be irregular, the walking possession charges unlawful and prohibiting further enforcement against the claimant.

7.7 Criminal Remedies

There is no reason why a bailiff acting under a warrant may not commit, or be accused of, a criminal offence (*R v Beacontree JJ ex p Mercer* [1970] Crim LR 103). Experience suggests that the police are often reluctant to become involved in anything that may be classed a 'civil matter' and, other than a warning against a breach of the peace, they are unlikely to take criminal proceedings.

7.7.1 *Forced entry*

Under s6 Criminal Law Act 1977 it is an offence for any person to use or threaten violence, without lawful authority, in order to secure entry into any premises. On summary conviction a person can be fined up to level five and/or be sentenced to up to 6 months in prison. For the entry to be criminal there must be someone on the premises opposed to the entry and the bailiff seeking to enter must know this. It is immaterial whether the violence was directed against the premises or person. If such an entry is in progress the police may be called by the debtor and under subsection 6 a uniformed constable is empowered to arrest, without warrant, anyone with reasonable cause suspected of committing such an offence.

Note also that a criminal entry may also involve criminal damage under Criminal Damage Act 1971. This offence arises wherever another's property is intentionally or recklessly destroyed or damaged without lawful excuse, or threats to that effect are made. The offence is triable on indictment and on conviction the penalty is imprisonment for up to ten years. Self defence or defence of another are lawful excuses for the offence but it is doubtful if the existence of a warrant per se would assist the bailiff. There is no power of arrest by constable at the time the offence is being committed, as with forced entry.

7.7.2 *Unlawful wounding*

Unlawful wounding or other bodily harm can be prosecuted if a bailiff's actions cause any malicious injury. For example, in *ex p. Smith* (1890) 7 TLR 42 a bailiff broke open a door with excessive force whilst trying to levy execution. The bailiff was convicted by the magistrates.

7.8 Statutory remedies

There are various remedies unique to distress for rent and related common law forms of distress that are provided by a number of venerable statutes. Partly because of their obscurity, and partly because of their limited application, they are little used today, but are worth brief notice, if only for the sake of completeness.

7.8.1 *Distress off demised premises*

Under cc2 & 15 Statute of Marlborough 1267, if a landlord distrains 'out of his fee', in other words not upon the premises in respect of which the rent is due, he is liable to a fine "and that according to the quantity and quality of the trespass". The aggrieved tenant's remedy is to sue upon the statute for trespass. Replevin does not lie (Thel. Dig. 117).

7.8.2 *Distress on highway*

Statute of Marlborough 1267 c.15 also makes it unlawful for the landlord to levy distress: "in the king's highway nor in the common street". The tenant has the remedy of recaption (see 3.4 and *Smith v Shepherd* (1519) Cro Eliz 710) and also the right to bring an action for trespass on the statute.

TCEA 2007- commentary

It is in respect of rights of entry to premises that the new Act proposes the most far-reaching changes. In summary the provisions of Sch.12 paras 14-25 are as follows:

- Fines - agents will still be able to use force for initial entries - but the Revenue will lose their power of forcing entry;
- In all other cases agents will be able to apply to court for a forced entry warrant. Execution of this warrant may also permit the use of reasonable force against individuals;
- Re-entry may be forced to trade premises in cases of income tax, NICs, VAT and civil court execution;
- In all other cases, re-entry must be under a warrant granted by a court if force is to be used; and,
- Route of entry- the government has stated that regulations will restrict entry to doors and French doors and all other routes will be prohibited.

The changes to the law on entry to domestic premises were that aspect of the Act which attracted the greatest criticism and opposition during its passage through Parliament. It will be clear that, if fully brought into force, the new Act will profoundly alter bailiff's rights of entry. However, at the time of writing, the government has announced that it does not intend to implement to powers of forced entry or force against the person and will undertake further consultation on the matter. In any event, it was never the intention of the Ministry of Justice to extend the greater powers of entry to private bailiffs until they had proved themselves under the new system of regulation.

If the Act is brought into force as it is presently written, a number of results may be anticipated. It seems unlikely that courts will often grant warrants permitting initial entry to be forced (nor that enforcement agents will often expend the time and resources to apply). However, the threat of being able to make such an application will probably prove extremely effective in overcoming resistance by individuals. The new requirement to seek a warrant in order to be able to force re-entry is a regrettable and unnecessary development. The current law on this worked perfectly well (see 10.4) and the addition of an application to court will probably make removals even less common than they are now- or will encourage enforcement agents to remove at the first opportunity, at the time of initial seizure, in order to avoid any possible problems of regaining access at a later date.

Chapter 8

CONDUCTING LEVIES: PROCEDURE

Levies are the crucial stage in the process of either distress or execution as they give the bailiff a claim over goods which entitles him to remove and sell them, make further charges and which pressure the debtor into paying. Unfortunately the levy procedure is uncertain and ill defined: for instance, in *Evans v South Ribble BC* [1992] 2 All ER 695 Simon Brown J remarked "what constitutes impounding on the premises is ... unclear, as also is the effect of a walking possession agreement". The broad elements of the levy process are nonetheless concisely summarised in the same judgment: "the process of distress consists of three stages: the entry into the premises, the seizure of the goods there and the subsequent securing of the goods (generally called impounding)... Impounding can take a number of forms". Entry has been described in the last chapter. The elements of seizure and impounding are analysed in the following sections. In respect of these elements of the levy process, there seems no reason for differentiating between the different forms of distress and execution. Many of the problems that arise with seizure stem from bailiffs' failure adequately to distinguish between the separate elements in the procedure.

In brief, seizure is identifying goods and taking possession of them whilst impounding is keeping possession of those goods. The cause of this seems to be the widespread use of walking possession. The result is that seizure and impounding both occur in the home at the same time, so that, in the words of Wightman J in *Johnson v Upham* (1859) 2 E&E 250, "these acts are very nearly if not quite concurrent".

8.1 Seizure

8.1.1 *Theory*

Seizure describes the process of identifying the goods being seized, usually by recording them on an inventory, though the term can also refer to both seizure and impounding as a process- here levy has been preferred to avoid confusion. The act of seizure of the debtor's goods will involve some process of selecting and securing items: a bailiff is not necessarily entitled to all the goods on the premises and has to select sufficient to cover the debt and costs whilst ensuring that the levy is not excessive. Thus in *Rai & Rai v*

Birmingham City Council (1993) reported in *Legal Action*, a deputy stipendiary magistrate held that bailiffs have a duty of care to exercise when seizing goods: they must act with discernment and judgment as the power of distraint is not "a dragnet trawling all within it". If put on notice that certain goods do not allegedly belong to the debtor, the bailiffs must act with 'caution and circumspection'. The goods seized must be available for seizure, that is, not exempt in some way.

In finding items suitable for seizure the bailiff is under a duty to employ "reasonable diligence" in searching premises for goods (*Mullet v Challis* (1851) 16 QB 239). As part of this the bailiff may break open any inner door, cupboard or other receptacle both to find goods (*White v Wiltshire* (1619) 79 ER 476; *Browning v Dann* (1735) Bullers NP 81c) and to escape if he is locked in (*Pugh v Griffith* (1838) 7 Ad & El 827). In one case it was held that legal entry through an outer door then justified not only the breaking of internal doors, but also windows in the property (*Lloyd v Sandilands* (1818) 8 Taunt 250). Because of the huge inconvenience it could cause to bailiffs, no demand need be made before forcing each inner door, though this precludes the unnecessary use of force where a door is broken despite the debtor's offer to open it (*Hutchison v Birch* (1812) 4 Taunt 619). If force were used despite an offer to open the door, damages would probably be recoverable.

8.1.2 *Practice*

In practice there are two forms of seizure:

- *actual*: as the name suggests this will involve the bailiff actually seeing, even touching or moving, the goods that are to be seized and listed for sale. It may well be coupled with a clear declaration of the bailiff's intention. For example, in a bill of sale case effective possession was taken by the claimant by marking the goods with his name and taking the keys to the room containing them (*Robinson v Briggs* [1870] 6 Exch 1). It may be that seizure by a distinct act in this manner may relieve the bailiff of the need to do much more in the way of impounding (e.g. *Firth v Purvis* (1793) 5 TR 432, in which the bailiff impounded goods in an unlocked cellar with his mark upon them).

- *constructive seizure* is far harder to define. The bailiff's intentions may be inferred from his actions, e.g. making and presenting an inventory of the goods seized or by some means preventing the removal of goods. The process is summarised by Chisholm J in *Noseworthy v Campbell* [1929] 1 DLR 964: "...to constitute seizure it is not necessary that there should be physical contact with the goods seized....Some act must be done to intimate that seizure has been made." A good example of this is *Cramer & Co v Mott* [1870] 5 QB 357. A lodger in the defendant's house hired a piano from Cramers. He failed to pay the hire charges therefore two men were sent to collect the piano. They were met by Mrs. Mott who said, in the tenant's presence, that the piano should not be removed until her rent was paid. It was held that there might be a distress without actual seizure and what occurred amounted to distress as it was enough for the landlord to prevent removal: if the firm had ignored her words, Mrs Mott was at the door of her tenant's room and could have barred the way, i.e. her words could have been carried into action. A similar case, cited by counsel for the defendant in Cramer, is *Cotton v Bull* (1857) CP, in which a lodging house keeper prevented a tenant in arrears removing personal items from the premises, which detention was held to amount to a distress. It will be clear that, whilst physical contact is not necessary, the bailiff must at least be in a position to be able to remove goods if s/he needs to for constructive seizure to be effective. It follows that seizure cannot be achieved by merely looking through a window and listing goods inside (*Evans v South Ribble BC* [1992] 2 All ER 695).

The bailiff can seize one item or part of the goods in the name of all (*Cole v Davies* (1698) 1 Ld Raym 624), but the whole must be in his power: he must know what items have been distrained and have power to take possession of them (*Re: Meehan* [1879] 6 Nfld LR 172). At least one item must be taken into actual possession it seems - in *Re: Henley ex p. Fletcher* [1877] 5 Ch D 809 Mellish J stated that "it may be by construction of law that his taking of one of the things in deed will amount to possession of all" but there must be actual possession by the bailiff before it can be said that there is formal possession of the rest.

8.1.3 *Problems with seizure*

Seizure involves a bailiff touching – or being able to touch (if required) - the goods sufficient to cover the debt and costs. Seizure therefore fails, and a levy cannot be effective, if this is not achieved. This may occur where:

- there is no access to the premises- for instance, household goods cannot be seized without actual entry to the house (*Evans v South Ribble BC* [1992] 2 All ER 695);

- there are no goods, or insufficient goods; or,

- the process of seizure is not begun or is not fully or clearly carried through. Seizure must involve some initial process of selection and where this fails to happen the levy may be challenged (*Brintons v Wyre Forest D.C.* [1976] 3 WLR 749). Seizure will fail also where the levying bailiff does not make his intention to seize clear. Thus in *Nash v Dickinson* [1867] 2 CP 252 the sheriff went to the debtor's house and, without saying or doing anything more, produced the warrant and demanded the debt and costs. It was held that this did not amount to a levy because the bailiff did nothing, such as leaving a notice or a possession man, to indicate that seizure had occurred. Equally in *Re: Williams ex p Jones* (1880) 42 LT 157 a sheriff went to Williams' house and allegedly seized a horse and cart. It was held there was no seizure as no warrant was produced, there was no inventory that identified what had been seized and it was insufficient to touch items without informing the debtor that they were being seized by bailiffs. These were cases of execution, but similar principles apply in distress. For example in *Whimsell v Giffard* [1883] 3 OR 1 the landlord made two visits to the house, declaring he had seized everything. He touched nothing and made no inventory. There was no valid seizure. Finally, the case of the *Warden and Scholars of New College, Oxford v Davison* (1933) 49 TLR 579 concerned the manner of levying a distress for tithes which had been employed by the county court bailiff. He had gone to the defendant's farm and had seen 14 heifers in a field. He spoke to no-one there and left no notice of seizure, merely writing in a notebook an entry that there were 14 cows on the land. Mr Justice Swift held this not to have been an effective levy of distraint. Nothing expressing the bailiff's intention had been done; the bailiff would have been unable on a return visit to distinguish the cows he had seen from any others. As the judge put it: "he did nothing except what any of us walking in the countryside might do - walk through a gateway and get a look at a likely lot of heifers." It followed that there had been no effective sale of these unidentified cows and no offence of rescue when the beasts were later removed by unidentified individuals.

Equally, in some cases bailiffs manage to gain entry to premises but merely spend their time discussing the debt with the debtor, without doing anything to indicate that a levy is occurring. In such cases there will have been no levy. The court held in *Brintons v Wyre Forest D.C.* [1976] that no valid seizure occurred in a case where, when calling at the claimants' offices, the bailiff simply demanded payment of the rates and costs. He never said that all or any of the goods were seized, no effort was made to inspect or select suitable assets and nothing amounting to the taking of possession was done, e.g. there were no threats to leave a possession man on the premises. See also *Central Printing Works v Walter* (1907) 24 LT 88 which confirmed that if all the bailiff does is wait on the premises whilst the debtor seeks to arrange payment of the sum due, without any indication of any seizure, there will be no levy. See too *Ancona v Rogers* [1876] 1 Ex D 285 in which a mere demand for possession after default on a bill of sale failed to alter actual possession.

Even though a valid seizure may have occurred, it must be stressed that the levy process is not yet complete. Seizure gives the bailiff immediate control of the goods, but they must now be impounded for the seizure to have any effect on the debtor, i.e. for the bailiff to exert and retain title and control.

8.2 Impounding - theory

8.2.1 *Definition*

A distinct act of impounding is necessary in order to exert control over the seized goods. Although a bailiff may purport to levy distress by making a list of goods that he has 'seized', this alone does not alter the debtor's rights over the property. The bailiff must acquire some legal control over the goods to have the power to return later, break into the premises, remove the goods on the inventory and sell them. This is achieved by impounding.

Impounding is said to be place the goods in the 'custody of the law'. It affects ownership of the seized goods in the sense that they are still the debtor's, but his/her rights are now qualified by the rights of the creditor. The bailiff now has a claim to possession and control of those specific goods against which the creditor's claims have been secured (see for example *Re: Pearce* [1885] 14 QB 966; *Re: Davies ex p Williams* [1872] 7 Ch 314; *Slater v Pinder* [1871] 6 Exch 228). This security protects the goods from interference by the debtor (see 3.4) and seizure by other bailiffs (see 6.6.3 and 9.9). The need to give the goods legal protection is especially important for private bailiffs. Unlike officers levying execution (see 8.2.3) bailiffs levying distraint do not have the same legal status and some distinct act is needed to give them greater powers over goods than any other private individual.

8.2.2 *Forms of impounding*

The common law rule is that seized goods may not be impounded on the premises, but should be removed to a suitable pound. On this see for example the *Year Book case* M.21 Hen.VII fo.39b pl.55 (1505) and the later case *Peppercorn v Hofman* (1842) 9 M&W 618; (see also Kruse, 1999). This rule has, in subsequent centuries, been modified by statute in respect of certain forms of seizure with the result that the law now recognises four different forms of impounding:

* *immediate removal*: a bailiff may take away the selected goods at the end of the first visit. Impounding is the physical act of locking the debtor's goods within a secure place. Only in distress for rent is the debtor entitled to know where the goods have been taken (s.9 DRA 1737). In fact, except against businesses, this method is rarely used because of the

expense and trouble involved (when the goods are impounded off the premises the bailiff is liable for them - see *Wilder v Speer* (1838) 8 Ad & El 547);

- *securing in a room* or other suitable place on the premises as a means of impounding is permissible only in distress for rent (s.10 DRA 1737). There is no duty on the landlord to collect goods together in one room to impound them (*Washborn v Black* (1774) 11 East 405) and it is seldom done. It is not permissible for a bailiff levying any other form of distraint or execution to lock up goods in a room on the premises. Further, it is illegal for any bailiff to impound goods by locking up the entire premises, thus completing excluding the occupier. This is tantamount to eviction and there is no power to do this. The warrant licences the bailiff to seize goods, not to seize a property, and to endeavour to take exclusive possession of premises in this way is trespass. See for example *Woods v Durrant* (1846) 6 M & W 149 in which the landlord impounded in the whole house by locking and bolting the doors and windows and expelling the claimant. This lasted until the sale twenty one days later. The landlord was found to have trespassed by impounding in the whole house when one room would do. The seizure was thus invalid. See also *Watson v Murray* [1955] 1 All ER 350 or *Smith v Ashforth* (1860) 29 LJ Ex 259. It has been held that excluding the tenant in this way can be treated as surrender by operation of law by the courts (*Planned Properties v Ramsdens Commercials* (1984) Times March 2nd). This of course would terminate the tenant's liability for rent and the right to continue any distress, but it seems a double-edged sword with advantages and disadvantages for both parties.

- *close possession*: a bailiff may be left on the debtor's premises guarding the goods as 'possession man'. Nowadays the cost and staffing problems associated with close possession and the small fees allowed by statute mean that it is virtually never used. Close possession is not trespass if the debtor does not consent (*Washborn v Black* (1774) 11 East 405) though without any agreement no daily fee for close possession will be chargeable; or,

- *walking possession*: walking possession is a process whereby the debtor agrees (usually in writing) that the goods will remain in his/her premises, subject to the bailiff's possession and right to return and remove them for sale and also subject to payment of a small daily fee to the bailiff. For the debtor the inconvenience of losing the use of items is avoided (and continued use of the goods is not contradictory to them being impounded - see *Dimock v Miller* [1897] 30 NSR 74 and also *ex p. National Guardian Assurance Co Ltd In Re: Francis* [1878] 10 ChD 408). For the bailiff the inconvenience of leaving a bailiff or removing goods is overcome. Both parties benefit from the breathing space during which arrangements to pay can be explored. As stated earlier seizure is the taking of possession, whilst the walking possession agreement functions as evidence and confirmation of this act and its ongoing effectiveness (e.g. *Husky Oil & Refining Ltd v Callsen Re: Weber & Sheriff of Battlefield* [1964] 45 DLR 396).

The legal effect of walking possession may be easily characterised by stating that the debtor is appointed as 'possession man' by the bailiff, i.e. an agent of the bailiff in 'close' possession of his/her own goods (*Federal Bank v Kretschmann* [1886] 7 NSWLR 183). Debtors are appointed as custodians of the goods and as agents for the creditor (*Dimock v Miller* [1897] 30 NSR 74). Davies LJ in the judgment in *National Commercial Bank of Scotland Ltd v Arcam Demolition & Construction Ltd* [1966] 2 QB 593 suggested that the wife who signed a walking possession agreement was appointed as the sheriff's agent and remained in possession as "a sort of bailee". If this is so, care must be taken by bailiffs when agreeing to such bailment that the debtor must be left in possession as 'mere servant' of the bailiff and not left in full, independent possession (*McIntyre v Stata & Crysler* (1854) 4 CP 248).

Many of the relevant regulations provide for walking possession and for the debtor to pay for this (though the fee may be small and its duration limited). Some regulations provide either a definition of the nature of walking possession. For example for council tax see para.2 of Sch.5 of the 1992 Administration & Enforcement Regulations; the same is done for indirect taxes - for example see s.68(2) of the VAT Act 1994. Alternatively, a standard form of agreement may be prescribed by the regulations. See for example county court form N334, Sch.4 of the High Court Enforcement Officers Regulations 2004 and the form prescribed by the Distress for Rent Rules 1988 which is also used in levies of execution for road traffic penalties. These statutory forms should of course neither be adapted nor used for levies of debts other than those for which they prescribed. Both however do happen and advisers should be alert to this technical error in the documentation.

8.2.3 *Executions*

Execution by the HCEO or county court bailiff is seizure by officers of the court. Because of their status, the goods are in the custody of the law as soon as, and at the same time as, they are seized by such a bailiff. An individual such as a landlord needs to undertake a further distinct act to achieve the same effect. Thus a bailiff levying execution who looks through a window may validly and legally seize and impound the items seen (*Giles v Grover* (1832) 1 Cl & Fin 72 and *Wilbraham v Snow* (1670) 2 Saund 47). However despite this, court bailiffs generally choose not to exercise this power and will, like private bailiffs, prefer possession agreements to evidence what has occurred so that no disputes can arise. What an officer levying execution must do to validly seize goods is very unrestricted:

- *an officer remains with warrant.* It was held that if a man enters under a warrant, not as a trespasser, with the intention of seizing, then the entry and his remaining must be held to be seizure (*Bird v Bass* (1843) 6 Scotts NR 928). The sheriff attended to execute and, as the defendant was out, the officer, without saying anything, left a man with the warrant to wait.

- *verbal seizure.* In *Gladstone v Padwick* [1871] 6 Exch it was held that "It is clear that it is not necessary for the sheriff to lay his hand on a single article ... I am of the opinion that ... if the sheriff gives and makes known that he has come to seize and does, as far as words and intention go, seize all the goods ... he has done enough". The court also held that seizure in one part of a property is equivalent to seizure of goods in the whole property. This verbal seizure may be accompanied by production of the warrant as in *Balls v Pink* (1845) 4 LTOS 356. The sheriff attended and stated that all chattels were in his possession, so that subsequent removal was at the debtor's peril, produced the warrant and then left. This amounted to seizure as the debtor understood his intentions.

The officer who is seeking to levy execution must totally fail to make his intentions clear to render the process ineffectual, such as a lack of any indication of seizure as in *Nash v Dickinson* [1867] 2 CP 252 or a failure to indicate his purpose as in *Re: Williams ex p Jones* (1880) 42 LT 157 (see 8.1.3 earlier for details). In levying under a second writ there is no need for actual seizure as the second writ's issue binds the goods already seized under a prior writ (*Jones v Atherton* (1816) 7 Taunt 56). By seizure, the HCEO gets a special property in the goods, and thus acquires sufficient legal possession to be entitled to claim in conversion and trespass (*Clerk v Withers* (1704) 6 MR 290). In addition, the HCEO gets a security over the goods (see *Re: McColla ex p McLaren* [1881] 16 ChD 534).

8.3 Impounding: practice

8.3.1 *Walking possession*

Walking possession is the form of impounding used almost exclusively and attention must therefore be concentrated on its operation in more detail. If the premise behind distress or execution is borne in mind - that the debtor is made to pay through the inconvenience of being deprived temporarily or permanently of his/her goods- for a possession arrangement made for the parties' convenience to have any meaning, an agreement to impound must be made (*Black v Coleman* [1878] 29 CP 507). An explicit agreement is also important to permit the bailiff to charge for this form of impounding, to secure the creditor's rights and provide evidence of the continuing existence of the levy in the bailiff's absence. However once goods are impounded by leaving them in situ in the debtor's house, for his/ her benefit, it will not be possible for him/ her later to complain that there has been no impounding (see Macnaghten J in *Lavell v O'Leary* [1933] 2 KB 200).

In respect of the making of these agreements, the following principles may be elaborated. The effect of failure to comply with these is discussed at 8.4.2.

- *any responsible person* on the premises, including the spouse, partner or adult relative of the debtor, can in most cases make the agreement. See *National Commercial Bank of Scotland Ltd v Arcam Demolition & Construction Ltd* [1966] 2 QB 593 in which the sheriff's officer obtained the signature of the debtor's wife. It was argued that she was not authorised to sign and thus the goods had been abandoned. On appeal it was decided that she was a responsible person capable of signing even without her husband's authority and against his will. The debtor's authority or consent is not necessary as the person is being appointed as an agent of the bailiff, not the debtor. "Responsible" was defined as knowing the goods should not be moved by anyone else, stopping them being removed and telling the bailiff if they are.

- The relationship between signatory and debtor is not important so long as that person is capable of understanding the implications of the agreement and is able to transmit that information to the debtor (or any other bailiff who might call) should they wish to remove the seized goods from the property.

- *children* cannot make such agreements, nor, arguably, can individuals only temporarily present in the property at the time the bailiff calls (*Lumsden v Burnett* [1898] 2 QB 177).

- *for local taxes* much stricter requirements are laid down in the regulations. The only acceptable signatory is the debtor named on the liability order, and s/he must sign at the time of the levy. If the debtor does not sign, no charges may be made for walking possession, although a valid impounding will still have occurred.

- *trading businesses*: where distress is levied upon a business that continues to trade the stock and materials seized and subject to walking possession must, if the business is to continue, be sold by the firm. In theory, this would be a breach of the possession agreement by the debtor (see 3.5) and to allow it would be abandonment by the bailiff (see 8.4.1). At the same time, to permit the firm to trade is likely to raise income to satisfy the debt. The bailiff must therefore find a means of taking possession that is both apparent and yet permits the business to continue to operate.

A solution to this is allowing the trader to dispose of seized items so long as they are replaced immediately. The bailiff must make any such arrangement very carefully or else he risks abandonment of the goods. Upon initial seizure a detailed inventory should be taken and the fact that stock will change noted on it. Limits on the amounts of stock that may be sold over a given period may be imposed. Regular repeat visits will need to be made to the premises to check on the goods. On such occasions it will be necessary for the bailiff to either up date the inventory by seizing more goods or receive the proceeds of sale of the items that have been sold by the trader. If sold stock is not being replaced by the trader, it will be necessary for the bailiff to consider removal, if no funds are available to make payment to cover the value of the missing goods. Such successive levies may be permissible for execution and distraint, but it is doubtful that the procedure could be legal in distress for rent (see 10.7).

This kind of approach has been sanctioned by the courts in *Re: Dalton ex p Herrington & Carmichael v Trustee* [1963] Ch 336. See also *Re: Hunter* [1912] 8 DLR 102 in which the sheriff, instead of seizing and selling the assets of a liquor business, placed a bailiff in possession to receive the daily receipts of the business as a going concern. Where the receipts were handed over on a daily basis, the court was prepared to place on this the legal construction that each taking was a levy of execution. However where the debtor is allowed to trade with no indication of any alteration in possession, and no accounting for proceeds to the man in possession, the seizure is voided and the goods are abandoned (*Paget v Perchard* (1794) 1 Esp 205).

See also *Toussaint v Hartop* (1816) Holt NP 335 in which the sheriff was in possession but the seizure and possession were both "concealed from the world" by the fact that the debtor was allowed to keep trading with the seized goods over an extended period of five months. When the trader went bankrupt the trustee's claim to the goods defeated that of the sheriff. A similar conclusion was reached in *Jackson v Irvin* (1809) 2 Camp 48 the debtor's employee acted as possession man of his stock and carried on the business as normal. When the debtor went bankrupt the trustee's claim to the goods defeated that of the execution creditor. In *Edwards v Edwards* [1876] 2 Ch 291 a receiver failed to take effective possession of a business when trade was continued ostensibly by the debtor and the change of possession was not publicised. Such a 'mere nominal possession' was not enough to defeat a later execution. These cases suggest that walking possession will not operate to remove the goods from the "order and disposition" of the debtor. In contrast two bills of sale cases show that publicly apparent possession of business assets will be effective seizure (for example *Re: Basham* (1881) WN 161; *Gibbons v Hickson* (1885) 55 LJQB 119). Numerous commonwealth cases give the same impression.

8.3.2 *Constructive walking possession*

The passing of s.10 DRA 1737 initiated (or endorsed) the practice of securing goods on the debtor's premises. From this point the link between impounding and real possession began to weaken, and it is clear from authorities already quoted that by the late eighteenth century the need for ongoing physical possession had diminished to a point where impounding could be achieved by quite simple steps on the part of the bailiff. Thus, even if there is no written possession agreement, a valid impounding will have occurred if the debtor, or a responsible person, is present during the levy and it is made quite clear to them what is happening.

So it is now that any act or word expressive of the intention to assume control of the goods is likely to be sufficient to take goods into (using the words of Sir John Allen CJ spoken with prescience in *De Grouchy v Sivret* [1890] 30 NBR 104) the 'virtual control' of the bailiff. This form of possession may be taken because of the inconvenience or impossibility of seizing items more fully. Nevertheless if the bailiff does act in this way, he has a valid possession of goods and all the rights that spring from that even though there is no signed agreement. The following cases give examples of how this form of possession may be taken:

- *seizure with written notice of impounding:* Service of a notice confirming a seizure amounts to impounding. In *Thomas v Harries* (1840) 1 Man & G 695 a bailiff had entered a field and touched one of the cattle in it stating that it was distrained for rent as a representative of all the cattle. A list was made but the cattle were not moved or the gate locked. Notice that the cattle were impounded was then given to the tenant. This was held to be valid distress. Tindal CJ cited *Firth v Purvis* (1793) 5 TR 432 in support of his judgment that giving notice amounted to impounding (however Lord Hanworth MR in *Lavell v O'Leary* [1933] 2 KB 200 treated the marking of the goods by Firth as the act of impounding- see 8.1.2). Furthermore we may note that Maule J dissented from the judgment as he felt that impound and secure were equivalent terms and that in this case the seizure thus fell short of this.

Similarly in *Swann v Earl of Falmouth & Jennings* (1828) 8 B&C 456 it was held that an effective levy occurred as notice to the tenant indicated an intention to leave the goods on the premises in the custody of the law without abandoning them. On arrival at the rented premises the bailiff announced his intention to levy for rent arrears, walked round the wharf and departed, leaving a notice listing the goods that had been seized, although they were left behind on the premises.

It seems that any notice will be valid whether given to the debtor or to a third party or agent. In *Re: Cooper* [1958] Ch 922, a dispute arose as to whether the sheriff's officer had indeed conducted a levy and was therefore entitled to reimbursement for the costs of execution from the bankrupt's estate. The sheriff levied by leaving with one of the bankrupt's employees forms stating that two tractors had been seized in execution. The bankrupt was asked to sign two walking possession agreements (though it appears he did not). One week later (after the bankruptcy order) the tractors were removed. Danckwerts J held "it is not necessary that the actual goods be taken into possession by the sheriff's officer. Also it is not necessary that he should retain possession of the goods...There is certainly one authority (*Lumsden v Burnett* - see 8.3.1) which shows that very little in the way of actual seizure would be sufficient to satisfy the requirements of delivery in execution ... it does indicate the way in which very simple acts would be sufficient to satisfy the requirements of taking and retaining possession. But it is, in each case, a question of fact ... events (in this case) entirely negatived an intention to abandon possession because everything was consistent with completing the process of execution." In addition to leaving the four documents at the debtor's premises, the sheriff had taken all the necessary steps to arrange removal, again indicating his intentions.

- *verbal notice of impounding*: a landlord, hearing a tenant and a stranger disputing ownership of a lathe on the rented premises entered, touched the item and said "the article shall not be removed until my rent is paid". It was held that from the time of this declaration the lathe was in the custody of the law, so removal later by the stranger was wrongful (*Wood v Nunn* (1828) 5 Bing 10).

It seems that this will apply even where the notice is given for the creditor by a third party or agent. See *Werth v London & Westminster Loan and Discount Co.* (1889) 5 TLR 520 in which a tenant had given a bill of sale over his furniture to the defendant company, who then seized the furniture and left a man in possession. The landlord, Werth, heard of this and claimed his rent arrears by requiring the tenant, on his behalf, to hand a letter in respect of the arrears to the man in possession. The tenant declared "I distrain for rent due to my landlord". Later the defendants removed the goods. The landlord claimed wrongful removal, which was upheld on appeal as it was held that the landlord's actions constituted valid seizure against the company.

- *assent by debtors*: In *Finn v Morrison* (1856) 13 UCR 568 the bailiff went to a shop and the owners told him to proceed as they would replevy. He listed some barrels at their request, but did not touch them or leave a possession man, relying on the tenants' assent and their stated intention to replevy. This was held to be a valid levy. A similar case heard in the same year is *Tennant v Field* (1856) 8 E & B 336. The bailiff attended to levy at the debtor's premises and, in order to avoid disturbing lodgers in certain of the rooms, based the seizure on an inventory of goods drawn up in consultation with the debtor's spouse. The court held this to be a valid seizure and impounding. The key element of this levy was that, after entry to the house, the bailiff could have gone into every room if he had wished but agreed not to do so, partly out of courtesy and partly out of convenience. A way of proceeding was agreed, to which the debtor later assented, and which avoided doing unnecessary injury to the claimant by leaving the goods in place so that lodgers were not disturbed - and thereby also avoiding any risk of damage to the goods that might arise during removal. In *Washborn v Black* (1774) 11 East 405 the courts held that there is no duty on a landlord to collect goods together in order to impound them and that they will still be impounded though not collected together by consent between the parties. See also *Kemp v Christmas* (1898) 79 LT 233 where a comparable process of impounding seems to have been used, or at least implied by the court, so that the claimant could maintain an action for poundbreach. Note may also be taken of *Vicarino v Hollingsworth* (1869) 20 LTNS 780 or *ex p National Guardian Assurance Co Ltd In Re: Francis* [1878] 10 ChD 408: the fact that possession is 'friendly', in the sense that the debtor does not object (and may even find it convenient) does not make it any less real and absolute.

- *during interpleader proceedings*: a more modern example of the possibility of the bailiff's possession being deemed to continue whilst he was out of possession is found in *PB Manufacturing v Fahn* [1967] 2 QB 1059 in which the court held that possession held before interpleader claims were made was restored without any need for a new writ once the claims were dismissed.

Recently this form of walking possession has been termed possession by 'operation of law'- see Cooke J in *McLeod v Butterwick* [1996] 1 WLR 995. However, as it is by its nature implied, rather than either agreed in writing or physically apparent, regular steps must be taken by the bailiff to ensure that possession continues, otherwise it will be 'abandoned'. This may be by regular and frequent return visits to the property, letters, phone calls etc (e.g. *London & Scottish Finance Ltd v Modern Car & Caravans (Kingston) Ltd* [1966] 2 All ER 732). It is not uncommon to encounter this sort of impounding. Bailiffs prefer to make written possession agreements so that they may charge the statutory fee for the impounding, but if this cannot be done, they may still retain their rights by this route. If an 'oral' form of possession agreement is not diligently followed up in this way the bailiff's claim over the goods will soon be lost in the absence of a written agreement. A claim of abandonment may arise within only a few days, judging by the decision in *Lloyds & Scottish Finance Ltd* (see also 3.4.5 & 8.4.1).

8.3.2 *Impounding for different debts*

It is important to stress that the forms of impounding allowed for different forms of distraint and execution depend upon the specific statutory powers granted for these debts. Failing these, the common law rule against impounding on the premises will apply. A number of forms of seizure of goods deserve particular attention.

- *Magistrates' courts* impounding off the debtor's premises should be the norm. However, a special procedure exists for the securing of household goods- this is discussed later at 8.4.7, as are the new clamping orders for fines enforcement (see 8.4.8).

- *Distress for rent* section 10 of the Distress for Rent Act 1737 explicitly overrode the common law to make it lawful "for any person...to impound or otherwise secure distress [made for rent]...in such place or on such part of the premises chargeable with the rent as shall be most fit and convenient for the impounding and securing of such distress." This provision has been found to be wide enough to justify not only impounding goods in rooms, closets or outbuildings on the demised premises, but to support the development of close and walking possession and (it would seem) to permit a landlord lawfully to clamp a motor vehicle found upon the land (see 8.4.6).

- *County court executions* county court bailiffs may, under s.90 CCA 1984, impound goods until sale by one of three means. The goods may be deposited by the bailiff in some fit place, they may remain in the custody of a fit person approved by the district judge to be put in possession by the bailiff or they may be safeguarded in such other manner as the district judge directs. From this it will be clear that county court bailiff may utilise close or walking possession and may (with the court's sanction) lock in rooms or use vehicle clamps, as alternatives to immediate removal.

- *Execution for road traffic penalties* s.90 of the County Courts Act 1984 does not apply to execution for road traffic penalties. Instead art.11 ERTDO 1993 enables the enforcement officer to "deposit" the goods seized in "some fit place" until sale. Contrasting this article with the county court provision from which it is derived, it will be apparent that narrower powers of impounding are permitted to private bailiffs enforcing these penalties than are granted to HMCS staff. Considering the wording of the provision alone, the use of the verb 'deposit' in conjunction with the specification of 'some fit place' appears to imply some process during which the goods are (re)moved and placed in a different location.

8.4 Impounding: problems

8.4.1 *Abandonment*

Abandonment occurs when the bailiff fails to remain adequately in possession or delays his return and thus loses any right to return and remove goods seized. Any abandonment, however urgent and necessary, must be satisfactorily accounted for if the bailiff is to retain his rights (*Ackland v Paynter* (1820) 8 Price 95). Any sort of agreement or arrangement with the debtor is likely to be evidence of impounding contrary to a claim of abandonment (*Anderson v Henry* [1898] 29 OR 719; *Black v Coleman* [1878] 29 CP 507). However four situations where the bailiff leaves will not be held by the courts to be abandonment:

- *withdrawal under false representation* by the debtor to the bailiff does not amount to abandonment (*Wollaston v Stafford* (1854) 15 CB 278).

- *temporary withdrawal*: it is not abandonment to go out of possession briefly with the intention of returning: the bailiff went out to get a drink of beer (*Bannister v Hyde* (1860) 2 E & E 627). The bailiff was held to retain a 'constructive possession' during his brief absence from the premises. Another example is *Coffin v Dyke* (1884) 48 JP 757 - Coffin was left as a 'possession man' in premises under a warrant of execution. No refreshment was provided for him therefore he went to a pub one mile away taking the warrant with him. His absence was only temporary. On return he was assaulted by Dyke to prevent re-entry. The court found that Coffin was in execution of his duty in re-entering and Dyke could be convicted for assault on a court officer.

- *Walking possession*: the courts have been prepared to treat walking possession, whether by agreement or not, as a form of ongoing constructive possession that survives the bailiffs' absence from the premises, even though that may be prolonged. However in one case where the bailiff withdrew simply on receiving from the debtor a letter (rather than signed agreement) acknowledging the possession and permitting him to re-enter as and when he wished. It was held that the bailiff went out of possession and did not retake it, so that the goods were abandoned (*Bower v Hett* [1895] 2 QB 337). Even where walking possession has been taken, it may be regarded as having been abandoned if the creditor does not take adequate steps to protect and maintain the levy. In *LCP Retail Ltd v Segal* [2006] EWHC 2087, Chancery Division felt that a landlord's failure to protest when impounded goods were sold by the debtor company, and later to notify the liquidator in the company's winding up of the existence of a walking possession agreement, amounted to an abandonment of the claim over the goods.

The walking possession may be either 'oral' or written. The latter is preferable as the possession will be short-lived in the absence of a signed agreement. Nevertheless, an adequately established and maintained 'oral' walking possession will defeat claims of abandonment (*Lloyds & Scottish Finance Ltd v Modern Car & Caravans (Kingston) Ltd* [1966] 2 All ER 732).

- *payment*: there may be no abandonment where there is an arrangement to pay, such as by instalments. If distress is then withdrawn such abandonment at the debtor's request is not voluntary (*Thwaites v Wilding* [1883] 12 QBD 4).

To conclude, whether goods have been abandoned is a question of fact (*Eldridge v Stacey* (1863)15 CB NS 458), and depends on the court deciding whether there has first been impounding and secondly whether there has been an intention to remain in possession (*Jones v Biernstein* [1900] 1 QB 100).

8.4.2 *Ineffective agreements*

To be valid a possession agreement must be in accord with the minimum statutory and common law requirements. If it is not, the bailiff may fail to retain possession and may abandon the goods. There are three main ways in which an agreement may be invalid.

Wrong place & time

A possession agreement must be made at the correct stage in the levy process and in the correct circumstances in order to be valid. Thus the following agreements will be vulnerable to challenge by the debtor:

- posted to the debtor- an agreement must follow a legal entry and levy and that paperwork dropped through the door for signature and return by the debtor is unacceptable and ineffective (*Evans v South Ribble Borough Council* [1992] 2 All ER 695). Evans was an appeal by a community charge payer against the magistrates' court decision dismissing her complaint against bailiffs levying for S. Ribble B.C. The bailiffs attended for £341 arrears and as Evans was out, posted an envelope through her letter box containing a notice of distress, a draft walking possession agreement signed by the bailiff which required her signature and return plus various documents explaining methods of payment, the level of the debt etc. Evans ignored this and instead sought advice, leading to her complaint as to the method of seizure. In his judgment Simon Brown J reviewed the law as described earlier and concluded "once entry is made, little in the way of seizure and impounding is required ... (but) there must in the first instance be an entry" thus "it is my clear conclusion that external inspection and posting through the letter box is a course of action insufficient to bring about the legal consequences of distress".

- It is clear therefore that the mere posting of documents by bailiffs levying distress has no effect whatsoever on the debtor's goods. A person cannot retrospectively make an agreement transferring rights over their property. A 'walking possession' agreement signed by the bailiff alone and posted to the debtor cannot an agreement binding on the debtor. Even if s/he subsequently signs and returns the document, as is usually requested, the debtor does not waive any irregularity in the manner of levy or adopt the agreement. Signing the agreement retrospectively will not estop the debtor from any subsequent objection to its legality. Even if the documents constitute a valid agreement it may be a voidable contract which could be set aside by the court because of fraud or misrepresentation by the bailiff. Even if distress had been successfully levied it would effectively be abandoned by the procedure (see *Dod v Monger* (1704) 6 Mod 215; *Spice v Webb & Morris* (1838) 2 Jur 943). If the agreement is invalid or there has been abandonment, no walking possession fee may be charged and the goods are not effectively seized. The debtor may thus continue to deal with goods as s/he wishes as they are not in the custody of the law and cannot be until the bailiff has at least entered the property.

- Readers should note one case that appears to suggest that 'constructive impounding' after external inspection is a valid levy. This is *United Counties Trust Ltd & Duncombe v Swaffield* (1939) 6 LJCCR 79 - this case is of great interest as it is the only recorded case where a bailiff has successfully impounded by looking through a window. However, the circumstances are significant. Swaffield attended to distrain for rent. He entered through an open window and legally seized furniture in the house. He then entered the garden where a motorbike was locked inside a greenhouse. Swaffield read the number plate through the glass and added it to the inventory. The bike was later sold but Duncombe claimed that there was no effective seizure. It was held that "it is not necessary for the bailiff physically to seize every chattel on which he distrains; constructive seizure is enough and may be effected by taking any chattel on the premises and making clear an intention to seize everything there, or so much as will satisfy the rent. In this case the defendant seized some chattels and made an intention to seize the bike clear by including it on the inventory. The true test therefore seems not to be ... whether the bailiff can physically seize if so minded, but whether he can impound them in the sense that he can prevent the tenant removing or dealing with them." Clearly constructive seizure can be valid following an entry and as part of a more normal impounding, but will not be effective as the only means of taking possession of goods at a property.

- * *local tax & child support* agreements must be made "at the time that distress is levied". If this is not done, there is no valid agreement as defined by the law.

Wrong signature

As seen at 8.3.1 in most forms of distraint and execution any 'responsible person' may sign. If a suitable person cannot or will not sign, no walking possession fee may be charged. However the goods may still be impounded constructively (7.3.2) and the agreement with the 'third party' is evidence of this, provided that it is left on the premises. If the bailiff endeavours to take possession and does so by means of an arrangement that is defective, it still demonstrates an intention to remain in possession and not to abandon the impounded goods. In *Lumsden v Burnett* [1898] 2 QB 177 the claimant's goods were distrained by collector of taxes but the bailiff went out of possession after getting the claimant's thirteen year old daughter to sign the walking possession agreement without authority from her father. However the bailiff did not abandon distress as he returned daily to the property to ensure nothing was removed. The seizure was valid and the agreement (though not binding on L) showed the bailiff's intention not to abandon possession and his return visit showed the goods were not abandoned. However as the possession was "constructive" rather than "real", no charges for a possession man could be made.

However for local taxes only the signature of the person named on the liability order will be acceptable. The signature of a spouse or partner will not do as a substitute. See for example the decision in *H v Sandwell MBC* (1993) Legal Action August p.15. A husband and wife were both in arrears with community charge. The husband signed a walking possession agreement in respect of a levy for his debt. The bailiff later sought to remove goods under this in respect of the wife's debt. A complaint was made to magistrates' court. At the hearing the council conceded that there was no valid walking possession agreement in respect of the wife and the magistrates made an order declaring the attempted levy to be irregular, the walking possession charges unlawful and prohibiting further enforcement against the claimant.

8.4.3 *No written agreement*

If it is not possible to find, or persuade, the debtor or another person to sign, it may still be possible for a bailiff to impound the goods by an oral agreement, though there is no direct authority on this. Charges could not be made for such an arrangement. However, despite the oral agreement being evidence of an intention not to abandon, in the absence of a written agreement as evidence of this impounding, the bailiff's rights will be quite short lived. If steps are not taken to keep the possession in existence, e.g. follow up visits, letters or phone calls , or of course prompt removal, within a relatively short time the bailiff's rights will be lost. The goods are then abandoned and the seizure process will have to be begun again from the start.

If no agreement is made at all, either written or oral, the bailiff can leave notice on the premises that seizure has occurred and this will operate to adequately impound the goods for a brief period. The notice and the debtor's presence during the seizure will be enough for the bailiff to have asserted his legal rights and for the debtor to understand what was intended. However the right to return and remove will be transitory and soon lost unless the levy is quickly followed through by the means described above. Of course, no charges can be made for possession in this situation.

A good example of this sort of procedure is *Lloyds & Scottish Finance Ltd v Modern Car & Caravans (Kingston) Ltd* [1966] 2 All ER 732. The sheriff's officer went to a caravan occupied by the judgment debtor to execute a writ of fi fa. The sheriff gained entry and informed the debtor of his purpose, saying the caravan should not be moved. The debtor refused to sign any walking possession agreement so the sheriff restated the position, left a notice and departed. The sheriff left but did not abandon the goods as he could demonstrate he had returned to the site nine times in one month to check the caravan was still there. Note that the courts have emphasised that possession should be actually, visibly retained wherever possible (i.e. even walking possession might not be enough- see discussion earlier at 8.2.1) but a notice left at the premises may be sufficient if the bailiff cannot remain (*Young v Dencher, Bank of Toronto v Adames, Sheriff of Acadia* [1923] 1 DLR 432).

This case may be contrasted to *Blades v Arundale* (1813) 1 M & S 711 in which a sheriff's officer seized a table by touching it and saying "I take this" but then locked the warrant in the drawer, removed the key and left. The court held that although the seizure was good, the sheriff did not then remain in constructive possession: locking the writ up could not amount to continuance of possession. Readers may also wish to note the judgment of the Divisional Court in *Brown v LB Haringey* (1986) cited by Simon Brown J in *Evans v South Ribble BC* [1992] 2 All ER 695. In this case bailiffs had been allowed to enter to levy for general rates by the appellant's wife. They left a draft walking possession agreement with her. The Court found this agreement to be unsigned and therefore ineffective.

8.4.4 *Conduct of impounding*

A bailiff should not remain in possession an unreasonable period or without the debtor's consent (*Re: Finch* (1891) 65 LT 466, where possession for a period of ten days months was felt more reasonable than five moths). The circumstances of the possession should not be unreasonable (*Griffin v Scott* (1726) 1 Barn KB 3 - eight bailiffs in possession for six days led to an award of damages for trespass).

Where ever goods might be impounded, a definite place must be chosen and must be fit, as the bailiff is responsible for taking care of seized goods and can be sued for any damages caused by the pound's unfitness. The place chosen must not only generally be fit, but must be fit at the particular time in question i.e. it should be checked before hand and regularly during impounding (*Wilder v Speer* (1838) 8 Ad & El 547). If it becomes unfit the distrainor must find an alternative location (*Bignell v Clarke* (1860) 5 H&N 485).

8.4.5 *'Remote levies'*

Individual bailiffs and enforcement agencies now and again devise novel means of levying, primarily as a means of saving time on individual cases. These 'short cut' methods of impounding seldom are effective because, as was outlined in *Evans v South Ribble Borough Council* [1992] 2 All ER 695, a successful levy of household goods requires entry, seizure and impounding. A levy through a window and a posted notice will be wholly ineffective (see 8.4.2). Similarly ineffective will be:

- levies of household goods conducted on a doorstep - the most that might be seized would be personal items from a debtor. The seizure of a watch or ring could be legal, unless it could be argued that the item seized was exempt as basic clothing, wearing apparel in use or, perhaps, valueless (see 9.1).

- levies conducted by signing forms whilst sitting outside the house (or elsewhere) in the bailiff's vehicle;

- levies made at the bailiffs' office - 'walking possession agreements' signed at an office without entry or even visits to premises will be void.

A related practice which has developed is the so-called 'drive-by levy.' A bailiff purports to seize motor vehicles by noting down the registration numbers whilst driving past debtors' premises. Typically, no notice of this is served on the debtor- as the essence of the process is getting through large numbers of cases at speed- and they will be entirely unaware of the fact of a levy. This again falls far short of the established essential elements of a levy and cannot be regarded as valid.

8.4.6 *Clamping*

The use of clamping to immobilise motor vehicles may be encountered in a number of contexts. Clamps may lawfully be applied in exercise of statutory powers:

- to an illegally parked car under Traffic Management Act 2004;
- to a car with no valid vehicle fund licence (tax disc) by agents appointed by Customs & Excise under s32A and Sch 2A Vehicle Excise and Registration Act 1994; and,
- to a car being seized by a bailiff enforcing a fine by means of a clamping order (see 8.4.8).

In the case of distraint no statutory provision exists to confer the power of clamping on the clamper. Given the common law situation outlined in 8.2.2, this suggests that the application of clamps is not a lawful action by bailiffs.

Clamping is a process equivalent to impounding. It is not removal (though it may be preparatory to it). The argument that the costs of immobilising cars could be recovered as a removal expense was rejected in *Culligan v Simkin & Marstons Group* (2008) which confirmed that clamping is part of the act of levying. Of the forms of impounding that have been endorsed by statute, clamping is clearly not close or walking possession, which require the physical presence of an individual to guard the goods. In fact, for private bailiffs, clamping can probably only be justified in distress for rent, as Distress for Rent Act 1737 s.10 overrides the common law rule and makes it lawful to impound "or otherwise secure" goods on the tenant's premises.

Thus. although the right to clamp may be useful - especially if the alternative for the debtor is the expense and inconvenience of removal, and the risk for the bailiff is poundbreach by the debtor removing a highly mobile and valuable asset - this cannot justify the current use of a procedure that lacks Parliamentary sanction. As a result, must be treated as trespass *ab initio* to the debtor's vehicle (see *Welsh v Bell* (1670) 1 Vent 37 and 7.5.2). The act of clamping is initially trespass when wrongful possession of the car is taken, and its continuing immobilisation is a wrongful detention of goods (see 9.27). Faced with such torts, the debtor has four possible remedies. Recaption would be one: self help measures may be employed to release the car. The clamp may be removed by taking 'reasonable' steps, including the use of 'reasonable' force. This should only be done if it can be achieved without any damage to the clamp e.g. letting down the tyre. The criminal cases arose because the drivers failed to take such care and were guilty of criminal damage. One levered off the clamp with a crow bar and dropped it over a twelve foot high parapet (*Stear v Scott* (1984) unreported), the other set about the clamp with a disc cutter (*Lloyd v DPP* (1991) Independent 21/6/91). If, however, the clamp can be freed without marking or injuring the clamp, and if it can be put in a safe place for the bailiff to collect, there seems to be no problem with a self-help remedy. The vehicle has been wrongfully immobilised, and one may properly remove that restriction. It is even possible to use reasonable force to resist a bailiff found in the act of trying to apply a clamp. In either case, as defining 'reasonable force' is difficult and such situations may easily escalate, self help is best avoided (see also 3.4). Other remedies would include suing for wrongful interference (see 9.27), paying the debt and then suing (see 9.32) or replevin (see 9.29).

8.4.7 *Magistrates' court - household goods*

In magistrates' court distraint there is no concept of walking possession. Instead, the Criminal Procedure Rules provide a wholly different procedure for the enforcement agent to follow when impounding household goods - unless the warrant itself directs that a different procedure is used. If the bailiff levies upon household goods, they cannot be removed from the house before the day of the sale without the person's written consent but must instead be impounded upon the premises with a conspicuous mark (Crim PR Part 52.8(11)). It is an offence, punishable by fine, to remove the goods or remove or deface the mark (MCA s78(4)). If other forms of impounding were to be used, they would be wholly ineffective, for the reasons explained in 8.2.2.

8.4.8 *Magistrates' court clamping orders*

Schedule 5 Part 9 paragraphs 38 and 41 of the Courts Act 2003 created a new regime for the collection of fines. Amongst the 'further steps' permitted for the recovery of an unpaid penalty is an order allowing the fitting of an immobilisation device to, and eventual sale of, a motor vehicle. The detail of these clamping orders is contained in the Fines Collection

Regulations 2006 Part 4 - all subsequent references are to these regulations unless otherwise stated.

Before a clamping order can be made the court's fines officer must be satisfied that the defendant has the means to pay and that the value of the car exceeds the fine outstanding plus the likely costs of clamping and sale (reg.16). The order is sent to a clamping contractor along with details of the defaulter's address and vehicle (reg.18).

Vehicles may be clamped in any public place as well as on any private land to which access may be gained without opening or removing any gate, door or other barrier. A right to enter such land is granted by the regulation 19. Vehicles not registered in the defaulter's name, those which display a disabled badge or which appear to be for a disabled person's use and those which are used by a doctor or the emergency services cannot be clamped (reg.20). If the vehicle to be clamped would contravene any traffic or parking regulations if it were left clamped, the contractor can move it to the nearest suitable place and, if that is out of sight of its original position, should leave a prominent notice indicating that the vehicle has been moved and clamped. Regulation 22 requires that a notice should also be put on the clamped vehicle specifying certain prescribed information, such as the details of the order how to arrange release and contact details for the court and contractor. Interference with an immobilised vehicle is an offence (see 3.4).

If the sums due are paid either to the contractor or to the court office, the vehicle should be released- within a maximum of 4 hours if payment is made to the court or contractor's office and within 2 hours if the clamper himself is paid. Part payments go first to the costs of the process. A receipt in prescribed form is issued.

A clamped vehicle must remain in place at least 24 hours. Then, if the fine remains unpaid and if no challenge has been made to the clamping, the clamper must remove the vehicle to secure and suitable premises. Notice of this must be posted to the defaulter (reg.24). The vehicle must be stored for one month from the date of the clamping before it can be sold. Ten days after the clamping the fines officer must apply to the court for a sale order. The defaulter will receive notice and a hearing will take place no earlier than 21 days after the clamping. The court may order sale of the vehicle or may order its release to the defendant (with or without payment of the charges due). If sale is ordered the contractor will be instructed to make the arrangements. On sale the ownership vests in the purchaser and the contractor will arrange registration of the transfer with DVLA. The contractor receives the proceeds, deducts the costs due and passes the balance to the fines officer. After paying the outstanding penalty, any remaining balance is remitted to the defendant within 10 working days with a written statement of account. If all or part of the fine still remains unpaid, other enforcement action may follow (reg.26).

If a vehicle is wrongfully clamped, removed or stored in breach of the regulations a person can seek its release or return. Request should be made to the fines officer (if the breach was in the content or making of the order) or to the contractor (if the manner of execution of the order is challenged). If a request is made to the wrong person, s/he should refer it to their counterpart. A written decision should be supplied within seven working days. If the request is accepted, the vehicle is released without charge. If the request is refused, or if no decision is made within the time scale, the court can be asked to order release. Application should be made within 10 working days of the refusal- though the court may allow more time. The court may order release without charge or may refuse the application (regs 27 & 28). Neither defects in the form of the order, nor its execution, invalidate the immobilisation (see 10.8).

8.4.9 *Permitted interference*

Permitting sale or removal of goods by the debtor may constitute abandonment. In the first case to be considered (*Bagshawes v Deacon* [1898] 2 QB 173) the sheriff seized goods from Bagshawes Bros. but was persuaded to withdraw from possession on learning that the business's goods were to be sold to a limited company. He received part payment and a written promise from Bagshawes to allow him to re-enter. The sale took place and then eight days later the sheriff once more seized the goods but the limited company initiated interpleader (see 9.26). The court held that as the sheriff withdrew to enable the goods in the custody of the law to be sold, without being able to demonstrate any urgent necessity to do this, he had abandoned the goods. Secondly in *Re: Dalton* [1963] Ch 336: a sheriff levied on the stock of a shop and took walking possession but gave limited permission to allow the trader to sell goods as long as they were replaced. The court held that the goods sold under that agreement were abandoned and the value of the execution thus reduced. It went on to make recommendations as to how such levies should be conducted.

However allowing temporary removal need not be abandonment (*Kerby v Harding* (1851) 6 Exch 234). The bailiff permitted a person to take seized goods off the premises for a temporary purpose, with the intention on the part of the bailiff that they should be returned, which was done. It was held that there was no abandonment if the claimant restored goods to the bailiff voluntarily.

8.4.10 *Summary & conclusion*

It will be clear from the foregoing discussion that the current state of the law on impounding is highly unsatisfactory and that, largely as a consequence of this, but partly as a result of bailiffs own failure to follow strict procedures with care, many seizures are potentially invalid. This is normally as a result of failure to impound seized goods adequately. Possession agreements should always be checked and the circumstances in which such agreements were made should always be investigated in detail.

To summarise the basic steps that the bailiff should take - the predicating element is a legal entry to the premises. Once inside little need by done either to seize the goods effectively- or to impound them. There can be a pound whilst the goods remain in situ i.e. walking possession (*Washborn v Black* (1774) 11 East 405); this impounding serves to secure the goods against both the occupier and strangers (*Lavell v O'Leary* [1933] 2 KB 200) and there does not need to be any ongoing real or actual possession (*Jones v Biernstein* [1899] 1 QB 470). However failure to enter, failure to indicate that seizure is intended and the use of procedures too much at variance with established authority will mean that the levy may be invalid.

8.5 Remedies for wrongful seizure

If seizure itself is not rendered illegal by any earlier unlawful act, such as forced entry, it will be the nature of what is seized that makes a levy wrongful. These issues are discussed in the next chapter at Part Four, 9.25 *et seq*. Remedies will arise in respect of the illegal taking of the goods and further may follow if removal or sale occur.

TCEA 2007- commentary

One of the most significant changes being made by the 2007 Act is the welcome simplification of the process of seizure of goods. The unnecessarily complex two part process of seizure and impounding is being replaced by a one stage act of 'taking control of goods.' Taking control of goods will be effected by one of four means under Sch.12 para 13. An enforcement agent may:

• Remove & secure goods;

• Secure on premises;

• Secure on highway (clamp vehicles, presumably); or,

• Make a controlled goods agreement (the future equivalent of walking possession).

It is to be hoped that, by this rationalization of the process, many of the technical errors in levies and cases of abandonment will not longer arise. The simplified procedure for taking control will make matters clearer and more definite for both debtors and bailiffs. The parties will benefit from the greater choice of forms of impounding available. The doubt over the legality of clamping of vehicles is also removed.

Chapter 9

CONDUCTING LEVIES: GOODS

PART ONE - DEBTORS' PROPERTY

9.1 Saleable goods

9.1.1 *Goods with value*

The bailiff can only seize such things "where the valuable property is in somebody" (Coke, 1 Inst 47) and that can be sold (*Francis v Nash* (1734) 95 ER 32). As a consequence items that cannot be sold, such as deeds or personal papers, should not be the subject of a levy. Equally personal effects of minimal worth (and very likely not attractive at public auction, as is the case with much jewellery) should not be taken (see 9.1.3). The sorts of goods typically worth seizing are office furniture, cars, high quality domestic furniture, garden equipment and antique and 'art' items. These will be seized based on a valuation of their sale price at auction. Only enough to cover the execution can be seized (*Pitcher v King* (1844) 5 QB 758). However, it is difficult to sell many second hand goods by auction because of controls, such as Consumer Protection Act 1987, over the electrical safety of audio visual and white goods, the fireproofing of furniture and safety of children's items. The effect of this is that it may often not really be worth removing any items from the average home.

9.1.2 *Equitable interests*

As they cannot be sold, equitable interests should not be seized (*Scarlett v Hanson* [1883] 12 QBD 213; *Miller v Solomon* [1906] 2 KB 91). In *Schott v Scholey* (1807) 8 East 467, the court reasoned that whilst a legal interest in property such as a lease could be seized and sold, the same could not apply to equitable interest through simple practical considerations of inconvenience - for example the difficulty of valuation and the impossibility of delivery of possession (In *Re: Duke of Newcastle* [1869] 8 Eq 700). Although the court in Schott did question if the case might be different for equitable interests in goods rather than land, the case law is that any equitable interests, whether under an equitable mortgage (*Re: Lusty* (1889) 60 LT 160), under a bill of sale (*Holroyd v Marshall* (1862) 10 HL Cas 191) or otherwise are protected from seizure and may be protected by interpleader etc. Older practice was to grant an order to the sheriff allowing seizure of an equitable interest or to validate a prior seizure, for example from a trustee (*Pit v Hunt* (1681) 2 Cas in Ch 73). The High Court may therefore still have the power to grant leave to seize such property (see also *Horsley v Cox* [1869] 4 Ch App 92).

9.1.3 *No valuable goods*

It has been a long accepted aspect of bailiffs' practice that, in some cases, insufficient goods will be found on the premises to justify a levy. In such cases the instruction is returned to the creditor with the report that there were "no goods" (*Dennis v Whetham* [1874] 9 QB 345). This is explicitly referred to on cases of execution for road traffic penalties. In CPR Part 75.1(2)(b) and Part 75.10 to use any of the alternative means of enforcement available in the county court, the authority needs to confirm that execution was tried but failed. The authority must certify that 'no relevant return' was made to warrant- for example because the goods seized were insufficient to cover the sums due or that the goods were insufficient to cover the costs of removal and sale.

The willingness of bailiffs to admit that there is nothing worth seizing seems to have declined in the last decade. It is not infrequent to encounter levies where only a few goods of little or no value are listed on the inventory- or where exempt goods pad the list out. Sometimes these are backed up by 'catch-all' phrases in the inventory (see 10.2.2) and may be justified as 'two tier levies.' Inventories should always be checked and challenged where appropriate.

9.2 Financial assets

9.2.1 *Money*

Bailiffs are granted the power by statute to seize money, in the sense of cash, in the following cases - execution on judgments and for road traffic penalties, and distraint for child support maintenance, magistrates' courts orders and for income tax (*E India Co v Skinner* (1695) 1 Botts PL 259). Note that case law suggests that this power may exist for local taxes as well (*Hardistey v Barney* (1696) Conb 356). In the case of distress for rent loose money cannot be taken- that is, money not in a wallet, purse or other container (*Wilson v Ducket* (1675) 2 MR 61). This is because, as distress was originally held only a security for the debt and had to be returnable in the same condition, any cash seized had to be distinguishable from the seizor's own. In other cases the money is of course simply paid over to the creditor.

The sums seizable must be in the debtor's actual possession, but this will include the daily takings of a business (see 8.3.1 earlier) and bank notes on a bank counter being paid out to a customer (*Hall v Hatch* [1901] 3 OLR 147). Thus proceeds of sale of a property held by a third party cannot be taken (*Robinson v Peace* (1838) 7 Dowl 93), nor can sums paid into court for the debtor (*France v Campbell* (1841) 9 Dowl 914) or cheques written out by HMPG but not yet issued to the debtor (*Courtoy v Vincent* (1852) 15 Beav 486), proceeds of sale held by the HCEO or county court bailiff for the debtor (*Padfield v Birne* (1822) 3 Brod & Bing 294) nor money held by an agent of the debtor (*Bell v Hutchinson* (1844) 8 Jur 895; *Re: Fort Frances Pulp & Paper Co v Telegram Printing Co* [1923] 4 DLR 204). As any goods seized do not become the judgment creditor's, neither does this happen to money seized, so a bailiff holding money taken in execution cannot in turn set that against a judgment debt of the execution creditor (*Collingridge v Paxton* (1851) 11 CB 683). If the HCEO is holding proceeds of sale for a judgment creditor, if he has appropriated and set apart sums to pay over to that creditor, they may be seized under a writ issued against that party (*Wood v Wood* (1843) 4 A&E 397).

9.2.2 *Bills of exchange etc.*

Some provisions also allow bailiffs to seize bills of exchange, promissory notes, specialties, bonds, cheques and other financial securities. Such instruments may be seized in execution and by the CSA. In road traffic distraint bills can be seized (art 9) but promissory notes, bonds, specialties and securities cannot (art 9(b)).

Bills of exchange and the like partake of the nature of money, but have the character of chattels and choses in action as well. It is as chattels that they may be seized by bailiffs. It is as choses in action that they may be converted in to the proceeds of execution. At common law negotiable instruments and cash were not seizable, and it is only by statute that this situation has been changed. This was done originally for HCEOs by means of s12 Judgments Act 1838. This section provides a model for the later civil court provisions (e.g. s91 CCA) and, it is suggested, for the procedure to be followed by other bailiffs in this position.

The instruments (or sufficient as are necessary to cover the judgment debt) may be seized and held as security by the bailiff. When the time for payment on the bill, bond etc arrives, the bailiff may sue upon it in his/ her name to recover the sums due (and may even issue execution upon such a judgment). The sums raised are paid over to the original creditor. Any surplus after the expenses of the execution shall be returned to the debtor. Note however that the HCEO is not bound to sue on the instruments unless indemnified for all the costs of the action by the execution creditor.

9.2.3 *Other assets*

A life assurance policy has been held not to be security for money and thus not seizable (*Re: Sargent's Trusts* [1879] 7 LR Ir 66), nor is any money payable under it (*Re: New York Life Assurance Association & Fullerton* [1919] 45 OLR 606). The common law principle that choses in action cannot be taken in execution has not been altered by statute other than in respect of bills of exchange (*Dundas v Dutens* (1790) 1 Ves Jnr 196) so it seems that it is not possible to seize the debtor's debts (e.g. *Willows v Ball* (1806) 2 Bos & Pull 376), stocks and shares (*Dundas v Dutens* above; *Taylor v Jones* (1734) 2 Atk 600; *Nantes v Corrock* (1802) 9 Ves 177), dividends (*Evans v Stephen* [1882] 3 NSWLR 154), patents (see *Brown v Cooper* [1870] 1 VR(L) 210; *British Mutoscope & Biograph Co Ltd v Homer* [1901] 1 Ch 671) or trade marks and copyright (*Re: Baldwin* (1858) 2 De G & J 230). Goods held on pawn by the debtor cannot be seized, but the debtor's interest in them can. The bailiff may then receive monies paid to redeem pledges or sell the pawned items when the time for redemption is passed (*Squire v Huetson* (1841) 1 QB 308; *Re: Rollason* [1887] 34 Ch D 495).

9.3 Jointly owned goods

Only those goods belonging to the debtor may be taken (*Glasspoole v Young* (1829) 9 B & C 696). This means that jointly owned goods may also be seized (*Farrar v Beswick* (1836) 1 M&W 682) though the proceeds must be divided between the owners according to their shares (*The James W Elwell* [1921] P 351). Most regulations for statutory distraint refer to seizure of the "goods of the debtor" so that it is possible that jointly owned goods cannot be seized in such cases.

9.4 Chattels

In income tax and VAT distraint and in execution the bailiff may seize not only goods but chattels (for tax see *Earl of Shaftesbury v Russell* (1823) 1 B&C 666). Chattels can include more than just tangible property and covers leases (but not interests in leases - *Scott v Scholey* (1807) 8 East 467) and rights under contracts. Where this wording is found in the relevant legislation the bailiff may seize the debtor's interest in such as goods on hire or hire purchase (see later). Most regulations for statutory distraint refer only to the "goods of the debtor" so such property may not be taken.

9.5 Fixtures

The case law on fixtures differentiates between execution and distress for rent. For the latter see 9.23. This section will describe the rules for execution and assume that these are likely to also apply to statutory distraint.

9.5.1 *Basic rules*

The basic principle is that as execution cannot be levied on real property, fixtures which are attached to the property have ceased to be chattels and as a result cannot be taken (*Hulme v Brigham* [1943] 1 KB 152). In *Boyd v Shorrock* [1867] 5 Eq 72 the definition given in ex p Barclay (1855) 5 DM & G 410 was quoted with approval - fixtures are "things ordinarily affixed to the freehold for the convenience of the occupier, and which may be removed without material injury to the freehold", for example machinery and cupboards. Chattels actually built into the structure of a property become part of it, such as doors, windows, hearths and chimney pieces (*Boswell v Crucible Steel Co* [1925] 1 KB 119).

Help may also be derived from the definition found in *Hellawell v Eastwood* (1851) 6 Exch 295. Whether an item is a fixture is a question of fact. The court must firstly consider the mode of annexation and the extent of annexation- whether an item can be removed easily, safely and without damage to itself or the building; secondly the court must examine the object and purpose of the annexation and the intention of the person fixing them- whether it was for the permanent and substantial improvement of the property or for a temporary purpose. These elements may be examined in detail:

- *degree of annexation*: articles simply resting on the ground by their own weight are not normally regarded as fixtures. This is so even though the ground may be specially prepared to receive them or though a base is built (see *Re: Richards ex p Astbury & Lloyds Banking Co* [1869] 4 Ch App 630 later) and even though they may sink into the ground by their own weight (*Wood v Hewett* (1846) 8 QB 913). If an item can be removed without great damage, even though they may be well attached and the process of removal may involve digging, it is not a fixture (*Provincial Bill Posting Co v Low Moor Iron Co* [1909] 2 KB 344). Items screwed, bolted or nailed down are generally fixtures, but the purpose can be a very important factor. Consequently even if the chattel is cemented it will not be a fixture if the purpose is not permanent (*Elitestone v Morris* [1997] 1 WLR 687). The importance of degree as a factor will vary also with the size of the item in question, so that a house, though not fixed, will probably be a fixture. Unfixed articles essential for the use of the property may be treated as fixtures, such as keys (*Liford's*

Case (1614) 11 Co Rep 46b; *Hellawell v Eastwood* (1851) 6 Exch 295). Items simply plugged into a power supply aren't fixtures (*Vaudeville Electric Cinema Ltd v Muriset* [1923] 2 Ch 72) but light fittings wired in probably are (*Gray v Fuller* [1943] KB 694; *Young v Dalgety* [1987] 1 EGLR 117).

• *purpose of annexation*: increasingly in modern cases degree has been replaced by purpose as the important factor in determining the nature of a chattel (*Berkley v Poulett* [1976] 241 EG 911). If the purpose of the annexation of a chattel is its better enjoyment as a chattel, it is not a fixture. An item affixed for permanent improvement of a property is a fixture (*Walmsley v Milne* (1859) 7 CBNS 115). Thus items such as paintings, tapestries and antique panels are not fixtures, but a wall, though simply resting by its own weight, is a fixture if the intention is to make it part of the realty (*Holland v Hodgson* [1872] 7 CP 328). The purpose of annexation is to be ascertained not from the motives of the person fixing the chattels but from the circumstances of the case (*Re: De Falbe* [1901] 1 Ch 523). The circumstances can include current tastes and fashions as well as the property interest of the person (*Leigh v Taylor* [1902] AC 157). Direct evidence of intention is inadmissible, instead the court's test should be objective.

This analysis was adopted in the modern case *TSB ex p Botham* [1996] EGCS 149 in which the Court of Appeal repeated that the two main factors to be considered when determining whether items were fixtures were method and degree of annexation, and object and purpose of annexation. On this basis it was concluded that fitted carpets, curtains, gas fires and white goods are not fixtures, whilst, on the facts of the case in question, light fittings, bathroom fittings and fitted kitchen units had become fixtures. The existence of a hire purchase agreement in respect of a chattel, or an agreement that it will not become a fixture, does not prevent it becoming one.

We may therefore identify the following as classes of fixtures:

• *barns, sheds & greenhouses*: these are not fixtures even if they are bolted down (*Billing v Pill* [1954] 1 QB 70). A conservatory however will be a fixture;

• *machines*: engines and parts fitted to them are fixtures. Looms nailed to the floor are affixed (*Boyd v Shorrock* [1867] 5 Eq 72) as are beer machines in a pub (*Dalton v Whittem* (1842) 3 QB 961), but a printing machine simply standing on a floor remains a chattel (*Hulme v Brigham* [1943] KB 152). Freestanding equipment does not become a fixture solely because another machine supplying power to it is affixed (*Hulme v Brigham*);

- *other business equipment*: fixtures may include stills set in brickwork, fixed ladders, swimming pool equipment, an alarm and video door entry system and a lift (*Melluish v BMI (No 3)* [1994] 2 WLR 795); a cinema screen fixed to a wall, advertising boards and tip up seats fixed to the floor, all equipping a cinema (*Vaudeville Electric Cinema Ltd v Muriset* [1923] 2 Ch 72); millstones (*Wystow's Case* (1523) YB 14 Hen VIII fo 25 pl 6); a skating rink floor especially installed by the tenant (*Howell v Listowel Rink & Park Co* [1886] 13 OR 476); items, such as an emulsifier, cream separator and ice chopper used in a dairy ice cream business (*Assiniboia Land Co v Acres* [1915] 25 DLR 439); an inn signboard (*Re: Thomas* (1881) 44 LT 781); post office fittings such as lockable letter boxes (*Bruce v Smith* [1923] 3 DLR 887), and railway tracks (*Turner v Cameron* [1876] 5 QB 306). By contrast chairs lent on hire for a limited period but screwed to the floor for safety reasons (*Lyon & Co v London City & Midland Bank* [1903] 2 KB 135), a machine fixed by brickwork to a factory floor (*Parsons v Hind* (1866) 13 WR 860) and a railway laid on piles (*Chamberlayne v Collins* (1894) 70 LT 217) are not fixtures. Nor are horses, and by extension motor vehicles, used by a firm off their premises (*London & Eastern Counties Loan & Discount Co v Creasey* [1897] 1 QB 768).

- *fuel meters and fittings* are fixtures (*Lee v Gaskell* [1876] 1 QBD 700); light bulbs are not (*British Economical Lamp Co v Empire, Mile End* (1913) 29 TLR 386);

- *shop fittings*: a counter and rack lightly screwed to a wall are not fixtures (*Horwich v Symond* (1915) 84 LJKB 1083);

- *domestic fittings*: kitchen units are fixtures, but appliances within them such as fridges and gas cookers are not (*Allan v Lavine* [1942] 1 DLR 731). However items such as ranges and ovens are fixtures (*Winn v Ingilby* (1822) 5 B & Ald 625). Bathroom fittings in a fitted bathroom are fixtures (see *TSB v Botham* above) as are fitted wardrobes and cupboards, mirrors, shelves and towel rails (*Gray v Fuller* [1943] 1 KB 694). The same case also indicates that parquet floors and linoleum or vinyl flooring are also likely to be treated as fixtures.

In summary items simply resting on the premises or lightly attached are unlikely to be fixtures but once an item is a fixture, any other article which is an integral part of it also becomes annexed, even if not attached to the fixed item (such as the drive belt on a machine) and the whole assemblage then remains a fixture permanently and can't be seized in distress or execution. A bailiff can be sued for trespass to land for removing fixtures (*Moore v*

Drinkwater (1858) 1 F&F 134), but mere constructive seizure without severance or removal is not enough to found an action (*Beck v Denbigh* (1860) 29 LJCP 373).

9.5.2 *Other examples*

The above examples can be supplemented by case law looking at various situations in which claims are made to property affixed to the freehold by the owner- for example, between mortgagor and mortgagee or tenant for life and remainderman (*In Re: Sir Edward Hulse* [1905] 1 Ch 406).

The principle in mortgage case law is that items annexed by the mortgagor pass as fixtures with the freehold to the mortgagee (see for example *Meux v Jacobs* [1875] 7 App Cas 481; *In Re: Yates* [1888] 38 Ch D 112; *Gough v Wood* [1894] 1 QB 713). This seems to apply even when partnership property is annexed to the premises of one partner (*Sanders v Davis* [1885] 15 QBD 218). Thus from mortgage cases we gather that if machines are fixtures which pass automatically with the land, so is every part of them, such as drive belts (*Sheffield & South Yorkshire Permanent Benefit Building Society v Harrison* [1885] 15 QBD 338); that the degree of annexation is an important factor to consider- so even an item on HP secured by bolts to prevent rocking ceases to be a chattel and becomes a fixture (*Hobson v Gorringe* [1897] 1 Ch 182); that even if fixtures are intended only as temporary improvement, they can still become part of the land but the onus of arguing this lies with the person seeking to protect them (*Holland v Hodgson* [1872] 7 CP 328); that items set into, but not attached to property, are not fixtures- nor are spares for machines that are not actually attached to them (*In Re: Richards ex p Astbury & Lloyds Banking Co* [1869] 4 Ch App 630); that all machinery affixed in a 'quasi-permanent' manner becomes part of the property (i.e. the items are intended to remain on the premises for their better use and enjoyment), even though the purpose of annexation was steadying the items and that they could be removed without injury to them or to the freehold (*Longbottom v Berry* [1869] 5 QB 123); and that even if goods are simply annexed for their more convenient use, not to improve the property, and may be removed without any appreciable damage to the freehold, they are fixtures (*Climie v Wood* [1868] 3 Exch 257- in this case an engine screwed to thick planks laid on the ground and set in brickwork).

Note that items do not need to be separately mentioned to pass as fixtures with a mortgage (see *Re: Yates* above). If they are separately described, it will not make the mortgage a bill of sale (*Re: Armytage* [1880] 14 Ch D 379), nor will the right of a mortgagee of a leasehold to remove fixtures as against the lessor - for which see below (*In Re: Rogerstone Brick & Stone Co Ltd* [1919] 1 Ch 110). However if the mortgage allows the mortgagee to sever and sell fixtures apart from the land, it is a bill of sale - for which see 3.7.3 (*Small v National Provincial Bank of England* [1894] 1 Ch 686).

The above rules are complicated by the further principle that, in execution against a tenant, whatever the tenant could sever, as between landlord and tenant, can be seized by the bailiff (*Day v Bisbitch* (1595) 78 ER 622; *Pooles Case* (1703) 1 Salk 368). Therefore, having determined that an item is a fixture, in some cases it will be necessary to move onto consideration of the separate issue of whether it is a fixture removable by a tenant.

9.5.3 *Tenant's fixtures*

Generally tenants are permitted to remove those chattels that they have affixed for the purposes of trade, and those put up for ornament or domestic use, and which are physically capable of removal without substantial damage to the land or to the chattel (*Webb v Frank Bevis* [1940] 1 All ER 247). All such items may be seized in execution (*Dumergue v Rumsey* (1863) 2 H&C 777). However these rights may be modified by the lease, in which case the HCEO cannot remove if the tenant cannot (*Duke of Beaufort v Bates* (1862) 6 LT 82). The rules on tenant's fixtures apply to licencees just as much as tenants (*Never Stop (Railway) Ltd v British Empire Exhibition* (1924) Inc [1926] Ch 877). The authorities on landlord and tenant fixtures give a contrasting picture of what can be removed from premises, but the case law may be summarised as follows. Trade fixtures include:

- *business equipment* such as machines, plant, vats and utensils (*Whitehead v Bennett* (1858) 27 LJ Ch 474) but not chemical plant; engines for collieries (*Lord Dudley v Lord Ward* (1751) Amb 113); petrol pumps- though bolted down and linked to underground petrol tanks (*Smith v City Petroleum* [1940] 1 All ER 260); pub fittings (*Elliott v Bishop* (1854) 10 Exch 496); brewing equipment (*Lawton v Lawton* (1743) Atk 13);

- *small buildings* such as sheds built on brickwork in the ground (*Penton v Robert* (1801) 2 East 88), glasshouses in a market garden (*Mears v Callender* [1901] 2 Ch 388) and pre-fabricated buildings;

- *electrical & gas fittings* including fluorescent light boxes screwed to a ceiling (*Young v Dalgety, Elliott v Bishop* earlier);

- *shrubs & trees* which are the stock of a market garden (*Mears v Callender* [1901] 2 Ch 388), but not fruit bearing trees in an orchard or trees which would be destroyed by removal.

The purpose of this right of removal is the protection of trade. Accordingly it has been held that locks, keys, bolts and bars to secure premises are not fixtures that can be taken by a tenant.

There is also a right to remove fixtures installed for ornamental purposes or for the domestic convenience and utility of the tenant. In determining whether the fixture is removable a number of considerations should be taken into account. Has the method of fixing made it permanent, as a more secure method of annexation may indicate that purpose of affixing was improvement of the premises? Would the chattel still be usable after removal? Would removal do serious damage to the structure of the property, rather than just the decoration? Ornamental items should be specifically ornamental and not an ordinary accessory of the property. Thus a conservatory was not a removable fixture (*Buckland v Butterfield* (1820) 2 Brod & B 58). This class of fixtures includes such items as: panelling, suspended ceilings and chimney pieces installed by a tenant in a flat (*Spyer v Phillipson* [1930] 2 Ch 183); bookcases and ornamental fireplaces (*Bishop v Elliot* [1885] 11 Exch 113); pictures and frames screwed to walls (*Buckingham v Pembroke* (1672) 3 Keb 74; blinds (*Colegrave v Dias Santos* (1823) 2 B&C 76); cupboards (*R v St Dunstan (Inhabitants)* (1825) 4 B&C 686; *Re: Gawan ex p Barclay* (1855) 5 De G M & G 403); bookshelves (*Birch v Dawson* (1834) 2 A&E 37); cornices, wainscotting and stoves, ranges ovens and boilers (*Grymes v Boweren* (1830) 6 Bing 437).

The HCEO may also seize any interest that the tenant has in fixtures which are included in the lease. All fixtures removeable by a tenant may be taken, whatever their description (*Place v Flagg* (1821) 4 M&R 277) unless they are simply too unwieldy to remove. Upon seizure fixtures should be separated from the rented property and sold (*Barnard v Leigh* (1815) 1 Stark 43).

The HCEO cannot seize fixtures unlawfully severed by the tenant (*Farrant v Thompson* (1822) 5 B&Ald 826). A tenant's right to remove items as against the landlord ceases on termination of the lease (*Pugh v Arton* [1869] 8 Eq 626) and on disclaimer by the tenant's trustee in bankruptcy (*In Re: Lavies ex p Stephens* [1877] 7 ChD 127; *In Re: Roberts ex p Brook* [1878] 10 ChD 100)- though it has been held that the tenant (and his/ her trustee) has a reasonable time to remove after termination (*In Re: Moser* [1884] 13 QBD 738). At the time of termination of the lease, property in the tenant's fixtures vests in the landlord (*In Re: Maryport Haematite Iron & Steel Co Ltd* [1892] 1 Ch 415). The tenant may still remove fixtures if s/he is holding over at the end of the term (*Weeton v Woodcock* (1840) 7 M&W 14).

Remember that these categories are only of relevance to execution. In distress tenant's fixtures, and fixtures in general at common law, cannot be seized (*Darby v Harris* (1841) 1 QB 895).

9.5.4 *Agricultural fixtures*

One class of tenant's fixtures requires separate consideration; that of chattels affixed to premises by tenants of agricultural holdings. At common law such fixtures were not removeable, but statute has intervened to alter this, with the consequence that these items will be seizable in execution. Two statutory codes apply, depending on the nature of the tenancy.

If the tenancy is of an agricultural holding regulated by Agricultural Holdings Act 1986, the rights of tenants to remove fixtures are controlled by s10. The basic rule is that a tenant farmer may remove:

- any engine, machinery, fencing, or other fixture of any description fixed to the holding by the tenant, whether for agricultural purposes or not; and,
- any building erected by him on the holding (s10(1)).

These rights apply to any fixture or building acquired by the tenant as well as erected by him/ her (s10(7)), but do not apply to any buildings or fixtures put in place as a result of an obligation; any fixture or building replacing one belonging to the landlord; a building in respect of which the tenant is entitled to compensation under the Act or a building or fixture dating to before 1884 (s10(2)). The tenant's common law right to remove trade or ornamental fixtures is unaffected (s10(8)).

If the tenancy is a farm business tenancy regulated by Agricultural Tenancies Act 1995, the Act provides a complete code relating to all tenant farmers' fixtures (s8). The basic right to remove applies to:

- any fixture of whatever description affixed to the holding by the tenant, whether for agricultural purposes or not; and,
- any building erected by him on the holding (s8(1)).

As under the 1986 Act these rights to remove do not apply to certain fixtures - specifically any buildings or fixtures put in place as a result of an obligation; any fixture or building replacing one belonging to the landlord; a building in respect of which the tenant is entitled to compensation under the Act or a building or fixture to which the landlord gave consent on the condition that it was not removed by the tenant (s8(2)). These provisions apply to any buildings or fixtures acquired by the tenant as they apply to items fixed by him/ her (s8(5)). Tenants of farm business tenancies are deprived of their common law rights regarding fixtures (s8(7)).

There is also a common law right for tenants of agricultural properties to remove certain items which may at first glance appear to be fixed buildings. These are Dutch barns (*Dean v Allalley* (1799) 3 Esp 11); barns resting on the soil (*Culling v Tufnal* (1694) Bull NP (5th Edn) 34; *Wansborough v Maton* (1836) 4 A&E 884) and barns resting on staddles (*Wiltshear v Cottrell* (1853) 1 E&B 674). These structures are not regarded as fixtures as normally soil is not displaced in their erection, nor is there any cementing or fastening of them to existing structures in the soil. Readers should however note that the Court of Appeal felt it could derive little assistance from these cases because of their age in determining *Elitestone v Morris* [1997] 1 WLR 687.

9.6 Statutory exemptions

Since the early 1990s Parliament has deliberately extended the protection given to basic tools and household items. The statutory exemptions are:

- "such tools, books, vehicles and other items of equipment as are necessary for use personally in business, employment or vocation". Attempts to limit this exemption to tools only capable of being carried by the debtor are incorrect. However in the unreported Court of Appeal decision in *Sheriff of Bedford & Toseland Building Supplies Ltd v Bishop* (1993) it was held that if a tool was occasionally used by another, it was not protected; and,

- "such clothing, bedding, furniture, household equipment and provisions as are necessary for satisfying the basic domestic needs of the person and family". It may be difficult to argue that personal jewellery or watches are protected as basic items of clothing.

These exclusions are both phrased very broadly. Naturally there have been various attempts to define what is meant. Lord Chancellor's Department has provided guidance on these categories for county court bailiffs. For example it is suggested that:

- tools will only be protected if they are so essential that without them there is no way that the debtor's present business or job could continue. It has been held under the bankruptcy legislation that this protection was intended for the tools of a workman's trade so that he might not be prevented from earning a living, and does not extend to items that are not implements, such as documents, patents, address books and references (*Re: Sherman* (1915) 32 TLR 231). Nevertheless, the exemption of tools was extended to record books and ledgers in *Gauntlett v King* (1857) 3 CBNS 59). Some commentators have doubted this decision. The case is an appeal which proceeds on the basis that the exemption was accepted by the parties and by the earlier judge and jury- an assumption that is questioned but not overturned in the judgment. The exemption of tools also extends to materials (Co Litt 47). It has been held that a trader's stock includes the safe, cash register and counter of the business, so that these items are not exempt from seizure (*Endrizzi v Peto & Beckley* [1917] 1 WWR 1439). In *Burns v Christianson* [1921] 60 DLR 173, tools where defined as being such items as the instruments used by a carpenter, mason or blacksmith. Tools of the trade do not include samples held by a commercial traveller or representative (*Addison v Shepherd* [1908] 2 KB 118). Having these is helpful to the individual but not essential to their business, so they are not exempt.

- motor vehicles will only be treated as a necessity in exceptional cases. Either the vehicle will be needed to continue a job or business or to get to work, and there will be no reasonable alternative; and,

- household necessities are not likely to include stereos, televisions, videos and microwaves. A fridge has been held to be household furniture (*Canadian National Railways v Norwegian* [1971] 1 WWR 766).

The key aspect of the statutory exemptions is that their definition will be subjective and will depend upon the circumstances of each individual debtor. The broad worded exemptions enable many particular needs to be accommodated and it will be necessary for the bailiff to assess each case- and for advisers to do likewise.

Note also that the statutory exemptions are modified in three cases:

- under NNDR distraint the only goods protected are basic household items, not tools of the trade (reg 14(1A));

- under CSA distraint it is provided that the goods needed to satisfy the basic domestic needs of the debtor include those needed by any member of the family with whom s/he resides (s35(4) CSA). This unique provision presumably is intended to protect any new spouse and children the liable person may have; and,

- in fines distraint, the exemption for motor vehicles applies but not the exemption for basic household goods- for which see next paragraph (Crim PR Part 52.8(6))

The standard exemptions do not apply in the following cases:

- *magistrates' court distraint* (household goods). Under Crim PR Part 52.8(2) the bailiff may seize the money or goods of the named person, but is required by Part 52.8(6) to leave bedding and clothing of the person and family. The term beds may be construed to include bedclothes as well as the bed frame (*Davies v Harris* [1900] 1 QB 729).

- *income tax distraint* All goods and chattels may be seized, including tools of the trade (*Macgregor v Clamp & Son* [1914] 1 KB 258). The claimant in this case tried to extend the distress for rent exemptions under LDAA 1888 to a distraint for tax. The court rejected this partly because common law rules don't apply to statutory distraint (see chapter 2) and partly because the rights of the crown are unaffected by statute unless expressly provided. See also *Swann v Sloan* (1895) 29 ILT 109: in an action against a poor rate collector for seizing a plough horse HHJ Fitzgibbon stated that "the contention that distress [for rates] is analogous to distress for rent is not correct: the rule of law which exempts instruments of husbandry from distress for rent does not extend to cases where the distress is given in the nature of an execution by a particular statute"; and,

- *VAT distraint* All 'goods and chattels' that belong to the debtor may be seized except those exempted by reg 6 and Sch 1 of the Distress for Customs & Excise Duties Regulations 1997. These apply to any of the following which are located in the home at which distraint is levied and which are reasonably required to meet the domestic needs of any person living there. The exempt goods are beds and bedding; household linen; chairs and settees; tables; food; lights and light fittings; heating appliances; curtains; floor coverings; furniture, equipment and utensils used for cooking, storing and eating food; refrigerators; articles for cleaning, pressing and mending clothes; articles for cleaning the home; furniture used for the storing clothing, bedding or household linen, cleaning articles or utensils for cooking and eating food; articles used for safety in the home; toys for the use of any child in the household and medical aids and equipment. On business premises the exempt goods are fire fighting equipment for use on those premises and medical aids and equipment for use there.

Another approach to the problem of definition has been through codes of practice which often list specific exempt items. The problem with any of these is that they can come to be seen as definitive lists. In fact each case must be decided on its individual facts and merits. The bailiff will have, at each levy, to exercise discretion in weighing up the interests of the debtor and family and the creditor for whom they are enforcing.

The previous statutory exemptions were based partly on the value of the protected goods. This no longer applies and there is no reason why assets of considerable value might not be protected by the above categories. See for example *Brookes v Harris* (1995) Times April 22nd in which the defendant successfully argued that, as a presenter of musical programmes on television and radio, his collection of records, cassettes and compact discs was exempt from seizure because it was a tool of his trade. The High Court accepted this, irrespective of the fact that the total collection was valued by the defendant at between £10,000 and £20,000.

In the High Court if a dispute arises as to whether goods fall within the exempt categories under para.9(3), Sch.7 of the Courts Act 2003, the HCEO may apply for directions from the Court by way of interpleader (see CPR Sch.1 RSC O.17 r.2A & 9.24). The procedure is for the debtor to give written notice of the claim that the goods are exempt within five days of their seizure. The HCEO must then serve notice of this claim on the execution creditor, who has seven days to accept or dispute the exemption. If the creditor does not respond or admits that the items are exempt, the HCEO withdraws from possession. If the claim of exemption is disputed, the HCEO seeks directions from the High Court and may also apply for an order protecting himself from any action. The Court will normally hear and determine the claims summarily. In the county court in the event of any dispute the matter is referred to the bailiff manager and ultimately a district judge's directions could be sought. The High Court provisions not apply to the county court, or to road traffic execution, but under s76 CCA and CPR Sch.2 CCR O.1 r.6 the county court could adopt similar procedures to resolve such disputes.

It would seem reasonable to insist that any claim to exemption should be made within a reasonable time of seizure, and certainly before sale takes place. Otherwise the exemption will be presumed to have been waived (*Pilling v Stewart* [1895] 4 BCR 94; *Roy v Fortin* [1915] 26 DLR 18 - in which a delay of several months before making a claim was held too long). It is probable that only the debtor can make such a claim for exemption (*Young v Short* [1883] 3 Man LR 302).

9.7 Personal items

Wearing apparel in use, in the sense of clothing, may not be seized (*Wolfe v Summers* (1811) 2 Camp 631; *Sunbolf v Alford* (1838) 3 M & W 248). Whether this exemption extends to items such as jewellery and watches is unknown. Nevertheless the courts may be prepared to extend these authorities as their primary purpose was not to protect specified items but to avoid levies which would almost necessitate an assault and breach of the peace in order to obtain them. However if the clothes have been removed, for instance in getting ready for bed (*Bissett v Caldwell* (1791) 1 Esp 206) or for the purpose of washing them (*Baynes v Smith* (1794) 1 Esp 206), they may be seized.

9.8 Assets of deceased debtors & their personal representatives

If the debtor dies a number of extra rights and liabilities come into effect. In execution if the debtor dies after the judgment, but before issue of a writ or warrant, leave of court is needed to issue (see 6.3 earlier). If the judgment debtor dies after the writ is issued the bailiff may proceed and seize the debtor's goods, whoever may be holding them. Goods of a testator in the hands of an executor or administrator can be taken in execution against that person as executor/ administrator. Presumably something similar to the latter principle will apply to statutory distraint. Note that money belonging to the late debtor is not bound by the writ (see 6.1.3) and therefore can't be seized in execution against the judgment debtor who dies pending the levy (*Johnson v Pickering* [1908] 1 KB 1).

9.8.1 *Trustees*

Execution against a trustee cannot be levied on the trust estate (*Duncan v Cashin* [1875] 1 CP 554). Note also that in this case the settlee had replaced some of the items left in trust for her by her father. It was suggested that these were bought by her with her own money as agent for the trustees and also could not be seized. The same rules will no doubt apply in statutory distraint. If a trustee runs up debts whilst administering the business of the assignor, the trust property cannot be seized (*Jennings v Mather* [1901] 1 QB 108). However the trustee has a right and interest in the goods and has a right of indemnity in the nature of as lien. A creditor of the trustee can in turn demand an indemnity for trade debts out of the business estate held on trust (*Re: Johnson* [1880] 15 Ch D 604).

9.8.2 *Personal Representatives*

Where execution is levied against a debtor acting as personal representative for a deceased third party, the bailiff cannot seize the deceased's goods in the debtor's hands (*Farr v Newman* (1792) 4 TR 621; *In Re: Morgan* [1881] 18 ChD 93). In the latter case, the fact that the executor carried on the deceased's business as his own was held not to entitle the judgment creditor to seize the deceased's assets. However, it was stressed that lapse of time and enjoyment of assets in a manner inconsistent with the trusts in the will, coupled with the consent of the beneficiaries, may raise an inference of a gift of assets to the executor by them, thus entitling the judgment creditor to seize them. If the business is carried on in line with trusts in the will, the lapse of time will not be relevant (*Ray v Ray* (1813) Coop 264). If the business is continued for the benefit of the estate, but debts are accrued, it appears that creditors of the business may enforce against the assets of the estate (*Moseley v Rendell* [1871] 6 QB 338; *Abbott v Parfitt* [1871] 6 QB 346). If the personal representative and spouse treat the testator's goods are if they were their own, they may be seized in execution against the spouse (*Quick v Staines* (1798) 1 B&P 293). If the executor incurs debts in the course of such trading, these are his/ her personal debts, and execution must be against his/ her own property (*In Re: Evans* [1887] 34 ChD 597). Evans also makes it clear that the creditors have a lien on the personal representative's interest in the estate, so as s/he is entitled to be indemnified out of the estate (*Dowse v Gorton* [1891] AC 190), they may also claim the benefit of that right (*In Re: Johnson* [1880] 15 Ch D 548). Creditors are also entitled to an indemnity if the assets of the testator are used for the benefit of the executor (*In Re: Oxley* [1914] 1 Ch 602). Goods in the hands of an agent of the executor cannot be seized (*Sykes v Sykes* [1870] 5 CP 113). Where a receiver or manager is appointed in an administration action to carry on the business in succession to the executor, the same principles apply (*In Re: Brooke* [1894] 2 Ch 600).

9.8.3 *Heirlooms*

Heirlooms require special mention apart from fixtures, for which see 9.5. They are chattels which are so associated with real property that they are regarded as an essential feature of its ordinary enjoyment and use, and are accordingly treated as inseparable from the land in any settlement. A settlement may thus annex furniture and household chattels, goods and effects to a house as heirlooms and give them a heritable character which they would not otherwise possess. Because of this nature as real property, heirlooms cannot be seized.

9.9 Goods subject to prior levies

Those items already seized in execution or distress cannot normally be seized again (e.g. *Grant v Grant* [1883] 10 PR 40; *Kingston City v Rogers* [1899] 31 OR 119) as an interest in the goods has been vested in a third party by the prior seizure. For instance goods seized in distress for rent cannot be seized in execution (*Haythorn v Bush* (1834) 2 Cr& M 689) though the landlord could consent to waive his rights (*Belcher v Patten* (1848) 6 CB 608). There is an exception to this general rule for the Crown, for which see 6.6.2. There is also an exception in respect of execution, as later writs bind earlier (see 6.1.3), even though the goods are already seized and in the custody of the law under a prior writ (*Belcher v Patten*, as above). Goods already distrained cannot be seized in execution whether for rent (*Edmunds v Ross* (1821) 9 Price 5) or for taxes (*Dicas v Warne* (1833) 10 Bing 341). Goods already seized in execution cannot be seized unless the execution has been abandoned (*Crowder v Long* (1828) 8 B&C 598), the levy was irregular (*Blades v Arundale* (1813) 1 M&S 711) or the execution has been satisfied (*Harwell v Burwell* (1640) Sir W Jones 456). An illegal seizure does not disturb the debtor's possession (*Barrow v Bell* (1855) 5 E&B 540; *Re: Cuthbertson ex p Edey* [1875] 19 Eq 264) so they may still be seized in subsequent levies. If goods already subject to a levy are seized again it is poundbreach, for which see 3.4 and *Reddell v Stowey* (1841) 2 Moo & R 358.

9.10 Motor vehicles

Motor vehicles are available for seizure like any other asset, and are frequently the most valuable and easily accessible of a debtors' possessions. There is almost no case law guidance as to the procedure to be followed in seizing vehicles. It would appear that the same rules of location and entry apply as in any other levy. Whilst the vehicle itself may be levied upon, it does not seem safe to assume that items within it may be taken if that involves forced entry. Impounding may be by notice, walking possession or removal as already described (see 8.4.6 earlier in respect of clamping).

It may be possible for the debtor to successfully claim that his/ her vehicle is an item exempted by statute as necessary for his/ her trade or employment. Again there is little English authority on the matter, but Canadian cases are very instructive. Vehicles have been held to be exempt in the following instances:

- when used by a pedlar for travelling around selling goods - even though the car was bought for a different business- for use in connection with the debtor's shop (*Re: Bell* [1938] 2 DLR 754);

- when used by a self employed person to transport his/ her equipment and materials - see *York v Flatekval* [1971] 3 WWR 289 (a musician) and *Hayward Builders Supplies Ltd v Mackenzie* [1956] 2 WWR 591 (the debtor was a floorer and the car was held exempt, even though it was not registered as a commercial vehicle and was used as a 'pleasure car' for the debtor and family at weekends);

- if the vehicle itself is the sole source of the debtor's income- such as a car equipped as a taxi and used by a one man taxi service (*Metro Cab Co Ltd v Munro* [1965] 48 DLR 701); or,

- where owning a vehicle is a condition of the person's employment and it would be virtually impossible for them to do the job without: see for instance *Bank of Nova Scotia v Jordison* [1963] 40 DLR 790 (the debtor was a salesman) or *Armstrong v Terry* [1967] 1 OR 588 (the debtor was an estate agent).

Note that in these cases the wording of the exemption in the relevant statutes referred to tools or 'necessaries' required in a person's trade or 'calling', which latter term was interpreted as meaning a person's ordinary occupation or business. As seen in 9.6, the exemption in England and Wales is for vehicles used in "employment, business or vocation." The wording of the English and Canadian provisions is very similar and the principles applied by the Canadian courts should be transferable.

A motor vehicle will not be regarded as exempt from seizure where:

- it is used for convenience and not as a necessity (such as, to carry a salesman's samples) and car ownership is not a condition of employment (*Langdon v Traders' Finance Corporation Ltd* [1966] 1 OR 655; see also *Re: General Steel Wares Ltd v Clarke* [1956] 20 WWR 215);

- the debtor's contract of employment neither requires the employee to have a car nor defines the person's duties as involving the use of one. See for example *Goldsmith v Harris* [1928] 3 DLR 478: the claimant was a manager in a house building firm, and used his car to travel from site to site within the city where he supervised the construction work. The vehicle was claimed as a necessity, but it was not required by the terms of his contract, nor was it essential because of the nature of his occupation. Denniston JA held "A saw, a plough, an anvil, a fishing net, a truck are necessary to a carpenter, farmer, blacksmith, fisherman or carter if he is to follow his occupation at all. A vehicle for a country doctor, books of account for a business man...are recognised as necessaries as soon as mentioned, for without them pursuit of their respective occupations is impossible. The mere statement that a person is a manager of a building company does not import that a private motor car is necessary; it is only after special evidence is given to show special circumstances relating to a particular position, which involves special duties, that one may say that the work cannot be done without a motor car." In this case there was no such evidence that the person would be unable to hold his position or perform his duties. The debtor may have suffered inconvenience, and may have had to curtail his activities, but that was a matter for arrangement between him and his employer and was not the concern of the judgment creditors.

- The debtor is no longer trading. In *McLeod v Girvin Telephone Association* [1926] 1 DLR 216 a telephone line repair man claimed that his car was an exempt tool of his trade. The court refused his claim, partly because he could not show he was actually following the trade at the time of seizure. He had been sacked by the defendants and was working part time as a farmer.

Issues of ownership are very likely to arise in respect of cars as they may be subject either to HP or leasing agreements (see 9.16 & 9.17). Before removal therefore the bailiff will check ownership with HPI and DVLA and if the results of this are satisfactory is then likely to remove promptly. One issue to note in respect of execution for road traffic penalties is the difference between who may be held liable for such a penalty, and ownership of a vehicle. Under the regulations the registered keeper of the vehicle can be regarded as the owner for the purposes of imposing a penalty (see also *R v The Parking Adjudicator ex p L B Wandsworth* (1996)). These provisions apply solely to liability for the penalty and cannot be held to alter the rights of a person with legal title to a vehicle. Not infrequently, problems arise because the liable person has sold the car but has failed to notify DVLA. In *Ba Tu Dinh v Drakes Group Ltd* (2000), a car was sold to an acquaintance. Although sale was agreed in early August 1998; the log book was not passed over until the full purchase price was paid two months later. The court held that this was the date at which title passed.

When removing a vehicle any personal contents in the vehicle should be either returned to the debtor or listed in the presence of a witness. If possible the registration documents and keys will be obtained from the debtor or another responsible person. Forced entry to premises is possible in order to remove the vehicle, but the use of force to enter the vehicle itself is probably not justifiable, as other means exist for transporting cars and vans - i.e. by towing or loading on a transporter. The only English case law on the subject of cars relates to removals. It indicates that the bailiffs should use reasonable care when arranging a contractor to move the vehicle, but, provided this is done, they are not liable generally for any negligence on the part of the contractor. Arranging removal by a reputable garage or haulage firm should be seen as discharge of the duty of care (*Rivers v Cutting* [1982] 3 All ER 69 CA).

9.11 Partnership assets

The rule in the civil courts is that execution under a judgment against a firm can be levied against any property of the firm, against the property of any person who admitted to being a partner or was held by the judgment to be a partner, and against the property of any person who was served with the writ or summons and who failed to respond to the action or to attend hearings (CPR Part 70 Practice Direction 6A.1). The fact that membership of a partnership has changed is no bar to enforcement. By analogy from *Re: Frank Hill ex p Holt & Co* [1921] 2 KB 831 retirement will not prevent execution, nor will death of a partner after issue of the originating process (*Ellis v Wadeson* [1899] 1 QB 714). Each individual partner can be separately pursued by execution (*Clark v Cullen* [1882] 9 QBD 355) but an action against a firm must lead to a judgment against the firm, not just one partner (*Jackson v Litchfield* [1882] 8 QBD 474). In this case an action for wrongful execution and detention of goods was successfully taken. Similarly if judgment is obtained against several named individuals, the warrant must also be issued against them all (*Penoyer v Bruce* (1697) 1 Ld Raym 244; *Clark v Clement* (1796) 6 TR 525). That said, it does not have to be levied on all or any one or more of those joint judgment debtors (*Herries v Jamieson* (1794) 5 TR 556). If execution against one partner clears the debt, the others may not of course be pursued. There is no requirement that partnership property be seized before the private property of partners, or vice versa.

Execution may not be issued against a person who was out of the country when the writ or summons was issued unless s/he was served within England & Wales; who with permission was served outside the jurisdiction, or (High Court only) who responded to the writ as a partner. Partners who were out of England & Wales when the action commenced are not otherwise affected. Permission can be sought to issue execution against a person claimed to be a partner (CPR Part 70 Practice Direction 6A.3 & 6A.4). This gives the alleged partner an opportunity to contest the claim of liability, and the dispute may be tried as the court directs. Permission cannot be given to issue execution against a person who leaves the firm before an action begins (*Wigram v Cox* [1894] 1 QB 792). Permission may be given where a person has 'held themselves out' to be a partner (*Davis v Hyman & Co* [1903] 1 KB 854).

Execution made not be made against partnership property for the separate debt of a partner (s23(1) Partnership Act 1890). If this were to happen the partners could interplead - see later (*Peake v Carter* [1916] 1 KB 652). Note that in *Flude Ltd v Goldberg* [1916] 1 KB 662 a person interpleaded over goods claimed as his sole property. On hearing the case it was decided that the goods were in fact partnership property of the claimant and the defendant, but as the claimant had not claimed on this basis the claim was barred.

These basic principles will apply in statutory distraint whilst in execution for road traffic penalties CPR Part 75 applies the county court practice. The situation is different in distress for rent, for which see 9.24 - no protection is given to goods of a business partner.

9.12 Business assets

There are a number of specific provisions dealing with different items of equipment or stock that may be liable to seizure from a business or farm. These provisions are in addition to the exemptions for tools of the trade by statute (see 9.6), for motor vehicles used in trade (see 9.10) and for items subject to third party interests such as debentures and reservation of title clauses (see respectively 9.20 & 9.21).

9.12.1 *Railway rolling stock*

Under s.4 Railway Companies Act 1867 the "engines, tenders, carriages, trucks, machinery, tools, fittings, materials and effects constituting the rolling stock and plant" used by a company on its railway for the purposes of public traffic cannot be taken in execution (though the judgment creditor may obtain the appointment of a receiver). If a dispute arises as to whether items are covered by this exemption, application may be made on summons for summary determination in the county court or to a Judge in the High Court (s5).

Under s.3 Railway Rolling Stock Protection Act 1872 rolling stock (which is defined in s2 as wagons, trucks, carriages of all kinds and locomotive engines) may not be taken in distress for rent if they are found on any rented premises, such as a colliery, quarry, mine factory, warehouse or wharf, and they are not the tenant's property (see *Easton Estate & Mining Co v Western Wagon & Property Co* (1886) 50 JP 790). If stock is seized, application may be made to the magistrates' court for an order against the landlord to restore the goods or pay their value and costs. If the tenant has an interest in any rolling stock, this may be distrained for rent and disposed of. If a disagreement arises between landlord and tenant as to the best way of disposing of the tenant's interest, application may be made to the magistrates' court for directions (s5). Any order of the magistrates' court may be appealed to the Crown Court (s6).

9.12.2 Farming Stock

Special provision is made for officers levying the 'process of any court of law' (which presumably must include warrants issued by magistrates' courts) against a farm by Sale of Farming Stock Act 1816 (N.B. the Act does not affect levies by the crown - *R v Osbourne* (1818) 6 Price 94).

Generally the officer levying execution can seize any '*fructus industriales*' - that is, any crops which are reaped at maturity (*Cameron v Gibson* [1889] 17 OR 233). This includes such crops as corn and similar produce such as potatoes (*Evans v Roberts* (1826) 5 B&C 829). It does not include trees (*Scorell v Boxall* (1827) 1 Y&J 396), grass (*Late v McLean* [1870] 8 NSR 69), seeds unsprouted in the soil (*Bagshaw v Farnsworth* (1860) 2 LT 390) or fruit on trees (*Rodwell v Phillips* (1842) 9 M&W 501). Standing crops are bound by the issue of a writ (*Belair v Banque d'Hochelaga* [1923] 2 WWR 771) though they cannot be sold until they have been harvested (*Kidd & Clements v Docherty* [1914] 27 WLR 636).

However under s1 of the 1816 Act an officer cannot in any levy seize any straw, chaff, turnips, manure, compost, ashes or seaweed. Also under s1 if the terms of a tenant farmer's lease require that any hay, grass, tares, vetches, roots and vegetables are not to be removed from and consumed off the premises, the execution must be conducted subject to these conditions provided that the HCEO or county court bailiff has been given notice of such covenants before sale takes place. The tenant is required to give written notice to the bailiff of the terms of the lease and the landlord's name and address (also it is the bailiff's duty to make enquiries on this - s5) and the bailiff should then notify the landlord of the seizure and delay sale until a reply is received (s2).

Produce may be disposed of by the HCEO provided that the purchaser agrees in writing to use them on the premises in accordance with the lease (or in accordance with the 'custom of the country' if no such conditions apply) and that person shall be entitled to have barns etc on the premises allocated to their use by the bailiff (s.3). The requirement to respect the terms of the farm lease as to the use of such produce as hay, straw, grass, turnips, roots, manure, compost or seaweed is repeated by s.11, which applies to any sale of farming stock contrary to the lease, not just those in execution (*Wilmot v Rose* (1854) 3 E&B 563), for instance by the trustee of a bankrupt tenant farmer. Neither the bailiff nor the purchaser shall be liable in trespass for coming onto the premises in order to use produce (s.10). Furthermore, the landlord may not levy distress upon any of the corn, hay, straw or other produce sold under the execution, nor any horses, sheep, cattle, carts, wagons or other implements of husbandry brought onto the premises by the purchaser (s.6).

If the terms of the lease are breached, the landlord may sue in the name of the bailiff having provided an indemnity for any costs or losses that may be incurred (s.4). The HCEO is not liable to damages under the Act except for any wilful breach or omission (s.9). If under any contract a tenant farmer may remove straw, turnips etc. the Act will not apply (s.8).

PART TWO - THIRD PARTIES' GOODS

Other than jointly owned and partnership property, other third parties' goods cannot be taken as a rule. However, the third party may be estopped from recovering damages if s/he intentionally induced the bailiff to seize the goods, either by expressly or impliedly representing that the goods were the debtor's (*Pickard v Sears* (1837) 6 A&E 469). There must be something equivalent to a licence from him/ her (*Freeman v Cooke* (1849) 4 Exch 654; *Dawson v Wood* (1810) 3 Taunt 256). However once notice of the true situation is given, the bailiff will be liable for any subsequent wrongful acts such as proceeding to sell (*Dunstan v Paterson* (1857) 2 CBNS 495).

9.13 Utility fittings

There are statutory exemptions from seizure for fixtures and other property belonging to utility suppliers. The details are as follows:

- *Gas Act 1986* Sch 2B, para 29(1)(a): any gas meter connected to a service pipe and any gas fitting in a consumer's premises which is owned by a gas transporter or gas supplier and is sufficiently marked with an indication of ownership shall not be subject to distress or execution. Fittings for gas include hired cookers (*Gas Light & Coke Co v Hardy* [1886] 17 QBD 619; and *Gas Light & Coke Co v Herbert Smith & Co* (1886) 3 TLR 15). It is also an offence under para 10 Sch 2B to injure, or allow to be injured, any gas fitting or service pipe, whether intentionally or by culpable negligence;

- *Electricity Act 1989* Sch 6 para 9: any electrical plant, line or meter owned or hired by a supplier to a customer and marked with a sufficient indication of their ownership shall not be deemed to be landlord's fixtures, notwithstanding that they may be affixed to any part of the premises in which they are situated and shall not be taken in distress or execution. As with gas fittings, it is an offence to damage electrical fixtures (para 4); and,

- *Water Industry Act* 1991: s179(4) provides that any water fittings let for hire by a water undertaker shall, if they are properly marked, continue to be the property of the undertaker even if they are fixed to some part of the premises and shall not be taken in distress or execution. Water fittings are defined by s93 as including pipes, taps, cocks, valves, ferrules, meters, cisterns, baths and toilets.

These exemptions may be referred to in specific legislation (reg 45(8) CT and reg 14(8)NNDR state that the 'provisions shall not affect the operation of any enactment which protects goods of any class from distress') but will apply generally to all forms.

9.14 Children's goods

Children may be given personal property in any manner- for instance by will or by gift. Thus "if property be put up on a boy, this is a gift in the law, for the boy hath capacity to take it" (*Hayne's Case* (1614) 12 Co Rep 113). Whenever property is given to a child, it becomes the child's as soon as the gift is made (*Hunter v Westbrook* (1827) 2 C&P 578). At common law there is a presumption in favour of the validity of a gift by a parent or grandparent to a child (*Garrett v Wilkinson* (1848) 2 De G & Sm 244; *Beanland v Bradley* (1854) 2 Sm & G 339) provided that the gift is complete, such as by delivery (*May v May* (1863) 33 Beav 81).

Purchase of property by a child is valid and effectual (*Holmes v Brigg* (1818) 8 Taunt 508). Children can deal with property in the same manner as adults, whether disposing of it by gift or by sale of goods in the normal fashion (*Manby v Scott* (1663) 1 Mod Rep 124).

The National Standard restates the common law principle that enforcement agents should not remove anything clearly identifiable as an item belonging to a child but adds additional protection by exempting any goods which are for the exclusive use of a child. In consequence, therefore, items bought by children, or for children, and presents to them, should not be taken in distress or execution unless the bailiff can successfully challenge any of the above principles or show a particular transaction to be invalid. Subject to special procedural provisions (CPR Part 21), the child may take court proceedings to protect their property.

9.15 Spouses' goods

It is not unusual for bailiffs to seek to seize the property of one spouse to satisfy the debts of the other. The existing case law relates to the rights of a married woman, but the general principles will apply to cohabitees as well.

A married woman is capable of acquiring, holding and disposing of any property in all respects as if she is a single woman (s1(a) Law Reform (Married Women & Tortfeasors) Act 1935. All property belonging to woman at marriage or acquired by or devolving upon her after that date belongs to her as if she is a single woman (s2(1)). Clearly such goods cannot be seized. However s4(2)(c) provides that none of the above stops couples jointly owning goods, which could be seized.

In respect of gifts from one spouse to another, it used to be a presumption that a gift had been made where the husband bought property in his wife's name. This is not now presumed. It will be assumed to be owned jointly if bought with joint money. If the wife buys property in her husband's or joint names, there is no presumption of a gift if it is acquired with her money. If the items are bought by the husband for the wife's own personal use (e.g. for birthdays, anniversaries or Christmas), they will be gifts. Note however the arrangement made by the spouses in *Rondeau Le Grand & Co v Marks* [1918] 1 KB 75 where execution creditors against a wife were unable to seize her personal effects because she had made a valid agreement with her husband that he would purchase items for her in his own name and simply lend them. Jewellery etc given to the wife by relatives and friends are her property. Wedding presents from the wife's family are hers, and those from the husband's family are his, unless there is evidence of the donor's intentions. Gifts to the couple give each a separate share. If the one spouse makes a gift to the other, the items become the other's absolute property. In *French v Gething* [1922] 1 KB 236 the gift was by means of a post nuptial deed. Although the chattels transferred were furniture in the marital home which both continued to use, the goods were the wife's.

If one spouse purchases chattels from the other there is no reason not to treat this as a valid transfer that would defeat an execution creditor. In *Ramsay v Margrett* [1894] 2 QB 18 the husband sold furniture and personal chattels to his wife. She received a receipt for them, though there was no formal delivery of the goods as they remained in the marital home. The wife succeeded in an interpleader claim against an execution as the court held that the intention of the deal had been to pass her absolute title which was demonstrated by her separate dealings with the goods (some were removed prior to the execution) and which was combined with sufficient possession.

The above principles do not just apply to married couples but could apply to any parties living together or sharing accommodation. See for example *Koppel v Koppel* [1966] 2 All ER 187 in which the court upheld an interpleader claim by Mrs Wide the housekeeper to the contents of Koppel's house. They had been made over to her in return for her coming to live in the property to care for his two children and to replace items of her own that she disposed of before moving in. In this case the court held that there was no need for delivery to be demonstrated as the transfer was not a gift but was for money or money's worth. See also *Antoniadi v Smith* [1907] 2 KB 589 - a case of a man and his mother in law.

The real problems arise in respect of items bought by the couple after marriage (or after beginning to live together). The courts generally assume an intention to share any property acquired, and allocate interests in it equally. Housekeeping money or property acquired with that will be treated as shared equally unless it is clearly intended to be shared otherwise (s.1 Married Women's Property Act 1964). Where there is a joint bank account or other common pool of income, the wages of one spouse are generally seen as being earned on behalf of both and to be joint property, and the sums paid in or withdrawn by each are irrelevant . For instance see *Jones v Maynard* [1951] Ch 572- the husband withdrew sums from a joint account to buy investments in his sole name. The court held the wife to be entitled to half their value. By way of contrast see *Re: Bishop deceased* [1965] Ch 450 in which a husband and wife opened a joint account to which each contributed in unequal amounts. Money was withdrawn for housekeeping purposes and for investment, in both their sole and joint names. On his death the trustees sought to determine the wife's interest and it was held that as the account had been opened on terms that either could withdraw from it, with no evidence of any specific or limited purpose, then any item bought in sole name was for that person alone. Items bought from such an account therefore would be regarded as jointly owned and seizable. This is not the case where one spouse provides all the income in a joint account, which is simply used as a matter of administrative convenience. The money (and thus the acquisitions) belongs to the person providing it (*Heseltine v Heseltine* [1971] 1 All ER 952).

9.16 Hired goods

Goods subject to a hire or leasing agreement are not the property of the debtor and on the face of it are not available for seizure. In distress for rent, though, they were not regarded as exempt until a recent Court of Appeal decision (see later). In execution where the bailiff is permitted to seize the goods and chattels of the debtor, the debtor's interest in the goods may be seized if it is saleable. In those cases of statutory distraint where chattels cannot be seized rented or hired goods are exempt (see for example the rates cases of *Prudential Mortgage Co. v St. Marylebone (Mayor)* (1910) 8 LGR 901; *Carter v Vestry of St. Mary* (1900) 64 JP 548). The owner's interest may not be seized.

Thus the debtor's interest for a term (i.e. the remaining rental period) may in theory be seized and sold. The owner can not sue the bailiff for selling (*Gordon v Harper* (1796) 7 Term Rep 9; *Pain v Whittaker* (1824) 1 Ry & M 99) or for simply seizing them (*Duffil v Spottiswoode* (1828) 3 C&P 435). The Duffil case also determined that the hirer is under a duty to notify the bailiff of his/her limited interest in the goods. If after notice from the owner the bailiff purports to sell the absolute property in the goods, s/he may be liable for damages in conversion (*Ward v Macauley* (1791) 4 D&E 489; *Lancashire Wagon Co Ltd v Fitzhugh* (1861) 6 H&N 502). To succeed in such an action the owner would have to show that as soon as the goods were seized the bailiff was notified that the goods were on hire so that the bailiff knew only a qualified property could be sold (*Dean v Whittaker* (1823) 1 C&P 347). If the hire is of such a nature that the debtor has no saleable interest (*Cooper v Willomatt* (1845) 1 CB 72) or if the interest is determined by the seizure, the bailiff cannot legally seize (*Manders v Williams* (1849) 4 Exch 339) and could be sued for conversion for so doing. If goods are sold, the owner can recover a proportion of the proceeds of sale paid to the creditor (see *Jones Bros (Holloway Ltd v Woodhouse* [1923] 2 KB 117). Another remedy for the hirer would be interpleader (*Ford v Baynton* (1832) 1 Dowl 359 and 9.26 later).

Goods hired out by the debtor cannot be seized and the hirer's quiet possession can't be disturbed (*Garstin v Asplin* (1815) 1 Madd 150; *Izod v Lamb* (1830) 1 Cr&J 35).

9.17 Hire purchase goods

The same principles that apply to the seizure of hired goods also apply to those subject to hire purchase (HP) agreements i.e. the debtor's interest can be sold if the bailiff is entitled to sell chattels as well as goods. In respect of HP this would be the debtor's 'equity' in the goods - the difference between its present value and the outstanding balance on the agreement. Distress for rent is again a special case (see 9.22).

Only the debtor's interest, not the finance company's, may be sold. Where the bailiff does sell the absolute property the finance company may sue the creditor for a proportion of the proceeds relative to the proportion that their goods formed of the total value of the goods seized (*Jones Bros (Holloway Ltd v Woodhouse* [1923] 2 KB 117). If, by a term of the contract, any distress or execution ends the agreement, the goods can't be seized. The bailiff may be sued for conversion for seizing goods in such circumstances

(*Jelks v Haywood* [1905] 2 KB 460). However in *Times Furnishing v Hutchings* [1938] 1 KB 775 the HP company was defeated in its claim because, despite the fact that the agreement terminated automatically on the issue of distress by the landlord, as no steps were taken to recover the goods they remained in the possession of the debtor with the owner's consent and were seizable under s.4(1) LDAA 1908. Interpleader would be another remedy available to the finance company (see 9.26 later and *Green v Stevens* (1857) 2 H&N 146). The Inland Revenue is entitled to seize goods on HP but chooses not to exercise the right.

Although road traffic penalties are recovered by a form of county court execution, the common law rules on execution do not seem to apply. Rather, ERTDO art.5(2) gives bailiffs the power to seize 'the goods of the respondent' - that is, property owned by the individual liable for the PCN. This must exclude the right to seize vehicles subject to hire purchase. It is, however, a regular occurrence. Moreover, finance houses often seem to participate in these wrongful seizures by agreeing terms of sale with the bailiffs. The remedies would be a claim by the hirer against the bailiffs for wrongful interference or, possibly, a claim under the Consumer Credit Act 1974 against the lender for a wrongful repossession of goods.

9.18 Goods subject to pledges and liens

It is a very long established principle that goods subject to pledges and charges may be seized in execution, but subject to those claims (22 Ed IV 11). Thus goods subject to a lien for work done upon them are seizable, subject to that lien (*Duncan v Garrett* (1824) 1 C&P 169). The lien has priority over both the debt and the bailiff's fees (*The Ile de Ceylon* [1922] P 256). If such goods are sold, the bailiff is liable for the amount of the lien (*Proctor v Nicholson* (1835) 7 C&P 67) and can be sued if he fails to settle it from the proceeds (*Adanac Tire & Retreaders Ltd v Sheriff of Edmonton* [1979] 9 Alta LR 66). A lien cannot have any effect if it has not yet come into effect. In *Byford v Russell* [1907] 2 KB 522 it was agreed between builder and client that if work was not completed quickly enough notice would be served and a lien would be created on the builder's plant. The sheriff levied on the plant before the notice was served and the court held the client had no lien or interest and could not defeat the judgment creditor. Goods held by a debtor subject to a lien that s/he claims against a third party cannot be seized in execution (*Legg v Evans* (1840) 6 M&W 36). It has been said that a lien is no bar to seizure in distress for rent, given the rules on landlords' rights to seize any property found on the demised premises (*Theatre Amusement v Reid* (1920) 54 DLR 35).

In execution it is also lawful to seize goods subject to mortgages (*Massey Manufacturing v Clement* (1893) 9 Man LR 359). The bailiff will dispose of the judgment debtor's equity of redemption. If there is any doubt as to the validity of the security, the bailiff should request evidence of the charges so as to be able to seek instructions from the execution creditor or seek an indemnity- such diligence will protect him/her from any charge of negligence in execution. An equity of redemption, as well as being an estate in land, may also be sold in execution (*Dunn v Bank of New South Wales* (1866)).

Goods given in pledge by the debtor to a third party cannot be seized in execution against the debtor, and the pawnbroker could sue the bailiff in conversion (*Rogers v Kenmay* (1846) 9 QB 592). Mather however speculates that pawn tickets, though not seizable or saleable as such, could be taken in execution in order that the bailiff could redeem the goods and sell them (para 9, p96). If execution is levied against a pawnbroker, pledged goods can be seized. The High Court enforcement officer has a right of possession in the pledges arising from the pawnbroker's qualified property, and when the redemption period has passed the High Court enforcement officer's interest permits him to sell. If the pledgees redeem their goods the High Court enforcement officer may receive the redemption monies: if the pledges are not redeemed, the High Court enforcement officer may sell the goods (*Squire v. Huetson* (1841) 1 QB 308; *In Re: Rollason, Rollason v. Rollason* [1887] 34 Ch D 495).

9.19 Bills of Sale

Bills of sale are unlikely to be encountered as commercial arrangements very frequently. This is because the technicalities of the procedure mean that they are not a widely used form of security, and conditional sale or HP will be a preferred arrangement. Bills of sale may still be encountered in respect of loans on motor vehicles as a way of avoiding some aspects of Consumer Credit Act regulation. As discussed in chapter 3, they may also be encountered as a way of trying to avoid the impact of seizure.

9.20 Reservation of title clauses

There are a number of modes in which title to goods being sold may be subject to provisions reserving title in the seller. For instance, if goods are supplied to a prospective buyer on approval or on 'sale or return', the property only passes to the buyer when s/he signifies approval or acceptance to the seller, or does any other act adopting the transaction- this may be by retaining the goods for a reasonable period of time (see rule 4, s18 Sale of Goods Act 1979 but note that the mere fact of seizure of the goods in execution is not such retention to render the property passed - *Re: Ferrier* [1944] Ch 295). The most common means of reserving title are the so called 'Romalpa clauses'.

The rule regarding sale of goods is that title of the goods passes only when the parties want it to. Consequently, by agreement, title is reserved until certain conditions are satisfied, typically that the goods (and sometimes others) are fully paid for, rather than passing when the contract is made or when the goods are delivered. Such agreements are often called 'Romalpa clauses' (see *Aluminium Industrie Vaassen v Romalpa Aluminium Ltd* [1976] 2 All ER 552) but such clauses are sanctioned by s19 Sale of Goods Act 1979.

In any of these situations if property in the goods has not passed to the purchaser who is then subject to distress or execution, the relevant goods will not be seizable. This will even apply in distress for rent as they are either held "in the course of business" or as "third party goods" (see later). In reality it is often difficult for the seller claiming under a retention of title clause to identify which specific items are covered. When a firm is supplied with stock in the course of business invoices rarely specify serial numbers or even models. Furthermore where the goods being supplied subject to the reservation of title clause are materials rather than finished items, successfully asserting any claim may be even more difficult for the seller as the goods to which they claim title may no longer have any identifiable separate existence (*Borden (UK) v Scottish Timber Products Ltd* [1979] 3 All ER 961 CA). In all cases the exact terms of the sales contract will need careful scrutiny to see if it does in fact protect the vendor against the enforcement being levied against the customer (see also *Re: Bond Worth* [1979] 3 All ER 919 CA).

9.21 Floating charges

Bailiffs may, in the course of levies against limited companies, endeavour to levy on goods subject to floating charges. Such a charge is created by a debenture- a document acknowledging the company's indebtedness and giving security over some or all of the present and future assets of the firm. The assets will change over time as the company trades in the normal fashion but the charge will apply to the changing plant and goods in stock. However, if the firm defaults in payment of its debt, an administrative receiver can be appointed and the floating charge 'crystallises' and becomes fixed, giving the creditors the power to recover their money. If the property charged is far less in value than the sum charged, it can mean that property loses the protection of the debenture and may be distrainable. This is because effectively the firm loses any interest in the goods and they cease to be the firm's assets (*Re: New City Constitutional Club Co ex p Russell* [1887] 34 ChD 646). The effectiveness of a floating charge in protecting goods against distress depends on the stage that has been reached in the process of making and enforcing the charge when distress or execution begins. The debenture will be regarded as valid and will defeat execution even if it was issued without authority (*Duck v Tower Galvanising Co Ltd* [1901] 2 KB 314).

9.21.1 *Contract to issue*

Where a firm has contracted to issue debentures but before this is done goods are seized, the intended debenture holder is in the same position as if the debenture had been issued, i.e. the goods are seized subject to all equities upon them (*Simultaneous Colour Printing Syndicate v Foweraker* [1901] 1 KB 771).

9.21.2 *Prior to crystallisation*

Prior to crystallisation of the charge execution or distraint on the charged goods cannot be prevented as they are still the company's property (*Re: Roundwood Colliery Co* [1897] 1 Ch 373). If goods are charged to a value far in excess f their worth, the rights of the debenture holders will defeat those of the execution creditors if the debentures are valid, even though the charge has not crystallised (*Davey & Co v Williamson & Sons* [1898] 2 QB 194) and the debenture holder may interplead to safeguard the security. If the debenture holder fears that their goods are in jeopardy, they may appoint a receiver if it is reasonable - this could be because a judgment creditor is in a position to issue execution (*Wildy v Mid-Hampshire Railway Co* (1868) 16 WR 409; *In Re: London Pressed Hinge Co Ltd* [1905] 1 Ch 576). This intervention must be in such a way as to crystallise the whole security: a particular asset can't be claimed from the enforcing creditor whilst the security remains a floating charge against the other assets (*Evans v Rival Granite Quarries* [1910] 2 KB 979). If goods are seized in execution prior to crystallisation, the debenture holder may interplead if the HCEO is disputing the validity of the charge (*Taunton v Sheriff of Warwickshire* [1895] 2 Ch 319). If the bailiff has levied and completed execution by sale the debenture holders cannot compel the creditors to restore the money (*Re: Opera* [1891] 3 Ch 260). If the company pays the bailiff to get rid of a man in possession or under threat of removal and sale, but before the money is passed to the creditors the debenture holders appoint a receiver, as the company has an implied power to settle its debts the creditors may receive the money from the bailiff (*Heaton & Dugard Ltd v Cutting* [1925] 1 KB 655 or *Robinson v Burnell's Vienna Bakery Ltd* [1904] 2 KB 624). It does not make any difference whether the agreement reached over payment is for instalments or for a lump sum (*Heaton v Dugard Ltd & Cutting Bros Ltd* [1925] 1 KB 655).

9.21.3 *After crystallisation*

Where a floating charge has crystallised on the appointment of a receiver, the goods are transferred to the debenture holders' receiver and are no longer the company's property. Accordingly, they are no longer available for seizure (*Re: ELS* [1995] Ch 11). There is one case at variance with this - *Cunliffe*

Engineering v English Industrial Estates [1994] BCC 974. Here a landlord was held to be entitled to seize goods from a receiver partly because the debenture holder was held to have an interest in the tenancy and partly because the goods were in the reputed ownership of the firm and thus excluded from protection under s4 LDAA 1908 (see later).

Generally the bailiff will not be able to levy and if he does, for instance, in ignorance of the receiver's appointment, he will have to withdraw (*Edwards v Edwards* [1875] 1 ChD 454). A creditor may appoint a receiver and begin winding up proceedings after seizure and before sale by a bailiff and assert his/ her priority over that bailiff against the proceeds of sale of the goods by the liquidator (*Re: Standard Manufacturing Co* [1891] 1 Ch 639).

If there has been a change of occupation of the premises as a result of the AR's appointment, s/he will become liable for any rates and may be subject to distraint for them (*Richards v Overseers of Kidderminster* [1896] 2 Ch 212). Normally, though, the terms of the debenture will not make the AR an agent of the company and thus s/he is not liable for any rates due after the date of the appointment (*Taggs Island Casino Hotel Ltd v Richmond upon Thames Borough Council* [1967] RA 70). The company will remain liable, though possessing few seizable assets. See in this connection *Re: Beck Foods v Rees* [2001] EWCA Civ 1934. The actions of a receiver and manager were held not to amount to rateable occupation of a company's premises and cannot therefore found a claim of rateable occupation from the local authority. There was thus no basis for a liability order being made against the receiver, who should not be threatened with a levy of distraint (see also *Re: Marriage Neave & Co* [1896] 2 Ch 633).

9.21.4 *Agricultural charges*

Assets on a farm may be subject to charges that may be either fixed or floating created by banks with tenant or owner farmers, charging all the livestock, crops, machinery, seeds and manures, fixtures and other produce of the farm as security for short term credit, under s5 Agricultural Credits Act 1928. Such charges, whether crystallised or not, do not prevent distress on the charged items for rent, rates and taxes (s8(7)).

However these charges, even if uncrystallised prevent execution. In the county court, the execution creditor may be required by the court to conduct a search at the Land Registry to ascertain whether any charges are registered under the 1928 Act prior to seizure taking place (CPR Sch.2 CCR O.26 r.3). This will enable the court to determine whether there are any sufficient goods available for seizure, and is it obviously important for the debtor farmer to alert any bailiff levying execution to such charges. A similar procedure is followed by HCEOs.

PART THREE - DISTRESS FOR RENT

There are many detailed rules applying to what may be taken in distress for rent. There has been a tendency to seek to extend these categories to other forms of distress. However in chapter 2 it was shown why this should not be done. Over and above this, it should be noted that in statutory distraint the legislation usually only ever speaks of the debtor's goods alone and there is no suggestion that anything broader than that is intended. In the absence of such indications, the rent classifications should not be applied.

The basic common law rule is that any item on the premises may be taken to a value sufficient to cover the rent arrears and costs (see Blackburn J in *Lyons v Elliott* [1876] 1 QBD 210). This right to seize in distress is regardless of ownership (*Gorton v Fuller* (1792) 4 Term Rep 565) and, it would seem, regardless of the fact that the occupier is now a person such as a squatter who has disseised the tenant (*Humphry v Damion* (1612) Cro Jac 300). This right has been modified by statute and some goods are now exempted, or privileged, as the following sections describe. The rules often seem inexplicable as Phillimore J observed in *Crossley Bros v Lee* [below] "It is a strange thing, and I see no principle in it...That, however, appears to be the law, and it is due partly to the fact that the law of distress is partly archaic and very technical." (*Crossley Bros. Ltd v Lee* [1908] 1 KB 86) and the courts, when an opportunity presents itself, attempt to modernise the privileges.

Readers should note that all the categories of exemption (or privilege) are separate exclusive clauses i.e. tools are protected even if they are not in use. It is however possible for lease to vary the protection afforded by the various privileges, either by permitting distress on privileged goods, as in *Re: The River Swale Brick & Tile Works Ltd* (1883) LJ Ch 638 (but only after a delay of a certain period, during which the right to exercise the common law remedy was unaffected), or by agreeing not to distrain on certain goods such as cattle (*Horsford v Webster* (1835) 1 CM & R 696) or third parties' goods (*Welsh v Rose* (1830) 6 Bing 638).

9.22 Qualified privilege

The items granted conditional privilege can only be taken if there are insufficient other goods. If it appears that nothing else seizable is present on the property the landlord may take items with qualified privilege, as he is by right entitled to whatever distrainable items there are actually available at the time of the levy (*Piggott v Birtles* (1836) 1 M&W 441). The landlord may be sued for seizing goods with qualified privilege unless s/he genuinely believed that there were no alternative items (*Jenner v Yolland* (1818) 6 Price 3). The privileged items include:

- *tools of the trade* in excess of the limit of absolute privilege (see 9.23 below) (*Nargett v Nias* (1859) 1 E & E 439);

- *sheep and beasts* which 'gain' the land (i.e. plough beasts) (*Simpson v Hartropp* (1744) Willes 512). However if the beasts are too young to be used for this purpose, they are not privileged;

- *agisted beasts* i.e. livestock belonging to a third party taken in commercially by the tenant for grazing. These are protected under s18 (2) Agricultural Holdings Act 1986. The agistment must be for a fair price, but this need not be in cash - payment in kind will be sufficient to give the privilege (*London & Yorkshire Bank v Belton* [1885] 15 QBD 457) but cattle taken under a contract for the grazing of land will not (*Masters v Green* [1888] 20 QBD 807). Under s18(3) a ceiling is placed on how much the landlord can realise by the seizure of agisted beasts. S/he cannot recover more than the (balance of the) sum agreed to be paid for the feeding of the stock. If, before sale, the owner of any such agisted stock pays to the landlord a sum equal to the above amount, the animals can be recovered and any amount due from the third party to the tenant is released (s.18(4)).

- *growing crops* already seized in execution (s2 Landlord and Tenant Act 1851). A landlord may seize growing crops seized and sold by the HCEO if they are still on the farm and if there is insufficient distress to cover any rent due after the date of the HCEO's seizure and sale of those crops. The crops lose all privilege if the purchaser from the HCEO allows them to remain an unreasonable time on the premises after they are ripe (*Peacock v Purvis* (1820) 2 B&B 362).

9.23 Absolute privilege

Items given absolute privilege are totally exempt from seizure. They include:

- *incorporeal chattels* - such as the rights of an owner of a patented chattel under letters patent to make and use the chattel and to licence others to do so (*British Mutoscope & Biograph Co Ltd v Horner* [1901] 1 Ch 671). This is because the right to distrain arises out of the demised premises and distress can be levied on goods on such premises. Just as distress cannot be levied under a demise of an incorporeal hereditament, it cannot be levied on chattels that have no local position and that cannot be physically seized.

- *wild animals and other items of no value* (*Davies v Powell* (1738) Willes 46);

- *perishable items* - those which cannot be returned to the tenant in the same condition (*Wilson v Ducket* (1675) 2 Mod Rep 61). This will exempt such items as fruit and meat, but extends also to items that will be scattered by an attempt to remove, such as corn in a sheaf, or items whose exact quantity may not be easily ascertained at the time of seizure, such as removing some grain or flour from a sack. Wine in bottles are not protected by this privilege (*Re: Russell* (1870) 18 WR 753), so *Woodfall on Landlord & Tenant* speculates at paragraph 9.055 that food in tins, jars or vacuum packs similarly will not be exempt. The item containing the privileged goods is also privileged e.g. a lorry transporting fresh fruit (*Muspratt v Gregory* (1838) 1 M&W 633);

- *fixtures* - as described at 9.5 the courts have recognised two categories of fixtures: those that are irremovable (which are never distrainable) and those that may be removed by the tenant but are otherwise part of the freehold (*Turner v Cameron* (1869) 5 QB 306). The basic rule is that the latter category of fixtures (items such as kitchen ranges and stoves) which the tenant may sever from the freehold and remove during the term cannot be seized in distraint (*Darby v Harris* (1841) 1 QB 895). This seems to apply even if the fixed item is removed for some purpose at the time of seizure (*Gorton v Fuller* (1792) 4 TR 567). The landlord can only seize items which may be restored in the same condition as before seizure, and the ability of the tenant to remove and the landlord to restore are different questions. It is irrelevant that the goods were, or may become, the tenant's chattels. If they are affixed to the premises for the purposes of the tenant, they may not be seized (*Provincial Bill Posting Co v Low Moor Iron Co* [1909] 2 KB 344). Those fixtures that are removable by the tenant become the landlord's if the tenant does not take them at the end of the lease, but despite this curious feature that the latter will ultimately become the landlord's they still may not be seized (*Crossley Bros Ltd v Lee* [1908] 1 KB 86);

- *public utility fittings* see 9.13;

- *loose money* (i.e. not in a purse or wallet) which cannot be kept separate;

- *things in actual use* (*Read v Burley* (1597) Cro Eliz 549) including clothes being worn (*Baynes v Smith* (1794) 1 Esp 206) and machinery (*Simson v Harcourt* (1744) Esp NP);

- *household goods and tools of the trade* as protected in the county court (see 9.6 earlier) as s4 LDAA 1888 exempts from distress the same goods that are protected from execution. Tools of the trade can include items hired or on HP in the spouse's name so that the other spouse can earn a living for the whole family e.g. a sewing machine (*Churchward v Johnson* (1889) 54 JP 326; *Masters v Frazer* (1901) 85 LT 611). Even if there is only one tool of considerable value, it is still privileged (*Lavell v Richings* [1906] 1 KB 480). By the proviso of s4 this protection does not apply to any case where the lease, term or interest of the tenant has expired, where possession of the premises in respect of which the rent is due has been demanded and where the distress is levied not later than seven days after that demand. It seems that these conditions are cumulative rather than separate. The proviso relates to those tenancies where the landlord may distrain under ss6 & 7 L&TA 1709 (see 3.2);

- goods already seized in execution (*Eaton v Southby* (1738) 7 Mod Rep 251);

- *crown property* - there is almost no authority on this privilege, which was interpreted by Wills J as an argument in favour of the long established and undisputed exemption of the Crown (*Secretary of State for War v Wynne* [1905] 2 KB 845);

- *goods in the mail* under s.64(1)&(3) Post Office Act 1969;

- *goods held in the course of business on trade premises* as a direct part of the tenant's business (*Challoner v Robinson* [1908] 1 Ch 490). This exemption is based on the need to protect trade by not allowing distress to close businesses down. The trade must be 'public' i.e. anyone can approach the trader to use his/her services. Thus in *Tapling & Co v Weston* (1833) Cab & El 99 a sales agent acting for one firm alone was not held to be in public trade. Public trade will include a butcher (*Brown v Shevill* (1834) 2 Ad & El 138), a wood mill (*Guy v Rankin* [1883] 23 NBR 49), a book binders (*Munster v Johns* (1850) 16 LTOS 245) and a restaurant or shop where the business is open to any customer.

The exemption covers all goods delivered to the tenant to be "carried, wrought or managed in the way of trade or employ" (*Simpson v Hartopp* (1744) Willes 512). There is no need for the goods to be physically altered whilst in the trader's hands, but for the goods to be privileged it must be necessary for them to be on the premises for the trade to be conducted (*Parsons v Gingell* (1847) 4 CB 545). Goods left at the premises for the owner's convenience, and not to be worked upon by the tenant, are not privileged (see *Joule v Jackson* (1841) 7 M&W 450- beer barrels left at a pub until the beer was drunk, or *Mitchell v Coffee* [1880] 5 AR 525 - machine left a hotel by customer in his absence).

The privilege will cover the following categories of goods:

- items left for repair or alteration (*Clarke v Millwall Dock* [1886] 17 QBD 494);

- goods in the hands of a public carrier (*Gisbourn v Hirst* (1710) 1 Salk 249);

- furniture held in store (*Miles v Furber* [1873] 8 QB 77);

- goods on pawn or at an auctioneer's (*Findon v M'Laren* (1845) 6 QB 891; *Adams v Grane* (1833) 1 Cr & M 380);

- goods held by a sale agent acting on commission (*Gilman v Elton* (1821) 3 B&B 75; see also *Thompson v Mashiter* (1823) 1 Bing 283);

- goods held by a shopkeeper on sale or return, as the arrangement is a 'notorious' trade practice which will prevent any claim that the goods are in the reputed ownership of the tenant (*Re: Florence ex p Wingfield* [1878] 10 Ch D 591; see also *Perdriau Rubber Co Ltd v Sadek* [1928] SRQ 114).

The protection does not apply to:

- goods purchased by a retailer from a wholesaler;

- goods on sale in a shop rather than in a public market (*Bent v McDougall* (1881) 2 R&G 468); or,

- second hand goods sold on commission by a dealer (*Lawrence v Turner* [1934] 3 WWR 353).

There must be delivery of goods to the tenant's own premises, so if goods happen to be on premises for use in the manufacture of products, they will not necessarily be privileged nor will goods being worked on at the owner's own premises. Although materials sent to be worked upon may be privileged (*Gibson v Ireson* (1842) 3 QB 39), machines delivered with them will not, nor will the vehicles in which they were delivered (*Joule v Jackson* (1841) 7 M&W 450), unless there are sufficient other distrainable goods on the premises (*Wood v Clarke* (1831) 1 C&J 484).

The premises upon which the goods are seized must be occupied by the trader. Goods are privileged if they are on premises which the trader is hiring temporarily for the purposes of trade (*Brown v Arundell* (1850) 10 CB 54). The goods to be worked on by the trader may be stored on his/ her premises (*Williams v Holmes* (1853) 8 Exch 861) or in a warehouse without losing their privilege (*Matthias v Mesnard* (1826) 2 C&P 353) as long as they are also worked upon and not just stored (*Re: Russell* (1870) 18 WR 753). Goods held for trade may also have protection from their third party status (see below).

- *agricultural items* various items that a bailiff may find on an agricultural holding or farm are completely exempt from seizure. These include:

- agricultural machinery owned by someone other than the tenant or left on the premises under a hire agreement or for use in the farming business (s18(1) Agricultural Holdings Act 1986);

- livestock of all descriptions belonging to a third party and present on the farm solely for the purposes of breeding (s.18(1)(b) 1986 Act);

- cattle belonging to a third party and consuming 'eatage' which, with the landlord's consent, have been sold to a third party on condition that rent is paid from the proceeds of that sale (*Horsford v Webster* (1835) 1 Cr M & R 696);

- cattle pastured overnight on the demised premises, whilst being driven to market (*Tate v Gleed* (1784) 2 Wms Saund 290a; *Nugent v Kirwan* (1838) 1 Jab & Sy).

- certain produce & implements subject to execution (ss3 & 6 Sale of Farming Stock Act 1816 - see 9.12 earlier).

- *goods on hire purchase or conditional sale* subject to a Consumer Credit Act 1974 default notice (s.4A(2) LDAA 1908), a suspended delivery order or a termination notice. If the goods are subject to an agreement in the tenant's spouse's name, they are protected (*Rogers, Eungblutt & Co v Martin* [1911] 1 KB 19), but not if they are in joint names (*Shenstone & Co v Freeman* [1910] 2 KB 84; *A W Garnage Ltd v Payne* (1925) 134 LT 222). In some cases goods may be protected without the need to serve any form of termination notice (*Perdana Properties v United Orient Leasing* [1981] 1 WLR 1496). A written notice clearly indicating that consent to continued possession has been withdrawn by the finance company takes the goods out of 'reputed ownership' (see below) and will be sufficient to protect them from seizure (see also *Hollinshead v Egan* [1913] AC 564 - a bills of sale case). Any such notice is operative from the date that it is posted by the finance company, and from this date the goods will be exempt from distress (*Drages Ltd v Owen* [1935] All ER Rep 342).

- *hired and leased goods*: In *Salford Van Hire (Contracts) v Bocholt Investments* [1996] RTR 103 the Court of Appeal ruled that changes in commercial and financial practice meant that goods hired or leased by firms can no longer be regarded as being in their "reputed ownership" and were to be regarded now as exempt from distress for rent. It is likely that these same principles will apply to goods on hire purchase or conditional sale, thus offering a more complete protection for such items than the above paragraph, and overruling earlier cases such as *Chappell v Harrison* (1910) 103 LT 594 in which a piano on HP was seized as the existence of an HP agreement did not prevent 'reputed ownership' of the goods by the tenant.

The courts have also held that, on the terms of some agreements, even after default and termination and until further steps were taken to recover the goods, they still remained in the order and disposition of the debtor (*Times Furnishing Co v Hutchings* [1938] 1 KB 775), so that no action would lie against the landlord for, respectively, damages for illegal distress or for the recovery of sums paid to release the hired goods as money had and received. Conversely, it has also been held that consent to possession of goods under a hire purchase agreement may be withdrawn without the need to terminate the agreement itself (*Perdana Properties v United Orient Leasing* [1981] 1 WLR 1496- see above).

- *third party's goods:* the property of lodgers and sub-tenants and strangers (i.e. "any other person whatsoever not being a tenant of the premises or any part thereof and not having any beneficial interests in any tenancy of the premises or any part thereof") is absolutely privileged under s1 LDAA 1908. Also case law provides some protection e.g. strangers' goods cannot be seized if brought onto the premises by the stranger personally (*Paston v Carter* (1883) Cab & El 183). These individuals must make a written declaration to the landlord in a set form accompanied by an inventory stating that items levied upon are theirs. On receiving a declaration the landlord should return the goods and to continue to distrain would render it illegal. If this is not done the person may apply before two JPs for a restoration order (for more detail on this procedure see 9.30 later).

  The protection only applies to subtenancies where the subtenant is liable to pay a rent not less often than quarterly which represents the whole annual value of the property or such proportion of it as s/he occupies (s1(a) LDAA 1908). The protection also does not apply to subtenants whose tenancy has been created in breach of a term of their landlord's lease or tenancy agreement (s5 LDAA 1908). Lodgers and licencees are not affected by this exclusion.

One considerable problem with the protection given by the LDAA 1908 is that 'lodger' is not defined within it. A lodger is clearly not a tenant, subtenant or stranger, and is probably being referred to in the ordinary sense of a person living and sleeping on the premises (see *Heawood v Bone* [1884] 13 QBD 179). This question of status is for the person claiming the Act's protection to prove. There is considerable authority on the meaning of the expression, which it may be helpful to note for both residential and business licensees:

- if the user of the premises does not have exclusive possession, for example, accommodation can be used by others in their absence, and if possession is given on sufferance and is provisional, at the owner's pleasure, even though a rent is paid for it, the user is not a tenant (*Allan v Overseers of Liverpool* [1874] 9 QB 180);

- though an arrangement may be termed a subtenancy and involves the letting of nearly an entire property, if the landlord retails possession of part of the property, the 'sub-tenant' is a lodger (*Phillips v Henson* [1877] 3 CPD 26);

- if the tenant shares accommodation with the landlord, even though no service or attendance is provided, s/he is a lodger (*Bradley v Bayliss* [1881] 8 QBD 195);

- where the landlord let all the property except for ground floor shop accommodation which he retained and used for trade, the tenant was held to be a lodger under the Act. The landlord does not have to be resident, the tenant's power of separate and unrestricted access will not have an impact. The important point is control: if the landlord retains some control of occupation and access, the tenant is a lodger. Control is, however, not retaining common parts and the right to enter to do repairs (*Ness v Stephenson* [1882] 9 QBD 245);

- in contrast to *Allan* above, it was held that a person occupying business premises is not a lodger, even where they do not occupy the whole premises and access is given by the landlord who holds the key (*Heawood v Bone* [1884] 13 QBD 179);

- if the landlord occupies a separate flat in the same building, the occupier is not a lodger (*Kent v Fittall* [1906] 1 KB 60); and,

- even if accommodation is shared with others, if the landlord does not reside but calls weekly to collect rent from the tenants, each of whom occupies individual rooms with their own keys and rent books, the person is not a lodger (*Honig v Redfern* [1949] 2 All ER 15).

Additionally, the goods of a third party are protected if that person is agent of the landlord and occupies the demised premises as such, for instance as a caretaker (*Wheeler v Stevenson* (1860) 6 H&N 155).

9.24 Goods with no privilege

No privilege from being levied in distress is given to the goods of the following:

- *the tenant's spouse* (s4(1) LDAA 1908);

- *a person who has lent goods* to the tenant, but note the absolute privilege of agricultural machinery and the recent exemption of hired and leased goods (see 9.23).

  This exclusion from privilege is provided by s.4(1) LDAA 1888 which refers to "goods in the possession, order or disposition of such a tenant by the consent and permission of the true owner under such circumstances that such tenant is reputed owner thereof". Reputed ownership is a question of fact. It is to be inferred in situations where, by exercise of reason and judgment on the facts capable of being found on enquiry, a reasonable person would have to conclude that the goods in the possession of the debtor were fully owned by that person (*Re: Fox* [1948] Ch 407). Equally if it is to be disproved, the real owner must show that steps had actually been taken to terminate ownership and recover the goods so that no grounds could exist on which to form such an impression. Goods on 'permanent loan' with no conditions attached would be seizable. Property held on trust is not in a person's reputed ownership (*Re: Sibeth ex p Sibeth* [1885] 14 QBD 417).

  Traders with goods on 'sale or return' will be able to rebut any claim of 'reputed ownership' provided that they can demonstrate that such terms of trade are a 'notorious custom' in their business (*Ex parte Wingfield In Re: Florence* [1879] 10 Ch D 591). A person who receives goods on sale or return receives them with the option of becoming owner, which can be exercised by buying the goods at the vendor's price, by selling to a third party or by keeping the goods so long that it would be unreasonable to return them. If he sells or attempts to sell, he does not do so as owner, but as having the option to take the goods if they are sold. The trader needs to show that customers would understand that possession does not necessarily indicate ownership.

- *a business partner* (s4(2)(a) LDAA 1908). Their separate property, if on the rented premises, may be seized. Application may be made by a claimant to magistrates' court for a determination as to whether goods are covered by this subsection. Readers should however note the decision in *Re: Potter* [1874] 18 Eq 381 in which it was held that a landlord may seize chattels, but not a partner's potential interest in chattels. The distress had to be limited to property of the debtor solely as their joint property was subject to payment of their joint debts, until satisfaction of which, it was impossible to quantify the interest of each partner in the chattels.

- *various goods on business premises*: under s4(2) LDAA 1908 no privilege is given to goods jointly owned by a tenant and subtenant found on trade premises; goods left in offices and warehouses one month after notice from the landlord to remove them, and goods belonging to, and in the offices of, any company which are located in premises rented by a director, officer or employee of the company. Application for a declaration as to protection may be made to the magistrates' court.

- *a farmer or smallholder* may have any of the following items seized in distress for rent:

  - sheaves of corn and hay if it is in a barn or granary, and not subject to replevin (s2 DRA 1689). In light of this provision Gilbert (at p213) questions whether the common law privilege of goods liable to deterioration no longer applies to goods which will not be ruined during the five day delay before sale. Such produce must be impounded on the farm and, it would appear, must be sold after an optional appraisement;

  - cattle or stock feeding on the commons or roads on the premises (s8 DRA 1737). Once the landlord has entered to seize such beasts, the tenant may not drive them off (*Clement v Milner* (1800) 3 Esp 95). Horses being kept by a third party in a stable let by the tenant may also be seized (*Crosier v Tomkinson* (1759) 2 Keny 439);

  - all produce (i.e. corn, grass, hops, roots, fruits and pulses) growing on the holding (s8 DRA 1737). This right does not apply to trees, shrubs and bushes, only such crops as ripen and are harvested (*Clark v Gaskarth* (1818) 8 Taunt 431). The landlord may both seize the crops when growing (*Glover v Coles* (1822) 1 Bing 6) and also cut this produce when it has ripened, but not before (*Owen v Legh* (1820) 3 B & Ald 470) and store it either on the holding or off the holding in suitable premises as close by as possible if there are no adequate storage facilities in the farm. A cart loaded with sheaves may also be seized (*Horton v Arnold* (1731) Fortes Rep 361). The produce must be appraised and must be sold. However, if the tenant makes payment or tender of the full rent and costs due before the produce has ripened and been cut, the distress shall cease (s9 DRA 1737). If produce is sold before it is in ripe, but the tenant can show no loss to have been caused by this, no damages may be recovered (*Rodgers v Parker* (1856) 18 CB 112). This power to seize growing crops does not extend to the grantees of rentcharges unless there is an express power in the grant (*Miller v Green* (1831) 2 C&J 142). Grantees may however distrain on oats and hay in stacks under DRA 1689 s2 mentioned above (*Johnson v Faulkner* (1842) 2 QB 925);

- *a stranger's cattle* that have been allowed on the premises or have strayed onto the farm by breaking through sound fences or unsound fences if the tenant was not responsible for their repair (*Jones v Powell* (1826) 5 B&C 647). If however they enter through defective fences that the tenant should have repaired, they may not be seized until they have been on the premises for a day and a night ('levant et couchant') and notice to remove has been given to the owner, to which he has not responded (*Kempe v Crews* (1697) 1 Ld Raym 167). If they are removed after notice, it is not rescue (*Fowkes v Joice* (1688) 2 Vern 131).

PART FOUR
REMEDIES FOR WRONGFUL SEIZURES   OF
GOODS

If any exempt goods are seized, the onus of proof in any case is on the debtor to show that they are exempt because they fall in any particular category or below any financial limit (*Gonsky v Durrell* [1918] 2 KB 71). However note that in *Rai & Rai v Birmingham City Council* (1993) Adviser 44, on appeal under reg 40 of the community charge regulations, a deputy stipendiary magistrate held that bailiffs have a duty of care to exercise when seizing goods and must act with discernment and judgment. If, during a levy, the bailiffs are put on notice that certain goods do not allegedly belong to the debtor, they must act with due caution and circumspection. As they did not in this case an illegal levy occurred. See also *Dunstan v Paterson* (1857) 2 CBNS 495- the HCEO may be justified in seizing the wrong person (or goods) if he is misinformed or mislead as to their identity, but they must be released as soon as the true state of affairs is known.

The remedies to be described apply to most forms of distress. Thus, if unlawful distraint for income taxes takes place, the debtor can sue for damages in the county court and return of the goods (*Berry v Farrow* [1914] 1 KB 632) or seek replevin. Equally where a remedy is provided by the relevant statutes, this does not exclude the general remedies. It was noted in *R v Hampstead Magistrates Court ex p St Marylebone Property Co plc*

(1995) Legal Action Sept 1996, p21 that "the statute clearly incorporated distress as a well established remedy. It can be assumed that it was intended that the established incidents of the remedy would apply except as specifically provided." Hence there is a right to sue for damages as much as the statutory right of complaint. A complaint against the levying bailiffs' certificate might also be appropriate (see 6.8.3)

9.25 Complaint to magistrates' court

Under the regulations for local taxes (reg 46 CT & reg 15 NNDR) and child support maintenance (reg 31) any person aggrieved by a levy, or an attempt to levy, can appeal to the Magistrates Court. The existence of this statutory remedy does not however exclude the right to sue for wrongful distress (*Governor of the Poor of Bristol v Wait* (1834) 1 Ad & El 264) and the local authority may be liable for trespass for any distraint levied in unlawful circumstances (*London & North Western Railway Co v Giles* (1869) 33 JP 776).

The case is commenced by making a 'complaint' and requesting the issue of a summons directed to the creditor. The complainant need not specially argue that the distraint was wrongful, as the onus lies on the defendant to show the legality of their actions (*R v Justices of Devon* (1813) 1 M&S 411). At the hearing, if the court is satisfied that the levy was irregular, it can order the return of the goods distrained. Although the regulations speak of irregularity alone, it has been held by the courts that this term includes any wrongful act by the bailiff i.e. illegality, irregularity or an excessive levy (*Steel Linings v Bibby* [1993] RA 27).

As an alternative to ordering return of goods the court may order an award of compensation for the goods sold equal to an amount which, in opinion of the court, would be awarded by way of special damages if proceedings had been taken for trespass or otherwise in connection with the irregularity. (N.B. in assessing the level of compensation the court is required to act reasonably and to give proper attention to any evidence placed before it: *R v Epping Magistrates ex p Howard & Leach* (1996) 7 CLY 521). It has been held by the High Court in *Steel Linings v Bibby* (and endorsed in *R v Hampstead Magistrates Court ex p St Marylebone Property Co plc* (1995) Legal Action Sept 1996, p.21) that the reference to special damages has a wider meaning in the regulations than just special damages as opposed to general damages and covers all damages caused by the wrongful levy, including damages for annoyance, injury to credit and reputation. The court can also order the creditor and bailiffs to desist from any levying in an irregular manner.

Several cases have been reported in respect of community charge:

- *Crosby v Wandsworth London Borough Council* (1991) Legal Action 3/91 - goods belonging to the son, Wayne Crosby, were seized and sold. He was awarded £310 compensation and the council ordered to better supervise their bailiffs;

- *Rai v Birmingham City Council* (1993) Adviser vol.44: the detail of the case is discussed at 5.5. The deputy stipendiary magistrate, on finding a "threefold commission of irregular levy" ordered that the goods removed by the bailiffs be returned.

- *H v Sandwell MBC* (1993) Legal Action August p.15: see 8.3.1 for details. On hearing the case the magistrates made an order declaring the attempted levy to be irregular, the walking possession charges unlawful and prohibiting further enforcement against the claimant.

If a complaint is dismissed, appeal may be by way of case stated.

9.26 Interpleader

9.26.1 *Applicability*

Interpleader is a process by which a person faced with competing claims for goods, and who may be sued by different people in respect of those claims, may start an action in court to settle the claims. It is a way of compelling claimants to pursue their claims, not for their benefit but for the relief of the person interpleading - who takes no further part in the case (*De La Rue v Hernu, Peron & Stockwell Ltd* [1936] 2 KB 164). There are two forms of interpleader, but we shall only be concerned with execution interpleader which applies to HCEOs, county court bailiffs and bailiffs enforcing road traffic penalties. Before the process is examined, a number of observations on general principles may be made.

- *claimants*: claims to property seized from the debtor may be made by a wide range of individuals - for example, partners, spouses, relatives, friends, lodgers, trade suppliers, trustees or liquidators in insolvencies, mortgagees under bills of sale (*Usher v Martin* [1889] 24 QBD 272) and hire or HP firms. These groups may all assert that the assets in question are owned solely by them. A claim does not need to be based solely on an assertion of absolute ownership. A person with an equitable interest in the goods, such as a lien or right of possession, may also make a claim. A debenture holder may thus make a claim. An assignee of a debt may not claim the proceeds of sale of an execution on a judgment for the debt (*Plant v Collins* [1913] 1 KB 242). In all cases, the claimant should put their claim in writing.

- *goods*: relief can be given in respect of any debt, money, goods or chattels. This can include choses in action such a share certificates

(*Robinson v Jenkins* [1890] 24 QBD 275) and money paid out under protest to prevent execution (*Smith v Critchfield* [1885] 14 QBD 873). A claimant may not be able to use interpleader to protect their goods if they have allowed the debtor to use them as their own- for instance, in the course of trade (*Engelbach v Dixon* [1875] 10 CP 645). Application can be made in the High Court even if there is only an intention to seize though there has been no actual seizure and regardless of whether the bailiff is actually in possession (CPR Sch.1, O17 r1 RSC; *Day v Carr* (1852) 7 Exch 883). Alternatively, where the bailiff suspects that a claim may be likely to be made by a third party, no seizure has to be made. Instead a return of no goods may be made, thus avoiding the need to interplead, even though the debtor may have some interest in the goods e.g. the equity of redemption in goods covered by a bill of sale (*Scarlett v Hanson* [1884] 12 QB 213).

- *investigation*: the bailiff should enquire into the validity of the claims made as failure to do this may disentitle the bailiff to protection from court action.

- *delay*: allowing for the above investigations, it is nonetheless important for the bailiff to seek interpleader as quickly as possible. Delay may mean the court refuses any protection or penalises the bailiff with costs (*Cook v Allen* (1833) 2 LJ Ex 199). The claimant may also be penalised for delay - for example it was held in *Watson v Park Royal (Caterers) Ltd* [1961] 2 All ER 346 that the defendants failed to act with "reasonable promptitude" in starting interpleader three and a half months after becoming aware of the competing claims.

Interpleader is not applicable where:

- the bailiff is no longer in possession of the goods, either because they have been abandoned or released to the claimant or the bailiff has been withdrawn (*Lea v Rossi* (1855) 11 Exch 13);

- the goods have been sold and the proceeds have been passed to the creditor; or,

- the claimant is the landlord seeking rent arrears. A special procedure applies (see 6.6.1).

9.26.2 *Procedure*

Application in the case of civil court executions is under CPR Sch.1 RSC O.17 for HCEOs and under ss100-101 CCA and CPR Sch.2 CCR O.33 for county court bailiffs.

N.B: In cases of the recovery of road traffic debts (as applied to the latter by Enforcement of Road Traffic Debts Order 1993) it seems that it will be necessary for an interpleader claimant to initiate a claim under Part 8 of the CPR. However, no deposit is required from the claimant in advance under s.100 of the County Courts Act.

In civil court cases, the bailiff seeks protection by initiating proceedings:

- to determine whether the property belongs to the debtor and thus may be seized or belongs to the claimant and is thus protected; and,

- to gain protection against other court actions arising out of any real and substantial grievance caused by his wrongful acts (see damages later). The bailiff will be protected in respect of actions which could result only in the award of nominal damages (*Cave v Capel* [1954] 1 QB 367). Thus even though the HCEO may, by a honest mistake, have entered third party premises and seized a third party's goods, if there is "mere nominal trespass" the HCEO will be protected unless there is an aggravating factor, such as insolent or oppressive behaviour (*Smith v Critchfield* [1885] 14 QBD 873).

The procedure will then follow the course described below.

Notice
In the High Court the third party must give notice of the claim, including a full description of goods, to the HCEO, who must forthwith notify the execution creditor, sending a copy of the claim. It is better to enter into specifics about the items claimed, rather than relying on a general claim such as to "all goods and money seized under the warrant", unless perhaps the costs of listing all items would be disproportionate (*Richardson v Wright* [1875] 10 Ex D 367). The creditor must then, within seven days, give notice whether or not the claim is admitted or disputed. If the creditor admits the claim, the HCEO withdraws. If the HCEO then fails to withdraw he may be liable to be sued and the court may refuse protection (*Sodeau v Shorey* (1896) 74 LT 240). The creditor is only liable for fees incurred by the HCEO until the notice was sent. If the creditor disputes the claim or fails to reply, the HCEO can apply to the Court for protection against any proceedings relating to the seizure and should withdraw from possession of the goods claimed. Protection from proceedings will normally be granted as the HCEO is protected by para.11, Sch.7 Courts Act 2003, but relief will not be granted where there is a substantial grievance against the HCEO which seems serious enough to override this immunity (see 'damages' later). On withdrawal the goods cease to be in legal custody and may be distrained (*Cropper v Warner* (1883) Cab & El 152), the execution creditor's remedy being against the

deposit (*Wells v Hughes* [1907] 2 KB 845). Even though the HCEO has withdrawn, the claimant may not remove the goods as this would be contempt.

In the county court the claimant serves notice on a county court district judge if the levying bailiff will not accept his/her claim. The district judge then notifies the creditor and requires a reply in four days. If notice is received within four days admitting the claim the bailiff is withdrawn and the creditor is only liable for fees incurred before the notice was served (CCR O.33 r2). The district judge may then seek an order from the Circuit Judge restraining any action being brought as a result of the disputed seizure. Normally the district judge will be protected under s.98 CCA but, as with the HCEO, this may be overridden (see later).

Application
In the High Court, if the claim is disputed by the execution creditor the HCEO applies for 'interpleader' by Part 8 claim, serving it on the creditor and claimant. It is good practice at this point for the bailiff to supply all parties with a copy of the inventory taken- certainly the HCEO should act impartially as an officer of the court and not supply an inventory to one party only (*Fredericks Timber Buildings v Wilkins* [1971] 1 WLR 1197). Within fourteen days, the claimant must serve on the other parties an affidavit specifying goods and chattels claimed and the grounds for the claim. S/he can also claim damages and give details of any grievance against the HCEO. The court may order a deposit as security (RSC O.17 r.5 and see below). In the county court if no reply is received or the creditor refuses to return of the goods then an interpleader summons is issued on N88 to the parties and a hearing of the case is arranged (CCR O.33 r4).

The effect of the issue of interpleader proceedings is to stay enforcement of the debt by any means (*Re: Ford* [1886] 18 QBD 369). If there is any concern about the safety of seized goods, application will have to be made to court for leave to remove or otherwise protect them.

Security deposit
The High Court may order payment of a deposit or the provision of security, and the county court must require this under CCR O.33 r.1(2)(b) and s.100 CCA when accepting any interpleader claim. The security may be a solicitor's undertaking, a bond from a bank or insurance company or a guarantee from a person with two other sureties. The purpose of the deposit is to place in the court's control a sum equivalent to the value of the disputed goods and, if the claimant wishes the bailiff to withdraw, a sum representing the possession costs that the bailiff has incurred up until that date. This fund then becomes the subject matter of the dispute and the goods are released to

the claimant and cannot be seized again by that creditor, even if the value is less than the debt due (*Haddow v Morton* [1894] 1 QB 565). In the county court if no deposit is paid the goods must be sold and the proceeds paid into court to await the judge's decision (s.100(3) CCA) unless the judge decides otherwise in the circumstances. Such a sale will pass good title to the goods (*Goodlock v Cousins* [1897] 1 QB 558). If less than the value is deposited the bailiffs must not withdraw from possession and the court can order the bailiff to retake possession (*Miller v Solomon* [1906] 2 KB 91). If the deposit does cover the debt and costs though not the value of the goods, the bailiff must not remain in possession after the date of the deposit and is not entitled to possession fees from then on (*Newsum Sons & Co Ltd v James* [1909] 2 KB 364). If a second execution occurs on goods already the subject of interpleader proceedings, the existing deposit cannot be relied on in further proceedings and the claimant will have to provide a further sum of security (*Kotchie v The Golden Sovereigns Ltd* [1898] 2 QB 164).

Sale of goods

As an alternative to requiring the deposit the court may order sale of the goods and that the proceeds be applied as it thinks just (RSC O.17 r.6). This may be done where:

- the goods are subject to a bill of sale;

- they are perishable;

- the safety of the goods is uncertain, for instance because the debtor will not agree to walking possession;

- it would be just and reasonable in order to save costs; or,

- as seen, where the claimant fails to provide the security required by the court.

The division of the proceeds is to be as the court sees fit, including interest at whatever rate and for whatever period is thought appropriate (*Forster v Clowser* [1897] 2 QB 362). If money remains in the hands of the HCEO after sale, this may only be released to the claimant or debtor on order from the court, and until then the bailiff cannot be sued (*Discount Banking Company of England & Wales v Lambarde* [1893] 2 QB 329). If the claim is then settled out of the proceeds, the claimant is not entitled to demand other sums from the HCEO not included in the original claim (see *Hockey v Evans* [1887] 18 QBD 390 in which the holder of a bill of sale demanded interest and extra costs and charges that would have been recoverable from the debtor under the agreement). Another option for the court is appointment of a receiver and manager of the disputed property if it seems that forced sale would lose value and where, most probably, the items claimed are business assets that can continue to be used to earn money by the claimant whilst the case is pending (*Howell v Dawson* [1884] 13 QBD 67).

Damages
In county court cases under CCR O.33 r.5 the claimant may enter a claim for any damages s/he feels were incurred within eight days of receiving the summons. In the High Court any such claim for damages will be made in a separate action. If it is proved that there is the basis for a 'substantial grievance' or that substantial injury has been suffered, damages should be awarded as it will not be just and reasonable to protect the bailiff. Factors to be taken into account when considering an award of damages will include:

- where there has been a sale at undervalue (*London, Chatham & Dover Railway Co Ltd* (1899) 80 LT 119);

- where the bailiff has entered the premises of a stranger and seized goods in belief that they are the debtor's, he may be protected against an action for trespass if no substantial grievance has been done. Thus a bailiff may be protected from an action by a person whose premises were wrongly entered or wrongly seized- but only so long as there was no insolent or oppressive behaviour or other misconduct (*Smith v Critchfield* [1885] 14 QBD 873). If only nominal damages could be recovered by the claimant, the bailiff should be protected (*Winter v Bartholemew* (1856) 11 Exch 704). The bailiff is not protected where they are guilty of a moral fault and substantial grievance is caused (*De Coppet v Barnet* (1901) 17 TLR 273); or

- where the claim arose from the bailiff's own wrongful actions- for instance, there has been forced entry or trespass against the person (*Cave v Capel* [1954] 1 QB 367), goods were seized in the knowledge that they were not the debtor's (*Tufton v Harding* (1859) 29 LJ Ch 225) or that they were already seized in distress (*Haythorn v Bush* (1834) 2 Dowl 641).

Even if the bailiff acts mistakenly, s/he will not be protected where the circumstances aggravate the wrongs done. Damages can be awarded even though the goods have been sold and are no longer under the court's control (*Hills v Renny* [1880] 5 Ex D 313). The fact that action is stayed against the bailiff will not prevent the claimant suing the purchaser- this cannot be stopped as part of interpleader proceedings (*Hills v Renny ante*). See also the discussion at 10.5.6 under 'Title on sale'.

A damages claim in the county court must be made before the hearing of the interpleader claim. If it is not, it will be too late afterwards as the decision on the matter by the county court under s.101 CCA is treated as final and conclusive (*West v Automatic Salesman Ltd* [1937] 2 All ER 706). Section 101(3) requires that the judge "shall adjudicate on the claim"- this renders the matter effectively '*res judicata*' (*Death v Harrison* [1871] 6 Exch 15). Whether the claimant forgets to claim or fails to particularise the claim, once the decision has been made the court is '*functus officio*' however good the claim for damages (*Kershaw v Automatic Salesman Ltd* (1937) 4 LJCCR 60).

Hearing
The court can summarily determine the matter when the HCEO applies, where all parties consent or one so requests or where the question at issue is one of law, not fact, and the case is thus straightforward and speed is important. Summary determination does not mean that no time will be given to gather evidence or to cross examine witnesses. A special hearing date should be set, discovery should be allowed etc (*PB Manufacturing v Fahn* [1967] 1 WLR 1059). If, on the basis of the evidence in the claimant's affidavit, the issue appears to be a dispute as to the ownership, the court may direct it to be tried either before a High Court Judge or in the county court (RSC O.17 r.5). Summary determination is not appropriate where the claimant's affidavit raises a serious claim to goods of an overall considerable value and the prospect of difficult points of law (*Fredericks & Pelhams Timber Buildings v Wilkins* [1971] 3 All ER 545).

If the claimant fails to attend or fails to comply with the order made, the Court may bar him/her from any future claims. If the execution creditor does not appear the HCEO is ordered to withdraw from possession. The HCEO will of course be told to withdraw if the third party's claim is established. If the claimant only establishes title to some of the goods, s/he is entitled to be paid from the deposit a sum representing the value of those goods, though the execution creditor will receive the balance (*Tellus Super Vacuum Cleaners v Ireland* (1938) LJCCR 54). If the claimant fails to establish the title claimed, he is not normally precluded from relying on a different title that is found by the court. See for example *Peake v Carter* [1916] 1 KB 652 in which the claimant asserted that goods were his sole property but which turned out to be joint property of a partnership with the judgment debtor and thus protected by s23(1) Partnership Act 1890). Similar orders may be made in the county court.

Costs
If the claimant fails, the bailiff can receive costs from the date of notice of claim or from the sale, which is earliest. If the claimant succeeds, the bailiff gets costs from the creditor from the time when the latter authorised

interpleader proceedings. All costs are awarded at the judge's discretion under either CPR Sch.1 RSC O.17 r.8 or Sch.2 CCR O.33).

9.27 Interference with goods

Any misappropriation of goods should properly be referred to as wrongful interference with goods (under the Torts (Interference with Goods) Act 1977), which provides common remedies for a range of wrongs against personal property that were previously actionable separately and are encountered in the older case reports as trover, detinue and trespass. Wrongful interference may be defined in three ways (conversion, trespass and negligence), though the offences are not completely exclusive and a seizure may turn out to be both conversion and trespass.

The remedies available through the court are:

- an order for delivery of the goods and the payment of any consequential damages (s3(2)(a) 1977 Act);

- an order for delivery with the alternative for the defendant to pay damages based on the value of the goods, with consequential damages in addition in either case (s3(2)(b)); or,

- damages alone, based on the assessed value of the goods plus any consequential damages (s3(2)(c));

- plus, if appropriate, an interlocutory injunction (s4) for recovery of the goods.

An order for specific delivery alone is at the discretion of the court and is rare unless the item is of special significance or value to the claimant, or it may be impossible for the claimant to find a replacement, perhaps because they are no longer made. The claimant may choose between the other remedies, though in cases were the goods are no longer in the defendant's hands, whether through destruction or disposal, damages are clearly the option to choose. The debtor can sue both the bailiff who commits the act and any person who is responsible for that action e.g. a creditor who has authorised wrongful seizure.

9.27.1 *Conversion*

Conversion includes three different forms of wrongful interference that involve appropriating another's goods or depriving that person of their use or possession. The gist of conversion is that there has been some wrongful act that interferes with, is inconsistent with, or deprives the owner of his/ her rights over, goods by asserting rights that are contrary to or negative them. Thus wrongfully taking goods into possession will be conversion (see *Tinkler v Poole* (1770) 5 Burr 2657; *Shipwick v Blanchard* (1795) 6 TR 298), as will wrongfully receiving goods, wrongfully selling them, wrongfully retaining them or any other dealing that leads to the loss or destruction of the goods or which denies the claimant's title. Taking under duress, such as obtaining property under a wrongful threat of execution can be conversion (*Grainger v Hill* (1838) 4 Bing NC 212). The duress must be equivalent to forcible taking and thus we must assume that taking property as a result of a lawful threat is not conversion.

Scope Conversion is any interference (whether by detention or dealing, whether temporary or permanent) which denies or is inconsistent with the rights of the owner of goods, whether s/he has actual possession of them or an immediate right to possession. These same principles apply in replevin (see *Smith v Mulcahy* [1934] 1 KB 608). Conversion can apply to execution (*Garland v Carlisle* (1873) 4 Cl & Fin 693) and distress (*Shipwick v Blanchard* (1795) 6 TR 298; *Clowes v Hughes* [1870] 5 Exch 160). Conversion will be more permanent than the possibly brief interference with possession that constitutes trespass. The three forms are:

- *wrongful dealing*: this is any dealing with or disposal of goods that is inconsistent with the owner's rights, whether in intentional or not. An illegal sale of goods is thus conversion (e.g. *Neumann v Bakeaway* later at 10.5.3). An auctioneer who knowingly receives illegally seized goods is also guilty of conversion by wrongful dealing.

- *wrongful detention*: this covers any detention of goods that consciously deprives a person of the use or possession of them. Thus a bailiff would be liable to an action if he refused to deliver up goods wrongly seized after being informed that this was the case or wrongfully impounded them after tender of the debt due (*Six Carpenters' Case* (1610) All ER 292). Refusal of tender after impounding is not conversion (*Singleton v Williamson* (1862) 7 H&N 747) nor is levying for more than is due (*Whitworth v Smith* (1832) 5 C&P 250). A mere threat to detain goods or prevent their removal by the rightful owner would not be conversion (*England v Cowley* [1873] 8 Exch 126). Seizing exempt goods is conversion (*Keen v Priest* (1859) 4 H&N 236). The claimant must make a demand for the goods which should be unconditional and specific and the refusal should also be unconditional. Unlawful keeping may also be implied if the defendant uses the goods in a manner inconsistent with the owner's rights. This could include 'abuse' of distrained goods (see 10.4.2).

- *wrongful destruction*: this term refers to any loss or destruction of goods that a bailee like a bailiff in possession has allowed in breach of his duty to the owner.

Claimants with a limited interest may sue a stranger with no interest in the goods for conversion, to the extent of the value of that limited interest (see *Chubb v Crilley* [1983] 2 All ER 294 CA). Thus a bailee can sue a bailor to the extent of his interest e.g. the value of the pledge. S/he must however account to the actual owner for any surplus recovered over and above the value of their own interest.

Damages
The measure of general damages in conversion is the market value of the goods lost at the date of conversion (*Chubb Cash Ltd v John Crilley & Son* [1983] 2 All ER 294 CA) plus any consequential or special damages incurred by the claimant provided that they are not too remote. If special damages are claimed there is no need to prove any financial loss in order to recover them. All such damages that are a natural and direct result of the conversion may be recovered, including damages for non-pecuniary losses such as inconvenience, distress and loss of enjoyment, loss of a purchaser, wasted expenses and standing charges, insurance excesses, lost no-claims bonuses, loss of use of a vehicle or the cost of hire of a substitute and loss of profit from an income earning chattel. An example of the assessment of the quantum of damages in a case of illegal seizure and sale of a car is the county court decision in *Ba Tu Dinh v Drakes Group Ltd* (2000). The judge referred to Parker's Guide to ascertain the market value of the car (rather than relying on the auction price). Loss of use was also allowed, plus interest on the total sum from the date of the levy.

Losses such as loss of profits on a contract cannot be recovered as they are too remote - unless the defendant could have foreseen them, for example, perhaps where tools of the trade are seized. Where the goods are on HP the measure is the market value or the sum still due under the agreement, which ever is the lesser. The best evidence of market value is the price fetched by sale at auction by the bailiff. If there is no market value, the cost of replacement should be used. If the value of the item has risen, this may be recoverable as consequential damages.

If goods are not lost but damaged the measure of damages is the reduction in their value (i.e. the reasonable costs of repairs to restore goods to their prior condition) plus loss of use until the repairs are done or the cost of hiring a replacement in the interim. These damages may be topped up if, despite the repairs, the market value of the goods is permanently reduced. If it is cheaper to replace rather than repair goods, the replacement price will be awarded. It does not matter that the repairs have not yet, and may never be done. No deduction from the damages may be made for the debt due (*Edmondson v Nuttall* (1864) 17 CBNS 280). It is not a defence that sums illegally raised were applied to a debt legally due (*Attack v Bramwell* (1863) 3 B&S 528).

Aggravated damages may be possible, such as damage to business or reputation. See *Brewer v Drew* (1843) 11 M&W 625 and *Smith v Enright* (1893) 69 LT 724 which support this, although *Dixon v Calcraft* [1892] 1 QB 458 is to the contrary. See too 7.5.2 for further discussion. Exemplary damages may also be awarded. An example of the potential level of an award of exemplary damages is the case of *Bhatnagar & Elanrent v Whitehall Investments* (1996) 5 CL 166. A landlord levied distress on the entire contents of business premises after both re-entry and a judgment for the rent arrears. It was held that the landlord's excessive and illegal levy, along with his obstructive behaviour, indicated that he was motivated by a desire to make a profit and, in addition to general damages of £54,500 for conversion based upon the value of the goods seized, the court awarded exemplary damages of £12,500 plus interest.

Exemplary damages arising from statute also have an application to conversion. As stated in 7.1 the goods of service personnel are protected from seizure. Section 13(2) of the Reserve & Auxiliary Forces Act 1953 allows the court to award exemplary damages for seizures in such cases (although it has been suggested that this relates to aggravated rather than exemplary damages - *Broome v Cassell & Co* [1972] AC 1027).

Redelivery
If goods are redelivered and accepted by the defendant an action is not barred but the damages will be reduced or mitigated. The same applies where the goods are returned after the action is commenced. The claimant may get nominal damages for loss of possession, as the fact of conversion cannot be absolved (*Lamb v Wall* (1859) 1 F&F 503), plus consequential damages and damages for any deterioration in goods. If there has been no substantial loss, the claimant may face the costs of the action. This is because, although the conversion vests a right of action, the recovery of the goods will be regarded as *pro tanto* satisfaction and will accordingly reduce the award (*Plevin v Henshall* (1833) 10 Bing 24). The claimant may refuse to accept redelivery as the action is for the value of the goods, not the goods themselves. The court may however stay an action on the basis that the goods are handed over and/ or grant an order for consequential damages only. The damages will also be reduced if the goods were never taken out of the debtor's use, such as the bailiff putting a man in possession (*Bayliss v Fisher* (1830) 7 Bing 153).

9.27.2 *Trespass to goods*

Scope Trespass to goods is direct, intentional or forcible interference that disturbs possession of goods. It will arise when there is an illegal seizure or removal or any other unpermitted impact upon or contact with them. This contact must be deliberate or direct, though as the tort is actionable without proof of damage, only very minor damage or contact will suffice (*Fouldes v Willoughby* (1841) 8M&W 540). This can include moving goods on the debtor's premises, although they may be moved only a very short distance (*Kirk v Gregory* [1876] 1 Exch 55). Trespass can also include direct acts causing damage to goods, but the onus of proof of such negligence will be on the claimant (the owner of the goods). The successful claimant is entitled as of right to recover general damages as there has been a trespass (as to land), but the award may also be exemplary or aggravated. Such trespass could arise if a bailiff seizes hire purchase goods (*Jones Bros (Holloway) Ltd v Woodhouse* [1923] 2 KB 117).

Damages
The measure of damages for trespass are as in conversion if the claimant is deprived of the goods. Special damages can thus be claimed for loss of employment as well as loss of tools if the trade implements of a self employed person were taken, or for fall in value of stock that could not be sold, or the loss of hire of a chattel. If goods are damaged without possession being lost, damages for trespass will only be the loss actually suffered as a direct result of the trespass- that is, any depreciation plus any consequential losses.

Aggravated damages will be recoverable to compensate for mental distress or injury to feelings arising from the defendant's manner of committing the tort, or his/ her conduct afterwards- for example, injury to a trader's reputation. Exemplary damages may also be recovered.

9.27.3 *Seizure of fixtures*

In cases of the severance of fixtures, the claimant may claim for either trespass to land or for wrongful interference. The choice depends on the relative values before and after severance. In the claims for trespass, the claimant may be entitled to claim not only general damages but also a figure for aggravated damages if fixtures have been removed. In conversion, even if the value of the item is greater as a fixture than as a chattel, that larger sum has not been allowed in claims for conversion because they are concerned with wrongful interference with goods and there is no such interference until fixtures have been severed and already have a lower value. Actions for trespass to land are therefore probably preferable. See for example *Clarke v Holford* (1848) 2 C&K 540; *Moore v Drinkwater* (1858) 1 F&F 134; *Barff v Probyn* (1895) 64 LJQB 557. In the latter action the measure of damages allowed was as in trespass, the figure being not a sum equivalent to the proceeds of sale of the severed fixtures but the amount that an incoming tenant would pay for them if they were *in situ*.

9.27.4 *Negligence*

Negligence is any mishandling of goods leading to their damage, loss or destruction (see *Watson v Murray & Co* [1955] 1 All ER 350). It could occur at any stage during the levy, from seizure (*Anon* (1572) 3 Leon Rep 15), during removal or at sale. The claim is for the value of the goods lost. The payment of the damages will extinguish the claimant's claim to the remains of their goods (*Attack v Bramwell* (1863) 3 B & S 520; *Keen v Priest* (1859) 4 H & N 236). A bailiff is not negligent if he has exercised reasonable care and diligence and the damage is done by third parties (*Willis, Winder & Co v Combe* (1884) 1 Cab & El 353).

9.28 Wrongful execution

Although illegal execution is trespass the levy remains good (*De Gondouin v Lewis* (1839) 10 Ad & E 117). Thus goods seized after a tortious entry are still validly taken (*Percival v Stamp* (1854) 9 Ex 167) i.e. illegal execution does necessarily not affect the validity of subsequent seizure or sale, but the person can sue. The remedy is for the debtor to apply for the execution to be set aside or amended or for restitution of the wrongfully seized goods to be ordered, if necessary (*Rhodes v Hull* (1857) 26 LJ Ex 265). There can be a claim for damages if there is evidence of malice, bad faith or actual damage which can be proved or if the goods had been sold (*Perkins v Plympton* (1831) 7 Bing 676). An (unusual) example of damages for wrongful execution is the case of *Keene v Dilke* (1849) 4 Exch 388). Goods wrongfully seized by a sheriff were then seized from his custody in a levy of distress. The owner paid off the second debt and then sued the sheriff for the amount paid.

9.29 Replevin

Replevin is an historic remedy to obtain recovery of goods that have been illegally seized, whether by distress or by other means (*Mellor v Leather* (1853) 1 E& B 619). It is used rarely because of its obscurity and cost and because interlocutory orders for the delivery up of goods under s4 Torts (Interference with Goods) Act 1977 (see 9.27) are now a preferable means of achieving the same result. A right of possession is not enough upon which to found replevin (*Templeman v Case* (1711) 10 MR 24), the claimant must have property in the goods, though a person with use or enjoyment of goods by the consent of the owner has enough special property to justify a replevy (Fell v Whittaker [1871] 7 QB 120). Thus a bailor may not replevy goods taken from a bailee (*Mennie v Blake* (1856) 6 E&B 842), though the bailee may do so (*Smith v Mulcahy* [1934] 1 KB 608). An agent cannot replevy (2 Co Inst 146). If separate individuals' goods are taken in one levy, each must replevy separately, though joint owners may initiate one replevin. Executors may replevy a testator's goods taken whilst s/he was alive (*Arundell v Trevell* (1662) 1 Sid 81).

Replevin is applicable to statutory distraint as well as to distress for rent (*Sabourin v Marshall* (1832) 3 B & Ad 440; *Rhymney Railway Co v Price* (1867) 16 LT 395; *London County Council v Hackney Borough Council* [1928] 2 KB 588). It is not applicable to execution in the High Court (see *George v Chambers* (1843) 11 M & W 149 or *Bradshawe's Case* (1597) Cro Eliz 570). However, the HCEO can be ordered to return wrongfully seized goods (see 9.26). Seizure under the order of an inferior court - i.e. either a county court or magistrates' court - cannot normally be replevied unless the warrant in question was issued in excess of or completely outside the court's jurisdiction (*George v Chambers* above; *Wilson v Weller* (1819) 3 Moore CP 294; *Fenton v Boyle* (1807) 2 Bos & Pul NP 391). For instance in *Hannigan v Burgess* [1888] 26 NBR 99 the court stated that replevin will not lie against distress for a fine as the conviction is conclusive and not questionable by replevin. To attempt to replevy a valid court warrant could be construed as contempt of court (*R v Burchet* (1723) 8 MR 208). At common law distress by the Crown could not be replevied (*Cawthorne v Campbell* (1790) 1 Anst 205) but it would seem that since the Crown Proceedings Act 1947 s.21 the remedy is possible against crown levies.

Replevin is not available where a distress is lawful but can be used in any case of illegal seizure, for instance, where there is no debt due, an illegal entry occurred or exempt goods were seized. It could also be used after a wrongful second distress (*Anon* (1702) 7 Mod Rep 118). The distress must be wholly illegal, therefore a replevin cannot be founded on a dispute over levy for a debt, part of which is admitted to be due (*White v Greenish* (1861) 11 CBNS 209). The use of replevin bars other remedies for the same distress (*Prude v Beke* (1310) Hil 4 Ed II) and is an alternative to an action for trespass to goods (*Solers v Wotton* (1405) YB 7 Hen 4 fo 27 pl.5). If replevin is commenced in error, an action may still be commenced (*Allen v Sharp* (1848) 2 Exch 352). However the bailiff may still be sued for trespass to land, even after a replevy, as the remedy relates to wrongful detention of goods and not to torts relating to land (*Gibbs v Cruickshank* [1873] 8 CP 454). Even if the goods are successfully replevied, they may be seized again by the same creditor for a debt that accrued subsequently (*Hefford v Alger* (1808) 1 Taunt 218).

A person can replevy within six years of seizure if the goods are un-sold (*Jacob v King* (1814) 5 Taunt 451; *Griffiths v Stephens* (1819) 1 Chitt 196). Action can be taken against the bailiff, the authorising person or both. It is begun in the county court for the district in which the goods were seized (*R v*

Raines (1853) 1 E&B 855; *Fordham v Akers* (1863) 4 B&S 578), the powers being found under s144 and Sch.1 CCA and consists of two parts.

9.29.1 *The replevy*

The owner (the replevisor) presents a notice stating the facts, provides a replevin bond and gives an undertaking that an action will be commenced within four weeks within the county court or within a week in the High Court. The bond will either be a sum deposited in court, or a bond with securities, that the action will be commenced "with effect and without delay". The level of security required is set by the district judge at a figure considered sufficient to cover the probable costs of the action and the alleged debt. The security could be a solicitor's undertaking to pay. Any fees payable are at the discretion of the district judge within limits of the county court fees scale.

The term 'with effect' means that the action must be pursued to a successful conclusion- if not the security is forfeit (*Jackson v Hanson* (1841) 8 M&W 477). Delay should be avoided as otherwise the action may be regarded as having been abandoned, in which case again the security may be forfeit for breach of the conditions (*Axford v Perret* (1828) 4 Bing 586 - a delay of two years; *Morris v Matthews* (1841) 2 QB 293; *Evans v Bowen* (1850) 19 LJQB 8). The district judge is empowered under CPR Part 25.12 to determine the terms and manner of the security, which must be accepted provided that it is adequate (*Young v Broughton Waterworks Co* (1861) 31 LJQB 14). All forms will need to be drafted from precedents by the claimant as standard court forms do not presently exist. The district judge then instructs the court bailiff by warrant to deliver the goods to the replevisor. The replevisor must then begin the action without delay and undertake to return the goods if ordered. If the bailiff does dispose of the goods, despite notice of the replevy, he may be sued (*Mounsey v Dawson* (1837) 6 A&E 752).

It is possible for the replevy to be challenged. The creditor may apply to set it aside (*Rhymney Railway Co v Price* (1867) 16 LT 394) or to attach a court officer for contempt (*R v Monkhouse* (1743) 2 Stra 1184). This would normally occur where an unreplevisable distress has been the subject of court proceedings (see above).

9.29.2 *The action*

The action must then be commenced by summons, with particulars of claim filed in line with CPR Part 8. A hearing follows with the bailiff (the seizor) as defendant.

If successful, the replevisor recovers the expenses of the replevy plus damages to be assessed as in an action for trespass (*Dixon v Calcraft* [1892] 1 QB

458). As the goods will usually have been returned, these will normally be the value of the replevin bond itself, though if the goods are not recovered the full value of the goods plus damages for detention may be awarded. It used to be held that the joinder of other causes of action with an action for replevin was at common law illegal and irregular (*Mungean v Wheatley* (1851) 6 Exch 88) and the county court rules included provisions requiring leave of court to join actions. However since *Smith v Enright* (1893) 69 LT 724 it has been the practice to assess damages as in illegal distress and thus to allow inclusion of any consequential damages suffered by reason of the distress (*Gibbs v Cruickshank* as above). Examples are *Brewer v Dew* (1843) 11 M&W 625 in which damages for injury to credit and reputation were also awarded, *Sperry Inc v CIBC* [1985] 17 DLR 236 in which the cost of maintaining a letter of credit as security for the goods was held to be a reasonable consequential loss and *Smith v Enright* (1893) 63 LJQB 220 in which damages were held to be allowable for loss, annoyance and injury to a person's reputation. No further action could then be taken in respect of damages. If the seizor is unsuccessful, it is not usually possible to appeal the decision, even on payment of the costs. This is because it is generally seen as unfair to the sureties to renew their liability and to expose the claimant once more to the risk of paying full costs, whilst there is normally some other remedy available for the debt due (*Parry v Duncan* (1831) 7 Bing 243; *Edgson v Caldwell* [1873] 8 CP 647).

If the seizor (the bailiff) is successful, s/he is entitled to an order for the return of the goods. Though it is usual to recover the seizor's costs, a money judgment in lieu of the goods is not possible (*Jamieson v Trevelyan* (1855) 10 Exch 748) unless for some reason it is impossible to recover the goods. If this is the case, damages for their value and for their detention may be awarded (*Ash v Wood* (1587) Cro Eliz 59).

If the conditions of the replevin bond are not satisfied distrainors have two remedies. They may either:

- claim the sum secured by the bond (*Dix v Groom* [1880] 5 Ex D 91); or,

- make a court claim for the damages caused by the breach (*Waterman v Yea* (1756) 2 Wils 41; *Turnor v Turner* (1820) 2 Brod & Bing 107; *Tummons v Ogle* (1856) 6 E&B 571). The action may be against all the sureties jointly or any one of them. Each surety or obligor is only liable for the amount of rent in arrear at the date of the distress and the costs of the distrainor (*Ward v Henley* (1827) 1 Y&J 285). Their total liability cannot exceed the amount of the penalty on the bond and the costs of the action on the bond (*Hefford v Alger* (1808) 1 Taunt 218). Any award of costs and any decision as to the basis upon which these are calculated is completely at the discretion of the court. Proceedings on the bond may be stayed by payment of the penalty and costs, even though the claimant's costs in the replevin action are bound to exceed the penalty (*Branscombe v Scarborough* (1844) 6 QB 13) and if the rent due is argued to be less than the sum secured, the court may rule on this (*Dix v Groom* [1880] 5 Exch 91). The fact that the distrainor has obtained judgment for the rent due in the trial of the replevin action is no defence to an action on the bond (*Turnor v Turner* above).

Breach of the bond may occur, for instance, the claimant does not prosecute the case within a reasonable time, but the court will protect the claimant if the reason for delay has been delay by the seizor (*Evans v Bowen* (1850) 19 LJQB 8) or simply the death of the replevisor (*Morris v Matthews* (1841) 2 QB 293).

9.30 Restitution order

One further remedy applies only to inner London. Under s27 Metropolitan Police Courts Act 1839, a magistrates' court district judge has the power to order the return of goods that are being illegally detained within the Metropolitan Police area. The court may make an order for the return of the goods either absolutely or on terms as to payment of such sums as the judge thinks fit. If the order is not complied with, or if the goods are disposed of despite the order, the defendant shall forfeit the full value of the goods as assessed by the magistrate. The defendant may, within six months, seek to recover any goods delivered up under this summary remedy. This remedy is clearly of limited applicability, both in terms of the area and circumstances to which it applies, but it may be a relatively quick and inexpensive means of recovering goods if it is available to a client.

9.31 Rent remedies

A number of little used remedies apply to distress for rent for the protection of goods that have been wrongfully seized for one reason or another.

9.31.1 *Exempt goods*

A restitution order can be made where any of the tenant's clothing and bedding within the statutory exemption (s4 LDAA 1888) have been seized by the landlord. The court may order either restoration of the goods if not sold or a sum to be paid in compensation by the bailiff, the figure being assessed by the courts (s4 LDAA 1895).

9.31.2 *Lodger's or stranger's goods*

If the property of any third parties such a stranger and lodgers (see 9.23) are removed by the landlord, despite service of the written notice application may be made to the magistrates' court for a declaration that the goods are exempt and for an order for their return. It has been held that as landlords' common law rights were altered by these provisions in favour of lodgers and subtenants in the LDAA 1908, the Act should be construed strictly and in landlords' favour (*Lawrence Chemical Co v Rubinstein* [1982] 1 WLR 284).

These individuals must make a written declaration to the landlord in a set form accompanied by an inventory stating that items levied upon are theirs. It is an offence under the Perjury Act to make a false declaration (s2 LDAA 1908). Such declarations can only be made within a reasonable time after distress- they are not effective against a distress which is not yet authorised or threatened (*Thwaites v Wilding* [1883] 12 QBD 4). If the declaration fails to state that the goods are exempted from seizure by the 1908 Act, it is a fatal defect and the goods lose the protection given by s1(c) (*Druce & Co Ltd v Beaumont Property Trust Ltd* [1935] 2 KB 257). A declaration that includes an inventory of goods that is unsigned is not defective providing the declaration itself is signed (*Godlonton v Fulham & Hampstead Property Co Ltd* [1905] 1 KB 431). A declaration made by a person without declaring their status (a lodger) or without stating whether rent was due to the landlord was sufficient as the Act requires no statement on the declarant's status and failure to make any assertion about rent due must be interpreted as implying that no rent was due (*ex p Harris* [1885] 16 QBD 130). If the declaration is made by a company, it can be made by a duly authorised agent such as a solicitor as well as by a director or company secretary (*Lawrence Chemical Co Ltd v Rubinstein* [1982] 1 WLR 284). If the declaration is made by a partnership there is no need for all partners to sign it; nor does it have to be in the form of a statutory declaration (*Rogers, Eungblutt & Co v Martin* [1911] 1 KB 19).

The declaration must include a claim to the goods seized, plus a statement of the rent payable to the mesne landlord, and the periods for which it is due, plus an undertaking to pay this rent direct to the head landlord until the rent arrears of the mesne landlord are cleared (s1). Additionally under s6 of the 1908 Act the landlord may serve notice on a sub-tenant requiring direct payment of future rent. Such a notice is not a levy of distress, but has been described as a 'statutory assignment of a chose in action' (Lord Greene MR in *Wallrock v Equity & Law Life Assurance Society* [1942] 2 KB 82). Sub-tenants must then pay any rent direct to the landlord until the tenant's arrears are cleared. If the sub-tenant then fails to pay, distress may be levied upon them directly.

On receiving a declaration the landlord should return the goods and to continue to distrain would render it illegal. If this is not done the person may apply before two JPs or one stipendiary magistrate for a restoration order, which should be granted if the court is satisfied that the applicant is entitled after enquiry into the truth of their declaration and inventory. In either case if the bailiff does not comply, he faces committal or daily penalties until the goods are returned.

Whilst if any goods belonging to a stranger are seized by the landlord the owner can be reimbursed for their value by the tenant owing the rent (*Exall v Partridge* (1799) 8 TR 308 - and see 9.32 later), it does not seem that there is any implied indemnity for the rent by the mesne landlord to the subtenant upon which the latter may sue (*Schlenker v Moxsy* (1825) 3 B&C 789; *Baber v Harris* (1839) 9 Ad & El 532). A lodger may sue the landlord and bailiff for selling even if s/he has not served the declaration described earlier (*Sharpe v Fowle* [1884] 12 QBD 385). The claimant to the goods has the option also to sue for illegal distress (*Lowe v Dorling* [1905] 2 KB 501; affirmed on appeal [1906] 2 KB 772 CA). The Court of Appeal held that the summary means of restitution before the justices does not prejudice the right to sue for the tort, or replevy (though the summary remedy supplements the right to replevy, which is hampered by the need for security).If the landlord does continue to distrain after notice from the lodger, an action for illegal distress lies against him/ her but not against the bailiff (*Page v Vallis* (1903) 19 TLR 393).

9.31.3 *Exempt beasts*

At common law plough beasts were not seizable in distress for rent if other sufficient goods were available, and this rule was confirmed by the Statute of Exchequer of Henry III. If a levy occurs that is illegal in this respect the tenant may rescue the beasts or may sue on the statute, there being no action at common law (*Porphrey v Legingham* (1668) 2 Keble 290). This is for trespass against the provisions of the statute. It is for the defendant to allege that there was no distress available for seizure at the time of the levy (*Anon* Dyer 312). Even though the tenant may pay or tender the rent claimed in order to release their beasts, this will not prevent them suing for violation of the statute.

9.31.4 *Double damages*

In the case of a distress that was illegal because no rent was due, the owner of the goods (whether that is the tenant or third party) has a right by statute (s.4 DRA 1689), to recover double the value of goods taken and sold by an action of trespass or upon the case (*Chancellor v Webster* (1893) 9 TLR 568). This procedure is similar to the exemplary damages that might be recoverable in cases of unjustified statutory distraint. The offence is not complete unless actual sale occurs. This is an additional remedy to those discussed earlier. Nothing less than double damages may be awarded (*Masters v Farris* (1845) 1 CB 715).

9.31.5 *Agricultural holdings*

Wrongful distress against an agricultural holding attracts extra remedies for the tenant under s19 Agricultural Holdings Act 1986. If there is any dispute as to:

- whether any levy of distress for rent complies with the 1986 Act;

- ownership of stock or the cost of feeding agisted beasts (see 9.22); or,

- any other related question,

a county court or magistrates court may determine it. The court may order return of any stock or things unlawfully distrained, declare the price of feed, or make any other order justice requires.

9.32 Pay & claim

It would be open to a third party owner of goods to simply pay the debt due and then sue the debtor, as it is a principle of law that where one person's goods are taken to satisfy another's debts, the owner shall have a remedy against the debtor for an indemnity (*In Re: Button ex p Haviside* [1907] 2 KB 180; *Edmunds v Wallingford* [1885] 14 QBD 811). This will be encountered in the older case reports as an action for '*assumpsit*' (e.g. *Exall v Partridge* (1799) 8 TR 308). The action would be either for the sum paid out to the bailiff or the value of the goods if they have been sold (*Groom v Bluck* (1841) 2 Man & G 567; *Lampleigh v Brathwaite* (1616) 1 Sm LC 151; *Dering v Winchelsea* (1787) 1 W&T 106). An exception may be made by the courts where the claimant is personally liable to the debtor or where s/he has left goods at the debtor's property for his/ her own convenience and could have removed them to avoid seizure (*England v Marsden* [1866] 1 CP 529).

If the debtor denies the validity of the seizure or feels exempt goods have been seized, it is also open to him/ her to pay off the debt and costs to the bailiff and then sue to recover those sums from the creditor. Although payment under protest in such circumstances is not the only option open to the debtor to alleviate an alleged unlawful interference with his/ her property (replevin and the like are arguably more apposite), any such payment is involuntary, being made under coercion, and an action may be commenced to recover it (*Kanhaya Lal v National Bank of India* (1913) 29 TLR 314). For the use of this remedy to recover disputed fees, see 11.5.

TCEA 2007- commentary

It is not expected that the regulations made under the new Act will alter the categories of statutory exemption from seizure, although these classes of goods will be extended to all forms of 'taking control' without any of the current variations from form to form.

This being the case, it is likely that current problems experienced with levies may continue to be encountered. The most significant is the very frequent practice of including numbers of exempt goods on inventories. This is often justified on the grounds that, although listed, there was no intention ultimately to remove these items. It should be apparent from all the foregoing discussion that this is argument has no substance or support in the laws of distress. If items are exempted from being levied, they are exempted from being seized and impounded - that is, from being listed on an inventory and covered by any form of possession agreement. Removal is, in a sense, irrelevant to this. It would seem that the main reason for the practice of listing exempt goods in inventories is to make it appear that a levy is more extensive than may actually be the case - that the debtor has goods worth seizing when in fact s/he has not. If such inventories are encountered, they should be challenged.

Chapter 10

CONDUCTING LEVIES:
REMOVAL AND SALE

10.1 Conduct after seizure

Once goods have been seized, the bailiff cannot remain an unreasonable time (*Cartwright v Comber* (1728) 2 Ld Raym 1427; *Cooke v Birt* (1814) 5 Taunt 765; *Winterbourne v Morgan* (1774) 11 East 395). In the latter case a bailiff stayed fifteen days on the premises and was held to be a trespasser for remaining too long and disturbing the claimant's possession. In *Aitkenhead v Blades* (1813) 5 Taunt 198 unreasonable possession by the sheriff was held to render the execution trespass *ab initio*. The sheriff entered into the property on April 10th and remained twelve hours. This was repeated on diverse days thereafter until May 6th. Sale of the seized goods was held on the premises, without the debtor's consent, on April 26th, but the sheriff remained constantly on the premises for a further ten days even though the goods could have been sold and removed in only a few hours. This major disturbance of the debtor's possession was held to be wholly illegal (see also *Ash v Dawnay* (1852) 8 Exch 237; *Lee v Dangar & Co* [1892] 1 QB 231). It may not, though, be trespass *ab initio* in most forms of distraint (*Smith v Egginton* (1837) 7 A&E 167) though the HCEO remaining in possession for nearly six months was held to be trespass *ab initio* (*Reed v Harrison* (1778) 2 Wm Bl 1218). The common law position is altered for distress for rent by s10 Distress for Rent Act 1737, which requires removal and sale after a minimum of five days (*Griffin v Scott* (1726) 2 Ld Raym 1424/ Stra 717). It is trespass to expel the occupant after entry (*Bissett v Caldwell* (1791) Peake 50). Conversely, it amounts to trespass for the debtor to exclude the bailiff (see 7.5).

10.2 Notice of Seizure

Having completed the seizure the bailiff will commonly leave the debtor with a notice of seizure confirming what has occurred. Notices will commonly include the following information:

- the debt due and costs incurred so far;

- an inventory of the goods seized, and;

- often, a walking possession agreement. Though strictly speaking this is a separate document, it is often incorporated in to the notice of seizure for convenience.

Other information may also be required to be left by statute: for example the Distress for Rent Rules 1988 contain a prescribed form for use in distress for rent and road traffic execution. It would not appear that the seizure or impounding can be invalidated just because the debtor refuses to accept the notice or inventory (*R v Butterfield* (1893) 17 Cox CC 598).

10.2.1 *Notice*

No notice of distress at all is required from the Magistrates' bailiff, Inland Revenue or Customs and Excise - though the latter both do provide one as a matter of good practice. Where notices must be provided, the contents are usually prescribed, for example:

- *High Court execution* On a first levy the HCEO will leave a prescribed notice of seizure at the premises or hand it to the debtor. This has been introduced under CPR Sch.1 RSC O.45 r.2 and draws the debtor's attention to his/ her right to seek interpleader if it is felt that certain goods should be treated as exempt from seizure.

- *distress for rent* Under r12(2)DRR the distrainor must present a signed notice in prescribed form setting out the amounts levied for - arrears plus authorised costs, and also give an inventory of goods seized (*Tancred v Leyland* (1851) 16 QB 669). A bailiff must give details of the certificate held and the right of replevin. The notice should be left at "the chiefe mansion house or other most notorious place on the premises" (s1 DRA 1689), though it is usually handed to the tenant or owner of the goods. To sell without serving such a notice is irregular (*Trent v Hunt* (1853) 9 Exch 14). Also details of costs of removal should be left with the tenant using Form 9, DRR. It may be difficult to prove the facts if the notice is simply left at the premises, and a witness to prove the regularity of the distress may be necessary (*Walter v Rumbal* (1695) 1 Ld Raym 53). If and when removal occurs, the goods should not be removed from the county in which they were seized. The landlord or bailiff may be subject to a penalty if this is wrongfully done (c.4, Statute of Marlborough 1267).

- *local tax distraint* After seizure, the bailiff must hand to the debtor, or leave at the premises, a copy of the relevant sections of the appropriate enforcement regulations, a copy of the schedule to those regulations showing permissible costs, a copy of any possession agreement that the debtor has signed and a memorandum setting out the sums due (reg 45(5) CT; reg 14(5) NNDR). Alternative documentation will not be acceptable.

- *county court execution* CPR Sch.2 CCR O.26 r.12 requires the bailiff to deliver or send to the debtor a sufficient inventory of the goods seized. The form, N332, can be handed or posted to the debtor at his/her home or premises where the goods were seized.

- *CSA distraint* On completing a CSA levy the bailiff should hand to the debtor or leave at the premises copies of regs 30, 31 and Sch 2, which contains the charge scale, a memorandum setting out the sums due, a memorandum setting out any possession agreement made at the time of the levy in accordance with para 2(3) of Sch 2 and a memorandum detailing the debtor's appeal rights (reg 30(2)).

Certain errors on notices will not invalidate them- in the name of the debtor (*Wootley v Gregory* (1828) Y&J 536), in the date the debt fell due (*Gambrell v Earl of Falmouth* (1835) 4 Ad & El 73) or in not including the date at all (*Moss v Gallimore* (1779) 1 Doug KB 279). Generally minor mistakes that neither prejudice nor mislead the debtor will be ignored (*Rutherford v Lord Advocate* [1931] 16 Tax Cases 145). The fact that exempt items are included in the list does not give an aggrieved person a right to sue as an intention to sell is not a cause of action (*Beck v Denbigh* (1860) 29 LJCP 273). A notice does not have to be presented personally to the debtor in distress for rent or local taxes, but if it is some flexibility in contents may be allowed (*Chesterfield v Farringdon* 11 Ann CB per Trevor CJ).

10.2.2 *Inventories*

No inventory need be given in distress for income tax, VAT or local taxes. Where a notice is mandatory, failure to provide one or provision of an inadequate notice will make the distress irregular (see later at 10.8). The CSA require that all items seized should be listed in duplicate on an inventory attached to the walking possession agreement. All reasonable steps should be taken to verify ownership and an estimated sale value should be endorsed on the inventory.

Case law has established that where an inventory is supplied, it must make it clear what goods have been seized. In *Davies v Property & Reversionary Co. Ltd* [1929] 2 KB 222 it was held that a notice should either:

- (preferably) list and identify each item seized; or,

- imply that all goods on the premises have been seized. In *Wakeman v Lindsay* (1850) 14 QB 625 a notice mentioning certain goods 'and any others on the premises' was held not to be illegal, though it was perhaps excessive and was certainly condemned as a manner of proceeding which was unprofessional and not to be recommended. Despite the court's censure this form of inventory may still appear to be lawful (if scarcely to be advised); however, this decision predated the introduction of statutory exemptions of categories of goods and is therefore probably no longer to be relied upon.

The purpose of an inventory is to alert all interested parties to what has been seized so that they may take whatever steps are necessary. Thus, in *Kerby v Harding* (1851) 6 Exch 234 a list of 'all goods on the premises that may be required' was held to have been too vague because neither the debtor, nor any later bailiffs attending to levy, could with certainty identify the goods intended. This problem of an inventory being too vague has been exacerbated by the modern, very broad categories of exempt goods.

The validity of the decision in *Davies* was confirmed recently in *Ambrose v Nottingham City Council* (2004) Adviser no.107. In this unreported decision by a stipendiary magistrate it was confirmed that bailiffs continue to have a duty to complete inventories which detail every item seized (and, it would seem, indicate which items are exempt). The inclusion of a 'catch-all' phrase at the end of an inventory claiming 'all goods except those exempt' was held not to constitute a lawful seizure of goods other than those specifically identified. In such cases the bailiffs will only be entitled to remove the items which are listed on the notice and any attempt to levy or remove other property should be challenged as illegal. It should be noted that several large firms still use the form of wording condemned by the courts in *Davies* and *Ambrose*.

10.3 Tender & payment

As suggested before, the purpose of distress is to provoke payment through the threat of goods' sale and removal rather than those steps actually being taken. Consequently the bailiff aims either to either receive a lump sum or to agree instalment payment. The latter is the most common result of the bailiffs' call. For example it seems that, for HCEOs, about ninety percent of levies lead to instalments being arranged.

10.3.1 *Instalment arrangements*

Difficulties may arise for both parties when an affordable payment cannot be agreed. This is often because of the timescales for recovery laid down by creditors. Local authorities may, in respect of local taxes, be happy to see instalments accepted, but will often want them only to run for two or three months. Magistrates' courts and local authorities collecting road traffic penalties do not tend to accept instalments. In either case if the debtor is on low income the options open to the bailiff may be limited.

Bailiffs in the civil courts can be made to accept instalments and withdraw if the court consents to suspending the execution on terms (see 3.1.1 & 3.1.2). The terms of such suspensions can be quite low offers over extended periods. In other forms of distress there is no option for the debtor to make application to the court and s/he will have to rely on negotiation with the bailiff or creditor.

10.3.2 *Tender or payment before seizure*

Over and above any contractual requirement imposed on the bailiff regarding payments, there are both common law and statutory restrictions as to how payment may be made by the debtor, when it must be accepted by the bailiff or creditor and the impact thereof. Reference is often made in the regulations to 'tender' of payment of a debt and costs. It is required that tender should be accepted and that this should end the levy process. For example if the sums due to the CSA are paid or tendered to the SoS or bailiff before seizure, the payment should be accepted (reg 30(4)). If the amount of local tax due is paid or tendered before distraint, then goods cannot be levied (reg 45(3) CT; reg 14(3) NNDR).

Tender may be defined as an unconditional offer to pay, whether by means of cash or a banker's draft or building society cheque, and the money should be produced at the time of making such an offer. If there is no actual tender, the debtor's mere presence on the premises will not prevent a levy taking place (*Horne v Lewin* (1700) 1 Ld Raym 639). Equally the readiness to pay must have continued until the moment of seizure (*Cranley v Kingswell* (1617) Hob 207). Tender must be of the full sum of debt and costs, though less than the full sum due may be accepted without prejudice to the right to pursue the outstanding balance (*Finch v Miller* (1848) 5 CB 428). Tender may be to the creditor or bailiff (*Smith v Goodwin* (1833) 4 B & Ad 413; *Hatch v Hale* (1850) 15 QB 10) and either should accept. The bailiff can receive the rent and cannot be told to refuse it by the landlord (*Hatch v Hale* (1850) 15 QB 10), but a man in possession cannot receive a tender (*Boulton v Reynolds* (1859) 2 E&E 369). In execution it seems tender should be to the HCEO or the creditor (*Taylor v Bekon* (1678) 2 Lev 203). In *D'Jan v Bond St Estates* [1993] NPC 36 the Court of Appeal held that a landlord was not entitled to reject a tender by banker's draft either because it is less than the full amount claimed or because s/he feels that a large sum should be paid in cash.

A tender under protest, reserving the right to dispute the sum claimed later, is good tender provided that no conditions are imposed on the creditor

(*Manning v Lunn* (1845) 2 C&K 13; *Greenwood v Sutcliffe* [1892] 1 Ch 1).
The creditor should not refuse the tender, simply because the payer preserves
the right to take legal action later (*Scott v Uxbridge & Rickmansworth
Railway Co* [1866] 1 CP 596). Where the sum due is disputed, a request for
a receipt is not such a condition as will invalidate a tender (*Richardson v
Jackson* (1849) 8 M&W 298), unless the receipt is requested to specify that
it covers rent for a certain period and the periods for which rent is due are
disputed (*Finch v Miller* (1848) 5 CB 428). Tender by a third party who is
neither co-debtor (*Smith v Egginton* (1855) 10 Exch 845) nor co-tenant
(*Smith v Cox* [1940] 2 KB 558) is only acceptable if they act as agent for the
debtor - whether their agency has prior authorisation or later ratification. In
Smith v Cox an action for illegal distress for rent by the claimant failed when
he admitted that payment of the rent had been made by a stranger without
his knowledge or consent.

Offering a current account cheque or other means of payment does not
qualify as valid tender, though of course the bailiff or creditor may accept
such a method of settling a debt and may suspend enforcement until the
cheque is cleared, rather than withdrawing the levy altogether. Payment by
instalments is handled in the same way as payment by cheque. It is not valid
tender with the consequences that flow from that, but enforcement may be
stayed whilst payments are maintained. Where a landlord did accept a bill of
exchange from a tenant for rent due, it was held to be evidence of an
agreement to suspend the remedy of distress during the currency of the bill
(*Palmer v Bramley* [1895] 2 QB 405). The tenant was therefore entitled to
replevy his goods (see 9.29). Equally the ordinary rule is that acceptance of a
cheque is not absolute satisfaction of a debt but conditional payment and
operates to suspend a creditor's remedies until it is either met or
dishonoured. The creditor would have the choice, if the cheque was
dishonoured, of either suing on the cheque or pursuing the debt as normal
(*Re: Romer & Haslam* [1893] 2 QB 286; *Gunn v Bolckow, Vaughan & Co*
[1875] 10 Ch App 491). Thus in *Bolt & Nut Co (Tipton) Ltd v Rowlands,
Nicholls & Co* [1964] 2 QB 10, a judgment entered after receipt of a cheque
to settle the claim was set aside as irregular. The court however suggested
that, if judgment had been entered before the cheque was taken, it could
have been argued that a better course of action for the creditor might be to
levy execution rather than sue on the cheque. The court also noted that the
situation is different in distress for rent. The acceptance of a cheque or bill in
such cases is not conditional payment and until it is met by the bank the
landlord may still pursue the debt by distress, his 'better remedy' of seizure
of goods not being suspended (*Davis v Gyde* (1835) 2 A&E 623; *Belshaw v
Bush* (1851) 11 CB 191; *Henderson v Arthur* [1907] 1 KB 10). Note also
that payment by tender of a cheque that later is dishonoured has been held

not to be obtaining pecuniary advantage by deception under s16 Theft Act 1968 (*R v Locker* [1971] 2 QB 321).

If tender of the full sum due is made before seizure, the levy is illegal (*Branscomb v Bridges* (1823) 1 B&C 145). No costs need be included in the tender as none can be recovered before the levy (*Bennet v Bayes* (1860) 5 H&N 391). Refusal of a valid tender gives the debtor the right of rescue (*Bevills Case* (1585) 4 Co Rep 6a and see 3.4), to sue in trespass (*Bennet v Bayes* above), to replevy (see *YB* (1347) 21 EIII 56b pl.7 and 9.28) or to sue in conversion (*Smith v Goodwin* (1823) 4 B & Ad 413). The time for valid tender in such cases may be extended by bringing replevin in order to establish the validity of the distress (*YB* (1333) 7 EIII 28a pl.20).

In the magistrates' court distraint or sale cannot proceed if the person pays or tenders the fine on the warrant (plus costs) to the distrainor (Crim PR Part 52.8(10)). The same applies if the defendant tenders to the bailiff a receipt for the correct sum from the clerk of the court (Part 52.8(14)). Sometimes courts refuse to accept payment from the defendant when the warrant is with the bailiff. This is justified by r55(1) MCR. However this provision deals with payment in the circumstances laid out in s79(2) MCA which applies only when a period of committal has also been imposed by the magistrates. This is unlikely to apply in the case of most warrants being enforced by bailiffs and the debtor should therefore be free to pay whoever is most convenient to them, which may often be the bailiff.

10.3.3 *Tender or payment after seizure*

If tender is made between seizure and impounding, it would be illegal for the bailiff to proceed to impound. After seizure, but before removal, if the debt and costs are tendered any removal or retention of the seized goods is illegal (*Loring v Warburton* (1858) EB&E 507). Tender of the rent and costs after seizure but before impounding makes possession and removal wrongful (*Vertue v Beasley* (1831) 1 Mood & R 21; *Evans v Elliot* (1836) 5 Ad & El 142).

If the tender is made after the goods have been impounded, it is too late for the levy to be rendered wrongful (*Six Carpenters' Case* (1610) 77 ER 695). After removal but before sale tender of the debt and costs renders any sale irregular (*Johnson v Upham* (1859) 2 E&E 250). If tender is made any goods removed must be returned, otherwise the debtor could sue for conversion, though the continuing possession is not trespass (*West v Nibbs* (1847) 4 CB 172). Tender after impounding does not render it wrongful (*Six Carpenters Case* above) as such a tender of rent and costs is invalid at common law (*Tennant v Field* (1857) 8 E&B 336; *Firth v Purvis* (1793) 5 D&E 432). A tender after impounding but within the five day period for replevin would make a sale irregular and the tenant may sue on the 'equity' of the DRA 1689 (*Johnson v Upham* (1859) 2 E&E 250). If the distress were to be continued the tenant could apply to the county court for an order returning the goods. The HCEO can receive the debt due and therefore if payment or tender is made, he must withdraw from possession. If the debtor tenders or pays the debt, execution is discharged and the HCEO may not then sell (*Taylor v Baker* (1677) 3 Keb 788/ 2 Lev 203; *R v Bird* (1679) 2 Show 87; *Brun v Hutchinson* (1844) 2 D&L 43).

The amount outstanding which must be cleared will include the bailiffs' costs. It is therefore important to determine the precise amount of costs which should be paid or tendered in a situation where the recovery action is an ongoing process and costs are mounting. The Court of Appeal gave helpful guidance on the issue of costs and the calculation and acceptance of tenders to discharge the sums due in *Wilson v South Kesteven DC* [2000] EWCA Civ 218. The case concerned a claim for damages for an illegal distraint. During a levy for NNDR a sum in settlement of the amounts due was tendered by the debtor and refused by the bailiff, who was engaged in removing the goods from the premises. This refusal was held to have been wrongful by a county court circuit judge. The Court of Appeal reversed this decision and held that, under the relevant local tax regulations, there are two distinct opportunities to make payment. These are either:

- before any goods are seized; or,

- after seizure and before sale.

The county court judge had assumed there was a "continuum of opportunity" to pay, so that tender could be made lawfully during the process of seizure. Simon Brown LJ rejected this partly because of the form of the regulations and partly because of the practical difficulty of determining charges which could be accruing minute by minute. In terms of practice for bailiffs, he recommended that the required memorandum of charges is presented either:

- upon, or shortly after, first entry to the premises, giving the debtor a chance to pay "before the process gets fully underway and charges begin to escalate"; or,

- after seizure has occurred. A further memorandum of the charges incurred to that point would be required, detailing all costs added to the account so far and warning that further charges (such as removal) may be incurred.

There are provisions for payment of the full sum due after seizure in statutory distraint. If the sums of CSM due are paid or tendered to the SoS or bailiff before sale, the payment should be accepted and the distraint will not proceed, any sale being cancelled and the goods being made available for collection by the debtor (reg 30(5)). If, after seizure, the sums of local taxes due are paid or tendered, the billing authority must accept the amount and the goods cannot be sold. The debtor can then collect them (reg 45(4)CT; reg 14(4)NNDR). If the respondent pays or tenders the road traffic penalty due on the warrant plus the fees, or any sum that will be accepted as satisfying the debt, to either the local authority or the bailiff, the levy of execution is terminated and any seized goods must be released (art. 7(2)). This repeats s.87 CCA, which also applies. Payment cannot be made to the court (CPR Part 75.7(4)).

For fines it has been held that if goods are seized, bailiffs are not liable on payment of the penalty to return them until they are demanded by the debtor nor are they liable for any damage to the goods (*Hutchings v Morris* (1827) 6 B & C 464). If the bailiff is paid, or receives sale proceeds, the sums must be passed to the clerk of the court (Crim PR Part 52.8(3)) and it is an offence punishable by a fine up to level one (£200) for the bailiff to fail to do this by wilfully retaining improper fees (s78(5)).

10.4 Removal & Storage

Removal and sale is a last resort where acceptable payments cannot be agreed or maintained. As an indication of the frequency with which it is used, it is understood that HCEOs remove in only five percent of cases; CIPFA states that only three per cent of warrants lead to actual removal of goods; the CBA estimate that only two per cent lead to sale and the Lord Chancellor's Department states that less than two thousand of the million and a half warrants issued annually actually lead to auction.

In most cases where goods are to be sold, they will be removed from the debtor's premises and stored before disposal at an auction room. Very little is laid down in law as to how this should be done, despite the regularity with which it occurs.

10.4.1 *Removal*

This will not usually happen until at least five days after seizure, not including the day of the levy (*Robinson v Waddington* (1849)13 QB 753). This timescale is set by statute for some bailiffs, but has merely been adopted as good practice by others.

The bailiff may, following a valid seizure (see chapter 8), force entry on returning to a property, but only if the debtor is deliberately excluding them (*Khazanchi v Faircharm Investments & McLeod v Butterwick* [1998] 2 All

ER 901 CA). The Court of Appeal overruled both the previous decision made on this point in *McLeod v Butterwick* ([1996] 3 All ER 236) and the longstanding view on the matter, deciding that there was no general common law power, either in distress for rent or in execution, for a bailiff to force re-entry to premises in order to remove seized goods. On a review of the case law it was held that the right of forced re-entry only applied after forced exclusion (see also 7.4.4). If the debtor is unaware of the bailiffs' intended return, a locked door may not be treated as a deliberate exclusion. It will therefore be necessary for the bailiffs to give prior notice of a date and possibly time for their return (see also *Aga Kurboolie Mahomed v The Queen* (1843) Moo PC 239 on the need for prior demand for entry). It may be possible for bailiffs in certain circumstances to get round this need to make prior appointments by including some general clause in their walking possession agreements permitting forced reentry at any time (see Morritt LJ in *Khazanchi* at 911b and *Lavell v O'Leary* [1933] 2 KB 200) though there may be questions about the validity of such agreements made under duress and such amendments will not be possible for the walking possession agreements prescribed for distress for rent and execution for judgments and road traffic penalties. County court bailiffs require the permission of a district judge, even an indemnity from the claimant, before such entry. If the county court bailiff feels that the are goods of insufficient value to justify the expense of removal and sale, but the creditor insists upon it, the bailiff can refuse to proceed until the creditor has indemnified the court for any costs that might not be recovered.

On return only what was previously seized may be removed (*Smith v Torr* (1862) 3 F&F 505). If extra goods are discovered after the seizure and notice was presented, they cannot be included in the levy and to remove them would be trespass (*Bishop v Bryant* (1834) 6 C&P 484).

In distress for rent several procedural requirements apply at the removal stage. Firstly a detailed breakdown of the costs should be left by handing it to the tenant using Form 9 (r.12(3) DRR). This details the number of vehicles used, the number of men employed, the number and type of special removal machines, the time spent at the property and loading and unloading the vans and the basic charge for each item. This form also applies to road traffic execution (r.12(3) & Sch 2). Failure to present the form is an irregularity, which will not invalidate the entire levy (*Culligan v Simkin & Marstons Group* (2008)).

Secondly, under s.9 DRA 1737 notice of where the goods are lodged or deposited shall be given to the tenant or left at the house within one week of the lodging or deposit of those items (the week does include the day of removal). Furthermore, under c.4 Statute of Marlborough 1267 goods should not be removed outside the county in which they were seized. The statute provides that the landlord will be "grievously punished by amerciament". What this exactly means to day is not clear, but it is probable that the tenant will be able to sue upon the statute for penal (aggravated) damages.

Finally for rent under s.10 DRA 1737 "it shall be lawful for any persons whatever to come and go from such a place where any distress for rent be impounded and secured..., in order to view, appraise and buy, and also in order to carry off and remove on account of purchase thereof". This applies specifically to the right of prospective buyers to attend a sale at the tenant's home if the goods are impounded there, but more generally to their right to attend auction houses and confirms the general right of the bailiff to re-enter to remove goods for sale.

The bailiff must take care when removing and storing goods otherwise an action for negligence could be brought by the debtor (see 9.27). If the goods are stored at an auction house, the auctioneer must exercise ordinary care and diligence in keeping them and is liable for any damage or loss arising from default or negligence. Equally the auctioneer's possession gives an interest in the goods which entitles him/her to sue for any trespass or conversion of the goods, so, if a debtor sought to rescue the goods, the auctioneer could take action.

10.4.2 *Abuse of distress*

The bailiff may not use items distrained for his own purposes but may use items if necessary for their preservation and for the benefit of the owner e.g. milking cows. In *Bagshaw v Goward* (1607) Yelv 96 a defendant seized a stray horse and rode it. The court held such use to be a misdemeanour as seizure gives only a custody and no property in the items. Consequently, the seizure was wrong from the beginning and the claimant was entitled to damages for the value of the item. In *Chamberlayn's Case* (1590) 74 ER 202 the court held that cattle etc should be made available to the owner to feed during impounding.

If impounded items are damaged or lost as a result of the neglect of the impounder, the owner may sue for their value (*Perkins v Butterfield* (1627) Het 75- though note that in this case in a dissenting judgment Hitcham J felt that trespass did lie for such mistreatment and that loss of goods seized could render the levy trespass *ab initio*). More modern examples might include the fact that a bailiff may not drive a motor vehicle seized from a debtor but may be entitled to periodically operate certain equipment that would otherwise deteriorate if not regularly used.

10.5 Sale

The conclusion of the process of distress is sale, though there must of course be a valid seizure to entitle the bailiff to sell (*In Re: Townsend* [1880] 14 Ch D 132). Both execution and statutory distraint are defined by the fact that the purpose of seizure is to sell (Lord Wright in *Potts v Hickman* [1941] AC 212)- though the real purpose of distress is to compel payment, not to sell goods. Thus in execution if the debtor fails to pay, the bailiff must proceed at once to prepare for a sale. The goods cannot be handed over to the creditor (*Thomson v Clark* (1596) 78 ER 754) but both the creditor and the debtor can buy them at the sale (*Re: Rogers ex p Villars* [1874] 9 Ch App 432 or *Stratford v Twynan* (1822) Jac 418). A HCEO also cannot retain the goods and pay the debt with his own money (*Waller v Weedale* (1604) Noy 107).

10.5.1 *Timing*

In most cases except High Court and local taxes statute requires that there is a delay of at least five days between seizure and sale of goods (e.g. s93 CCA, which also applies to road traffic penalties; r65(4) for VAT; s61(4) TMA). In magistrates court Crim PR Part 52.8(7) sets limits upon when the sale may occur. The goods cannot be sold earlier than six days after the levy unless a person gives written consent. Further if a period for sale is not specified on the warrant, sale should be no later than 14 days after levy. There is no set delay in local taxes (*McCreagh v Cox & Ford* (1923) 92 LJKB 855) but the five day period tends to be followed. Sale may take place earlier if the goods are perishable or the debtor consents in writing.

In any event, the sale should be conducted within a reasonable time unless there is good cause (*Jacobs v Humphrey* (1834) 2 Cr & M 413; *Ayshford v Murray* (1870) 23 LT 170) and the bailiff will be liable in damages for an unreasonable delay (*Aireton v Davis* (1833) 9 Bing 740). If the goods are left an unreasonable time on the premises before sale they may have been abandoned, in which case the bailiff will be a trespasser if he tries to collect them (*Griffin v Scott* (1726) 1 Barn KB 3). Equally, if a sale is attempted on the premises of goods impounded there, after a reasonable time has elapsed, the bailiff will also be a trespasser (*Winterbourne v Morgan* (1809) 11 East 395). Ten days has been held to be reasonable period of time to prepare (*Re: Finch* (1891) 65 LT 466).

In distress for rent, although the DRA 1689 gives the power to sell, the landlord is under no obligation to sell (*Hudd v Ravenor* (1821) 2 Brod & Bing 662). However after five days from, but not including, the date of the distress, if the arrears remain unpaid or replevin has not been commenced, he may sell for the "best price that may be gotten" (s.1 1689 Act) and pass good title (*Harper v Taswell* (1833) 6 C & P 166). This period of five days can be extended to fifteen at the tenant's request, in order to allow replevin (s6 LDAA 1888). Sale before the five day 'waiting period' mentioned above has elapsed is an irregularity.

10.5.2 *Appraisement*

There is generally no requirement to set a reserve price before sale (for example in the High Court see *Bealy v Sampson* (1688) 2 Vent 93) except for taxes (s.61(5) TMA- the collector will have this done by an auctioneer or some other qualified person such a private bailiff). In most cases 'appraisement' can be requested by the debtor, at his/her own expense. For example in distress for rent the tenant can in writing request that competent persons carry out an appraisement of the goods (s5 LDAA 1888), but s/he must meet the costs (*Pitt v Shew* (1821) 4 B & Ald 206). In distress for rent it has been held that appraisers need not be professionals (*Roden v Eyton* (1848) 6 CB 427), but they should be impartial (*Westwood v Cowne* (1816) 1 Stark 172), so it is irregular for the bailiff to be both appraiser and broker (*Lyon v Weldon* (1824) 2 Bing 334). If there is loss due to failure to (properly) appraise, the debtor can sue for special damages based on the value of the goods less any sums due (*Knotts v Curtis* (1832) 5 C&P 322; *Whitworth v Maden* (1847) 2 C&K 517). Even though there may have been an appraisement, the resulting valuation is not conclusive proof of the goods' value (*Cook v Corbett* (1875) 24 WR). Appraisers may buy the goods at their own valuation price.

10.5.3 *Mode & conduct*

Sale is normally by public auction. Sometimes this is the only method permitted by the regulations (e.g. VAT reg 65(5); road traffic penalties art 13 ERTDO; s61 TMA). Sometimes other modes of sale are possible:

*   in magistrates. court the sale shall be by public auction unless the person consents in writing to some other method (Crim PR Part 52.8(9));

*   in High Court execution, unless the court orders otherwise, under para.10 Sch.7 Courts Act 2003, if the debt and expenses exceed £20 the sale must be by public auction which should be advertised for three days beforehand (Re: Crook ex p Southampton Sheriff (1894) 63 LJQB 756) but the HCEO should allow reasonable time before sale to allow claims for interpleader. Another mode of sale can be employed by order of court on application from any of the concerned parties (CPR Sch.1 RSC O.47 r.6). If the HCEO has notice of other executions, for example (it would appear) a warrant for a road traffic penalty, an application to sell privately cannot be considered by the court until the other creditors have been served notice of the application (para.10(3) & (4), Sch.7 Courts Act 2003). The sale can be on the debtor's premises with his/her consent. If a

sale is by any means other than public auction, without leave of court having been obtained first, it is valid until it is set aside by the court (*Crawshaw v Harrison* [1894] 1 QB 79). The court can set aside a sale under a fi fa if the HCEO did not take reasonable care to advertise it, leading to a sale at undervalue (*Edge v Kavanagh* [1884] 24 LR Ir 1). A sale is unlawful if the HCEO sells part of the goods without the authority of the execution creditor in order to recover possession money, fees and expenses (*Sneary v Abdy* [1876] 1 Ex D 299); and,

- in distress for rent there are no regulations as to the mode of sale, but an expensive method should only be employed when a better price can be expected. There is not a set order for sale- in other words, there is no need to sell all unprivileged items before conditionally privileged goods. In *Jenner v Yolland* (1818) 6 Price 3, a landlord took cattle, *inter alia*, but after the sale it transpired that there would have been enough to cover the rent and costs without needing any goods with qualified privilege. The distress was not illegal as there had been reasonable grounds for supposing (after qualified appraisement) that there would not have been sufficient otherwise. The sale can take place at the tenant's home (s10 DRA 1737), but if s/he requests transfer in writing and is prepared to cover the costs and any damages, it can be transferred to an auction room or other suitable place (s5 LDAA 1888). Irregular sale will make the landlord liable to account for the proceeds and the value of the goods and the tenant will be entitled to recover the full value less the rent and costs.

- in county court execution sale should be advertised for three days previously and is by public auction unless the court orders otherwise. Under CPR Sch.2 CCR O.26 r.12 the debtor must have four days' notice of the time and place of the auction on N333. Private sale cannot be ordered where the debt is less than £20 but otherwise the court can order this on application from the creditor, debtor or District Judge (s97). Any other creditor enforcing against the debtor should be given four days notice of the hearing and can attend to make representations (CCR O.26 r.15).

Only in the county court is the debtor actually entitled to notice of when and where the sale will occur. If goods seized under the same warrant are sold over several days, it will be treated by the court as one sale (*In Re: Rogers ex p Villars* [1874] 9 Ch App 432). If the goods are of a specialist nature, it is the bailiff's duty to obtain advice on the mode of sale- for instance advertising in specialist press to encourage bids by creating "an excitement or an opposition" (*American Express v Hurley* [1985] 3 All ER 564). The best price possible should be obtained (*Ridgway v Lord Stafford* (1851) 6 Exch 404). Restrictive conditions should not be laid down that will effect the sum raised (*Ridgway v Lord Stafford* (1851) as above; *Hawkins v Walrond*

[1876] 1 CPD 280). Any conditions preventing the best price being achieved are illegal. The best price is not necessarily that offered by the highest bidder if this is still greatly under the item's value and no reasonable price can be obtained (*Keightley v Birch* (1814) 3 Camp 321). If the goods have been appraised but do not reach the reserve price, the sale may proceed for the best price that can be obtained. It may be necessary for several attempts to be made to reach the appraised price at successive auctions before sale for a lesser sum is reasonable (Vin Abr vol.9).

An action can be taken for not selling at the best price, giving evidence of mismanagement in connection with the handling of the goods at the sale (e.g. in *Poynter v Buckley* (1833) 5 C&P 512 the goods were left in the rain and inadequately lotted). Improper lotting and hurrying the sale was held to invalidate it (*Wright v Child* [1866] 1 Exch 358). Care should be taken to properly advertise the sale (*Edge v Kavanagh* [1884] 24 LR IR 1). If a bailiff is to be sued for being negligent in the conduct of a sale only nominal damages will be recoverable unless actual loss and damage can be shown (*Bales v Wingfield* (1843) 4 A&E 580).

10.5.4 *Amount*

A bailiff acts wrongfully by seizing and selling more than is "reasonably sufficient" to cover the debt and costs (*Gawler v Chaplin* (1848) 2 Exch 503; *Cooke v Palmer* (1827) 6 B & C 739), though obviously there must be a margin for error and a reasonable amount may be seized in the first place. The bailiff should closely monitor a sale to make sure that too much is not sold (*Batchelor v Vyse* (1834) 4 Moo & S 552).

If goods are sold for greatly under their value the debtor can be assumed to have a substantial grievance upon which an action for damages in conversion could be based. However the onus is on the claimant to show that there was substantial difference between the price realised and the value at the date of sale. In the absence of such proof the bailiff will be protected from proceedings. The auction price is not conclusive proof of the value of the goods (*Neumann v Bakeaway* [1983] 1 WLR 1016) but, as confirmed by Morritt LJ in *Khazanchi v Faircharm Investments* [1998] 2 All ER 901 at 920f "The price realised at auction is not necessarily the best evidence of value at any particular date but if there is no evidence.. to the effect that the auction had not been properly advertised or conducted it is evidence a judge is entitled to accept". It was also confirmed that evidence as to prices fetched for goods on the second hand market may be acceptable, but in the absence of such indications of worth the value of goods if bought new at the time of seizure could not be relied upon as evidence as to the value of seized items sold some years earlier (Millett J @ 919). The judgment also contains useful guidance on the matter of accounting for VAT in the course of assessing the price obtained (Millett J at 921b & c).

If several items, each worth more than the debt due, are seized and all are sold, this is clearly trespass (*Wooddye v Coles* (1595) Noy 59). Thus in a case where the sale was extended over two days, where enough was sold by the HCEO on the first day, it was trespass to continue with the sale on the second day, even if there was a fear that actual delivery of the goods might somehow be prevented by loss or accident (*Aldred v Constable* (1844) 6 QB 370).

If the sale is irregular, damages can be claimed. If the sale is wholly void there is no basis for an action in damages (*Owen v Leigh* (1820) 3 B& Ald 470). Presumably if goods were sold in such circumstances a claim for money had and received by the debtor might be possible (see 9.32).

10.5.5 *Proceeds & surplus*

The proceeds should be paid over to the creditor promptly and the debtor is then entitled to receive any surplus and any goods that remain unsold- see for instance s1 DRA 1689; Crim PR Part 52.8(12); VAT reg.65 or TMA s61(5) and E. India Co v Skinner (1695) 90 ER 516. In *Lyon v Tomkies* (1836) 1 M&W 603 it was held that if no overplus is passed on, it may be a ground on which to question the reasonability of fees. The balance of the proceeds, after satisfying any debt and costs, constitutes a debt from the bailiff to the debtor (*Harrison v Paynter* (1840) 6 M&W 387). The HCEO may retain any surplus until it is demanded by the debtor- there is no need for the HCEO to search for him/ her or pay the amount into court (*Wooddye v Coles* (1595) Noy 59). A landlord who sells enough to clear the debt should leave any surplus with the HCEO and return any surplus goods to where they were seized or leave them at a more convenient location, details of which will be notified to the tenant, for collection (s1 DRA 1689; *Evans v Wright* (1857) 2 H&N 527). If money is paid direct to the tenant, his/her receipt of it is not necessarily acceptance in satisfaction and s/he may still question any fees charged etc. (*Lyon v Tomkies* (1836) 1 M&W 603). If the landlord fails to leave an overplus with the HCEO as required by DRA 1689, the tenant should sue for breach of the statute, rather than money had and received (*Yates v Eastwood* (1851) 6 Exch 805).

10.5.6 *Title on sale*

How good title is passed depends partly on the form of distress involved but some general observations can be made before examining the assorted forms. Sale by a bailiff is recognised as passing good title even though it is not sale in market overt. However (except for distress for rent) if the goods are on hire or HP even sale under an execution cannot pass absolute title if the debtor does not possess it. Such a sale is conversion (*Lancashire Wagon Co Ltd v Fitzhugh* (1861) 6 H&N 502). In other cases a true sale, however irregular, passes title to the purchaser in distress (*Lyon v Weldon* (1824) 2 Bing 334) and in execution (*Jeanes v Wilkins* (1749) 1 Ves Sen 195). If, however, the levy is void, good title cannot be passed (see below).

Execution
If goods are sold under an execution good title will generally be passed and the officer will be protected from any action against them for selling goods or paying over the proceeds, provided that no third party claim to them has been made (para.11 Sch.7 Courts Act 2003; s98 CCA; art.14 ERTDO). However if the sale occurs before a person has had any chance to make a claim to them, the sale will not pass good title (*Crane & Sons v Ormerod* [1903] 2 KB 37) but contrast this with *Goodlock v Cousins* [1897] 1 QB 348 where goods sold in default of a claimant complying with the conditions laid down in interpleader procedure were held to pass good title.

The protection for a bailiff selling under an execution is not available if there is a "real or substantial grievance" against the bailiff e.g. he was insolent or oppressive or the goods were sold at undervalue. See *Neumann v Bakeaway Ltd* [1983] 1 WLR 1016 in which an interpleader (see 9.26) was begun after wrongful seizure and sale by the bailiff, though with no misconduct on the HCEO's part. Good title will also not be passed if it can be shown that notice of a third party claim was received or that on 'reasonable enquiry' the HCEO should have ascertained that the goods were not the property of the judgment debtor. See for instance *Pilling v Teleconstruction Co Ltd* (1961) 111 L J 424 in which the defendants were held liable for damages in trespass and costs. They were judgment debtors at whose rented premises the claimants left industrial machinery. The equipment was seized by a county court bailiff and sold. As bailees the defendants should have notified the bailiffs and the court of the situation, whilst the court did all it had to try to establish the facts. Compare this with Observer Ltd v Gordon [1983] 1 WLR 1008 in which interpleader protection was granted to a HCEO as the defendants had failed to show a "fairly arguable" case that the sheriff was liable in conversion. The defendant had repaired pianos, which were seized and sold for a judgment creditor. The owners made claims and the sheriff was protected by the court. He was entitled to defend the action unless he had notice of ownership or it would have been reasonable for him to make enquiries. In this case, in the absence of notice as to ownership despite repeated visits to the shop, because it was not unreasonable of him not to enquire (removal and sale occurred after the judgment debtor's death so goods were removed from an unoccupied shop) and, because even if he had made enquiries, the true facts would not have been revealed in a reasonable period of time, the sale was valid. Sale in the county court passes good title and creditors making claims against the debtor cannot recover any sums for the sale of the goods unless the court had notice of their claims or "reasonable enquiry" would have shown that the goods were not the judgment debtor's (CCA s98). In such cases the owner may be entitled to sue the bailiff and the execution creditor who has received the proceeds for money had and received (*Curtis v Maloney* [1951] 1 KB 736) and anyone who converted the goods before sale (*Farrant v Thompson* (1822) 2 Dow & Ry KB 1).

The protection granted in execution is also subject to the right of any person (e.g. a hirer or HP company) to any remedy against any party other than the bailiff or county court district judge (for instance the purchaser) to which they may be entitled if they can prove good title at the time of the sale (para.11(3) Sch.7 Courts Act 2003/ s98(2) CCA). If the execution is regular the buyer is protected by statute, even if s/he had notice of some defect in title. See for example *Dyal Singh v Kenyan Insurance Ltd* [1954] AC 287- the appellant secured good title to a car purchased at auction and subject to a chattels mortgage, the registration of which was deemed to have given all parties notice.

If the execution is irregular for some reason (see 5.2), for example the HCEO deals wrongly with the proceeds, the execution creditor is not entitled to seize the goods again in order to recover the judgment debt once they have been sold as a bona fide buyer's title is secure (*Smallcomb v Cross & Buckingham* (1697) 1 Ld Raym 252). A purchaser in good faith is entitled to protection against other executions which should have had priority (*Imray v Magnay* (1843) 11 M&W 267), even if the writ itself is void through fraud unless s/he was aware of or party to this (*Bessey v Windham* (1844) 6 QB 166; *Shattock v Craden* (1851) 6 Exch 725). The title of a purchaser, even though s/he acted in good faith, is not secure if the irregularity made the execution altogether void (*Jeanes v Wilkins* (1749) 1 Ves Sen 194; *Bushell v Timson* [1934] 2 KB 79) for instance the levy is trespass *ab initio* (see for example *Lee v Gansel* (1774) 1 Cowp 1) or the goods seized were not those of the execution debtor (*Hoe's Case* (1600) 5 Co Rep 89b). In the latter case the owner may recover the value of the goods from the purchaser (*Tancred v Allgood* (1859) 4 H&N 438). In *Bushell v Timson* execution was issued without the necessary leave- the sheriff was held liable for damages.

Distress for rent
For title to pass by means of a sale under a distress for rent there must be actual sale to a third party. The landlord is guilty of conversion if s/he purchases the goods or takes them in satisfaction (*King v England* (1864) 4 B & S 782). In *Plas-y-Coed Collieries Co Ltd v Partridge Jones & Co* [1912] 2 KB 345 it was confirmed that a landlord purporting to buy does not get good title, even after an appraisement. The sale will be invalid and the tenant will be able to sue for wrongful interference. This will render the distress irregular and the measure of the tenant's special damages will be the full value of the goods.

Sale will also be irregular even if the form of an auction is gone through - in *Moore, Nettlefold & Co v Singer Manufacturing Co Ltd* [1904] 1 KB 820 it was emphasised that an auctioneer, as the landlord's agent, is not an independent vendor. It may be noted that the tenant may agree to cede goods to a landlord in full or part satisfaction (King v England above).

10.6 Accounts

There is almost no regulation on the provision of information to the debtor on the sums raised and the fees deducted by bailiffs. In the county court and magistrates' court the debtor is entitled, after sale, to a statement of the proceeds raised, the costs charged and the proportion of the debt cleared, though in the magistrates court the debtor must attend the court themselves to inspect this within one month of the levy at a reasonable time to be set by the court (Crim PR Part 52.8(13)). In the case of magistrates' clamping orders, any remaining balance should be remitted to the defendant within 10 working days with a written statement of account. In no other form of distress is there such an entitlement.

HCEO's returns

Special provisions apply in execution to the information to be supplied at the conclusion of the process. A writ of *fieri facias* contains a direction that it should be endorsed after execution with a statement of the manner of execution and that a copy of this 'return' should be sent to the creditor. A similar procedure also applies in the county court. There are three main forms of HCEO's return:

- *fieri feci* - goods were seized and sold, the debt being satisfied and paid to the creditor. A return of partial execution is commonly made;

- *nulla bona* - no goods or proceeds insufficient to cover the levy costs or prior writs were found. There must have been an attempted seizure for such a return to be made (*Doker v Hader* (1825) 2 Bing 479). If there are goods on the premises, but they cannot be seized due to prior insolvency, this return is appropriate (*Milner v Rawlings* [1867] 2 Exch 249) as would also be the case where rent is due, exceeding the value of the goods seizable (*Dennis v Whetham* [1874] 9 QB 345); and,

- *unsold for want of buyers* - no bid or satisfactory offer was made. The HCEO's valuation of the seized goods must be attached to the return and the HCEO should await an instruction to sell for the best price possible in the circumstances, known as '*venditioni exponas*' (*Keightley v Birch* (1814) 3 Camp 521).

If a debtor (or a creditor) is dissatisfied with the HCEO's action in an execution, s/he may give notice requiring a return to the writ (CPR Sch.1

RSC O.46 r.9- "Any party...against whom a writ of execution was issued may serve notice on the sheriff...requiring him, within such time as may be specified.. to indorse on the writ a statement of the manner in which he has executed it and to send that party a copy of the statement...If the sheriff fails to comply, he may apply to court for an order"). The debtor may only request this after execution (*Richardson v Tuttle* (1860) 8 CBNS 474). If, in making the return, the HCEO discloses a breach of duty on his part the return is bad and the HCEO is liable to an action (*Mildmay v Smith* (1671) 2 Wms Saund 343; *Stockdale v Hansard* (1840) 11 A&E 297; *R v Sheriff of Leicestershire* (1850) 9 CB 659). If by the return the HCEO discharges himself, the aggrieved person may still sue for a false return or for any alleged misconduct during the levy. A mere false return where there has been no breach of duty is not actionable (*Stimson v Farnham* [1871] 7 QB 175).

10.7 Repeat levies

Frequently stated rule is that a second levy cannot be conducted. In fact this principle deals with two issues under the same heading. A bailiff can't distrain again for the same debt after a completed levy. This is because the second levy is rendered illegal by the fact that no debt is any longer due. Secondly the bailiff may not split the demand and try more than once under the same warrant because he realises he has not seized enough the first time around. There is an exception to the second instance for execution (and statutory distraint too, if one argues on the basis of the execution/ distraint analogy) as repeat levies can be made in any circumstances where any portion of the debt is outstanding.

10.7.1 *Second levies*

The following principles on second levies of distress may be derived from the case law. A bailiff cannot levy more than once- even though the levies are only separated by a few hours (*Wallis v Savill* (1701) 2 Lut 493) - if:

- it is for the same debt after a complete levy has satisfied it already (*Wotton v Shirt* (1600) Cro Eliz 742; *Owens v Wynne* (1855) 4 E&B 579); *ex parte Shuttleworth & Hancock: In Re: Deane* (1832) 1 Deac & Ch 223);

- the bailiff has levied for too little previously (*Dawson v Cropp* (1845) 1 CB 961) and simply failed to get enough through his "own folly" (*Wallis v Savill* (1701) 2 Lut 493; *Anon* (1550) Moore 7, pl.26, Distress);

- the bailiff has abandoned seized goods (see 8.4.1). In *Bagge v Mawby* (1853) 8 Exch 641 a landlord withdrew after receiving a notice that another creditor intended to petition for the tenant's bankruptcy. After the order he distrained again. It was held that if there was no lawful cause for not following the levy through, he should have continued. The notice from the creditor was not a good cause or excuse, rather it was a mere idle threat from a stranger with no right to interfere in the distress. The landlord ought to have proceeded and couldn't levy again. The same would appear to apply in execution (*Castle v Ruttan* (1854) 4 CP 252). This may also happen where the bailiff is withdrawn by the creditor on reaching an arrangement with the debtor. A new warrant would be needed (*Shaw v Kirby* (1888) 52 JP 182);

- if seizable goods are lost to the creditor either because the goods that were seized were of inadequate value when the bailiff had a fair opportunity to levy for more or because those goods that have been levied upon have been lost through negligence on the part of the bailiff. This applies to landlords in distress for rent but does not seem to apply to execution. Here the bailiff may levy again, but may be liable to be sued by the parties to the execution; or,

- the total debt due is split between separate warrants to give a series of small levies (*Forster v Baker* [1910] 2 KB 636; *Rothschild v Fisher* [1920] 2 KB 243). Of course separate rents may be distrained for separately (Sheppard's Touchstone of Common Assurances p.81) as may separate instalments of rent (*Anon* (1550) Moore 7; *Gambrell v Earl of Falmouth* (1835) 4 A&E 73). This may be in any order, and does not have to be in the sequence in which the sums fell due (*Palmer v Stanage* (1661) 1 Lev 43) but multiple levies must be avoided (*Holt v Sambach* (1627) Cro Car 103; *Hunt v Braines* (1694) 4 MR 402).

A wrongful second levy could be resisted by the means described in chapters 7 and 8. However second levies of distress and execution are permissible where:

- there were insufficient goods on a first visit upon which to levy execution (*Anon* (1585) Cro Eliz 13; *Jordan v Binckes* (1849) 13 QB 757; *R v Sheriff of Essex* (1839) 8 Dowl PC 5). Writs of execution remain in force until the whole sum due has been collected- they are a continuing power to seize any goods that become available until such time as the debt is clear. In the former case above it was held permissible to complete the levy some eleven years after the first seizure. Thus a further levy may be permitted because on the first levy it was found that all the goods then available had been seized by another bailiff (*Edmunds v Ross* (1821) 9 Price 5; *Drear v Warren* (1833) 10 Bing 341) or because more effects are discovered at a later date (*Hopkins v Adcock* (1772) 2 Dick 443). The bailiffs may make a partial levy but are entitled to wait until the levy can be completed rather than make a return of no goods. Bailiffs may also distrain in 'instalments' where they are concerned to avoid an excessive levy (*Hudd v Ravenor* (1821) 2 Brod & Bing 662). This ability to make successive moderate levies is endorsed by both *Gilbert* and *Bradby* as to the advantage of the debtor, as otherwise items of great value may have to be seized on the first visit. Thus a further levy is legal if on the first occasion the bailiff acts out of 'moderation or tenderness' and does not levy for full value (*Hutchins v Chambers* (1758) 1 Burr 580);

- the bailiff made a reasonable mistake because of the uncertain or illusory value of the items (*Hutchins v Chambers* (1758) 1 Burr 580);

- the levy has been obstructed. This may be because the debtor obstructed or attacked the bailiff or refused entry (*Lee v Cooke* (1858) 3 H & N 203). On such a second levy the bailiff need not confine himself to goods seized on the previous occasion (*Gislason v Rural Municipality of Foam Lake* [1929] 2 DLR 386). Equally a second levy may be justified if circumstances at the auction prevented the best price being obtained. See for example *Rawlence & Squarey v Spicer* [1935] 1 KB 412 where demonstrations and threats by the debtor prevented a sale or *R v Judge Clements ex p Ferridge* [1932] 2 KB 535 where a crowd prevented the sale by attending the auction, harassing bidders and making ridiculous offers;

- seized cattle died in the pound by an act of God (*Anon* (1568) 3 Dyer 280 pl 14; *Anon* (1700) 12 MR 397; *Vaspor v Edwards* (1796) 12 MR 658). We may assume that if the bailiffs' warehouse were to be burnt down following a lightning strike, this would provide a more likely modern reason for a further levy;

- the first attempted levy was trespass and thus void *ab initio* (*Grunnell v Welch* [1906] 2 KB 555). This could be where a levy on goods was made, but it transpires that none of the goods were the judgment debtor's (*Re: A Debtor ex p Smith* [1902] 2 KB 260);

- the first distress is withdrawn, at the request of the tenant. This may be because the debtor simply asks the creditor to "forbear now and postpone the distress" (*Bagge v Mawby* above) or because instalments are agreed (*Thwaites v Wilding* [1883] 12 QBD 4). If the arranged payments are not made, the bailiff can distrain again; or,

- the debtor goes bankrupt so that the first levy is withdrawn, but the bankruptcy is later annulled (*Crew v Terry* [1877] 2 CPD 403).

10.7.2 *Second Warrants*

The previous section dealt with repeat levies under the same warrant. Various regulations on statutory distraint permit repeat warrants to be issued, as many times as are necessary, for the same debt (e.g. reg.52(3) CT(A&E) Regs). That this is permissible in these cases strengthens the analogy between statutory distraint and execution, as it is accepted in respect of the latter that an execution creditor may issue further or simultaneous warrants (*Lee v Dangar, Grant & Co* [1892] 2 QB 337). A second warrant should not be issued whilst the first is still in the bailiff's hands (*Chapman v Bowlby* (1841) 8 M&W 249) even if the levy has been abandoned (*Miller v Parnell* (1815) 5 Taunt 370). If the bailiff is withdrawn on the instructions of the creditor, following an arrangement between debtor and creditor, a new warrant will have to be issued to permit the bailiff to return (*Shaw v Kirby* (1888) 52 JP 182). A new warrant can be issued if the first was inoperative due to prior seizure and assignment of goods to a third party (*Dicas v Warne* (1833) 10 Bing 341). A second warrant cannot be issued whilst interpleader proceedings are pending upon the first warrant (*In Re: Follows ex p. Follows* [1895] 2 QB 521).

10.8 Remedies for errors in removal or sale

10.8.1 *Illegal & irregular distress*

At common law there was no distinction between an illegality and an irregularity in the conduct of a levy (see *Six Carpenter's Case* (1600) 8 Co Rep 146b). Both made the process void and trespass *ab initio*. Statute intervened, initially for the benefit of landlords (s.19 DRA- to avoid the "very great hardship upon landlords" that distresses should be rendered void by "mistake or inadvertency" during a levy), but the differentiation of illegality and irregularity has been extended to other regimes as well- for details see 10.8.2 below. The result is that:

- removal and sale will still be lawful despite an irregularity in any other aspect of the levy ;

- an irregular sale will still pass good title (*Wallace v King* (1788) 1 H Bl 13), therefore the debtor cannot sue for conversion;

- if the claimant fails to show any loss, s/he is not entitled to nominal damages (see *Rodgers v Parker* (1856) 18 CB 112); and,

- the normal measure of damages is the value of the goods less any sum actually due (by analogy from s.19 DRA). See for example *Biggus v Goode* (1832) 2 Cr &J 364 or *Rocke v Hills* (1887) 3 TLR 298. It will be possible to recover any consequential losses as well.

Readers should note that independent acts unconnected with the conduct of the levy are not effected by the provisions on irregularities and will still be illegal (for example, a wrongful eviction of the tenant - *Etherton v Popplewell* (1800) 1 East 139). Equally in those forms of distress where such provision is not made, any wrongful act continues to be a potential illegality. These forms are:

- execution by the HCEO (see *Aitkenhead v Blades* (1813) 5 Taunt 198). Execution follows the basic common law principle that anything not within the authority of the writ is illegal and therefore trespass or conversion. Irregularities tend to be treated as breaches of duty by the HCEO for which any actual damage can be recovered (see earlier); and,

- distraint for income taxes and indirect taxes.

For an irregular act to be an illegality it is going to have to be a 'positive' irregularity, rather than a 'negative' one - that is, the bailiff must do something wrong rather than fail to take an action he should have taken. For example, an irregularly conducted sale may be illegal where as failure to give a prescribed notice of distress is unlikely to be regarded as unlawful. See Lord Coke in *Six Carpenters' Case* (1600) 8 Co Rep 146b - "not doing is no trespass".

10.8.2 *Irregular distress*

The following regimes contain a provision distinguishing illegal from irregular distress:

- *distress for rent* - as already stated, under s19 DRA 1737 which gave the tenant the right to sue for special damages for any irregularity either by an action for trespass or on the case. The successful claimant is entitled to recover his/ her full costs, but if the landlord tenders amends before the action is commenced, any award of damages is barred (s.20 DRA 1737). Payment into court is thus unnecessary (*Jones v Gooday* (1842) 9 M&W 736) and the landlord is provided with a complete defence.

- *local taxes*: under reg 45(7) CT(A&E) Regs and reg 14(7) NDR(A&E)(LL) Regs a bailiff shall not be treated as a trespasser from the beginning because of any subsequent irregularity in distress, but the debtor sustaining special damages from such an irregularity can recover full satisfaction for the special damages (and no more) by proceedings in trespass or otherwise;

- *county court*: no officer trespasses because of any irregularity or informality in either any proceedings on which the validity of a warrant depends, or the form of the warrant or mode of execution (s125 CCA). However any person aggrieved may sue for any special damages sustained, though no costs will be awarded if the damages do not exceed £2. In an action for wrongful execution on goods, the owner need only show that the warrant did not authorise the officer to levy execution to the value of the goods in fact seized - see *Moore v Lambeth County Court Registrar* [1970] 1 All ER 980 / 1 QB 560 which demonstrated that execution is excessive if the warrant does not authorise it, even in the absence of malice on the part of the bailiff.

- *execution for road traffic penalties*: s.125 CCA is applied to this form of execution by art.4(1) ERTDO;

- *magistrates' court*: if there is any irregularity in execution of a magistrates warrant, the bailiff shall not be held a trespasser as a result (s78(2)), but the debtor could claim special damages ((s78(3));

- *magistrates' clamping orders*: under reg.21 of the Fines Collection Regulations 2006 no defect in the order invalidates it or renders the clamper a trespasser. Nonetheless, a person is entitled to make a claim for special damages arising from any defect in the order or irregularity in its execution; or,

- *child support maintenance*: s35(5) provides the bailiff is not a trespasser *ab initio* because of any subsequent irregularity in the levy, though special damages may be recoverable (s35(6)).

The bailiff may be sued and the creditor can be included in a claim if s/he authorised the distress, though not the irregular act, as the creditor's duty is to ensure proper execution. The debtor can only recover what 'special damages' can be proved and any action for trespass or conversion would be barred (*Wallace v King* (1788) 1 H Bl 13; *Whitworth v Smith* (1832) 5 C&P 250). The damages are based on the actual damage suffered, which is often said to be the full value of any goods lost or injury sustained less the debt and costs. In the absence of proof of special damages, the claimant cannot even get a nominal sum (*Rogers v Parker* (1856) 18 CB 112). Special damages need to be proved if, for instance, the bailiff sells within five days (*Lucas v Tarleton* (1858) 3 H & N 116), sells without appraising (*Biggins v Goode* (1832) 2 C & J 364) or sells without notice of distraint (*Whitworth v Maden* (1847) 2 Car & Kir 517). Any consequential losses such as for detention after tender of the sums due or for sale after tender is made but before the time for replevin has expired may also be recovered.

10.8.3 *Excessive distress*

An excessive distress has always been treated as wrongful at common law, for which an action will lie. The continuing relevance of this principle is underlined by the National Standard, which restates it in slightly more modern terms: it is required that bailiffs should take all reasonable steps to satisfy themselves that the value of the goods impounded is proportional to the value of the debt and charges due.

The common law rules on excessive distresses were confirmed and codified by two successive medieval statutes which remain in force. Chapter 4 of the Statute of Marlborough 1267 requires that distresses are reasonable and not too great: anyone levying an unreasonable distress will be 'grievously amerced' for the excess. This necessity for distresses to be reasonable and not outrageous is repeated by the Statute of Exchequer (date uncertain). Despite the reference to 'amercements' it is not an offence to levy in an excessive manner and no information or indictment can be laid (*R v Ledgingham* (1671) 1 Vent 604). *Viner's Abridgment* terms it a 'private offence' and rather than prosecution the remedy for excessive distress is an action in case founded on the statute. It will be conducted as for irregular distress above, the measure of damages being the excess. It is accepted that the above mentioned statutes deal generally with levies of distress for rent (see remedies at 7.8), but Bradby at p.275 cites Coke (2 Inst 107) to the effect that the operation of the statutes regarding excessive levies is general and applies to all cases of distress whatsoever. Readers should recall that execution is subject to separate rules (see 5.2).

If an excessive levy has taken place the claimant cannot sue for trespass (*Hutchins v Chambers* (1758) 1 Burr 580; *Lynne v Moody* (1729) 2 Stra 851; *Woodcroft v Thompson* (1683) 3 Lev 48), unless perhaps goods of very great value are taken for a very small debt (*Moir v Munday* (1755) at 1 Burr 590; *Crowther v Ramsbottom* (1798) 7 TR 658). Baron Gilbert in his analysis of *Moir v Munday* noted that the seizure was of gold and silver- assets of known worth- and that this serves to distinguish this decision from any distress on goods of 'arbitrary and uncertain value' (Gilbert p.60). Recovery of damages in a replevin will bar any action for excessive distress (*Phillips v Berryman* (1783) 3 Doug 286; *White v Wallis* (1759) 2 Wils 87; *Pease v Chaytor* (1863) 1 B&S 658). This is because replevin is founded upon the distress being illegal, whereas an action for excessive distress is founded upon there being a cause for the distress. However an agreement between landlord and tenant to prevent sale will not prevent a later action for an excessive seizure (*Willoughby v Backhouse* (1824) 2 B&C 821).

There is no need to prove malice in the action but the excess will have to be disproportionate rather than trifling. There is no cause of action if the value of the goods taken is less than the sum actually due (*Tancred v Leyland* (1851) 16 QB 669). No special damage need in fact be shown for the claimant to succeed (*Chandler v Doulton* (1865) 3 H&C 553), but if the claimant only establishes an entitlement to nominal damages s/he may be deprived of the costs of the action (*Crowder v Self* (1839) 2 Mood & Ry 190). The price realised at sale by auction, rather than in the normal course of the claimant's business, is *prima facie* evidence of the item's value (*Rapley v Taylor & Smith* (1883) Cab & El 150 and *Wells v Moody* (1835) 7 C & P 59) and will be the measure of damages. Again the debt and costs due will be deducted from the amount awarded (*Knotts v Curtis* (1832) 5 C&P 322). An action can be begun even when the goods are not yet sold (*Hooper v Annis* (1838) 2 JP 695) the measure of damages then being the loss and inconvenience to the debtor occasioned by the goods' removal, though this may be nominal (*Chandler v Doulton* (1865) 3 H&C 553; *Mudhun Mohun*

Doss v Gokul Doss (1866) 10 Moo Ind App 563). It may include excessive sums paid to prevent removal (*Fell v Whittaker* [1871] 7 QB 120). Consequential losses, such as for loss of use and enjoyment are also recoverable (*Piggott v Birtles* (1836) 1 M&W 441). If the person had to replevy in order to recover seized goods, the costs of replevying the excessive sum are also claimable as consequential damages (*Piggott v Birtles* above) unless these costs have already been taxed in the replevin action (*Grace v Morgan* (1836) 2 Bing NC 534). If there is no inconvenience as in walking possession, no damages may be awarded (*Watson v Murray & Co* [1955] 1 All ER 350). In this latter case the HCEOs had attended at the claimant's shop and said they must take charge of everything there. The claimant signed a walking possession agreement under protest and then sued. The court held the seizure to have been valid, if excessive. The excessive seizure caused no damage as the trader was able to carry on dealing with the stock in the course of business. If the distress is both irregular and excessive, damages can be substantial (*Smith v Ashforth* (1860) above). In an action for an excessive levy any bailiff should not appear as a witness for the creditor unless released from their agency (*Field v Mitchell* (1806) 6 Esp 71).

If an excessive amount of growing crops are seized, the measure of damages is not their value but the inconvenience and expense to the farmer of being deprived of the management of them, or the value of the farmer's replevin sureties. As growing crops can be levied under DRA 1689, they are covered by the common law principles of excessive distress under 52 H3 c4 (*Piggott v Birtles* (1836) 1 M&W 441).

Chapter 11

CONDUCTING LEVIES: CHARGES

Introduction

Of all the areas for dispute that will be encountered, the issue of charges is probably the most common and one of the most difficult. Money diverted into fees to which bailiffs are not entitled is money which is not discharging the debtor's liability, so that it unnecessarily extends repayment periods. For many centuries the courts have been concerned to protect vulnerable debtors from exploitation in this way (see for example *Roe v Hammond* [1877] 2 CPD 300).

In hearing challenges to fees, the courts have developed a number of general principles which should be applied when considering the legality and fairness of the fees under scrutiny. These are:

- are the fees lawful? Upon what basis are they charged?

- have the fees been earned? Did the bailiffs carry out the actions for which they are charging- and did they need to perform those actions?

- are the fees fair? Are they a reasonable reflection of the costs incurred by the bailiffs' company?

The issue of fees will now be considered in light of these principles.

11.1 Charge scales

The costs chargeable by most bailiffs are regulated by scales found in the various statutes and statutory instruments. The purpose of the scales is to regulate what is charged to debtors and to prevent the 'extortion' of 'helpless debtors' by the levying of any 'unfairly large sum' (*Roe v Hammond* [1877] 2 CPD 300; *Phillips & Another v Rees* [1889] 24 QBD 17).

11.1.1 *Elements of charge scales*

The charges allowable are found in schedules or appendices to the regulations, for example Sch 5 CT(A&E) Regs; Sch 3 NDR(A&E)(LL) Regs; Appendix 1 DRR; Sch 1 CS(C&E) Regs; Sch 1 ERTD(CB) Regs. The broad outline of each of these is the same, but readers are referred to the text of each as the specific wording and effect differs from scale to scale. The following paragraphs consider a few significant features, but the main focus of this chapter will be abuses of the charging system and the remedies available to the debtor.

Typical elements within the scales are fixed or set daily fees for certain activities such as visits to the debtor's property, 'reasonable' costs for activities like removal and storage and fees for levies and auctions based on a percentage of the debt due. The local tax and child support scale charges include VAT, whereas they are additional to charges for distress for rent and taxes. There is now a standard format of fee scale across most forms of statutory distraint, but there are a few major exceptions to this considered in the following sections.

11.1.2 *Magistrates' courts*

The fees charged by bailiffs enforcing magistrates' court orders are fixed by the regional contracts let by HMCS. The charges permitted cover more activities, and are set at a higher level, than those usually found in the statutory fee scales. Advisers should be able to obtain a copy of the scale applicable either from the court or from the enforcement agency.

Recently the question has been raised as to the legal basis upon which these fees are charged. The government's rather unsatisfactory response, given by the minister in the House of Lords on 2nd April 2009, was that the "necessary implication" of Part III of the Magistrates' Court Act 1980 is that proper costs associated with the execution of the warrant are recoverable. Equally HMCS cites the authority of *Cook v Plaskett* (1882) 47 JP 265/ 46 LT 383. Cook is, however, a rather unsatisfactory authority upon which to rely. It is a decision of the Queen's Bench Division on case stated from a magistrates' court. Plaskett was ordered to pay a sum of 5/-, which included a fine and court costs for an offence under the Elementary Education Act 1870. He did not pay and a distress warrant was issued for 8/-, comprising the original fine and 3/- costs of enforcement. Plaskett challenged the warrant on the basis that s.74 of the 1870 Act stipulated that no penalty imposed for breach of the statute should exceed 5/- (including costs). The JP felt that this precluded him from issuing distress for more than the maximum sum stipulated. On appeal, the two judges in Queen's Bench Division reversed this decision on the grounds that it would otherwise render the 1870 Act inoperative. If defendants refused to pay, the cost of enforcement would fall wholly upon the prosecutor and pursuing breaches of the statute would become uneconomic. There are two problems with this decision. Firstly, Plaskett was not represented by counsel on appeal and Grove J noted the lack of argument for the defendant's position. Secondly, this is a decision solely concerned with the interpretation of the Elementary Education Act- it is not concerned with the powers granted to magistrates' courts. The argument that there is no basis in the Magistrates' Court Act 1980 for bailiffs passing on to defendants the expenses of distraint remains plausible and this would appear to be an issue deserving of scrutiny by the Administrative Court.

11.1.3 *High Court execution*

The HCEO is entitled by statute to fees and costs for enforcing writs, unless the debt is below £600 (CPR Sch.1 RSC O.47 r.4), and the writ instructs him to levy for these and all legal incidental costs. A formal seizure must be made first (*Barker v Dynes* (1832) 1 Dowl 169; *Nash v Dickenson* [1867] LR 2 CP 252). The HCEO cannot include the cost of previous abortive executions as these are only payable out of proceeds of that execution and may not be carried over to another: the execution debtor is under no personal liability for them (*Re: W M Long & Co ex p Cuddeford* [1888] 20 QBD 316).

If the creditor loses the right to enforce, the HCEO cannot then sell goods to recover fees (*Sneary v Abdy* [1876] 1 Ex D 299). By the same token, if the creditor authorises release of the goods in possession, the HCEO cannot then seize them in respect of his fees, as such a release is treated as a release consented to by the HCEO as well and if the execution creditor's right to the goods is ended, so is the HCEO's (*Goode v Langley* (1827) 7 B&C 26). Whenever execution is withdrawn, satisfied, stopped or fails, the HCEO is entitled to the same fees from the creditor as if the execution had been completed (*Mortimer v Cragg* [1879] 3 CPD 216). If insolvency occurs between seizure and sale, the HCEO can claim expenses for possession and preparing for sale, but not poundage (*Re Craycraft* [1878] 8 ChD 596; *Re Thomas* [1899] 1 QB 460). It is up to the court to decide, when awarding damages for illegal execution, whether a HCEO should be allowed the costs of selling the goods wrongfully seized (*Clarke v Nicholson* (1835) 4 LJNS Exch 66).

Expenses not covered by the rules should not be incurred unless either the execution debtor or creditor has authorised them and agreed to pay for them (*Re: Woodham ex p Conder* [1888] 20 QBD 40). It is unlikely that the courts will support extra fees demanded from defendants. Expenses incurred without consent, even though they may be of benefit for a party, cannot be charged as part of the costs of an execution (*Buckle v Bewes* (1825) 4 B & C 154; *Joynson v Oldfield* (1847) 8 LTOS 468).

Under s20(2) Sheriffs Act 1887, para.12(3), Sch.7 Courts Act 2003 and
Schedule 3 of the High Court Enforcement Officers Regulations 2004, the
HCEO is entitled to the following fees:

- set allowances for actions taken, such as mileage at a statutory rate for
  one journey to seize and one to remove goods; set seizure fees; charges
  for enquiring into claims to seized goods by landlords and third parties
  and daily fees for close and walking possession. Possession money is
  chargeable between seizure and removal (*Howes v Young* [1876] 1 Ex D
  146). The fees are only payable for a reasonable period (*Davies v
  Edmunds* (1843) 12 M&W 31);

- incidental expenses of removal, storage, etc. The sums actually and
  reasonably incurred are allowed;

- auctioneer's fees and advertising costs, based upon a percentage of
  sums received and recovered. These are deducted by the HCEO to
  cover the reasonable out of pocket expenses of an auctioneer. If there is
  no sale the auctioneer still gets flat rate commission based on the value
  of the goods. Certain percentage fees are also allowed for sale of goods
  by private contract;

- 'poundage' calculated as a percentage of the amount recovered.
  Poundage is only payable on sums which the bailiffs "levy and deliver in
  execution"- this means getting payment under compulsion of the writ,
  however that may come about: there does not have to be a sale
  (*Mortimer v Cragg* [1878] 3 CPD 216). A levy is not complete until the
  goods are turned into money i.e. until after the sale (*Miles v Harris*
  (1862) 12 CB 550) or payment (*Re: Ludmore* [1884] 13 QBD 415).
  Without any seizure at all there can be no poundage (*Nash v Dickenson*
  [1877] 2 CP 252) so even though the money may be paid or tendered
  after the writ is delivered to him for execution no poundage can be
  charged upon it, and any poundage claimed in such circumstances and
  paid under protest by the defendant to prevent seizure may be recovered
  by action (*Colls v Coates* (1840) 11 Ad & El 826). If the money is paid
  after seizure but before sale, poundage can be claimed (*R v Jetherell*
  (1757) Park 176). The same applies if a compromise (i.e. instalment
  payments) is reached after seizure (*Alchin v Wells* (1793) 5 Term Rep
  470). The HCEO can take the poundage and fees out of the proceeds of
  sale of the property seized (*Curtis v Mayne* (1842) 2 Dowl. NS 37).

The HCEO is entitled to poundage if the execution is later withdrawn,
satisfied, stopped or stayed (*Union Bank of Manchester v Grundy* [1924]
1 KB 833) but the claim is made against the person issuing execution or
the person at whose instance the sale is stopped (e.g. the trustee or
Official Receiver). Poundage cannot be recovered if the judgment is set

aside after seizure but before sale (*Miles v Harris* as above). In all other cases, if judgment is set aside poundage and fees can be recovered (*Bullen v Ansley & Smith* (1807) 6 Esp 111).

• General fees for copies of any return made by the HCEO and to cover any 'miscellaneous' expenses. Para.12 of the fee scale states that this is to cover "any matter not otherwise provided for" and it is allowable upon application to the court. The case law indicates that this is to cover unusual expenses necessitated by the particular nature of the levy involved and is not to be used as a matter of course to supplement the standard fees allowed by Parliament.

• VAT is payable in addition

11.1.4 *County court costs*

County court fees are much lower than any other fees that will be encountered. For example there is a flat rate issue fee for a warrant of execution which is banded according to value. Other charges are then only made if a sale has to take place.

11.1.5 *Liability*

In *A.W. Ltd v Cooper & Hall Ltd* [1925] 2 KB 816 Salter J observed "In the absence of any special bargain [between bailiff and creditor], the rights of the bailiff to his fees are purely statutory. He may in some cases have contractual rights to fees arising by bargain...". As there was no bargain in this case, the bailiff could only claim the sums set in the relevant statutory scale. The statutory scales apply to both the creditor and the debtor, but, except in distress for rent, there is nothing in the legislation specifically precluding special agreements for extra remuneration, even though these may be contrary to the provisions of the law (*Robson v Biggar* [1907] 1 KB 690). However it will become clear that, whilst special arrangements with a creditor may be conscienced by the court, there will be great reluctance to endorse similar arrangements with debtors due to their weak bargaining position.

Advisers will encounter two categories of 'non-statutory' fees being charged. Firstly, there are those which are for activities permitted by the scale, but which are being charged wrongly - for example, multiple vehicle fees or levy fees, walking possession fees when there has been no agreement, higher daily fees than those permitted or levy fees when there has been nothing more than a visit to the premises. Secondly, there are those extra fees which simply do not appear on the charge scales at all (see below). These fees may be added on the initiative of the bailiffs' company or, in some cases, may even be sanctioned by the creditor in a contract.

There are numerous cases illustrating the court's attitude to the charging of fees extra to the scale figures allowable. Examples include *Usher v Walters* (1843) 4 QB 553, *Jenkins v Biddulph* (1827) 4 Bing 160 and *Braithwaite v Marriott* (1862) 1 H&C 591: these were all sheriff's cases and show the sheriff facing action to recover the wrongful overcharges. It is clear that in most cases the courts have felt that the statutory bar on extra fees should have been final and that there was exasperation that the rule was regularly flouted, with the result that the courts were still being called upon repeatedly to consider "complaints against auctioneers, bailiffs and all those locusts who prey upon the estates of necessitous defendants....": Grose J in *Woodgate v Knatchbull* (1787) 2 TR 148.

What extras are charged?
It is very frequent for bailiffs' companies to charge for additional activities such as vehicle immobilisation, damages to clamps or for taking payment by credit or debit charge. In order to decide whether there is a legal basis for such fees, the following issues must be considered.

Is there a statutory prohibition?
Many of the regulations dealing with statutory distraint state that the creditor may levy distraint for an appropriate amount, which is defined as the debt plus "a sum determined [as prescribed] in respect of charges connected with distress". The charges are then determined by reference to the appropriate charges scale. The schedule will contain a list of permitted charges, and is often headed "charges connected with distress". See for example reg 45(2)(b) CT(A&E) Regs, reg 14(2)(b) NDR (A&E) (LL) Regs 1989 or s35(2) CSA and reg 32 CS(C&E) Rs 1992. On the basis of this wording alone, it may be argued that additional charges are simply not possible.

In *Day v Davies* [1938] 1 All ER 686 the Court of Appeal reviewed the permissible charges a bailiff could make under the Distress for Rent Rules 1920. As under the current r10 DRR the bailiff could not charge fees for " for doing any act in relation [to a levy], other than those specified and authorised" by the rules. On this basis the court held that any charge for actions related to distress not covered by the rules was directly prohibited, and as the charge being made by the claimant was not in the rules, it could not be recovered. The principle of this case still seems applicable, despite slightly differing wording in some of the current regulations, and appears to represent a complete bar on extra charges. Other cases reinforcing the conclusion that extra charges are unlawful in respect of distraint are *Megson v Mapleton* (1884) 49 LT 744, *R v Smith & Others ex p Porter* [1927] 1 KB 478 and *Headland v Coster* [1905] 1 KB 219 (confirmed on appeal [1906] AC 286 HL).

Although there is limited case law on the legality of extra charges in distraint, there is extensive authority in respect of sheriffs' officers levying execution. Scales have been provided for their charges since the reign of Henry VI. It is clear that, whatever the reason, charges not in accordance with the scale are not permissible. This is the case whether:

- the bailiff has been put to extra trouble or expense: this will include extra costs of keeping possession, whether with extra bailiffs or for an extended period, (*Davies v Edmonds* (1843) 12 M&W 31; *Jones v Robinson* (1843) 11 M&W 758; *R v Fereday* (1817) 4 Price 131; *Halliwell v Heywood* (1862) 10 WR 780) or other extra expenses arising from inconvenience (*Lane v Sewell* (1819) 1 Chit 175; *Slater v Hames* (1841) 7 M&W 413);

- the extra fee is not excessive: however reasonable a fee may be, if it is contrary to law it cannot be allowed (Abbott CJ AT 566 in *Dew v Parsons* (1819) 2 B&A 562);

- it has become customary to make additional charges: usage and custom cannot be claimed as a defence however reasonable the extra fee may be (*Dew v Parsons* (1819) 2 B&A 562). See also *Gill v Jose* (1856) 6 E&B 718 where charging double the allowed mileage, as was the local practice, was deemed illegal; or,

- the fees are illegal: if there is no statutory authorisation for a fee it cannot be recovered as at common law the HCEO is entitled to no compensation (Best J in *Dew v Parsons* (1819) 2 B&A 562; see also *R v Palmer* (1802) 2 East 411.)

In all these cases the HCEO was ordered to repay the excess plus costs.

Is there a separate contract?
It has sometimes been suggested that a separate contract has been made for the payment of extra-statutory fees (in the walking possession agreement, presumably). Is such a contract is permissible, is it a genuine agreement and is it valid? The Court of Appeal in *Day v Davies* (above) stated "As for special agreements, where a prohibition under statute is absolute, it cannot be waived by the party for whose benefit it is made. If an act is prohibited, it cannot be the subject of a valid contract. No special agreement as to charges for an act of distress, other than those permitted by the rules, can be made and the agreement relied upon to justify a [non-statutory charge] cannot be enforced". From this, it would seem that the separate contract idea fails for the reasons already given. However attention should be paid to two cases that seem to reach different conclusions.

In *Robson v Biggar* [1907] 1 KB 690 the court held that it was permissible for a person and bailiff to agree to pay fees extra to the statutory scale as long as each party consented. However the case concerned a landlord making the agreement and the statute in question, the Distress (Costs) Act 1817, was aimed primarily at preventing the "great oppression of poor tenants". From this it would appear that the court may well not have upheld an agreement for extra fees by a debtor because of the risk of oppression, excessive charges and an unfair bargaining position. Creditors are in a different position as they can always refuse, negotiate or employ a different bailiff if they are unhappy with the service. In a dissenting judgment in *Robson v Biggar* Darling J held that separate fee bargains are outlawed by statute, which sets the maxima that can be charged, in order to protect the debtor "who [is] in too bad a position to be able to resist exorbitant demands".

Further in *Lumsden v Burnett* [1898] 2 QB 177 CA, in a dispute about possession charges, it was suggested by Chitty LJ that the court may sanction an agreement by the debtor to pay for a man in walking possession, which was then not allowable and therefore a wrongful charge, if such a charge was getting rid of the unnecessary inconvenience of man in possession and was therefore to the debtor's benefit. The learned Judge remarked that there is nothing in the statute to stop a debtor contracting out of the protection given to them if it would be to their advantage to agree to constructive rather than actual possession (and to pay for it). However this remark is obiter to the substance of the appeal so that the decision is not a clear authority. It must be contrasted with *Phillips v Viscount Canterbury* (1843) 11 M&W 619, a sheriffs case, in which it was explicitly decided that a charge not permitted by the scale is not recoverable, even though the action in question- private sale by bill of sale- was more advantageous to the parties than sale at auction. It is certain though that charges not to the debtor's benefit would still not be condoned by the court. It is also possible that charges made by the bailiff which would have been incurred by the debtor if the levy had not occurred, may be legal (see *R v Smith ex p. Porter* [1927] 1 KB 478: the bailiffs charged a range of extra fees not permitted by the scales but including the expense of feeding the horse seized. It was not argued that this was irrecoverable, perhaps because it would have been a cost met by Porter anyway.)

To conclude, the weight of opinion is against extra-statutory fees. A creditor may consent to pay extra, but it will be unlawful to charge such amounts to debtors unless (perhaps) it is an amount which the debtor would have expended anyway. Very recently, in a detailed assessment of a bill for charges made in executing a warrant for a road traffic penalty, a county court district judge disallowed a credit card charge on the grounds that it was not permitted by the fee scale and (there being no contract for the fees) was consequently illegal. The argument that the bailiffs were merely passing on a charge made to them by their bankers was rejected as being irrelevant to the question of their legal entitlement.

11.1.6 *Payment*

If a debt is paid, without the costs, before any seizure has occurred the right to distrain ceases (*Bennett v Bayes* (1860) 5 H&N 391; *Branscomb v Bridges* (1823) 1 B&C 145). If the debt is paid to the creditor and the bailiff is instructed to withdraw, the bailiff would not be able to proceed to recover any costs by sale as it would be conversion and would not pass good title (*Harding v Hall* (1866) 14 LT 410). If the creditor instructs the bailiff to withdraw any authority to sell is lost as the bailiff is acting as the creditor's agent. If the creditor loses the right to enforce, the bailiff cannot sell goods for fees (*Sneary v Abdy* [1876] 1 Ex D 299). Whenever a levy is withdrawn, satisfied, stopped or fails, the principle in execution law is that the bailiff is entitled to the same fees from the creditor as if the execution had been completed (*Mortimer v Cragg* [1879] 3 CPD 216). The costs of previous unsuccessful levies should not be included in later levies as these are only payable out of proceeds of the first and may not be carried over to another: the debtor is under no personal liability for them (*Re: W M Long & Co ex p Cuddeford* [1888] 20 QBD 316).

Where any proceeds are produced as a result of the use of distraint which total less than the full sum due, whether they are proceeds of sale or payment by the debtor, are applied first to the bailiff's permissible charges under the relevant schedule, the balance (if any) then going to the liability due to the local authority (reg 52(4) CT(A&E) Regs; reg 19(3) NDR(A&E)(LL) Regs). It is finally interesting to note that this order of distribution of proceeds provided for local taxes refers to the deduction of charges under the relevant schedule. From this it would appear that, even if 'non-statutory' charges are permissible (see 11.3 later), they could only be paid after the sums due to the local authority had been cleared in full.

11.2 Actual and necessary?

Charges should only be made for steps actually and necessarily taken by the bailiff. This is a specific provision in distress for rent under rr10 & 12(2) DRR; see also *Day v Davies* [1938] 2 KB 74. The same rule also applies to road traffic execution (reg 4). As stated earlier, in execution case law confirms that the same applies and steps must actually be taken to permit a charge (*Holmes v Sparks & Nicholas* (1852) 12 CB 242; *Cohen v Das Rivas* (1891) 64 LT 661). It seems from *Re: H K Stinton* (1900) 109 LT Jo 427 that the full fee should not be chargeable unless each item on the scale is fully performed but that a lesser amount may be allowable.

The question whether sums were "actually and necessarily" incurred often arises in respect of disputed van charges. The sorts of issues which should be considered in determining this question are:

- had any seizure taken place - was the bailiff in a position to remove the goods?

- what was seized- what sort of vehicle was necessary?

- was walking possession taken? Was there evidence of any real intention to seek to remove at the time of seizure, bearing in mind the great costs and inconvenience for the bailiff?

- what sort of vehicle, if any, did attend, and is the charge reasonable for it?

11.3 Reasonable charges?

The court can consider if the sums billed are a fair charge for the work done. In deciding this question the court must take into account the following factors.

- *the ratio between charges and sum due*: disproportionate charges will be disallowed (*ex p Arnison* [1868] LR 3 Exch 56). Where large attendance and enforcement fees can rapidly inflate what were originally quite small liabilities, this question of proportionality is becoming increasingly important;

- *the work involved*: for example, if one levy is conducted for several warrants simultaneously, charges may be restricted to those allowable for one levy (*Glasbrook v David & Vaux* [1905] 1 KB 615; *Frisch v Gateshead MBC* (1992) 25 Adviser 17). It is implicit in the local tax scales (Head B(i)) that less than a multiple of the percentage levy fee may be considered reasonable if multiple warrants are levied at once. The courts have held that multiple fees will only be allowed where there are separate seizures and one levy is not for the benefit of all creditors. In a recent county court detailed assessment of road traffic charges, the district judge disallowed the multiple levy fees added to the bill. Eight fees had been charged on eight warrants, but only one car had been seized. The court followed the principle applied in *Throssell v Leeds City Council* (see below) but added that, in any case, the fee scale only allowed a fee for 'levying distress' rather than for levying each warrant, so only one levy fee should be calculated, as a percentage of the total sums due.

If the same goods are taken to satisfy several warrants, only one possession fee is possible. If different goods are taken under several warrants, even though they are all seized on the same premises and are held in possession simultaneously by one person under the several warrants, the bailiff is entitled to possession money under each warrant (*Re: Morgan* [1904] 1 KB 68). In *Throssell v Leeds City Council* (1993) 41 Adviser 22 in which a county court allowed only one visit charge for an attempt to levy three warrants simultaneously. Although it was also argued that the scale sum is still only a maximum and that the reasonable figure the court might allow could be less, the court felt that the effort involved by the bailiff in preparation, travel, attendance and follow up reports meant that the sum in the scale was reasonable;

- *expense to the bailiff.* In the unreported case of *Flanagan v Crilley* (1987) a van charge was taxed down on the basis that the bailiff's firm could not justify a charge several times in excess of the commercial hire rate when the van was part of a fleet operated by them and any individual visit it made would also be combined with other visits to other debtor's homes.

- *the period for which charges are made*: in *Re: Finch ex p Sheriff of Essex* (1891) 65 LT 466 a sheriff remained in possession an unreasonable time without the debtor's consent. The court held that he couldn't charge beyond a reasonable period (held to be ten days). However where debtor and creditor agree a longer time, higher charges can be made, for example for up to fifteen months (*Re: Beeston* [1899] 1 QB 626; *Re: Hurley* (1893) 1 WR 653).

11.4 Current problem areas

There are currently two charging issues upon which most concern is focussed. One is specific to council tax, one is a more general problem which is particularly problematic in council tax and road traffic cases.

11.4.1 *Council tax 'redemption fees'*

Over the last few years concerns have developed amongst advisers about the charges that are made by bailiffs under Head H of the local tax fee scale: so-called 'redemption fees'. Such a practice is becoming increasingly common.

Seizure & removal?
Under Head H of the council tax fee scale bailiffs are permitted to charge an amount of £20 or "the actual costs" up to a maximum of 5% of the sum due under the liability order. The fee arises "Where no sale takes place by reason of payment or tender in the circumstances referred to in regulation 45(4)." Clearly the fee head in Schedule 5 of the Council Tax (Administration &

Enforcement) Regulations cannot be read or understood independently of the regulations themselves. Regulation 45(4) states that "Where an authority has seized goods of the debtor in pursuance of the distress, but before sale of those goods the appropriate amount...is paid or tendered to the authority, the authority shall accept the amount, the sale shall not be proceeded with and the goods shall be made available for collection by the debtor." The problem therefore is to determine the meaning of reg.45(4) in order to decide when the fee permitted should be charged. The regulation is not clear, as the wording at the start appears at odds with the concluding phrase.

Regulation 45(4) posits a situation where goods have been "seized" in distress. As has already been seen (8.1) seizure should be narrowly understood to refer to the process of selecting and identifying the goods upon which distress is being levied. Seizure in this strict sense precedes impounding by the taking of walking possession, close possession or the like. If seizure is understood in this manner, a charge under Head H would appear to be permissible at the very start of the process of levying. Potentially, no impounding need have occurred for it to arise. However, this is to read the start of regulation 45(4) independently of the last phrase "the goods shall be made available for collection by the debtor." If payment or tender is made, it seems that any planned sale will be terminated and the goods will be released to the debtor. From this it is clear that a prior relocation of goods from the debtor's premises has to be contemplated by both reg.45(4) and Head H; the goods will have been taken to a place of storage or to an auctioneer's showroom preparatory to sale and it is from here that they are to be recovered.

The last part of reg.45(4) is problematic as it requires us to understand "seized" to have a broader meaning than its accepted technical sense. 'Seizure' apparently denotes removal in reg.45(4). There is some legal support for such an interpretation of the word. In *Wilson v South Kesteven District Council* [2000] EWCA Civ 218, Simon Brown LJ several times distinguished levying and seizure from removal and sale, but towards the end of the judgment refers to "seizure (in the sense of removal)..." This is the non-specialist sense of the word and it seems to be used this way in reg.45(4). Others have contended that the word must be read in its technical sense, but regardless of this legal argument, it is still necessary for us to explain the goods 'being made available for collection by the debtor'- not a phrase which sits comfortably with walking possession.

Wasted auction costs
Support is lent to this interpretation of Head H by considering the previous forms of wording of the Head. In the original version of the council tax regulations (SI 613 of 1992) the fee was said to cover "Other expenses incurred in connection with a proposed sale where there is no buyer in

relation to it." These were the reasonable expenses incurred by the bailiffs other than auctioneer's fees. In the 1993 version of the fee scale (SI 773 of 1993) the sum allowed was for the "Reasonable costs and fees incurred in respect of advertising." This was amended in 1998 to the present 'fixed cost' allowance. Both predecessors of the current fee anticipated a situation where goods were capable of being sold - in one version the sale failed; in the other it was pre-empted by settlement of the debt. For matters to be so advanced there must have been removal - mere impounding on the premises and the mere making of an inventory cannot logically be sufficient to justify the charge. It is also worth noting that the present scale refers merely to "actual costs" without defining what costs are being referred to. If bailiffs are correct and no physical removal or preparation for sale is required, an allowance would appear to have been made for the bailiff doing nothing at all- or at most for relinquishing the claim to possession and removing the case from their system. As no fee scale makes any allowance for firms' administration costs in opening an account in the first place, an allowance for closing a case seems highly doubtful and the allowance for "actual costs" suggests something more tangible (i.e. cancelled sale expenses) was intended.

It seems that reg.45(4) has always been a provision concerned with events located firmly at the end of the distraint process. Its context is not a distant and only theoretically possible sale, but an imminent sale for which concrete arrangements have been made. Payment by the debtor renders these arrangements unnecessary and it is to compensate for wasted expenses that Head H was devised. Changes in wording to the fee scale have not altered this fundamental context. There has been no change in basic policy, nor in the regulations, despite the variations in wording in the statutory instruments.

Payment or tender
Even if all the foregoing is mistaken and these 'redemption fees' may be properly charged early in the levy process before removal, or even contemporary with levy fees, there is still an unavoidable condition imposed by the regulations. For the bailiff company to be able to charge the fee, payment of the full amount due (including other bailiff fees) has to be made, or at least offered, by the debtor. This might be a lump sum payment or the last payment in a series of instalments. In fact, most firms seem to charge this fee coincident with a seizure and impounding- if a 'redemption fee' is to be made at this point it will be necessary for the debtor to clear the entire balance due at the time of the levy. It should be noted that this interpretation is the one adapted by the ESA and which should be followed by its members.

Summary

To summarise and conclude this analysis of Head H:

1. The nexus of this fee is 'seizure', followed by full payment by the debtor of the debt and costs, and subsequent recovery of chattels from an unspecified location. Without this full payment, this fee can never arise in any situation.

2. To interpret the regulation, it seems necessary to give a non-standard interpretation to part of reg.45(4). It seems that the best reading is that seizure is used to denote removal rather than bearing its more technical and legal sense. This seems preferable to trying to interpret "the goods shall be made available for collection by the debtor" differently. The only sensible understanding of this phrase must be that the goods have been transported from the debtor's to the bailiff's premises; it is not possible to give it any satisfactory meaning in the context of impounding on the debtor's premises.

3. Finally, a fundamental principle of bailiff's law is that charges should only be made for work 'actually' and 'necessarily' done. As regulation 45(4) and Head H both refer to the cancellation of a sale, it seems reasonable to insist that before such a charge is exigible, a sale must have actually been arranged- and then cancelled. Neither a potential nor a contemplated sale will be sufficient.

11.4.2 *Attendance fees*

As has already been mentioned, there are considerable concerns on the part of advisers over the 'attendance' or 'van' fees which are added onto many debtor's accounts. The main concerns arise in the context of levies of council tax and of road traffic penalties.

In levies for council tax, a vehicle attendance fee is permitted under Head C of the fee scale. This allows for one charge to be made 'following a levy.' Two problems appear to arise in practice. The first should fairly easily be resolved. Some firms add on one (or more) attendance or 'enforcement' fees before any levy has been conducted at a property. It would appear that this often is done because the rather low fixed 'visit' fees that are allowed by the scale have already been used to cover the costs of postage and office overheads and a 'reasonable' fee for the physical attendance of the bailiff at the property allows a more 'realistic' fee to be recovered. Nonetheless, it is clear from the wording of the fee scale in Sch.5 of the enforcement regulations that a levy must precede an attendance fee being charged. All such fees added to accounts before there has been a seizure and impounding must be unlawful. More problematic is the question of when after the levy the attendance fee should be charged: should there be any delay between the levy and the attendance? This cannot be resolved by reference to the fee scale alone, but case authority may assist.

In levies of execution for road traffic penalties, attendance fees are a much more serious problem as the usual practice is to make multiple charges on accounts, at the same time as making visit charges, and usually before any goods have been seized. For assistance we can now turn to the decision in *Culligan v Simkin & Marstons Group* (2008). In the course of his judgment, the district judge analysed the detailed process of making a levy. He concluded that the stage of removal of goods was distinct and separate from their seizure. There must be a gap between these two stages and, the district judge said, "in my judgment the bailiff should not and, as a matter of law, cannot, take any steps to remove goods until he has given the debtor a reasonable opportunity to pay what is due at the time of seizure." He felt that this conclusion was supported by the fact that the relevant regulations (the Enforcement of Road Traffic Debts (Certificated Bailiffs) Regulations 1993) require the bailiffs to use two separate forms to record the costs incurred at the stages of seizure and removal (forms 7 and 9 in the Regulations). The bailiff had, in fact, failed to supply a breakdown of removal expenses to Mr Culligan on form 9; it was argued that this was a fundamental omission, but the district judge held that this error was not fatal to the validity of the whole levy.

The district judge's decision on this point is of the highest importance. Seizure and removal are found to be distinct stages in the levy process separated by a clear space of time but, as stated earlier, many bailiffs' firms charge fees for 'attending to remove' at the same time as charging fees for 'attending to levy.' There are now several clear objections to this practice:

- As stated in *Culligan*, removal cannot take place at the same time as a levy and even less so at the same time as a visit to levy when no levy is made;

- Bailiffs should not charge two fees for the same activity. This cannot have been Parliament's intention and cannot be supported by the fee scale. The 'attendance fees' are charged under paragraph 6 of the scale, the visit fees are charged under para.3. The latter allows a fee calculated as a percentage of the debt due for "attending to levy, but where the levy is not made." Paragraph 6 allows a reasonable fee for "Removing goods, or attending to remove goods, where no goods are removed." On careful consideration, the use of this latter fee to cover 'attendance costs' alone cannot be supported by the wording of the scale. It is not a mere attendance fee, it is a fee for turning up to remove goods with the necessary equipment (the removal vans, machines and men which are itemised on the removal form no.9), but then not needing to use them because the debtor pays on the doorstep.

- Finally, when the charge is made at the very beginning of the process, before any goods have been identified or seized, there must also be questions of proportionality given the fact that the fees added to bills can often exceed the initial liability under the court order.

This discussion is very important to cases of road traffic enforcement, but the judge's reasoning is clearly also applicable to attendance fees added in council tax cases.

11.5 National Standard for Enforcement Agencies

It is clear from the attention given to fees by the National Standard that the government is aware that it is an area of dispute between debtors and bailiffs. Various recommendations are made, which build upon the principles laid out in the *Introduction* earlier:

- agents should provide clear & prompt information to debtors. They should explain the consequences of seizure and the fees charged so far as well as those possible in the future;

- whenever a fee is incurred, notice of this and of any previous fees charged should be given. This need for notice is clearly an attempt to ensure that fees charged are for work actually undertaken, in order to try to deal with the problem of 'ghost visits' and the like;

- a detailed breakdown of fees should be supplied on receiving a written request from the debtor or that person's representative.

The latter clause of the Standard has proved particularly valuable since it was introduced in 2002. It is important for advisers to obtain this information and then to compare it to the statutory fee scale and to the debtor's account of what has taken place. This breakdown may thus provide the foundation for some form of challenge to the fees- see the next section.

It should also be noted that the OFT debt collection guidelines (where they are applicable) also make recommendations about fees. Licensed firms are warned that it is improper to:

- claim collection costs in the absence of express legal provision; and,

- apply unreasonable charges which are not based on actual and necessary costs or applying charges which are disproportionate to the main debt.

11.6 Remedies for disputed charges

Generally specific remedies will have to be employed for challenging disputed charges. It will probably not be possible to sue for trespass or illegal distress, as an overcharge alone is not such a tort as to render a distress unlawful (*Shorland v Govett* (1826) 5 B&C 485), though it should be noted that the court in *Hickman v Maisey* [1900] 1 QB 752 observed that the decision in *Shorland* might have been otherwise had the facts been slightly different. The sheriff left as soon as the full sum, including the wrongful costs, had been paid. It is conceivable that remaining in possession solely to receive the unlawful charges might have caused the court to view the bailiff's presence as no longer legitimate or reasonable, and hence trespass.

11.5.1 *Detailed assessment*

Detailed assessment (formerly taxation) is the process by which a county court district judge scrutinises and approves a bill. Wherever private bailiffs' fees are set by statutory instrument (most forms of distraint except for fines) the relevant regulations provide for a county court to assess any disputed charges. This applies in cases of distraint and to charges made in execution by the HCEO (reg.13(4) High Court Enforcement Officers Regulations 2004). In such cases application will be made by Part 8 claim, seeking detailed assessment under CPR Part 47. This should be done within three months of the bill being received. A fee of £150 will be payable to initiate the claim; there is also a risk of paying the bailiffs' legal costs if the court considers that a person acted unreasonably in disputing certain items on the bill or did not achieve a sufficient reduction in the sums payable (CPR Part 47.18(2)).

A detailed assessment is a paper based procedure; the basis of assessment is going through the bailiffs' file, checking that the letters and notices charged for are there and deciding on whether they were necessary and the fee fair. The onus of proof is on the 'receiving party'- that is, the bailiffs' firm which presented the bill- and if there is any doubt about entitlement to the charges it will be resolved in favour of the paying party and the charge will be disallowed. The court can allow the bailiff the costs of the taxation (*Butler v Smith* (1895) 39 SJ 406) or allow costs to a debtor who is successful in challenging the fees. A person cannot appeal sums decided by assessment (*Townsend v Sheriff of Yorkshire* [1890] 24 QBD 612), but the principles of that assessment can be appealed (*Re: Beeston* [1889] 1 QB 626).

In fact, the established principles of bailiffs' fees were developed in the context of detailed assessments over the last 100-150 years. When approaching the validity of a bailiffs' bill, the court conducting the assessment will ask itself a number of questions:

• Upon what basis is the fee charged? As the right to fees is statutory, if the fee cannot be justified by the scale, it will be disallowed. Accordingly fees for card payments have been disallowed as they do not appear in the statutory fee scales;

- Does the fee relate to an action which was actually and necessarily performed by the bailiff? In other words, did the bailiff do what he is claiming payment for- and did he need to do it? Fees for visits to premises where the bailiff has been unable to inform the court when they took place or to produce the associated notices or letters have been disallowed;

- Is the fee reasonable and proportionate? These are different questions. A fee may be reasonable if it is a fair charge for the action in question; whether it may be proportionate will depend upon a consideration of the fee in the context of the amount of debt being recovered. These are both highly pertinent questions in respect of levies of distraint;

- Finally, and most importantly perhaps, can the charge be justified? In other words, is the bailiff company capable of satisfying the judge that they are entitled to the sum, because the fee has been earned and because it is possible to show how they arrived at the amount for which they have billed. Fees for removal and for attendances to remove have been disallowed simply because bailiffs' companies have been unable to supply the court with any breakdown illustrating how they were arrived at- for example, hourly rates for the bailiffs or the costs of the removal vehicle.

As an example of the potential of this remedy to challenge unlawful or unreasonable fees, we shall consider the detailed assessment case of *Culligan v Simkin & Marstons Group* (2008). It involved a challenge to the defendants' inclusion in the claimant's bill of a fee of £100 for immobilisation of a vehicle. Mr Culligan denied their right to recover this under the fee scale; Marstons justified it as one of the 'reasonable charges and expenses' incurred in removal. The judge completely rejected this argument. He reviewed the case law on the conduct of distresses and concluded that, if clamping formed any part of the levy process, it had to be part of the act of seizure and impounding. Logically, it could not be part of the removal process, simply because the immobilisation of a car is the exact opposite of its removal. The £100 fee was therefore disallowed. In any event, the district judge added that, even if he was wrong on this basis, he would still have disallowed the fee because "the defendants have produced no evidence whatsoever that it is reasonable in amount." In a detailed assessment, this was "clearly not sufficient." In the absence of any such evidence or breakdown the judge rejected the fee as "a completely arbitrary figure which in reality should be substantially less."

Note that there is a link between certification and overcharging. Under r.11(3) DRR if, at the end of a detailed assessment hearing, a district judge feels overcharging has occurred of such magnitude that the bailiff's fitness to hold a certificate has been called into question, and the court where the hearing took place is not the court where the certificate was granted, a copy of the assessed bill endorsed with the district judge's opinion is sent to the relevant court and acts like a certification complaint (see 6.8.3).

11.5.2 *Pay & claim*

An alternative civil remedy for an aggrieved debtor would be to make a claim to recover unlawful fees paid to a bailiff. A number of cases illustrate the application of this remedy in the case of charges and confirm that there would be grounds for an action against a bailiff.

The debtor's course of action is to pay the disputed debt under protest and then start an action to recover any sums wrongfully paid on the grounds that they were paid under duress. This is technically known as an action for money 'had and received' by the bailiff and is found as such in the older case reports. The debtor sues for money for money paid to the bailiff but which rightfully belongs to him/ her. Such an action is not an action for damages: the defendant's liability to the claimant is that s/he has unjustly benefited from the claimant's money. The debtor may issue a claim against a private bailiff or an HCEO (*Jons v Perchard* (1797) 2 Esp 507); and, in the case of distress and distraint, against the principal who instructed the bailiff (*Dawe v Cloud & Dunning* (1849) 14 LTOS 155).

Payment under duress in the context of distress means compulsion under which a person pays money to a bailiff through fear for their property (or the property of a close family or household member) being wrongfully seized or detained. The distress in question may be threatened or actual. The payment must not be voluntary, defining which can be difficult, but the debtor should be expected to have made it clear that they were paying the sum claimed under protest (*Atlee v Backhouse* (1838) 3 M&W 633). Ideally the fact that payment was being made under protest should have been conveyed by unambiguous words or in writing, but the court may find that the circumstances of payment or the claimant's conduct are sufficient indication of their intention. Establishing that payment was made under protest is important to the claimant because the general rule is that seizure in a legal distress is not illegal pressure and any payment made by the debtor to release goods is simply submission to that form of legal process. Money paid to release goods in the custody of the law is thus not paid under duress and cannot be recovered (*Liverpool Marine Credit v Hunter* [1868] 3 Ch App 479). Consequently there must be some wrongful element in the levy and the debtor, in paying, would have to make clear that this was not seen as an end to the matter but simply a way of retaining use of the goods rather than being deprived of them during lengthy litigation over the alleged illegality (*Green v Duckett* [1883] 11 QBD 275).

There is some uncertainty whether the remedy applies to all forms of distraint. The authorities are as follows:

- *execution* It is clear that the debtor could sue in this way to recover excess fees charged in cases of execution (*Blake v Newburn* (1848) 17 LJQB 216). If a public officer such as a HCEO demands an illegal or excessive fee for performing his legal duties it is extortion '*colore officii*' and the fee or excess is recoverable (*Dew v Parsons* (1819) 2 B&Ald 562).

- *statutory distraint* In *R v Judge Philbrick & Morey ex parte Edwards* [1905] 2 KB 108 a bailiff distrained for rates on a gold watch and brooch, sold them and retained a sum for costs amounting to six times the debt and reputedly covering removal, storage, possession, delivery to sale yard and haulage. Edwards began a county court action claiming the sums were unreasonable, which the judge refused to hear. On appeal it was confirmed that there was indeed a right of action as noted in *Nott v Bound* [1866] 1 QB 405 - the bailiff "might be liable to be made to refund by an action in the county court charges which were unnecessary or not strictly lawful" (even if they had been charged in error for acts that had been done and were not excessive). See also *Maskell v Horner* [1915] 3 KB 106.

- *distress for rent* It may be harder to make a successful claim in cases of distress for rent in light of the judgments in *Glynn v Thomas* (1856) 11 Exch 870, *Yates v Eastwood* (1852) 6 Exch 805 and *Skeate v Beale* (1840) 11 Ad & El 983. These were cases of illegal or irregular distress and the claims for recovery were rejected on the grounds that such bailiffs' offences attract their own remedies such as replevin or an action for trespass and therefore, in such cases, payment by the tenant is to be deemed voluntary. It is more likely that an action would succeed where there has been excessive distress, where the measure of the money had and received is the excessive sum sought by the creditor (*Loring v Warburton* (1858) EB & E 507 or *Fell v Whittaker* [1871] 7 QB 120), or where the goods have been sold so that replevin is impossible. See also *Hills v Street* (1828) 5 Bing 37 in which a tenant requested a broker not to proceed with the sale of his goods on payment of his charges. A dispute however arose over the charges and Best CJ held that he would "allow the legal expenses of the distress and inventory but the other charges were made (and paid) improperly and the claimant was entitled to recovery" by an action for money had and received. The action is certainly appropriate where bailiff's fees are at issue and especially where an element of fraud could be shown in the purported contract between bailiff and debtor (*Clarke v Dickenson* (1858) EB&E 148).

This remedy would be pursued by the debtor issuing a Part 7 claim for a liquidated sum which the defendant must have received. There can be no claim where the defendant has received goods instead of money (*Leery v Goodson* (1792) 4 TR 687) unless the goods in question can easily be converted to money (e.g. securities). Electing to sue this way extinguishes any right to damages on the part of the debtor, although it is possible for a claimant to sue for trespass or money had and received on the same summons.

11.5.3 *Magistrates' court remedy*

It is not possible for a defendant to seek detailed assessment of charges made in the levy of magistrates' distraint as there is no statutory provision providing a scale of charges, but the Magistrates' Court Act 1980 provides an alternative remedy. Complaint may be made under the court rules against the court's own bailiff. From the proceeds of sale the magistrates' bailiff may retain their charges and should return any balance to the owner of the goods after clearing the sum due (Crim PR Part 52.8(12)). A bailiff can be fined up to £200 for exacting high or improper costs from a defendant (MCA s.78(5)).

11.5.4 *Complaint under the Sheriff's Act*

It is an offence under s29(2) Sheriffs Act 1887 for an HCEO to breach any terms of the Act (see 5.4.1). The HCEO may be sued by the complainant for a penalty plus damages, or action may be taken to punish the officer for a misdemeanour or for contempt. Under s20(2) of the Act the officer "may demand, take, and receive such fees as may from time to time be fixed". As stated at 11.1.3 the current fees are fixed by the High Court Enforcement Officer Regulations 2004. Any overcharge is therefore an offence though this remedy can't be used where the charges made had been imposed without malice or with reasonable or probable cause. Thus an innocent mistake may be excused where there is no culpability (*Lee v Dangar, Grant & Co* [1892] 2 QB 337) or there has been a clerical error (*Shoppee v Nathan & Co* [1891] 1 QB 245). An unintentional overcharge is not misconduct by the HCEO but an action can be taken for excessive fees (*Blake v Newburn* (1848) 17 LJQB 216). However see *Braithwaite v Marriott* (1862) 1 H&C 591 in which a sheriff was successfully sued for an overcharge and for contempt.

11.5.5 *Certification complaint*

A complaint against the certificate held by the bailiff may also be considered where there has been serious overcharging. This might be initiated by the aggrieved individual or may be initiated by a district judge at the conclusion of a detailed assessment hearing (see 11.5.1 and 6.8).

TCEA 2007- commentary

At present there is very little of substance which may be said about the new fees regime which will apply to all bailiffs under the 2007 Act. Schedule 12 para.62 of the Act states that a new unified scale will be drafted, that it will not be lawful to make charges which are not allowed for by the scale and that a court will have the power to assess fees in cases of dispute.

The Ministry of Justice has committed itself to developing a new unified scale of fees which is both remunerative to bailiffs and fair to debtors. Work is ongoing on this at the time of writing. Needless to say, getting this fee scale right will be fundamental to the success of the new regime, as it is the pressure to raise fees which drives almost all the questionable practice which has been noted throughout this text.

Part 4

General Remedies and Conclusions

Chapter 12

COMPLAINTS TO CREDITORS AND BAILIFFS

12.1 Contracts

In most cases there will be a written contract between creditor and bailiff. Contracts are the norm where local authorities are the creditors, and the Lord Chancellor's Department has recently recommended that magistrates' courts should adopt contractual relationships with their bailiffs, rather than the more informal 'non-binding agreements' that have been preferred in the past.

12.1.1 *Contractual terms*

The bailiff's power to levy derives from the warrant that is issued. The purpose of the contract is to regulate the general administration of enforcement by distress and to ensure that distress is conducted in an acceptable manner. Contracts will normally be for a fixed period of time. Typical terms in a contract will cover such issues as timescales for enforcement (the period of time which is to be allowed for a bailiff to execute a warrant and the number of visits that should be made to try to do that), the charges to be made, cash handling (the frequency with which monies should be remitted to the creditor), monitoring of the bailiffs' activities and the conduct of levies themselves (this latter issue is normally governed by a code of practice - see 12.2).

The National Standard gives particular attention to the relationship between enforcement agent and creditor. Creditors must be fully aware of their own responsibilities, which should be observed and which should be set out in terms of agreement with their enforcement agency. In particular NSEA stresses that, in the case of vulnerable individuals (see 3.8), both agents and creditors have a duty to protect such groups and they should accordingly have procedures to deal with such cases in a prompt and appropriate manner.

12.1.2 *Agency*

Regardless of the detailed terms of the contract, the effect of it will be to make the bailiff the agent of the creditor so that, besides all the explicit terms of any agreement, there will be certain terms implicit as a result of the relationship of principal and agent. One is that the agent has the powers of the principal, but cannot exceed those powers. Thus, where statute gives a local authority the power to levy distraint in a certain way, the bailiff may exercise those same powers, but may not go beyond them. There is an implied authority to do all subordinate acts necessary or incidental to the exercise of that authority - though these may be restricted by codes of practice and the like (see later). Where an agreement is vague, an agent acts in good faith if s/he uses discretion, places a reasonable construction on the principal's authority and seeks to act in the best possible manner for the principal. If the agreement is clear, there is no right to exercise discretion. Authority cannot be given to act illegally and the agent cannot seek reimbursement from the principal for performing any illegal act.

Secondly, as the agency relationship is a fiduciary one, there is an implicit term that the agent must not acquire any profit or benefit from the agency not contemplated by the principal at the time of making the contract. To receive such sums is a breach of duty (*Rogier v Campbell* [1939] Ch 766). This duty is combined with the requirement that the agent should not put their agency in conflict with their own interests and therefore must not enter into any transaction likely to produce that result (*Phipps v Boardman* [1965] Ch 992), unless it has been fully disclosed to the principal and consented to by him/ her. Any profit must be accounted for to the principal and the whole benefit paid over less any commission and expenses- it cannot be pocketed by the agent (*De Busscher v Alt* [1878] 8 Ch D 286). This appears to have implications for separate agreements with debtors over the payment of 'non-statutory' fees as discussed in chapter 11. Note *Erskine, Oxenford & Co v Sachs* [1901] 2 KB 504 in which it was held that such a 'secret' profit made out of a share deal should be accounted for to the creditor- and also that failing to separate private and agency elements in the deal and treating it all as one transaction to the benefit of the agent made the agents liable to make payment to the principal. The agent cannot defend such a claim on the basis that in acting for the principal, the agent incurred a possibility of loss (*Williams v Stevens* [1866] 1 PC 352).

Generally the principal will be responsible for those acts of the agent that are expressly authorised or procured or are within the scope of the agent's apparent or implied authority. Thus if the agent exceeds that authority, the principal may become responsible for acts of illegal distress and may be sued along with or instead of the bailiff (*Megson v Mapleton* (1884) 49 LT 744; *Re: Caidan* [1942] Ch 90). The principal will be liable whether the bailiff's wrongful act is deliberate or arises from carelessness, provided that it was in execution of the warrant and for the benefit of the principal (*Dawe v Cloud & Dunning* (1849) 14 LTOS 155). If the act in question is completely outside the agent's authority, there can be no joint and several liability. See *Richards v W. Middlesex Waterworks Co* [1885] 15 QBD 660 in which the company was not liable for an assault committed by a bailiff executing a warrant in their name as such an excessive action was not within the fair scope of the bailiff's duty. The principal is also liable for any acts of the agent that are ratified. S/he then becomes liable for any tortious act as well. For examples of acceptance of illegal distraint see *Carter v St Mary Abbot's Vestry* (1900) 64 JP 548 or *Whitehead v Taylor* (1837) 10 A&E 210. Ratification must be a clear adoption of the acts in full knowledge of the facts (*Green v Wroe* (1877) WN 130). Thus receipt of proceeds of sale of wrongfully seized fixtures without knowing the source of the money is not ratification (*Freeman v Rosher* (1849) 13 QB 780; *Lewis v Read* (1845) 13 M&W 834; *Haselar v Lemoyne* (1858) 5 CBNS 530), nor is offering to compromise an action (*Roe v Birkenhead Railway* (1851) 7 Exch 36). However keeping goods illegally seized with knowledge of the illegality is evidence of ratification (*Becker v Riebold* (1913) 30 TLR 142). Ratification relates back so an action done without authority becomes legal if it is later authorised - for example, a bailiff distrains without authority but later receives it and thus ceases to be liable (*Potter v North* (1669) 1 Wms Saund 347(c); *Hull v Pickersgill* (1819) 1 Brod & Bing 282). The principal will also be liable for acts that are a breach of his/ her personal duty as principal and, of course, for acts jointly undertaken with the agent.

Otherwise, the agent is personally liable for any wrongful act or omission done on behalf of the principal as if it was done on his/ her own behalf. Examples of such liability include:

- the bailiff signed a distress warrant and then after issue refused a tender of rent. The agent was personally liable for the illegal distress (*Bennett v Bayes* (1860) 5 H&N 391);

- the bailiff illegally seized a lodger's goods and was liable under s.2 LDAA 1908 (*Lowe v Dorling* [1906] 2 KB 772);

- an agent converted third party goods to the principal's use and was liable to the true owner for the full value (*Stephens v Elwall* (1815) 4 M&S 259);

The issue of the bailiff's authority as agent is linked to the next section on codes of practice. Where an agent purports to do anything as agent of the principal s/he is deemed to warrant that s/he has, in fact, received authority from the principal to act in that way. If there is no such authority the agent may be sued by the third party for "breach of warranty of authority". Thus if a bailiff acts outside a code of practice, even though those actions may not amount to wrongful distress, those actions may still form the basis for an action for damages by the debtor or other aggrieved individual.

The damages that may be obtained in an action for breach of warranty of authority are the losses engendered by the absence of authority. The measure is based on what normally applies in cases of breach of contract, i.e. any fair and reasonable loss actually sustained as the natural or probable consequence of the breach. These damages reflect the position that the claimant would have been in had the representation been true and the position the person is in because it is untrue.

Finally if the agent makes wilfully false statements about his/her authority an alternative course of action is for the debtor to sue for deceit or to consider prosecution for obtaining pecuniary advantage by deception.

12.2 Codes of Practice

It is now common practice for local authorities and central government agencies to impose codes of practice on bailiffs as part of the contract agreed between them. In addition, as described throughout the text, there is the National Standard whilst the formulation and publication of codes has been recommended for local authorities by professional bodies- for example the Institute of Rating, Revenues and Valuation has drafted and promoted a model code for use by all revenues departments - and by representative bodies.

Many codes are well-drafted and offer considerable additional protection, both by exempting vulnerable groups and by expanding upon the present legislation or clarifying or defining the law where it is either unclear or even absent. However criticisms may be made of some codes. In some cases codes (or even contracts) have endorsed practices by bailiffs that were either illegal or of dubious legality. Whatever the contents of any contract or code between bailiff and creditor, it cannot authorise illegal acts and with the bailiff acting as agent for the creditor, both will be liable for any wrongful act. In addition, in many local authorities codes are regarded as internal only, part of the private contracts between local authority and bailiff that may not be published. They are thus of little use either to the debtor or, indeed, to the creditor as a means of verifiable monitoring of bailiffs' activities.

If advisers are uncertain whether or not a particular public body has a code of practice in operation, request for it should clearly be made. If this fails, a formal demand may be made under the Freedom of Information Act. This has proved valuable for obtaining all kinds of documents relevant to relationship between creditors and enforcement agencies, not only codes of practice but also contracts and or service level agreements.

12.3 Public law remedies

There is little doubt that many of the actions of bailiffs when acting as agents for public bodies will be susceptible to public law challenges, whether on the basis of violation of public law principles, breach of the ECHR or because of general maladministration.

The remedies available are as follows:

- complaint to the relevant ombudsman- certainly the Local Government Ombudsman regularly investigates the improper use of distraint by local authorities and the misconduct of their bailiffs;

- complaint to the local authority's monitoring officer - as a preliminary to complaint to the LGO or to judicial review. Where little progress has been made with the relevant department, involving the monitoring officer (who is often the borough solicitor) can often be an effective strategy;

- judicial review in the Administrative Court- there is little authority on the use of this remedy in the context of enforcement. There is, though, one nineteenth century authority to the effect that the court will not grant prohibition against a magistrates' court issuing a warrant unless it has done so in excess of its jurisdiction (*Ricardo v Maidenhead Board of Health* (1857) 27 LJMC 73). Nevertheless, it would seem that unlawful actions, policies and codes of practice formulated in excess of lawful powers and violations of the articles and principles of the ECHR would all be suitable matters for judicial review proceedings.

No such remedy should be contemplated without first employing the public bodies' internal complaints procedure. All creditors, as well as their enforcement agencies, will operate an internal complaints procedure which will obviously in most cases be the first stage in any effort to resolve a dispute.

12.4 Trade bodies

Under the National Standard enforcement agencies are required to operate and to publicise complaints & disciplinary procedures. These should be in plain English, should have clear contact names and numbers and should specify time limits within which responses will be made by the firms involved. The complaints schemes should include an independent appeal process where appropriate (see the trade body schemes described below). All these trade associations (or their predecessors) signed up to the National Standard when it was introduced, thereby committing their members to complying with it.

12.4.1 *High Court Enforcement Officers Association*

The Association exists to regulate its members, maintain professional standards and lobby government. The Associations website states that, as a responsible professional association, it takes complaints about its members seriously. A robust complaints procedure is operated and those aggrieved by the actions of an officer should contact the Association's secretary at High Court Enforcement Officers Association Limited, PO Box 180, Winsford, CW7 2WP. The website is www.hceoa.org.uk.

12.4.2 *Enforcement Services Association*

The Enforcement Services Association, known as the ESA and formerly the Certificated Bailiffs' Association, exists to represent both individual certificated bailiffs and firms. It will be found that many large firms are corporate members of both the ESA and the ACEA (see below).

The ESA has a code of practice for its members and operates a complaints procedure for individuals aggrieved by the actions of a member. The complaint scheme culminates in a hearing by an independent complaints panel and can lead to the refund of fees or payment of compensation to complainants. Full details of all of these and of the Association's membership may be found on its website at www.ensas.org.uk.

12.4.3 *Association of Civil Enforcement Agencies*

The Association of Civil Enforcement Agencies (ACEA) exists to represent the larger firms operating nationally, lobbying on their behalf with government and other policy makers.

The ACEA has a code of practice for its members and operates a complaints procedure for individuals aggrieved by the actions of a member company. The three stage complaints procedure culminates in a hearing by an independent complaints panel and can lead to the refund of fees or payment of compensation to a complainant. Full details of all of these and the ACEA's membership may be found on its website at www.acea.org.uk.

12.5 Conclusions

Enforcement law has, for a century, been a neglected area. This has allowed various misconceptions regarding the law to develop, which have become embedded in practice. Changes to local authority funding, meanwhile, have had a deleterious impact upon the remuneration of bailiff companies. This has resulted in the development of a variety of strategies to complete more levies and to raise more revenue. The consequent corner cutting and the prevalence of charging practices of doubtful legality, based upon questionable readings of the legislation (or upon no reading at all) have brought the industry into disrepute.

Ultimately government felt obliged to act. The result was the Tribunals, Courts & Enforcement Act 2007. This proposes a complete reform of the law, creating a unified system operating under a single code of law, making charges from a single scale of fees and under the supervision of a single regulator. For this new regime to succeed, each of the elements must work. Weakness in one will undermine the others. There are presently two potential sources of concern. One is the regulator. The Security Industry Authority is the chosen body, but - although it will licence bailiffs, enforcement agencies and training providers - it will not operate as a full regulator with complaints procedures and disciplinary powers. This raises the possibility that some individuals will still be able to operate in an undesirable manner. Secondly, the fees scale must be workable. If the fees are set too low, or are not sufficiently rigorously worded, it will be possible for bailiffs to make extra charges or to charge fees inappropriately.

All of this is to come. In the short term however, the law described in this text remains in force with all its faults, and will continue to provide considerable scope for debate and dispute.

GLOSSARY OF ABBREVIATIONS

CCA 84   County Courts Act 1984
CCR 81   County Court Rules 1981 (now CPR Sch.2)
CPR   Civil Procedure Rules
Crim PR   Criminal Procedure Rules
CSA (the)   Child Support Agency
CSA (with
section number)   Child Support Act 1992
CS(C&E) Regs   Child Support (Collection & Enforcement) Regulations 1992
CT(A&E) Regs   Council Tax (Administration & Enforcement) Regulations 1992
DCED-   Distress for Customs & Excise Duties and Other Indirect Taxes Regs 1997
DRA 1689   Distress for Rent Act 1689
DRA 1737   Distress for Rent Act 1737
DRR 1988   Distress for Rent Rules 1988
ECHR   European Convention on Human Rights
ERT(CB) Regs   Enforcement of Road Traffic Debts (Certificated Bailiffs) Regs 1993
ERTDO   Enforcement of Road Traffic Debts Order 1993
HCEO   High Court Enforcement Officer
LDAA 1888   Law of Distress Amendment Act 1888
LDAA 1895   Law of Distress Amendment Act 1895
LDAA 1908   Law of Distress Amendment Act 1908
LGFA 1988/
      1992   Local Government Finance Acts 1988/ 1992
L&TA   Landlord & Tenant Act 1709
MCA   Magistrates' Court Act 1981
NDR(C&E)(LL)
 Regs   Non Domestic Rates (Collection & Enforcement)(Local Lists) Regs 1989
NNDR   National Non-Domestic Rates (business rates)
RSC   Rules of the Supreme Court 1965 (now CPR Sch.1)
VATA   Value Added Tax Act 1994

FURTHER READING

Bradby   *Law of Distress*, London, 1828;

G Gilbert,   *Law & Practice of Distresses & Replevin*, London, 1794;

Kruse J,   'Legal problems in the process of impounding of distrained goods by private bailiffs,' *Civil Justice Quarterly*, vol.17, 1998, pp.41-57;

'Further aspects of impounding of distrained goods considered,' *Civil Justice Quarterly*, vol.18, 1999, pp.58-64;

'The nature of legal custody- the implications & effect of impounding distrained goods in the custody of the law,' *Civil Justice Quarterly*, vol.19, 2000, pp.267-286;

'Replevin - repeal or retain?' *Liverpool Law Review*, vol.23, 2000, pp.95-115;

'Ships in distress,' *Lloyd's Maritime & Commercial Law Quarterly*, Part 1, 2000, pp.113-121;

'The transfer of powers of arrest by magistrates' courts', *Association of Civil Enforcement Agencies*, 2001;

'The legacy of Semayne - the sources of the present law on bailiffs' rights of entry,' *Civil Justice Quarterly*, vol.21, 2002, pp.42-56;

'Enforcement law reform & the common law' *Civil Justice Quarterly*, vol.27, 2008, pp.494-506;

A lawful trespass - Bailiffs' law volume 1, Wildy, Simmonds & Hill, 2009;

Persons of no value? - Bailiffs' law volume 2, Wildy Simmonds & Hill, 2009;

Powers of distress- a guide to the remedies unreformed by the Tribunals, Courts & Enforcement Act 2007, Wildy Simmonds & Hill, 2009;

McLennan &
      Cooke, *Eddy on the Law of Distress*, Sweet & Maxwell 1961;

Wigan &
      Maston   *Mather on Sheriff & Execution Law*, Gaunt & Sons, 1990;

Index